# Degrees of Separation

## Roger White

LEAF BY LEAF

Published by Leaf by Leaf
an imprint of Cinnamon Press,
Office 49019, PO Box 15113, Birmingham, B2 2NJ
*www.cinnamonpress.com*

The right of Roger White  to be identified as author of this work has been
asserted by him in accordance with the Copyright, Designs and Patent Act,
1988. © 2022, Roger White.
Print Edition ISBN 978-1-78864-940-7
British Library Cataloguing in Publication Data. A CIP record for this book
can be obtained from the British Library.

Designed and typeset in Adobe Jenson Pro by Cinnamon Press.
Cover design by Adam Craig © Adam Craig.
Cinnamon Press is represented by Inpress.

The quotation from the *Dancing Wu Li Masters* by Gary Zukav is used by
permission of .HarperOne publishers (US) and Penguin (UK).

## About the Author

After graduating from the University of York, Roger went into teaching. Early involvement with UNESCO catalysed a lifelong interest in international links and opportunities for encouraging cross-cultural dialogue and friendships through exchange programmes. Roger has written a number of educational books and articles, exploring different perspectives on schooling, including *In and Out of School, Absent with Cause* and *The School of Tomorrow*. Roger lives and works in Bristol.

# Foreword

Growing up on RAF stations in the 1950s, I was surrounded by people whose memories and experiences reached back to the second world war. My father had been a night-fighter pilot, flying Mosquitoes over occupied Europe to protect the Lancaster and Wellington bombers attacking Germany, and some of the escapades of him and his navigator filtered down to us children.

Historians continue to debate the role of aerial warfare in securing Victory in Europe. Whilst weighing the damage done to the Nazi war effort against the dreadful consequences for civilians from the bombing strategy approved by Churchill, what is not contested is the bravery of the crews flying the planes. As they strapped themselves to their seats, opened the throttle and climbed into the freezing desolation of the night sky, they knew the odds were stacked against them, and their chances of surviving a 'tour of duty' were small. 'Kill or be killed' was the over-arching mantra. They must have been scared beneath the stiff upper lip. As President Roosevelt observed at the time, 'Courage is not the absence of fear'.

Such courage was not the sole preserve of the Allies, of course. Flying across the Channel from occupied Europe, to bomb targets in the United Kingdom, German aircrew would have been aware of the destructive power of the Royal Air Force and the anti-aircraft batteries beneath. Like their Japanese and Italian counterparts in the other Axis powers, they would have been fearful of the military forces lined up against them. Nor was bravery confined to aircrew. Battles on land and sea would have tested the courage of everyone involved.

I am a trustee of an educational charity in Bristol that receives support from a foundation established by an ex-World War II army officer, Barry High. He fought in Burma as a young man. During one of my regular meetings with Barry, he talked about his involvement in the rescue of seven thousand soldiers of the British Army, surrounded by Japanese forces near Yenangyaung in April 1942.

As an engineer, his job was to secure a bridgehead across the Pin Chaung river to extricate trapped soldiers. Outnumbered and outgunned, surrender seemed inevitable, until a division of one thousand Chinese soldiers fought through the jungle to relieve the encircled British army. Before Barry told me this, I was unaware of the role the Chinese army played alongside Allied forces in WW2.

However, on a visit to the city of Chengdu in the west of China to celebrate the birth of our grand-daughter who has Chinese and British parents, we chanced upon a memorial to victims of Japanese air raids during eight years of bombing from 1937-1945. I was curious to know more about theWW2 alliance between China and Britain, and my research led me to a home for elderly war-veterans in Chengdu in May 2019. An ex-soldier called Zhang Li Yuan talked to me about his experiences fighting for the Chinese Expeditionary Force. He described being sent to Burma in April 1942, aged 17, to help the British Army.

Zhang Li Yuan was at the battle of Yenangyaung.

He died on June 28th 2019, in Chengdu, at the age of

94, two weeks after Barry High, who was 102. I have no idea if they ever physically met in the jungles of Burma, but I had the privilege of meeting them both—and realizing there was a connection between the successful British businessman, whose philanthropy was influenced by his experience in Burma, and the Sichuanese farmer, who responded to the call to defend his homeland and walked a hundred miles to enlist in the Chinese Army.

We hear a lot about the concept of 'six degrees of separation', the notion that all people are six or fewer social connections away from each other. In a world increasingly linked through 'social' media and confronting a common threat to humanity from a tiny virus, it feels like the number of degrees of separation may have reduced considerably.

The novel explores this theme through a contemporary love story set in China and the UK, interwoven with encounters in Egypt, China and Britain during the second world war. Although it draws some of its inspiration from the connected threads described above, it is a work of fiction, which acknowledges the bravery of combatants, who responded to the call to arms then—and during the eight decades since—in what are beguilingly called 'theatres of war'.

Equally importantly though, the book pays tribute to the many millions of civilians who have perished, often unknown and unmentioned, across the world—lives cut short prematurely by conflicts not of their making. It is to them this book is dedicated in the hope their passing can encourage us to focus on what unites us as human beings.

Roger White
Bristol, September 2022

# China, 1942

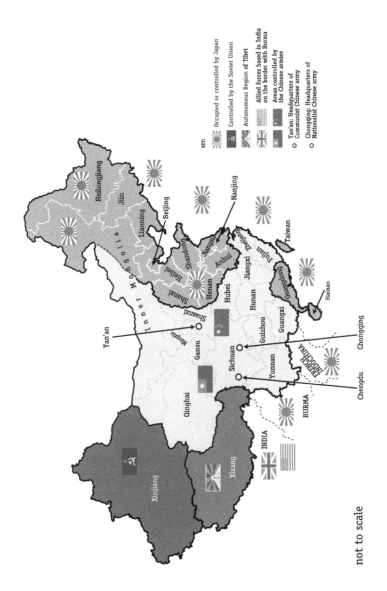

key:

Occupied or controlled by Japan

Controlled by the Soviet Union

Autonomous Region of Tibet

Allied forces based in India on the border with Burma

Areas controlled by the Chinese armies

○ Yan'an: Headquarters of Communist Chinese army

○ Chongqing: Headquarters of Nationalist Chinese army

Heilongjiang

Jilin

Liaoning

Beijing

Inner Mongolia

Hebei

Shandong

Jiangsu

Nanjing

Zhejiang

Anhui

Taiwan

Shanxi

Henan

Hubei

Jiangxi

Fujian

Shaanxi

Ningxia

Hunan

Guizhou

Guangdong

Hainan

Yan'an

Gansu

Sichuan

Chongqing

Guangxi

FRENCH INDOCHINA

Qinghai

Yunnan

Chengdu

BURMA

Xinjiang

Xizang

INDIA

not to scale

# Chengdu, 2019

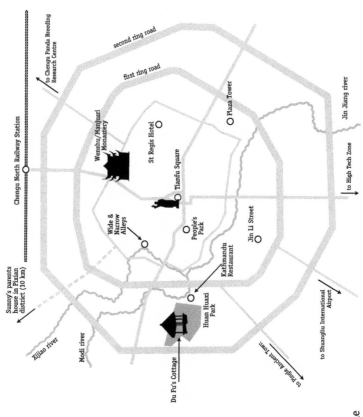

not to scale

# London, 2019

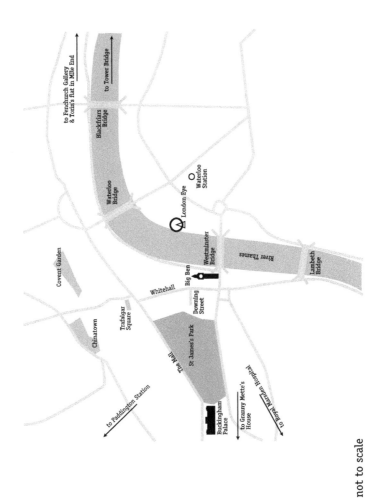

not to scale

Degrees of Separation

# Prologue

## Cairo: Wednesday 6th April 1942

Harry Winchester sat by the open window, towelling his hair after a shower. The sun had burnt out beyond the distant hills, and the water was turning black in the eddies behind the feluccas, whose white sails flapped limply as heat disappeared from the day. Beneath a cluster of palm trees a solitary ibis stood on the bank of the Nile, guarding the strip of sugar cane between the river and desert. Crickets interrupted the cries of playing children. A smell of burning charcoal drifted across the water.

Next to him a glowing mosquito-coil tracked the slowly-lengthening circle of ash in the dish below. Harry glanced at his wristwatch on the pillow. Better not be late for the General. He stubbed his cigarette and reached for a shirt. Before leaving his room, he checked himself in the mirror above the mahogany dressing-table. His fingers pressed down the collar-stiffeners either side of his knotted, black tie. Emerald irises looked back from beneath the tangled, brown eyebrows that arched above his nose. Not for the first time he wished he'd asked his mother about his ancestry.

His polished, black shoes clattered on the wooden walkway of the SS Sudan till he reached the entrance to the bar. Harry hesitated, his hand on the gleaming brass. Floating notes from a dance-band mingled with shouts of the Nubian crews tying their boats. Could he handle another drinking session? The blast of oxygen above the desert had cleared his hangover, but was he sharp enough for poker with a brass-hat old enough to be his father? There was something about the American though. Different to the stuffed-shirts in the Air Ministry.

Harry pushed the door. The waiters had closed the shutters to keep insects at bay, cutting out noise from the river, so the only sounds were the swishing of ceiling-fans, chinking of glasses, and voices raised above the music from the quartet on a platform. Coffee aroma mingled with the scent of perfume.

He scanned the rattan chairs clustered round wooden tables, taking in the peaked caps stacked against beer tankards, officers with gilded epaulettes, calloused knees beneath the frayed hem-line of khaki shorts, women with tanned legs and black sandals, fingers curled round the stems of their cocktails, a turbaned head puffing on a thick cheroot, whose smoke was sucked up to the gleaming chandeliers by orbiting fan-blades.

In the corner Chennault was already half way through a glass of beer. He looked up as Harry approached and lifted his index finger to attract a waiter. 'Pyramid for you, fella? They've been brewin it since King Narmer, so have had a whole bunch of years to get it right.' The voice was gravelly. 'How was the flight?'

'Fantastic, sir. Top hole.'

The General grinned. 'Try full bore?'

'Ruddy hell, sir. Over five hundred on the clock once I pulled up above the dunes.' Harry sat down, placing his forage cap on the table beside the arc of gold braid. As he described the rear end of the plane scuffing the sand with its slipstream, he noticed the General grinning. The craggy face looked like it had been carved from brown rock, with fissures of laughter-lines eroding the weather-beaten skin. 'Nearly blowing chunks with the G-force.'

'Jeez, son, where d'ya learn to talk like that?' Chennault shook his head. 'You sound like the King of England, with a poker up his jacksey.'

Harry frowned. The American corporal, who'd pulled open the canopy of the Warhawk, had said something similar, albeit in less colourful language. 'Blame the school I went to, sir.' The first line of a rhyme from the weekly elocution lessons with Ma Riley played through his head. 'My father's car is a Jaguar and Pa drives rather fast'. How had it continued?

'Must have cost a wad of bucks to teach you to rhyme farst with arse.' Chennault forced his lips into an oval, as he mimicked Harry's accent. 'At least it turned out a half-decent, limey flyer. Glad you enjoyed the Warhawk.'

'Some crate, sir. Threw it about the sky, and the wings stayed on.'

'Us Yanks are handy with rivets,' observed the General drily. 'Take it up top?'

Harry nodded. 'Smooth as a Roller, even at twenty-five thousand. I can see why a formation coming out of the sun would send the enemy into a blue funk.'

'The shark's teeth say it all.' Chennault drew his finger across his throat. 'We've been usin them on the front line in China. Three hundred enemy planes destroyed for the loss of just fourteen of our own pilots. Not bad odds, but the Japs are still comin for us.'

Harry noticed the prominent Adam's apple moving up and down as Chennault drained his glass. 'I didn't even know we were fighting in China.'

'That's because you're preoccupied with the punch-up across the English Channel.' The General's lips tightened. 'There's no doubt Hitler's an evil son-of-a-bitch, but what the Japanese have unleashed will change the world.'

'Like Singapore?' Harry thought of his cousin, Rupert, taken prisoner when the Allies surrendered two months ago. He'd been ferrying troops and equipment from the mainland.

Chennault snorted. 'You Brits only think in terms of friggin Empire. Malaya is a tiny part of the Japs overall plan. Do you know how much they've taken? Even before Pearl Harbour, they'd grabbed huge chunks of China. Heard of Manchuria?'

Harry was aware of the steely-grey eyes scanning his face, as he struggled to recall what he knew about China. Tea? Opium wars? The green-eyed villagers Archie had told him about? Something to do with captured Roman soldiers from a battle along the Silk Road.

'I expect you were still in diapers, son.'

Harry touched his reddening cheeks. He'd deliberately not shaved that morning, but the skin felt boyishly smooth. Before he could respond, a white-robed waiter with a red fez and matching cummerbund arrived with two beers and a couple of shots of whisky. There was an outburst of laughter at the next table. Harry saw a girl with black sandals rest her hand on a bare knee.

Chennault pulled a crumpled piece of paper from his pocket, smoothing it against the table top, pushing the drinks aside. It showed the countries to the right of the Mediterranean. 'Look at the map, fella. The Japs have grabbed most of the Far East. They've even put the old Chinese Emperor back on the throne here.' He pointed at the land-mass across the sea from Japan. 'Now the battlefront has shifted to Burma and we're takin a beatin.'

To the left of the nicotine-stained finger, Harry recognised the outline of India. Was that Ceylon at the bottom, where Rupert had been heading before the Japanese destroyed the runway at Paya Lebar? They'd heard nothing, apart from a Red Cross message listing him in Changi prison. Poor sod. Banged up in the tropical heat with mozzies and cockroaches for company. There were rumours prisoners were being offered paid work on a railway project, so maybe conditions would improve.

'Chinese armies are pinnin down a million Japs.' The gritty voice interrupted Harry's train of thought. 'The big question is whether they can hold the line in the south. They need air support. Which is why I'm here.' Chennault pressed his fingers against his temples. 'I've got fifty friggin Warhawks ready to roll to Sichuan, but if the Chinese troops cave in before we get em there, there's no way we can stop the Nips pushin across Burma into India.'

The booming Cajun drawl was drawing attention from people at adjacent tables. Harry noticed the girl with sunburnt legs looking at Chennault. The General glanced to the side and she raised her cocktail glass. Beneath the table, her other hand pushed up the hem of her white cotton-dress to scratch the red circle of an insect bite.

Harry watched Chennault's index finger trace a line from Turkey to Iran. 'There are Nazi supporters in both countries. If they ally with Hitler, German forces would have a direct corridor into India from the west.' Chennault tossed back the whisky and looked directly at the young pilot. 'The Indian Congress want you Brits out, so might welcome Adolf with open arms as the lesser of two evils. The country could fall faster than a hooker's drawers. Then we'd see the whole of Asia ruled by Axis powers, apart from bits the Soviets have grabbed.'

Harry tugged his ear lobe, struggling to understand what Chennault was talking about. When he'd joined up after Dunkirk, it was all so straightforward. Good versus evil. Britain against the Nazi fascists and their Italian poodle, Mussolini. 'I've only been thinking about the war in Europe.'

'Let's hope you can win that one, son, but this fracas in China is goin to be a longer haul.' Chennault called over the waiter again. 'Anyway, fella, how about this game you suggested last night? Brought the cards?'

Harry pulled the pack from his pocket. 'Five-card draw?'

'Suits me. Playin for dollars?'

Harry scattered his money on the table. 'I've got pounds and shillings.' He stacked the coins into piles, calculating it was close to a month's pay. 'And a couple of half-crowns.'

Chennault's eyes narrowed. 'You limeys think your currency is the only dough that matters. We'll go one for one.'

'Hang on sir,' Harry protested, holding up a green banknote with the King's profile. 'The exchange-wallah at the dockside would give me four dollars.'

'Maybe he would, boy. But you ain't at the harbour, and I call the shots, as the senior officer on this floatin bathtub.'

Harry figured he just needed to win. He dealt the cards

and studied the American as he sorted his hand. In the jutting chin and coils of hair sprouting from his nose and ears, there was a resemblance to the Desperate Dan character in the *Dandy* comic they'd clubbed together to buy at school.

Harry registered the US Army's star on Chennault's left shoulder and a silver emblem, showing a white sun against blue sky, on his right epaulette. An ivory scarf was tucked into the open neck of his tunic, with his wings visible above his breast-pocket. On the table, the cap-badge insignia was the same symbol as the epaulette. Intelligence Corps or Special Forces for sure.

Chennault twisted his head to the right as he looked at a card pulled from his hand. 'Jeez, fella, these pictures are somethin else. Look at this dame!' He flipped over the Queen of Hearts. A girl was kneeling forward on a carpet with her hands gripping the legs of a metal bedstead. She was wearing a black corset, unbuttoned to her midriff. From the edges of the lace, black straps ran across her bottom to the stockings at the top of her thighs. Her smiling face was turned towards the camera behind. 'Where did these cards come from, son?'

'Spanish pilot on flying training.' He recounted how Javier had fought with the International Brigades at Tarragona, and fled to France in 1939. He'd been part of the art scene in Barcelona, and moved in with Catalan painters in Paris. Harry took a long pull from his beer and wiped froth from his lip with the back of his hand. 'One of them had done a painting of a Basque city being bombed. He wanted to get it to the States to raise funds for refugees from Franco's Spain. Javier took the canvas to New York, where he cut a deal with the Museum of Modern Art. In return, his friend painted him a set of pictures.'

'What's that gotta do with this naked broad?'

'Javier's idea was to produce playing-cards, with an image on the face side he could sell to rich Spanish ex-pats as a limited edition.' Harry explained that Spades were portraits of the Kings of Spain from Philip the Fifth; Clubs were signed black and white sketches of famous pilots since 1903, starting with Orville Wright, whose mother was from Madrid; and Hearts were nude models in Javier's studio. 'So, he needed his chum's paintings for the Diamonds.'

'Ya mean these pictures are *originals?*' Chennault held up the red seven.

'Yes, each one has a title—that's l'*Homme aux cartes.*'

'Jeez, fella, they're pretty weird.'

'That's Modern Art for you, sir.' Harry raised his eyebrows. 'Lots of lines and curves, but nothing that actually resembles anything.' He described how Javier had contacted the US Card company in New York, who agreed to produce them as a collector's set. 'But soon after he returned to Paris, the Germans invaded France, and Javier escaped to England, taking the originals.'

Chennault swallowed the contents of his whisky glass. 'If I was young Javier, I'd have done precious little paintin with these dames around. How did you get your mitts on em?'

'New Year's Eve bet.'

'Tequila slammers play a part?'

'Not really.' Harry's fingers stroked the back of his ear. 'Flying under Brighton pier.'

Chennault's eyes narrowed. 'Should I be worried about you, son?'

'I planted your Hawk back on the deck in one piece, sir.'

'Yeah, but I've seen Brighton Pier. You couldn't squeeze a fart between the cross beams.'

Harry's laugh was an awkward bark. 'That was true till the Home Guard removed the middle section to prevent Germans using it for invasion. We reckoned the gap was big enough to fly a Blenheim between the stanchions. Javier went first. Turned out the wingspan was three inches wider than the uprights.' Harry pursed his lips. 'By the time air-sea rescue fished him from the sea, he was stiff as the proverbial board. Rotten show.'

'So you swiped his cards?'

'Seemed only fair. He lost the bet after all.'

Beneath the arched eyebrows, the deep-black pupils stared levelly back. 'Let's play, fella. See whether your poker's as good as your storytellin.'

The American tossed a dime in the middle and Harry matched it with a florin. He pushed two cards towards Chennault and dealt himself three replacements. The girl with the sandals was watching. Harry levelled Chennault's bet and they each drew another card, before a further round ended with Harry lifting the kitty on the back of a flush.

In the corner of the bar, couples jitterbugged to music beneath a blue-grey haze, and Harry caught snatches of references to Rommel and Monty from the officers behind his back. He had reckoned the game would be over quickly, but the tide of fortune kept the pile of money ebbing and flowing, while the waiter maintained the supply of drinks.

A boy in a black waistcoat, carrying a tray with plates of food, hesitated nearby, looking for the source of the order. A smell of fried bacon mixed with the sweetness of toasted cheese.

Harry noticed the girl drag her chair round, but kept his focus on the cards, half listening to Chennault talking about the difficulty of getting his planes to Kunming. Something about supply lines between India and China being cut by the enemy.

'If I try truckin them across the mountains, the Japs'll have a turkey-shoot. Only 'ternative is to assemble 'em in India and fly over the Himalayas.' It seemed to Harry that Chennault was addressing the girl in the white dress as much as himself. 'But everyone keeps tellin me it can't be done.'

Harry felt the room spin and took a long mouthful of beer. The clock on the wall showed past midnight. 'Maybe call it a day, sir?'

'I ain't a quitter, son. Ever heard of a boy from Louisiana throwin in the towel? Gotta be a way to shift these friggin planes into China.'

'I meant the poker, sir.'

The American checked his wrist watch. 'Okay fella. Try seven-card draw for a last round?'

Harry shuffled. His face was impassive as he glanced at his hand and then at Chennault. He accepted another shot of whisky. Surely he could hold his own against the American?

The pile of coins and notes in the middle of the table increased with each draw. Finally, Chennault pushed forward his remaining dollars. 'Up yours with this lot, fella.'

Harry totted up what he had left. He swallowed quickly to suppress the rising bitterness in his throat. 'I can't match that, sir.'

'Better cry uncle, then.'

Harry loosened his tie and leant back. He could feel the woven, rattan strips pressing against the back of his bare legs, sticking to his skin. He looked again at the five cards he held. If he hadn't agreed such a ridiculous exchange rate, he'd have been able to square the stake with Chennault. Damned if he'd let a single-pipped General put one over him. His jaw tightened. 'What if I bet I can fly your plane over the Himalayas?'

Chennault grinned. 'I'll see your hand, with that kind of parlay.'

Harry's pulse was racing as he laid down three kings and two eights. Chennault breathed out slowly, then pushed the kitty towards Harry. 'I swear I'd whip your ass with three queens. Trouble is these damn hearts are a distraction. I'm reluctant to let the broads go. And I was so close to gettin the friggin planes to Kunming.'

Harry couldn't resist pressing home the advantage. Maybe he wasn't so clued up about China, but he could show a Yankee penguin a thing or two about flying. 'The bet still stands, sir.'

'Is that the drink talkin, son?' Chennault's eyes bore into the young pilot across the table.

Harry stared back, determined not to blink. Did the Yank think he was a kid who could be teased about his accent? He'd probably gone to some two-bit academy in Louisiana. Had the General any idea what he'd been doing in England before ferrying Beaufighters to the squadron at

Alexandra? Did he know what it was like to watch runway lights disappear beneath you in the darkness, wondering if this was the night you were for the chop? He pressed down the resentment. There was a rumour in the mess-room Chennault had been a fighter-ace on the Western Front.

'My navigator's in Cairo General being treated for West Nile fever, so I'm not rushing back to Blighty. If I'm going to be stuck here for a couple of weeks, I might as well do something useful. I'll get your kite to China fast enough.' The rest of Ma Riley's rhyme ran through his head. *Castles, farms and draughty barns, all go shooting past. But I prefer Tom's classy cart to my Papa's fast car.* 'Flying over a couple of mountains can't be that difficult.'

'Whaddya want, if you make it, son?'

Harry glanced across the room. The quartet was playing a Glen Miller foxtrot. A soldier with three yellow pips on the epaulette of his khaki shirt caressed the exposed back of a girl in a floral dress. She'd kicked off her sandals and was squeezing one of his legs between her thighs as they turned on the spot, before gliding across the floor. Unbidden, an image of Amy floated into his mind, outlined against the moonlight from the casement window in the upstairs room of the *Angel*, as she drew her crumpled blouse over her head. Was it really just seven days ago? Four nights en route from Blighty and then three billeted on the Sudan?

'How about a week on this houseboat with my fiancée? We're due to be married in June, but the RAF won't allow us out of the country.'

'Should be able to fix it, fella.' The rasping voice softened.

Harry frowned. 'What do you mean?'

'I can speak with Keith Park or Hugh Dowding.'

Harry's eyes widened. 'You know our top brass?'

'Spent an evenin with both dudes at Bentley Priory last year. Park is now Air Commander Egypt, the biggest cheese in this neck of the woods. I'm due to see him tomorrow about these Hawks, before I fly back to Burma. I'll square it for you to be gone a while.'

Harry imagined Amy's reaction. Perhaps he could persuade a wireless operator at the airfield to relay a message to Blighty? He stretched out his hand. 'You've got a bet, sir.'

Chennault's grip was firm. 'Take the kite you flew today, son. The additional fuel-tanks give it fifteen hundred miles.' He flattened the map on the table and jabbed his finger at Cairo. 'Your route is across the desert to Bahrain, over the Gulf to Karachi, then Delhi and Calcutta, onto RAF Dinjin in the north of India, close to the border with Burma. Two days flyin if you start early enough and hot rod the engine.'

Harry smiled. 'Looks easy enough, sir. Just keep the setting sun behind me all the way. Can I take your map?'

Chennault chuckled. 'You might need more than this when you reach Dinjin. It's only five hundred miles to Kunming over the Himalayas, but that's the real challenge.'

'A couple of hours steady flying, sir.'

'Steady doesn't quite describe it, son, but the guys watchin you this afternoon told me you know a thing or two about aerobatics.'

Harry drained the dregs from his beer glass and stood. Maybe this Kunming place was near the Leechee Anne village Archie had mentioned. A punch up between Persians and Romans had ended with legionaries sold to the Chinese Emperor. Some had married local girls. 'If I can find a blower that works at Kunming, I'll call you Friday.'

Chennault raised his eyebrows. 'Custer had your sort of confidence at Little Bighorn, and that didn't exactly end well. What if you lose?'

'You think this mountain caper is risky, sir?' Harry reached for his forage cap and gathered the cards. 'If something happens, I guess I'll not be in any state to cough up.' He smiled wryly, pointing to the pile of money. 'Better take this lot now, just in case.'

'I'd rather have the cards.'

Harry was silent, thinking of the moonless night watching Javier's plane somersault into the sea. He pushed the pack to the American. 'As long as I get them back, after I touch down at Kunming.'

'If you disappear into the bundoo, I'm not sure how I'm goin to explain to Roosevelt that I swapped fifty-thousand bucks of Warhawk for a deck of playin-cards.'

Beside them, the girl was rubbing ointment onto her thigh.

Chennault traced the outline of the Queen of Hearts. 'Accomplish the mission, and I promise you'll see her again son. But if you don't make it, you'll know she's gone to a 'preciative home.' He glanced at the clock. 'I'll make sure the kite's ready by dawn. That gives you six hours shut-eye. Some of us might still be in the sack.' He winked at the girl in the cotton dress.

# Part One

Illimitable happiness,
But grief for our white heads.
We love the long watches of the night, the red candle.
It would be difficult to have too much of meeting,
Let us not be in hurry to talk of separation.
But because the Heaven River will sink,
We had better empty the wine-cups.
To-morrow, at bright dawn, the world's business will entangle
    us.
We brush away our tears,
We go—East and West.

Du Fu *A Toast for Men*

# Chapter One

## Chengdu:
## Thursday May 9th 2019

Torin clambered out of the taxi at the corner of Tianfu Square, waving off the two Germans working for Audi who'd travelled with him from the St. Regis hotel. They were going on to a breakfast sales-meeting in the south of the city. Torin paused to take in Chairman Mao surveying the crowds, right hand raised in acknowledgement, left hand behind his back.

His phone cursor pointed east. A traffic-controller's shrill whistle cut through the warm air and he followed the crowd over the striped crossing, dodging bicycles and scooters weaving around pedestrians. Green digits beside the traffic-light descended towards zero. Behind him, the whistle blew again and vehicles accelerated in a cloud of dust and exhaust fumes.

Threading along the crowded pavement, Torin followed a girl with a Dior bag slung across her shoulder. Auburn tints to her black hair lifted and fell in waves with each step as she hurried towards Xin street. At the corner of the road, she slowed to join a crowd waiting to cross to Burberry, and Torin walked past, registering her dark glasses above deep, red lips. She was studying an iPhone clasped in her right hand, manicured nails matching her lipstick.

He entered Plaza Tower, took a lift to the twenty-eighth floor and stepped onto the cushioned quietness of the carpeted corridor. Before going to the conference-room, Torin checked his reflection in the mirror in the rest-room. He adjusted his tie against the collar of his pink shirt, satisfied the alternating stripes of Oxford and Cambridge blue matched the navy Hawes and Curtis suit. Fortunately, there had been time to have it cleaned after arriving from Xi'an late on Tuesday night. His gold links were just visible beneath neatly-pressed cuffs. He ran his fingers over the designer-stubble, and smoothed his curves of blonde hair.

At the end of the corridor the sign on the door declared China UK Ventures, with '*Digital Apps for Effective Marketing*' underneath the company's logo. Torin turned the handle.

Two women stood beside the display of materials and resources. He recognised the taller from his meeting at the company's headquarters in the High-Tech Zone the day before. In contrast to the dark-green tailored-suit in the office, she now wore a full-length, black cheongsam, with plum-blossom brocade. Her brown hair was swept back from her face, and held in a bunch above her neck with a red clip. A pair of white pearls hung from her ears.

'Hi Gloria.' Torin moved forward, responding to her outstretched hand. The day before she'd talked about her hopes for involving the company in a joint enterprise with *Perfect Pitch*, promising to put him in touch with the British Consulate in Chongqing. He felt encouraged she'd come to the start of the event, especially as he knew she was hosting a lunchtime-reception for a UK trade-delegation. Torin pointed at the resources laid in front of a digital photo-montage. 'I love the banner. How did you create that so quickly?'

'Thanks to Chen Xi,' Gloria introduced the woman beside her. 'She sorted it with the printers after you left, and was here before seven o'clock, setting everything up.'

'*Xiè xiè*,' Torin inclined his head and pressed the woman's hand, struck by the firmness of her grip. Had he met her the day before? It was hard to tell. There'd been a lot of girls in the office when Gloria showed him round. He registered the discrete make-up beneath a sheen of raven-black hair and her finely-tapered, grey suit, complemented by ebony shoes. She was younger than Gloria, with wide brown eyes. 'Have you done many conferences like this?'

The girl smiled, revealing perfect, white teeth, but before she could speak, the entrance door opened and she turned to greet the first delegates, leaving Torin to check his presentation on the data projector. Gloria had said they'd be lucky to attract twenty people, but with a quarter of an hour to go, all forty seats were taken and Chen Xi had to request more chairs from reception.

Gloria spoke for ten minutes. Although Torin couldn't understand, he was impressed by her PowerPoint slides. Under the CUV logo, they illustrated a range of joint ventures between China and the UK. Finally, she turned to Torin and her hands swept in a wide circle, embracing the audience as she spoke. A ripple of laughter came from the delegates.

'I explained I must go back to our office in High-Tech Zone, but am hoping to return before you finish at four o'clock. Meanwhile I said they would be in safe hands. I told them you already visited Beijing, Dalian, Shanghai, Suzhou, Guilin and Xi'an, so you know China better than many Chinese people. That is why you have saved the best for last in Chengdu. We have a motivated audience, for an important subject, with an excellent speaker.'

As Gloria passed him the remote, Torin surveyed the expectant faces, confident about the workshop. Judging from previous events, the marketing managers would be enthusiastic about the opportunity to try the sequence of activities and interactive games.

Before the conference ended, Gloria had slipped back, reaffirming the company's potential for nurturing links between businesses in China and the UK. Many people stayed to look through the resources, and it was a further hour before the door closed behind the last delegate. Torin's pocket bulged with business cards. With help from Chen Xi, he packed the displays; Gloria phoned the conference help desk in the Plaza, with instructions to return the materials to the St. Regis.

'I'd like to take you both out to dinner to say thanks,' Torin addressed Gloria. 'You've done a brilliant job promoting the conference. Fifty-two delegates is more than twice the number at any other event. My boss is going to be delighted.'

In the conversation between the women, Torin noticed Chen Xi shaking her head. Gloria responded sharply. He stepped forward, interrupting the flow of Mandarin. 'It's okay. I understand if you're busy.' He wasn't that keen anyway. The sales managers from Audi had mentioned going to a French wine-bar and onto a nightclub, Octopussy. It sounded much less complicated. And there was always the football on telly. England were playing Montenegro in a qualifier for the Euros.

After a further exchange in Chinese, Gloria turned to Torin. 'I have to take my daughter for a violin lesson but Chen Xi has recommended a restaurant not far from here. *Chilli Peppers* is on the way to Tianfu Square, where you can take a metro to your hotel.'

Torin smiled; he'd ended up with the worst of both worlds. No Gloria and no Octopussy.

Chen Xi accompanied Torin into the settling darkness, wishing she'd been more assertive. She had planned to see a martial-arts tournament with friends, but Gloria had reminded her of the importance of hospitality. It was difficult to argue with her boss. As they weaved along the crowded pavement, she noticed Torin dragging his left foot. It was like he had a weight attached, although it didn't affect his pace.

'Do you live near Plaza Tower?' she heard him ask. Had he any idea of the cost of accommodation in downtown Chengdu? What did he think she was earning as an office worker? Chen Xi pressed her lips together, choosing her words carefully. 'Prices are high in city. Family living beyond third ring road in Pixian district. Long way north-west Chengdu. But last year new metro station opened next to our apartment. Line Two takes thirty minutes. Before it was more than one hour on bus. Very slow and crowded.'

'I guess it's the same in London,' he replied.

She was relieved he'd understood. When Gloria had asked for help with the conference, she'd been apprehensive because of her English. Although her marks on the language test were above the basic requirement for the organisation, she knew her conversational fluency was nothing like her written ability. This wasn't usually a problem. Most of her job involved writing reports and responses to proposals from British companies wanting to expand business from the Eastern seaboard into cities like Chengdu and Chongqing. With access to her language app, she could take her time editing text. But the *Perfect Pitch* event would mean being principal translator in real time.

However, Digital Apps had been a module on her business-management course at Sichuan University, and she'd been intrigued by the sample material from the UK. In describing the conference to the contact list provided by Gloria, her enthusiasm was rooted in a genuine understanding of the technical aspects of the product. As the bookings on her spreadsheet lengthened, Chen Xi noticed she'd personally spoken to most of the names. Her satisfaction and confidence about the product had been an effective counterbalance to her language anxieties.

In that sense she knew the conference had gone well. A web-designer from a tech firm in Hong Kong, familiar with the specialist jargon, had helped her interpret the questions and answers. Could she sustain a whole evening of conversation in English, though? It was the first time she'd hosted a visitor from the UK alone, and Mister Torin's accent was unusual. At least the restaurant would be lively and the service had been good last time with the girls from the office. With luck they wouldn't be late.

Gloria had told her that Torin was keen to try food typical of Chengdu, which was why she'd suggested *Chilli Peppers*. What could be more appropriate than Sichuanese hot-pot, renowned for its spice? A black-jacketed receptionist showed them to a table in one corner and reached under the cloth to fire up the cooker. While the young man filled the hot-pot bowl, Chen Xi studied the menu and ticked off her choices.

Torin looked round the restaurant, taking in a party of girls with ruby lipstick and brown-tinted bobs; parents of two toddlers in scarlet dresses, whose tiny topknots were clipped together by red butterflies; three men with white tee-shirts rucked above waists, clasping bottles of Snow beer; moonscape contours on the faces of grandparents sipping tea with their extended family; and a middle-aged businessman in his blue fitted-suit, puffing smoke rings above the styled, black hair of a young woman opposite.

From the kitchen behind the red-striped plastic-screens, he heard cutlery clatter as dishes dropped into washing-up bowls, and glasses clinked in the dryer. Waitresses with black aprons pushed through the red-streamers, carrying trays of food and calling out across the room. Two worn posters were stuck to the wall beside the kitchen entrance. One displayed a red arrow zigzagging through mountains, against an outline of a platoon of soldiers. Next to it were four faces beneath the national flag. He recognised one from the statue in Tianfu Square.

A smell of sesame oil and oyster sauce rose from the bowl in the centre of their table. Strips of pink pasta bobbed in the bubbling liquid, like pieces of flotsam rolling through rapids, sinking and rising to the surface. He watched Chen Xi expertly twirl a ribbon into a loose ball with her chopsticks, then pluck it from the foam and place it carefully in his bowl.

He hesitated with his fingers pressed around the pencils of wood. 'Try,' he heard her urge.

'Meat or vegetable?' asked Torin.

'Special Chinese food. *Yā cháng.*'

'Looks like chicken?'

'Similar. Soft and crisp at same time. Delicious.'

Torin saw her chopsticks hover over his bowl with another piece, as he struggled to chew the morsel in his mouth. An image of his father carving the Sunday joint, slicing the gristle from the meat beside the bone, drifted into mind. He nearly gagged, but managed to swallow the lump whole.

Chen Xi registered the raised eyebrows and tightened lips, so she dropped the second ball onto her own plate. Had she chosen wrong? He had said he wanted to try local food and *Yā cháng* was one of the must-order dishes if you were Chinese. When she selected a strip of sliced beef from the pot, she was relieved to watch him swallow it without grimacing. Were all foreigners so choosy?

'There is pork and more beef.' Chen Xi indicated the platter next to the steaming cauldron. 'And here is vegetables—cabbage, potato, mushrooms, bean sprouts, bamboo shoots, lotus, seaweed.' She lifted a tray from the serving trolley at the side.

'And these?' Torin's chopstick pointed at a white ball in the pot, tinged with yellow sauce, that had floated into view. It rolled over and sank.

'Eggs. Small bird.'

Torin frowned. 'Quail?'

'We call *Ān chún.* I think English is bamboo chicken.' Chen Xi passed him her phone. 'Look here!'

Torin pushed his spectacles down his nose and studied the stocky bird with its brown and buff plumage. 'Like a small partridge. Really expensive in the UK. I've only ever seen the eggs in Harrods.' He noticed Chen Xi frowning. 'Shop for very rich people in London. Sells unusual foods. Not many quail in the UK.'

'Here lots of bamboo chickens working for Chinese restaurants. Many eggs at bottom of hot-pot bowl.'

'Good news for me.' Torin fished into the bubbling broth, circling the edge of the bowl with his chopsticks. After three fruitless laps, Chen Xi reached across and deftly plucked an egg from the foaming liquid.

'You make it look so easy.'

'We learn when little. Same with bicycle. You just need hot-pot practice. This only your first time in Chengdu. Come again and be expert.' Chen Xi spoke her English sentences softly. 'Maybe build up confidence with beef, easier to lift with *kuàizi*. Take time to push end of chopsticks together. No hurry. Food not able run away.' She watched him lift a strip of meat from the pot.

When Gloria had told her Mister Torin was the marketing director for *Perfect Pitch*, she'd been expecting someone in his forties or fifties. She'd had plenty of time to study him during the day though, and he seemed closer to her own age. Beneath the wavy, blonde hair that seemed to sprout from a high forehead, bushy eyebrows merged above the bridge of his nose. With his wide-lipped smile and tortoiseshell spectacles, magnifying the sparkling blue of his eyes, he reminded her of Stephen Hawking in the *Theory of Everything*, which she'd seen last year with her boyfriend. The manicured stubble on his upper lip and chin stretched along his jawline, to blend with the light shadow of shaved hair above each ear. The only blemish on his face was a scar down his neck. The purple weal disappeared below the collar of his pink shirt.

With the beef finished, she watched Torin return his attention to the eggs. He dug his chopsticks into the yellow broth and a familiar oval shape rose to the surface. He chased it round the rim several times, till he succeeded in balancing it on the ends of his two sticks. She noticed the thick curls of fair hair on his forearm, as he lifted the egg towards his bowl, but it rolled off the wooden tips and plopped into the bubbling hot-pot. Chen Xi struggled not to laugh.

He glanced up. 'Despite your chopstick tutorial, I think I'll stick to anything that comes in strips, apart from the *Yā cháng.*'

'Maybe need more help.' Chen Xi turned to the waitress standing beside the posters. '*Měi nǚ! Nà gè sháo zi ma?*'

Torin was surprised at the shrillness in her voice, but it worked. The girl quickly came with a spoon. He smiled at the waitress. 'This feels likes cheating, but thank you anyway.'

Chen Xi translated and the girl bowed her head. '*Bù kèqì.*'

Torin grasped the spoon. 'Maybe it's time to focus on vegetables.' He scooped cabbage and potato, and pointed at a white circle, dotted with holes. 'Looks like bleached pomegranate?'

Chen Xi started to describe lotus fruit, but stopped, seeing his puzzlement. What had she said wrong? 'Sorry, my English not so good.'

'Damn sight better than my six words of Chinese.' Torin looked at the woman opposite, registering the deep whirlpools beneath the curved lids. 'It's not your English at all. I was just wondering how this pure-white vegetable could possibly come from the thick-leaved plants I've seen growing in muddy waterways.'

'Most healthy vegetable in China, probably in world.' Chen Xi passed him her phone with a photo of the lotus flower and the nutritional qualities of its roots.

Torin scrolled down the screen. 'My God, it does everything, including inducing peace and tranquillity through minerals and trace elements. I should eat this every meal. Tell me more about Chinese food—and about you as well.'

Chen Xi hesitated.

Torin loosened his tie. 'Perhaps your name? On all the conference documents it gives your Chinese name, but Gloria introduced you as Sunny.'

'Many people choose English name as well as Chinese.'

'Can I call you Sunny then?'

'Of course.' She smiled, then covered her mouth with the tips of her fingers. 'I like English name because Chen Xi means rays of morning sunshine.'

'Does everyone have a second name?'

'Most young people. We sometimes change, if we like different name. I was Lisa when little.'

'But what does it say on your passport?'

'Lu Chen Xi.' Sunny placed her chopsticks on her plate. 'Lu is my family name. My father called Lu Tian Yi. Family names always first and individual person second. Xi Jinping family name is Xi. Mao Zedong is Mao. My mother chose Chen Xi for my person-name, because when she came out the labour room and lay down on her bed, she saw the first light came into the hospital-window shining on me.'

Torin was struck by the poetic image. Although Sunny didn't stress syllables, there was a resonance in the timbre of her voice. 'Do children take their father's surname, like in western countries?'

She nodded. 'I am Lu, like my dad. Sometime I called Xiao Lu, which means small Lu, and my father is Lao Lu because older. But my mum keeps own name. Not change when married. She called Wang Yu Ling.'

'Are your parents from Chengdu?'

Sunny shook her head. 'They met at a village school year Chairman Mao died. Married twelve years later.' She talked about her parents and what it had been like growing up in the countryside. She described how life had changed when Deng Xiao Ping took over as Chairman, what the one-child policy meant for a generation, and how her parents moved to the city when she started school, so she could have a chance at university. She explained the importance of family-gatherings, to connect those in the city with relatives on farms, and celebrate shared roots on the land. 'It why *Fēng shuǐ* important to Chinese people; the words mean wind and water, and we need a balance with nature in our homes.'

Torin was intrigued. Previous conferences had been followed by evenings socialising with CUV executives in large groups. Conversation was about food and places of interest, but never strayed into social history. This was the first he'd heard anyone refer to life under Mao.

In return, he talked about growing up in Scotland and moving to London, where he went to university. After landing the job with *Perfect Pitch* he'd bought a small flat near Mile End. From her frown, he guessed the East End district didn't mean anything, but when he explained it was not far from the Olympic Park, her eyes flashed recognition. She had watched the opening ceremony of the Games with friends in 2012, even though it was five o'clock in the morning.

'We loved James Bond diving with the Queen. We didn't understand burning towers or hospital dance, but music worth waking for. And David Beckham driving his speedboat through the firework waterfall.' Sunny giggled.

Seeing her smile again, Torin was encouraged to ask about Tiananmen Square, on his mind ever since his Beijing hosts had taken him to the Forbidden City, and he'd seen the vast space opposite Chairman Mao's mausoleum.

'*Tiān ān mén guǎng chǎng?*' Sunny pronounced the words carefully. 'Gate of Heavenly Peace. I visited last year with a friend. Very large. Used for festivals and parades.'

'I mean the demonstrations... thirty years ago?' Torin hesitated. There had been a question in the pub-quiz, the night before he left London.

Sunny's chopsticks hovered over the hot-pot bowl. 'June 4th incident happened before I even born. We don't really know about this.' She paused and looked directly at Torin across the table. 'What I see and feel is that our country is getting better and better these years.'

During the long silence that followed, Torin watched her stirring the bubbling pot, thinking he didn't know much either. The business trip for *Pitch Perfect* had challenged his stereotypes about China. Life seemed free.

People weren't nervous about speaking to him, and the only police he'd encountered were directing traffic. Walking along city-streets, he'd seen children playing on pavements; bars full of young people smoking and drinking; men sat round mahjong tables, slapping tiles on the green beige as money exchanged hands; women dancing in the squares to music from cassette-recorders.

Torin looked round the restaurant, registering the laughter and chatter. He tried to engage Sunny in conversation about the music she liked, and what she did in her spare time. Her responses were measured and polite, but the sense of engagement had evaporated. He wanted to apologise for asking about Tiananmen Square, but was reluctant to mention it again. There were long silences.

Finally, he asked for the bill and they walked to the metro entrance in Tianfu Square. She bought tickets for them both. 'For St. Regis you take Line One to *Luó mǎ shì* and then change to Line Four for *Tài sheng nán lù*.' She pointed to the names on the map and explained it would take ten minutes. 'I take Line Two.' She accompanied Torin to his platform, grateful to see a train pulling in as they came down the escalator.

The cushioned doors opened. 'Thanks for everything you did today, Sunny.'

The train slid into the darkness and Chen Xi disappeared from view.

# Chapter Two

## Fenghuangshan Airfield, Chengdu:
## Thursday, September 20th 1942

Harry was stirring a small spoonful of sugar into his tea, savouring the spicy aroma in the coils of steam from the chipped mug, when a wailing siren arched across the airfield.

The haunting urgency ran like an electric current through the operations room. Arms reached through flying-jackets hung in readiness at first light. Already Lin Xiaobin had pulled on his boots and was moving to the door, parachute slung over his right shoulder.

Harry stood beside the young airman on the tarmac, staring at the blue sky. He breathed in deeply, savouring the freshness of the morning. From the hamlet of thatched buildings beyond the boundary of the airfield, a light breeze carried the tangy smell of wood smoke, blended with a sweet odour of pigs. Above the clucking of chickens came a sound unlike anything he'd heard in England: *ki-ko-kua... ki-ko-kua... ki-ko-kua...*

'Bamboo partridge,' explained Lin Xiaobin. 'More common in eastern China, where I grew up. Warning off other males.'

Harry glanced at the pilot. 'You know about birds?'

'Not much, but *Ān chún* are good to eat.' Lin brushed his hand over his shaved head, curling his fingers around the long pigtail at the back. 'My parents kept them behind our house in Nanjing. I expect the Japanese have killed them by now.' He spat onto the tarmac, and the ball of saliva gathered dust as it rolled towards the parked aircraft. 'Maybe today will be revenge for the partridge.'

'Let's hope.' Harry rubbed the corner of his white neck-scarf across his goggles to remove dust. 'Observers picked the planes up at Yichang and tracked them past the Wu mountains. Sichuan control can always tell whether it's Chengdu or Chongqing for the chop from the course the Japs take at the Han river.'

He studied the sky to the east, where wisps of cirrus cloud coalesced into cumulus. 'All week the bombers have been turning south to give Chongqing a pasting. But today the course is due west. The blighters will be over Chengdu in forty minutes.'

'Zǒu ba!' Lin Xiaobin pulled on his gloves. 'They will discover that Chengdu is no longer an easy target. Many Japanese pilots will not see the sun set this evening.' His right hand played with the zipper on his chest, and his other brushed away beads of sweat oozing from his smooth forehead. 'Hot already.'

Harry squinted at the yellow orb. 'It'll be very different at twenty thousand feet.'

'Commander Winchester, we will still keep the heat on the Japanese aggressors.' His tongue brushed the edge of his upper lip.

Harry registered the pilot's controlled determination. It was like the words were forged in his mouth, unconnected to any emotional space in his chest. There was a flatness to the resonance, chilling in its deadliness. From the start of training in July there had been a burning intensity to his eagerness to be in the first wave of Chinese pilots to take on the bombers. Lin Xiaobin knew, with smouldering precision, the specifications of the different makes of Mitsubishi and Kawasaki aircraft, and the best angle of attack to minimise the defending firepower of their gunners. He slept with silhouettes of the aeroplanes pinned above his bed.

Having attended a primary school run by Scottish missionaries in Nanjing, Lin Xiaobin had learnt to speak English before his teens, and Harry had come to rely on him as the translator for the squadron. His distinctive voice was higher pitched than the rest of the men, almost feminine, and the pace of his utterances conveyed an urgency that was sometimes harsh. But whenever he spoke, the men fell silent, knowing they were about to be told something important. The faint trace of broadened vowels reminded Harry of his grandmother.

On his first day in charge of the squadron, Harry had memorised the notes in the operations room's filing cabinet about each pilot. Xiaobin had joined the Chinese Air Force at eighteen, straight from High School, having secured the highest Gao Kao grades in the class of 1941. He had completed his basic training with the Flying Tigers in Kunming. Before he was combat-ready, Xiaobin had witnessed the final stages of the Burmese campaign, when the handful of surviving pilots from the American Volunteer Group stemmed Japanese attempts to cross the Salween River into China.

On the personal recommendation of General Chiang, Captain Lin had been assigned to the newly-formed Chengdu defence squadron at the beginning of July. In three months of training, he had emerged as the most proficient Chinese flyer.

Harry studied the airman looking at the Warhawks, lined up on the perimeter-track with their menacing sharks' teeth. He registered the mahogany-brown eyes and porcelain smoothness of the young man's cheeks. His lips were pressed together beneath the finely-manicured arch of moustache that matched the plaited braid of inky hair hanging down from the crown of his head. The only blemish was a line of dark moles running from his left jaw to underneath the ear. In his charcoal flying-suit, shifting his weight from foot-to-foot, he looked like a panther poised to spring.

Harry felt restive energy emanating from the lithe figure beside him, sensing the young pilot already had ambitions to take command. He'll need to prove himself first, though! Shooting at dummy targets dragged behind a stooge plane was one thing; holding your nerve as tracer arced towards you from the bomber in your sights, quite another.

'Once we're airborne, Control will confirm the enemy's height and bearing. We have twenty minutes to position for attack. We'll be coming out of the sun when I give the order to dive.' Harry knew Xiaobin was aware of all this, but it helped calm his own nervousness. It was eight months since his last enemy encounter above the south coast of England. Could he still hack it? Nervously, his fingers rubbed the curved indents of his ear lobe.

The breeze dropped and the sounds from the village quietened for a few moments. From the trees behind he heard the distinctive call of a cuckoo.

Within minutes of the siren sounding, the pilots stood

on the tarmac in a precise semi-circle. Harry scanned expectant faces. 'Well done men. B flight are on standby for any second wave, so we get first stab. Maintain close formation after take-off and climb with me until we have the bandits in sight below. No one break ranks. Surprise is our advantage. The bombers will be looking down for anti-aircraft fire and barrage balloons. They won't be expecting an attack from above. Good luck.'

Harry gave Lin Xiaobin time to translate, and then led the men towards the parked aircraft. He climbed onto the wing of the Warhawk to lower himself into the cockpit, reassured by the familiar rustle in the pocket of his jacket. He fired the cartridge to start the engine and the ground crew pulled away the chocks. As he taxied onto the perimeter-track, fourteen Warhawks manoeuvred into an extended Vee formation behind him.

'Bravo Three Six to Control.' Harry closed his gloved hand over the throttle-lever as he spoke into the intercom. 'Ready for take-off.' In the reflection from the shaded instrument- panel, a shaved line of dark-brown hair was just visible below his flying-helmet, and he could see the leather rim of its frame pressing against his cheekbones. From within the squeezed eyes, a tiny spot of sunlight gleamed from the depths of each black circle.

Harry scoured the horizon to the east, even though he knew they would see nothing till they were airborne. He glanced at his watch. Ten fifteen. Eight minutes since the siren. Good going. The twenty-one-year-old shivered, but knew it wasn't from cold; the temperature inside the cockpit was stifling, even with the canopy pulled back. Harry rubbed his eyes with the back of his glove.

Excitement mingled with apprehension; he drew comfort from the familiar sensations in his stomach, recalling the flash of wintry sunlight across his canopy as he'd turned onto the runway that day in January to lead the attack on the German intruders crossing the Channel.

'Control to Bravo Three Six. Hold in line.' The stretched vowels of the Midwest accent crackled over the intercom. He'd met the American in charge of the control tower at the briefing by the station commander two weeks ago, when the squadron had flown into Fenghuangshan airfield from their training base at Shuangliu. Douglass Walters' voice had become familiar to the pilots as they practised circuits and bumps in the new environment, preparing for combat.

'Roger Control. Bravo Three Six holding.' Harry enunciated each syllable, knowing Douglass would be holding his ears at the clipped, English accent.

'Fuel, ammo, revs, temperature.' Harry ran through final checks. He touched the trim wheel beside his foot, feeling it set to nose down. As he straightened up, his right hand brushed his pocket. Harry knew the poem by heart.

*'How do I love thee? Let me count the ways.*
*I love thee to the depths and breadth and height*
*My soul can reach, when feeling out of sight*
*For the ends of Being and ideal Grace*
*I love thee to the level of every day's*
*Most quiet need, by sun and candlelight'*

Beneath the text Amy had written, in purple ink, 'Stay safe, my darling.'

She had produced it from the ageing Remington in her office, the morning after he'd proposed. They would have been married on Midsummer's Day, a week before his twenty-first, but the order had come to fly to the Far East on the fifteenth of June.

In the upstairs room in the *Angel*, the night before he left England, they'd clung together, whispering endearments, aware that hope and promise could be snuffed in a second. It would only take one wrong turn, a miscalculation, or bullet, for Lady Luck to run her course. They had both known pilots now drinking at the bar in Valhalla.

'Control to Bravo Three Six. Clear for take-off. Cumulus one-tenths at Angels Eight. Latest report is twenty-two Nells at Angels Twelve, distance eighty miles, heading for Chengdu. Estimated arrival ten forty.'

'Roger, Control.' Harry knew Douglass was relaying information from the radio operators in the tunnels at Badong, under the bombers' path. He turned to see the jagged teeth of his wingmen visible behind his tail fin. Harry pulled the canopy closed, shutting away the world.

'A Flight rolling.' His gloved hand eased the throttle-lever forward, pressing the rudder-bar with his right foot to hold the nose straight against the torque of the airscrew, noting the rising pitch of the engine as the plane gathered speed along the makeshift runway. He watched the indicator pass a hundred and twenty and eased back the control-column.

With a final bump, the Warhawk leapt clear of the ground, propellor clawing the humid air to lift the aircraft from the sanctuary of the aerodrome. Harry released the pressure on the rudder-bar and held the plane in a steady climb. Beneath its belly, lines of ancient drainage-rhynes reached like silver fingers across the baked, red earth. Green smudges of woods dotted the land between the canals.

He glanced either side to check Lin Xiaobin and Xu Wen were in formation, before calling the flight to starboard. 'Bravo Three Six turning Zero Eight Five.'

Hungry jaws devoured the scattered cloud, pulling the planes upwards. Harry watched the altimeter sweep past ten thousand as they rose above the puffy cumulus. Already the cockpit was cooler and he pulled up the zipper of his flying-jacket, savouring the comforting warmth of the fur-lined collar against his neck.

'Bravo Three Six to Control. Passing Angels Eleven. Confirm height of bandits.'

'Control to Three Six. Bandits holding at Angels Twelve.' The air-traffic controller's voice was faint but clear. 'You're on course to intercept in five minutes. Good luck A flight.'

'Three Six climbing to Angels Eighteen.' Harry wanted the sun behind them when they dived towards the Japanese planes. 'See you for tea, Dougie.' In the cockpit it was silent, apart from the comforting hum of the Allison engine. The fifteen planes were flying towards Santai like a gaggle of wild geese.

# Chapter Three

## Giant Panda Breeding Research Base: Saturday May 11th 2019

Chen Xi stood beside the entrance gates, scanning the taxis that pulled off Qing Long Dao road. She had left home soon after seven o'clock to make sure there was time to buy tickets before Mister Torin arrived. It had meant two changes on the metro from Pixian and then a bus for the last two kilometres from the end of line 3. She glanced at her watch. It was only ten past nine, but behind her the ticket-queue was already lengthening.

As she left the office on Friday, Gloria had asked if she was free the following day. She'd said yes, thinking Gloria was going to invite her to the finals of the Sichuan boxing championships in the International Gymnasium. Chen Xi knew that China UK Ventures was one of the event's sponsors and Gloria had been given complimentary tickets, as well as being invited for dinner with the competitors in Howard Johnson's. It would be a chance to meet Han Feilong, one of her heroes.

When Gloria had said she wanted her to show Mister Torin the pandas, Chen Xi turned away to hide her disappointment. She knew it would mean an early start and take up the whole day, so she'd texted her friends to say she couldn't join them for lunch at the Global Centre. There had been talk of swimming with sharks in the Oceanarium afterwards.

Chen Xi had spent ages deciding what to wear,

worrying about appearing too casual. Her phone said it was going to be warm, so she thought it unlikely Mister Torin would come in his suit. In the end she'd chosen a loose, yellow cotton top over cream-coloured shorts and brown, open-toed sandals, with leather thongs tied round her ankles. On her head she wore a straw hat with a floppy brim. A red ribbon ran round the rim, tied into a bow, with the loose ends hanging over her ear.

Her phone vibrated. 'Two minutes. In green taxi.' She flashed back a smiling emoji. Maybe Mister Torin was unaware all Chengdu taxis were green? Chen Xi glanced towards the highway, where a row of market-stalls ran along the line of the slip road. She guessed he'd come round the Third Ring Road onto the highway to the panda base. The smell of freshly kneaded *bāozi* frying in palm oil mingled with barbecue smoke from the brazier beside her, with its wrapped parcels of blackening sweetcorn.

As each car unloaded passengers, Chen Xi pressed her mask against her cheeks, glad she'd taken her mother's advice. Although air quality was good in spring, the rutted mud at the edge of the highway was a dustbowl after two weeks of sunshine.

The last time she'd come to the Panda breeding centre was twelve years ago. It was the week before spring holiday and her junior high-school class had voted for this as their shared activity before the New Year. She'd queued with Huang Guo and Lin Ting, her two closest friends. Despite wearing thick, leopard-spotted fur-coats, they'd had to skip on the spot to keep warm, chanting the words of the English rhyme their teacher had taught them.

'*Salt, mustard, vinegar, pepper;*

*bread and butter for our supper,*
*eggs and bacon, salted heron,*
*pickled onions, apple pudding…'*

When their teacher explained the meaning of each word, the fourteen-year-old girls had a fit of giggles, imagining a dead heron on the same plate as apple-pudding, black eyes staring straight along the orange beak that pierced the fruit. Wang Laoshi showed them a picture of a heron in flight above a river bank in the south of England, and Chen Xi could see it looked like the storks and cranes that lived in China.

She thought English people must truly be barbarians if they ate such beautiful birds. In school they had read the *Fēngshén Yǎnyì* stories from the Ming Dynasty era and knew about the sacred role of cranes in Taoism. In their living-room her parents had a painting called 'Bamboo and Cranes' by Bian Jingzhao. Chen Xi had been fascinated ever since she could remember, trying to work out how the birds wrapped their necks so gracefully round the trunk of the young trees.

Wang Laoshi told them that not only did westerners eat birds, but also ate everything from an animal, including the heart, liver, intestines, and lungs, although they often disguised the food with names such as chitterlings or tripe so the connection with the body part was unclear.

Chen Xi recalled Mister Torin's expression as he'd swallowed the piece of *Yā cháng*. Instead of explaining it was duck's intestine, she should have described it as scratchy pork, which she remembered seeing on a packet in Mai De Long, the western supermarket beside the Second Ring Road. But he'd been adamant he wanted to try real

Sichuan food. Maybe she should have added *Máo dǔ* and *Huáng hóu* and watched his face as he'd chewed the strips of stomach lining.

A green taxi dragged a cloud of dust from the highway and pulled up beside her. She recognised Mister Torin through the windscreen. As he stepped out of the car and stood beside her on the pavement, Chen Xi again registered the thickness of his blonde eyebrows above the rim of his spectacles and the blue eyes. She was relieved to see he'd swapped his finely-tailored suit for jeans and a white tee-shirt, with the letters LSE above an outline of a building that looked like the pictures of the American White House she'd seen on television. The scar on his neck ran beneath his collar.

Chen Xi was conscious of an awkwardness, unsure how to greet him. Should she just offer her hand, like when they'd met at the conference on Thursday? As she hesitated, Torin resolved the dilemma, wrapping his arms around her and kissing her cheek. She caught the scent of aftershave from his trimmed beard. Chen Xi was blushing as she stepped back, but realised the mask was hiding her embarrassment. By the time she'd unhooked it from her ears, her cheeks had regained their usual colour.

'I see quite a lot of people wearing masks.' Torin glanced towards the queue, where several women had covered their faces. 'Is pollution that bad?'

'Only in winter because of cold temperature. Fog in the morning seals bad things in the air. Especially there's almost no wind in winter. Spring brings warm air and breeze that make the air flow. But dust from edge of road still bad.' As she spoke, another taxi pulled up on the concourse, so Chen Xi moved towards the entrance gates. 'I bought tickets already. We go through here.' She pointed at the barrier.

Torin pressed back his spectacles to focus on the animals on the billboard. 'Back home, everyone who has been to Chengdu says *you must see the Pandas*, so I rang Gloria last night. She had a business meeting today though, and said you might be busy as well.'

Chen Xi shook her head. 'All okay. Lucky today. Sunny wherever you are.'

Torin glanced at the puffy, white clouds drifting gently through the blue sky and then realised what Chen Xi was saying. He was relieved after what happened on Thursday night. 'Thank you for bringing sunshine.' He looked at the wisps of shiny, black hair that brushed the tips of her ears underneath the sun-hat, and the ribbon that fluttered behind her head. His eyes flickered down and he noticed the painted nails poking from her sandals. The colour matched the ribbon. He was glad he'd discarded his suit and tie.

'I came here once before and it raining, so no panda.' Chen Xi recalled how the heavens opened as the three girls walked along the drive. Wang Laoshi had ushered the whole class into the exhibition-centre, where water poured like stair-rods from the dragon-headed gargoyles at the corner of the ornate guttering. The three girls had watched all the films on the big screen in the separate cinema and studied the detailed descriptions beside each exhibit, but by the time Wang Laoshi called them to queue up for the bus back to school, they still hadn't seen a live panda.

This time Chen Xi was determined. Instead of

following the line of people into the exhibition-centre, she touched Torin's shoulder. 'Come. I know where pandas are.'

He followed her to the nearest enclosure.

'*I'm the national treasure and I hate noise.*' They stood beside the brown noticeboard with its neatly-painted, white lettering underneath Chinese characters, watching the four animals on their raised platform made from roped poles. Pieces of bamboo lay strewn across the wooden base. One of the pandas was leisurely chewing along the thin stick, while another was using the bamboo to scratch below his ear. A third lay back against the poles, strips of shredded bamboo criss-crossing the white fur of its belly, shiny eyes staring back at them from within the black patches. The fourth had its mouth open, contemplating the piece of cane it held in its right paw, like a conductor's batten. Chen Xi registered the milky whiteness of the lower white teeth and the moist, pink mouth beneath the button-nose.

Panda dung mingled with the scent of frangipani blossom as they walked round the sanctuary. In each compound, pandas were engaged in similar activities, either slowly shredding bamboo, working through chopped canes, or sleeping, stretched on the wooden platforms with a raised pole as a headrest. Occasionally, one rolled over onto the ground and ambled towards another platform, where the bamboo sticks seemed more appealing.

The path around the sanctuary meandered between the manicured lawns and clumps of carefully-tended trees, each with an information board giving its name in Chinese characters. Purple and red bougainvillea cascaded from the bushes.

They were walking through a glade of eucalyptus when Chen Xi stopped and clutched Torin's arm. 'Look,' she whispered, pointing up with her other hand. 'See animal? Maybe jump us!' Her voice was breathless.

Torin could feel Sunny's fingers digging into his skin. Above, a brown creature straddled two, thick branches. It resembled a large squirrel with its long, bushy tail, but the face was of a small bear, white markings round its mouth and fur covering its ears.

'Looks like a brown raccoon.'

'Raccoon?' Chen Xi let go of Torin's arm and reached into the pocket of her shorts for her phone. She tapped the keyboard and studied an image. 'Yes, bit like raccoon—but actually same as other panda. We call them xiǎo xióng māo—little bear cat. Also red panda. Eats same bamboo-food. Less lazy than black and white xióng māo.' As she replaced the phone in her shorts, the movement startled the animal, which leapt to a higher branch and disappeared.

They walked round a dense clump of trees to see a large building with a framed notice announcing it was sponsored by Coca Cola.

'This is baby panda house.'

They followed the line of visitors round the circular viewing-gallery. On the other side of the glass were cribs, each with a tiny creature—slug-like in the first phase, then morphing into the cuddly black and white balls of fur recognisable as miniature versions of the Giant Panda. In one compartment a girl was feeding a ball of fluff from a baby bottle. The milk bubbled as the panda tugged at the teat, guzzling the white liquid.

'So cute.' Torin raised his phone.

'Check no flash.' Chen Xi pointed to the large notice above the glass screens. 'Okay if just normal photo.'

They stood in the semi-darkness watching the baby animals suckle.

'Do they do this because pandas aren't very good at mothering? Or is there a risk of the male pandas killing the babies?'

'Giant Pandas very lazy. Mostly sleep or eat. You see in enclosures. Lots of lying down, with bamboo in mouth and eyes shut.' Chen Xi hesitated, choosing her words carefully. 'Baby-making too much effort.'

Torin grinned. 'I thought that was what motivated all animals, apart from moving to find food or escape from being eaten.'

Chen Xi was grateful for the dim-lighting so he couldn't see her blush. Maybe if she'd been with Lin Ting and Huang Guo it would have been different, but it wasn't a subject she wanted to discuss with a man—especially a foreigner. She looked at the tiny fluff-ball, whose eyes had glazed over as it finished feeding. 'Not panda. Is why dying.'

'Dying?' Torin chuckled. 'For lack of sex! Not very different to some humans then.' He smiled. 'Do you mean endangered?' He glanced at Sunny, who was tapping her phone.

'Bīnlín mièjué. Yes, mean endangered. Sorry.' Chen Xi turned away, flustered, and pushed through the plastic doors that sealed the incubation house.

The air was warm from the morning sunshine and

Sunny sat on one of the benches that ringed the brick-laid courtyard. She pulled out two bottles of water from her rucksack, and passed one to Torin. He unscrewed the cap and took a mouthful. Holding the drink to the sky, sunlight refracted through the glass; he was conscious the day had clouded over.

Torin touched the neck of her bottle in a silent toast. 'I needed that. Thank you.' He paused, then quietly added, 'I'm really sorry for embarrassing you.'

'It okay,' Chen Xi wished she'd not said anything about the mating habits. If it hadn't been for the darkness, she'd have kept quiet.

'Actually, it's not okay.' Torin rested his hand on her arm. 'Your English is brilliant, Sunny. You pronounce every sentence so clearly. For me to laugh because you used one wrong word was stupid.'

Chen Xi said nothing, struck by the intensity of his blue eyes. She was conscious of his fingers touching her skin.

'You speak English like you have spent time in England. Yet you said you learned it all at school in China? You must have had a very good teacher.'

She adjusted her hat, lowering the brim to shade her cheeks. 'Also from songs and films.'

He rubbed his forefinger across the bristles above his upper lip. 'If I spoke any language as well as you speak English, I'd be so pleased. Most British children learn French or German, but we hardly use it. Now there is discussion in some schools about learning Mandarin, because China is becoming such a strong country.'

'Mandarin not easy.'

Torin laughed. 'Say that again! Even if I know the

words, it's the pronunciation that's the real challenge. I struggle to say basic phrases like *nǐ hǎo* or *xièxiè* in ways that people understand.'

'Grammar is easy. No verb changes. One word same for everything in past, present or future. So only need learn once. But tones difficult. Meaning changes when tones change. Maybe I will teach you Chinese and you correct my English. Watch me.' Chen Xi stood in front of Torin and repeated the same word four times, '*mā... má... mǎ... mà.*'

Torin's brow furrowed as he registered the slight difference in emphasis. The first word remained steady, the third wavered, and the fourth dropped. He wasn't sure that the second was different to the first.

'Easier if you move finger when you say sound. Look at me.' Chen Xi opened her mouth and pointed her finger in the air, moving up and down, and left to right as she spoke. 'Hard for you, Mister Torin.' She smiled. 'Hard for us too, and we have Chinese class the moment we step into kindergarten. We are taught to move hands. High for mā. Moving up for má. Down and up for mǎ. Quick down for mà. High first one means mother. Straight up is plant; up and down means horse; quick down is cross. Important to use right tone. Even have fifth ma, which means question.' Chen Xi uttered the syllable quickly, and without emphasis.

Torin copied the movements with his hand as she repeated the words. 'This is really helpful, Sunny. Thank you for my first Mandarin lesson. The only thing is,' he took her hand as he lifted himself up to stand beside her, 'you don't need to call me Mister Torin you know. Just Torin will do.'

Chen Xi pulled her hand away. 'We are taught show respect. Often title with family name. *Lǎoshī* for teacher, *yīshēng* for doctor, and *xiānshēng* for Mister, although that bit old-fashioned. For man, we say brother or handsome; for woman, sister or beautiful, like in restaurant when I call waiter *měi nǚ*. Means beautiful girl.'

'It used to be the same in the UK, but we have become less formal in recent years,' explained Torin.

'Well, Mis… I mean Torin, shall we go to the information hall?'

On the path they passed four teenage-boys, laughing and joking. She noticed one nudge his friend as he glanced from Torin to her. She thought she heard "*wàiguó rén* and *nǚ péngyǒu*", and increased the space between them.

In the exhibition-centre, away from the sun, they studied the information-panels and videos about the Giant Panda. Most of the carefully-constructed visual displays had descriptions in English below the Chinese characters, so they took their time with each stand. As they came to the end, Sunny felt Torin's hand touch her arm again.

'I think I'm now so informed about the Giant Panda, I could give a lecture on its evolution, breeding-cycle, habitat and unique status as a vegetarian bear that is actually called a cat in Chinese!' He pointed at the clock, which was showing nearly midday. 'Should we have something to eat?'

They sat in the café with bowls of spicy beef-noodles, sharing photos on their phones.

'Sunny, that was such a great visit. Thank you for

sparing the time. Are you at home with your family this afternoon?'

Chen Xi was surprised. Gloria had asked her to keep the day free, so she'd told her mother she'd be back in the evening. She had thought Mister Torin might like to visit old streets like Wide and Narrow alleys. Or the Buddhist temple in Wenshu monastery. 'I can take you other places, if like?'

Torin shook his head. 'I need to go back to my hotel.'

Chen Xi walked slowly to the exit from the research base, taking a detour round the lake, ringed with lotus plants. She noticed again he was dragging his left foot. They passed the turnstile onto the concrete forecourt, where a zigzag of people queued for the ticket-office. She checked her phone and pressed a key. Moments later a white Toyota pulled up beside them. 'Your car, Mister Torin.' She smiled at his raised eyebrows. 'Sorry, I mean Torin. I order Didi. They are often round corner. No need to wait for taxi.'

'How about you? Can I drop you on the way?'

She hesitated. 'Not really same direction. I will get bus from main road.' Chen Xi pointed to the queue at the end of the slip-road. She was hoping he might insist; she wasn't keen to repeat the number of metro line changes. 'No big hurry.'

'Let me pay something though. You came all this way and bought the tickets. You didn't even let me take the bill for lunch.' His blue eyes fixed on her.

She shook her head. 'You our guest. Of course, we pay.'

She sounded abrupt, and he wondered if he'd offended her. 'If you're sure.' Torin pressed his cheek against hers, feeling her stiffen. He was getting it wrong again. 'I hope we can speak before I leave on Friday. How do Chinese say "goodbye for now"?'

'We say *zài jiàn*—means "meet again".'

'*Zài jiàn*, Sunny.' Torin waved through the open window of the Toyota as it accelerated towards the ring road, kicking up a dust cloud that drifted towards the Panda research base.

Chen Xi adjusted her face-mask, registering the faint trace of his aftershave. She watched his car join the stream of traffic heading to the centre of Chengdu. Then she walked slowly towards the bus-queue and rang her mother. She could tell Yu Ling was pleased to hear her daughter would be home earlier than planned.

# Chapter Four

## Chengdu airspace:
## Thursday September 20th 1942

Harry's eyes scan ned the horizon, searching for the enemy aircraft he knew would soon emerge from the haze to the east. At eighteen thousand feet the metallic tint to the blueness was surreal in its intensity, wisps of stratus clawing up to the beginnings of space. In formation beside him, the jaws of the Warhawks looked voracious.

'Red leader. Bandits three o'clock. Angels Twelve.' Lin Xiaobin's voice crackled in his ear.

Down to the right of his nose-cone, Harry saw dots of aircraft appearing like fruit-flies from empty sky. 'Squadron turn Zero Seven Zero. Hold at Angels Eighteen till we identify.'

Harry heard Lin Xiaobin translate the order and narrowed his eyes to analyse the approaching formation. Twenty-two Mitsubishi bombers. Exactly as Dougie predicted. With two dives they could destroy them all. The first would be a turkey-shoot as the pilots came out of the sun on the unsuspecting Nells, shredding cockpits and fuel tanks. That would leave seven, with the odds very much in favour of the Warhawks. He breathed slowly to counter the adrenalin rush, and fingered the intercom, ready to order the attack once he judged they were close enough.

'Commander, our bandits have company.' The voice was shrill in his ear. 'Joining one o'clock.'

Harry studied the distant aeroplanes converging on the Mitsubishis. With mounting foreboding, he identified twelve Zeros. How had Control missed the fighter escorts? He'd have ordered up B flight if he'd known. At close quarters the ageing Warhawks were no match for the agile Zeros. Plus ten pilots in the flight had never been in combat before.

'We now have Snappers to deal with as well as Nells.' Harry's voice was measured. 'Red wing, follow me to attack bombers, using one-seven pattern. Regroup at Angels Fourteen for second attack. Yellow wing, follow Lin Xiaobin towards the fighters.' Harry flicked off his safety catch and pushed the control-column. He could hear the engine screaming as the airspeed-indicator nudged five hundred. Harry glanced both sides of his canopy, noting Red wing in perfect formation. Grinning, pink mouths bared their rapacious teeth. Below, the Misubishis were like lumbering, grey elephants, with distinct, red circles on their extended ears.

'Fire when ready.' Harry edged the control-column to the left so the cockpit of the leading bomber was centred in his sights. The end of the hunt. He was conscious of a pervading calm. The same feeling as when they'd closed on their radar blip and emerged from the cloud to see the Heinkel several hundred feet below them.

At one hundred yards he squeezed the button and watched the cannon-fire arc towards the enemy aircraft, slicing a line along the fuselage from the cockpit to the rear gun-turrets. Smoke billowed from the starboard engine. Harry's plane screamed past the tail-fin of the bomber and he pulled hard on the control, feeling the G force press him towards the edge of consciousness. He eased back on the stick to avoid blacking out.

As he climbed through the blueness he looked back at the bomber. Flames licked the engine cowling of the Mitsubishi, which slowly corkscrewed to the right, its nose dropping. Four other bombers retreated east, trailing smoke. Another plane was spiralling, its cockpit engulfed in flames. Two figures leapt from its belly, parachutes deploying below the mayhem. A third parachute had caught on the fin and the figure was flailing like the tail of a kite as the plane plummeted towards paddy fields. Harry scanned the sky. Somewhere there must be a seventh bomber because only fifteen aircraft were holding their course towards Chengdu.

Less than a mile away he could see Yellow Wing engage the Zeros in a whirling dance of white and grey metal, teeth snarling as planes twisted and turned.

'Red wing. Regroup Angels Fourteen.'

It meant leaving Lin Xiaobin to manage the dogfight, but they had to take out the bombers. As the engine strained to climb steeply, he glanced downwards through the side of the canopy.

Three thousand feet below a Warhawk chased a Zero in a tight circle, both aircraft trying to reach a point where they could fire on the other. Tracer from the Warhawk shot across the cockpit of the Zero. Harry saw another fighter closing in from above.

'Yellow Two. Bandit on your tail.'

The Warhawk kicked into a steep dive, but the Zero was persistent and followed the aircraft, firing a burst as it turned. The Chinese plane zigzagged furiously, trying to shake off its pursuer, but the pilot of the Zero was more than a match. The Japanese aeroplane closed in. Tracer flashed from the guns of the Zero and coolant gushed from the engine of the Chinese fighter. Harry watched the pilot struggling desperately with the canopy, which fell away, knocking against the tail fin. The plane turned on its side, and his arms grabbed the edges of the cockpit to pull himself from the seat. He plunged headfirst into the empty void. Seconds later his parachute opened and Harry turned to concentrate on his own flight-path. Xu Wen would fight another day.

He glanced at his altimeter, watching the needle approaching fourteen thousand. Four Warhawks circled in readiness and another pair climbed from the west.

As he waited for the two planes to join them, Harry surveyed the dogfight. Aircraft spun and turned, metal flashing in the bright sunlight, rolling like seals in an aquarium. He watched a Zero plummeting, black smoke billowing from its engine, a Warhawk in pursuit, guns blazing. Orange flames burst from the engine and the Zero spun round, its tail falling away from the fuselage. Yellow Wing was doing its job.

Harry removed his goggles to wipe sweat from his forehead, conscious of the thumping in his temples. An image of Douglass sitting on one of the soft chairs in the bar next to the ops-room, beer in right hand and cigarette clamped between his lips, floated into his mind. It would be good to be back there in one piece. He eased the canopy open a few inches to feel the cool air on his cheeks.

'Red Wing repeat attack. Choose target and fire when ready.' Harry dipped his wing and was relieved to see the

Chinese pilots maintain close formation as the Tigers screamed down towards the Mitsubishis.

This time the bombers were ready and tracer flashed from gun-turrets. Harry twisted and turned, holding the aircraft in his cross-sights, guns blazing. There was a blinding flash as the cannon-fire hit the fuel-tanks and he felt his plane lifted by the force of the explosion and tossed across empty sky. He glanced beneath him. A huge fireball floated gently downwards like a dandelion-seed. For a fleeting moment Harry thought about the crew, vaporised into a pink cloud of atoms, drifting noiselessly across the blue sky. It had happened with the Heinkel over the English Channel.

'Red Leader. Break. Bandit behind. Break Commander.' Lin Xiaobin's voice crackled. Harry kicked the rudder hard to the right and pulled up. The Zero shot underneath and turned sharply back towards the Warhawk. Harry rammed the throttle forward as far as it would go, and climbed steeply to put distance between him and the enemy.

'Red leader. Second Bandit on your tail.'

Harry booted the rudder again. Tracer flashed over his canopy and he felt the aircraft shudder as cannon-fire smashed into the fin. He pushed the column forward to increase speed. The Zero raced above his head, with Lin Xiaobin on its tail, guns blazing.

The wisp of smoke from the Zero's engine thickened and flames licked the cockpit. Harry watched the pilot struggling to escape. The canopy tumbled away but the pilot was fighting with his straps. The orange-red flames danced along the fuselage as he flipped the plane onto its back and fell into the empty space below, turning over and over till the parachute billowed from his back, arresting his descent. The white circle of silk sank towards the paddy-fields beside the river, where tiny dots were following their buffalos along the lines of rice.

Harry scanned the empty horizon, turning through three hundred and sixty degrees in a clockwise direction and then back a second time. The dogfight had evaporated. The only other planes circling were Warhawks with their familiar nose-markings. In the shimmering haze above the distant city, he saw eight bombers on track for Chengdu, but no escorts.

Harry knew the Warhawks would struggle to catch the Mitsubishis before they reached their target. Maybe Shuangliu could be scrambled to intercept. He radioed Dougie, but there was no response. He repeated the message but the intercom mocked him with empty silence.

He could feel the adrenalin draining. Time to head home? Lady Luck had been with them so far. The arithmetic was impressive. Over twenty aircraft destroyed or damaged, for the loss of one Warhawk. Stop when you're up. He closed his eyes, massaging the side of his temples to ease the throbbing. A cloud of pink-mist drifted into view and he could feel the nausea rising in his stomach. Don't think about it, Harry. The job is to destroy enemy planes. It's you or them. There's no other choice. He snapped open his eyes and his gloved hand wiped the sweat from his forehead as he scanned the sky.

There was still a chance of catching the Nells if they flew at full bore. In any case they could nail the bastards as they turned for home. A final shoot-out was worth a try.

'Red leader to Yellow leader. At Angels Ten over Chong Wen village. Will pursue eight Nells heading Two Seven Zero for Chengdu. Confirm if okay to join.'

'Red leader, Yellow One, Yellow Three and Yellow Eight coming now.' Lin Xiaobin was the first to respond. 'Yellow Two missing. Yellow Five and Six returning to base damaged. Yellow Four and Seven out of ammunition.'

Calls followed from Red wing pilots. Dong Wen and Ma Hongsen were also limping back to Fenghuangshan.

Harry circled above the village, allowing the Warhawks to coalesce in loose formation. As he brought round the eight planes into line for Chengdu, there was a flash of sunlight from the east, a momentary glint gone in an instant. Harry narrowed his eyes, staring at the horizon. It could easily have been something moving on the ground, perhaps the windscreen of a turning vehicle. Harry noted the tightening in his chest and knew he should trust his instincts. 'Red Leader to all pilots. Suspect bandits Zero Nine Zero.'

Twelve dots appeared from the east, low in the sky to avoid the radar.

Harry breathed slowly, drawing air deep into his body. He knew his men would be feeling the same trepidation about taking on adversaries fresh off the starting block. He glanced at his watch. They'd already been airborne two and a half hours. Fuel and ammunition were low. It might be wiser to cut and run.

Harry glanced to his right. Lin Xiaobin was in perfect formation. He could see the outline of the young pilot's head through the perspex canopy, eyes fixed on the approaching Zeros. *'Many Japanese will not see the sun set this evening'.*

It was simple. Kill or be killed. Harry pressed the intercom as he pushed his control-column forward. 'Right ho, chaps. Choose your target. Plenty for everyone. Good luck.'

# Chapter Five

## Chengdu:
## Sunday 12th May 2019

Chen Xi was unable to focus, trying to fill the time till the weekend was over and she could get back to work, restlessly moving from one activity to another.

Early in the morning she went for a twenty-kilometre run on Sha Xi Lu Dao, part of her training for the Chengdu marathon. Two hours pounding the Green Way in Pixian left her drained, but with her brain still whirling. While her muscles settled, she went online to see if playing *Wéi qí* with her latest opponent in Qingdao would calm her thoughts. But she lost the match, after making errors well below her grading level.

To lift her mood she spent an hour talking to Huang Guo and Lin Ting on 'WeChat'. There was a plan to visit KTV with boys from the *Eye Pad* office where Lin Ting worked, near Computer City. It was one of the software companies she persuaded to attend the *Pitch Perfect* conference. Lin Ting mentioned that Zhao Han in coding was keen on her, but Chen Xi was not interested. Since splitting with Wang Yi three months ago, she wanted to spend time with the girl friends she'd neglected during her eighteen-month relationship.

After agreeing to meet them later for a coffee at Mama Chufan's by the metro, Chen Xi flicked on the *Táo bǎo* website to check if there was anything new in their range of skirts, but it was showing the same patterns as the previous week. For a while she listened to FanxyRed's latest album, *Activate*, but decided she preferred them when they were Acrush. They'd lost something with Min Junqian's departure. Their singing was less genuine now they'd moved to South Korea. The androgyny of the four remaining *měishàonián* performers and the way they danced and dressed seemed more important to the girls than the songs. Along with all her friends she'd admired the way that the group had broken ground with their challenge to gender stereotyping, but felt that leaving Zhejiang province for Seoul had been a betrayal of their nationality.

Chen Xi knew she should complete the report she'd agreed to write, following her PowerPoint presentation to the Chamber of Commerce on Friday. With Brexit approaching, they wanted a clear explanation about what the CUV could offer British companies planning to start up in Chengdu. A further event was planned for Thursday, so she had intended to type it on Saturday morning while the issues were fresh, but then Gloria had asked her to show Mister Torin the Pandas.

Since he'd driven away towards the third ring road, she'd been going over and over their conversations in her head to see if there was any particular reason why he'd left when he did. Was it her poor English? Did he think she was a bit stupid because she muddled her words sometimes—like when she'd talked about the pandas dying. She'd felt awkward when he mentioned sex, and then she'd used the wrong word, compounding her embarrassment.

Perhaps he just had other things to do? She knew at least one delegate had asked him to submit a project tender. She could have helped because she knew something about *Lucky Banana*. Lin Ting had a friend working there, who had told her they were struggling with marketing and had set aside nearly a million kuai to raise their profile in Chengdu and Chongqing.

She looked at the small, Jade dragon beside her bed, with shades of green visible in the whorls of its polished surface. It had been a present from a monk in the Taoist monastery in Qinsheng mountain, who had taught her how to use it as a focus for meditation. She stroked its back, seeking insight from the mysterious patterns.

She'd been surprised to enjoy the visit to the panda base. There was an attentiveness to Torin's expression when he'd asked about life in the countryside. He had listened quietly as she'd talked about starting at high school in the city and her subsequent experience as a student at Sichuan University. She closed her eyes and his face floated into focus, arched eyebrows above the red-rimmed glasses, raised scar on his neck.

She knew Gloria was arranging for Torin to meet the British Consulate in Chongqing on Thursday, and Sunny had wondered if she might be asked to accompany him. The trip would take all day. But Gloria had said nothing so she guessed she'd asked someone else. Torin was flying back to the UK on Friday. If the *Pitch Perfect* orders were mostly from Beijing and the eastern seaboard, he might never return to Sichuan.

She rubbed the head of the dragon, feeling the rough contours of its ears and jagged crown. It was surely wise to let it go. What was the proverb her English teacher taught her? *'Leave sleeping dogs to slumber'*? Everyone knew it was a mistake to become involved with westerners. They always wanted to ask questions about *Tiān ān mén guǎng chǎng* or tell you Taiwan was another country.

She pulled her laptop towards her and opened the file for the Chamber of Commerce. She persevered as the sun dropped behind the adjacent apartment block, casting a shadow across her wall.

'*Chen Xi!*' her mother called from the kitchen. '*Wài pó wài gōng huí yào lái chī fàn.*' She'd forgotten her grandparents were coming for food. For a moment she was tempted to shout back that she had to finish the report, but dutifully took off her headphones and went through to the kitchen to help her mother prepare. At least having her grandparents over meant she had an excuse not to join the gathering at KTV. Explaining again to her doting *wài pó* that she wasn't on the shelf at twenty-six was probably easier than handling Zhao Han.

Her mother was chopping bean-curd into squares, so she guessed *mápó dòufu* was one of the dishes, even though her grandmother was not keen on spicy food. Chen Xi looked at the clock in the corner. Quickly she pulled out the portable cooker from the cupboard, washed the rice-grains three times till the water lost its creamy colour, tested the depth of liquid in the bowl with her finger, and switched it on. '*Mǐ fàn zhǔ hǎo le.*'

Her mother smiled, reassured to know the rice would be ready in time.

Chen Xi put her hand on her mother's shoulder, wondering what else she was making. '*Wǒmén jīn tiān chī shén me?*'

'*Hóng jiāo ròu sī.*' Wang Yu Ling gestured with the knife

at the dining table, where a bowl of shredded pork and cabbage already sat on the hot plate, beside the *fān qié chǎo dàn* Chen Xi knew was her grandfather's favourite dish. The eggs would have come from the hen-coop in his tiny garden. On the cooker she could see a white sauce, bubbling over pieces of chicken, specially slow-cooked for her grandmother.

'*Kuài bāng wǒ xǐ cài!*' Yu Ling pointed at a plate of tomatoes, peppers and onions, and Chen Xi washed the vegetables and sliced them to add to the different dishes.

When the doorbell rang, everything was laid on the table. Chen Xi messaged the girls on WeChat with a photo of the meal.

She found it difficult to sleep that night, turning her pillow as she tried to find a cool haven for restless thoughts. Finally, with dawn breaking across the city on Monday morning, she showered and dressed and headed to the metro, deciding it was more important to be first into the office and access the file about *Perfect Pitch* than do boxing exercises.

There were no messages on the answerphone, but she discovered from the passport page in the file that Torin Cameron was born in December 1989. Three years older. His emergency contact was Mette Rasmussen. Relative or girlfriend? It wasn't the same address as on the invitation letter the company had sent to Torin for his visa. Still in London though.

Half an hour later she was sitting at her desk, working through notes from the Chamber of Commerce event, when her phone buzzed. The familiar opening of '*nǐ xiào qǐ lái zhēn hǎo kàn*' made her glance down from her computer. After watching Lu Xiao Le sing this at the Voice of China auditions, she'd uploaded it as her ring tone.

The green lettering flashed the caller's name. Chen Xi looked around the office. Apart from An Qi Qi, who had just come in and was sorting the mail in Gloria's room, she was alone. It was after eight, so the office would fill soon.

'*Nǐ hǎo.*' The fall and rise of the third tone was perfect. Had he been taking lessons, or just practising with Google translate?

'*Wǎ hěn hǎo. Nǐ ne?*' Chen Xi smiled as she pressed the phone to her cheek.

'Sorry if this is a bit early. I just wondered if you might be free at all this week—tomorrow perhaps?'

'*Míngtiān?* You mean Tuesday? In evening?'

'I was hoping during the day. I know that's work time, but I want to talk through how China UK Ventures might help with next steps. Maybe not in the office though. Somewhere quieter, perhaps?'

Chen Xi hesitated, wondering if Qi Qi was listening. 'In morning I am with guests from Manchester. Maybe afternoon is possible. I need to discuss with Gloria.'

'I thought she was happy to delegate to you?'

'That when she can't come eat hotpot, because of her daughter. Maybe she have other work for me than just meet Manchester visitors.'

'Could you say it's to follow-up on the ideas we were discussing over dinner?'

Chen Xi felt her pulse quicken. 'I will ask Gloria when I see her this morning.'

Gloria was hesitant. Sunny hadn't finished the report for the Chamber of Commerce, and they needed time to print it. But she acknowledged *Perfect Pitch* could be really successful in China, so it was worth trying to secure the countrywide franchise for CUV.

Sunny promised Gloria she'd have the report ready for printing on Wednesday. She was relieved Gloria didn't ask to see what she'd done so far. Returning to her desk, she texted Torin to confirm she'd meet him at his hotel at one o'clock, then pulled out the notes she'd made from the Chamber's discussions the previous Friday, sorting the headings for the report. She could finish it as long as there were no interruptions for the rest of the day.

When Qi Qi came over a few minutes later to say Gloria wanted her to host a mid-morning meeting, followed by lunch and a visit to Jin Li and People's Park, for a delegation from the British Council, Chen Xi smiled dutifully. She closed her eyes, focusing on her meditation exercises. The room quietened and her balance returned.

She still had Wednesday. If she could finish the report in the morning, there would be time to print it in the afternoon, or even early on Thursday since the conference didn't start till lunch. Quickly she made a decision about the headings of the different sections, then rang Zhao Han at *Eye Pad* to ask if he could help with the graphics.

That evening, watching television with her parents, she wondered what to wear the next day. She couldn't appear too casual, because Gloria expected standards in the office, but didn't want to dress too formally if they were strolling in the sunshine. She opted for the black jacket and skirt she'd worn at the conference and an embroidered blouse, barely visible beneath the jacket she could hang in her locker as she left the office.

It was just after one o'clock when the Mercedes turned into the forecourt of the St. Regis. Torin was waiting beside the doorman, dressed in cotton trousers and a tee shirt printed with '*If God is the answer, what on earth was the question?*'

He opened the door of the taxi and edged himself onto the seat, beside Chen Xi. 'Great to see you again Sunny. Where are we going?'

'*Wén shū yuàn* first. Monastery. Then *Dù fǔ*, in a big park.'

'Sounds good. How was your morning? Was it okay with visitors from Manchester?'

'Football team.'

He whistled approvingly. 'Marcus Rashford?'

Chen Xi smiled. 'Not players. Managers. Here about summer school for children in Sichuan. We visit sports stadiums in south of Chengdu to show possibilities.'

'You get around. All I've done is thirty lengths of the hotel pool. Have you been busy since Saturday?'

'A little.' She talked about the family meal on Sunday evening, smiling as she remembered her grandmother clicking her tongue when she told her there was no new boyfriend to replace Wang Yi. 'We had special food because grandparents been away on farm three months. Now they stay with us for a bit.'

Torin was intrigued. 'You said your parents grew up in the countryside and then moved to Chengdu, but are your grandparents still living there?'

Chen Xi was pleased he'd remembered. She explained that her story was similar to many of her friends who had been born on farms, often a long way from Chengdu. At least one of the parents had moved to the city before their children started high school.

'Schools not that good in the countryside?'

'They are okay.' Her eyes sparkled. 'I loved when I study in countryside. It has my best childhood memory. That not reason.' She talked about the migration into cities of people looking for work, where the money earned outweighed living costs, including education fees for people without Chengdu identity cards. When her parents had moved to Chengdu fifteen years ago, it had not been easy. Wages were low, housing poor and there were shortages. But things were changing fast. The population of Chengdu doubled in ten years. Many families now had money to spend. 'All parents want their children to be success. With only one child, it's very special.'

Torin shook his head thoughtfully. 'I can't imagine being an only child. It must be very strange in the evenings and weekends, when you just have your parents for company.'

'Since 1980, our government has said each family only allowed one child. Back then people think having a boy is important, because men carry on the family line. Girls will marry to some other family, no longer belonging with relatives. Most family want boy not girl. Before then lots of children in every family. My mom has four brothers and one sister. All now in Chengdu.'

'And your Dad's family?'

She described a similar story for her father, although his four brothers had moved to different cities—Xian, Chongqing, Wuhan and Beijing. But her father's parents stayed on the family farm, because her great-grandfather had lived there since he was born.

'He must be very old?'

'Ninety-five next birthday. We have a big party at farm.'

'That will be some gathering.'

Chen Xi smiled. 'Maybe fifty relatives, with all the cousins. Not sure I met them all yet, especially those in Wuhan and Beijing.' She glanced through the car window. 'Ten minutes to Wén shū. Tell me about your family.'

Torin hesitated; he could count his relatives on one hand. He described his childhood in the countryside around Forres, in the north east of Scotland. As the youngest of four he had only known the rough and tumble of sharing. Wearing his brother's hand-me-downs, he remembered acquiring his first new trousers on his tenth birthday. It wasn't that his parents were short of money; his father worked with one of the oil companies in Aberdeen, but they'd grown up as baby-boomers in the shadow of the Second World War, influenced by their parents' attitudes to rationing. One of his grandparents had lived in occupied Europe during the second world war. Making do was an artform, recycling a way of life.

The car stopped in front of a wide alley with a large sign in brown lettering.

'We here. Wén shū monastery that way.'

They walked along the wide lane past food-stalls. Above the high wall on their left they saw the curved, tiled rooves of traditional buildings. The wall gave way to an ornate pair of ten-foot, metal gates that were fixed open at the entrance of the monastery.

Beside the gates an old man was sitting in a wheelbarrow, stumps of severed legs hanging over the rim.

Next to him a younger man ate from a bag of sunflower seeds, chewing out the kernels and spitting the husks on the ground. The old man held a piece of cardboard with Chinese writing on his chest.

'What does it say?' asked Torin.

'Work accident. Sick wife to feed. Please help.'

'Should we give something?'

Sunny pressed her lips together as she looked at the old man. 'We often give change or buy food or water. We living much better life. If he have choice, he won't sit on ground, begging for money.'

Torin put a folded ten renminbi note in the upturned cap and they walked through into the monastery grounds. 'That's the first beggar I've seen. In London many homeless people live on the streets now, but mostly it's younger people.'

'He here because Buddhism temple. People who come should have a kind heart and be open.'

Inside Wenshu they walked past the Peace Tower, with its crenelations rising beneath the golden dome, towards the entrance to the maze of courtyards linking the ancient buildings.

'How old is this monastery, Sunny?'

'First built at start of Tang dynasty, so over one thousand years. But not all buildings very old I think. Some temples destroyed by emperors or fire. See here.' She pointed at a large noticeboard with the history of Wenshu in Chinese and English.

Torin read how the first temple had been erected in 605 when the monastery was called Xin Xiang Si. *In the year 845 Emperor Tang Wu Zong ordered it to be destroyed* because he feared Buddhism was brainwashing people to overturn the royal family. His successor Tang Xuan Zong took over in 845 and allowed Buddhism to remain on the site, but in 1644 a fire burnt every building to the ground. During Qing dynasty in 1697 strange red lights were seen and people who went inside came back saying they had seen the reincarnation of Manjusri Bodhisattva in the middle of the fire. Funds were raised to rebuild the monastery and the name was changed to Wén shū, which means Manjusri in Chinese.

'Wow. Long history.'

'Here is my favourite place in Chengdu. Sometimes come alone to sit in library. Just close eyes to think.'

Outside the temple of the smiling Buddhas, they watched people place lit sticks in the huge, black metal-cauldrons in the centre of the yard, before walking towards the embroidered cushions inside the temple, kneeling in front of the statue, and prostrating themselves on the ground. The smell of incense mingled with the chanting from behind the decorated screen at the side of the Buddha.

'Stay here.' Chen Xi walked across to the temple entrance where a brown-robed monk sat at a wide table surrounded by coloured wrappers. She came back with a packet of incense. 'Follow.' She took him by the arm towards the cauldron, drew three sticks from the packet, and lit them from one of the candles pressed into the sand. 'I show you.'

Holding the smouldering incense with both hands, she closed her eyes and lifted the sticks towards her forehead, then bowed to the Buddha inside the temple. Torin watched her repeat the actions three times, then she pushed the ends of her sticks into the sand and stepped back.

'Why do you close your eyes for so long after you bow?'

'Making a wish,' she said softly. 'Now you try.'

Chen Xi watched him move closer to the cauldron to light his incense. He raised them in front of his face. Beside him an old woman muttered quietly, oblivious to the foreigner awkwardly copying her example. Her dark-blue headscarf matched the colour of her long skirt.

Torin was smiling as he rejoined Sunny. 'That was a special moment. I could feel the power of her prayers.'

'She is Naxi tribe, from near Tibet. Different language and customs. Women in charge, not men.'

Torin looked back at the temple, where the woman was kneeling on the cushions. He noticed the richly-embroidered belt at the back of her jacket. 'This place reminds me of *The Last Emperor*.'

'*Mò dài huáng dì.*' Sunny nodded. 'You mean Pǔ Yí?'

'Like the Forbidden Palace. You enter a temple from the first courtyard, go through an archway into another courtyard, then through a second temple, which leads to more courtyards, each one laced with incense, chanting and mystery.'

'Except Pǔ Yí live on his own. Here hundreds of people! But not all buildings. Also garden. I show you.'

She led him through a stone archway onto a path winding through wooded glades and waterways edged with lotus plants. The sounds of the city beyond the walls were softened by the birdsong and distant chanting from a prayer hall. They passed a turtle pond where huge reptiles were motionless in their decorated shells, eyes unblinking as they waited for the day to cool. The track opened into a clearing surrounded by clumps of bamboo. Tables dotted the yard, with awnings providing shade from the sun.

'There is tea-house and then restaurant.'

A large sign in English explained about the vegetarian food. They took a plate each and went round together, with Chen Xi selecting portions of vegetables from the dishes. Sitting at a quiet table in the corner, they could see the Peace Tower through an open window.

'It's so beautiful and tranquil,' he breathed.

Chen Xi was relieved. She knew many tourists wanted to visit the Wide and Narrow Alleys, and Jinli Street, which were listed on the tourist websites about Chengdu—together with the Giant Pandas and Chairman Mao's statue. But once the excitement at seeing the old Chinese shopfronts had worn off, and visitors had captured images of hanging red lanterns on their phones, those places left people unsated. Maybe it was because of the crowds and incessant clamour of street vendors, which was more about the pocket than the soul.

She repeated a haiku poem Wang Laoshi had taught her class.

*'Come and buy, come and buy*
*But where happiness can be bought*
*None can tell'.*

Torin blinked, and turned from the open window. She sensed a heaviness and wondered what she had said to upset him.

Leaving the restaurant, they walked through the Sutra-Preservation Pavilion with its display of paintings and calligraphy by artists from the Tang and Song dynasties.

Sunny translated some of the sayings for Torin, struggling to convey the profound message contained in the simple characters. They stopped to watch an old man creating his own brush-strokes on a large sheet of paper pinned to the wall.

'He describe spring and flowers. Very beautiful. Now we go to see more beauty at Du Fu's cottage, where old poetry written. Also peaceful, but about words and stories. Another part of our culture. Important too.'

As they came through the high gateway, her phone pinged. She could see the caller's name. 'Sorry, Torin, this is Gloria. I need speak with her.' She stood against the wall, feeling the rough concrete pressing against her skin through the thin cotton.

When she put the phone in her pocket Torin could feel something had changed.

'I am very sorry, Torin, but must return to work.' She explained to Torin about the report for the British Chamber of Commerce.

'You have to do it tonight?'

She nodded. 'I plan to do tomorrow, but now Gloria asks me to run a meeting at the office in the morning, so must finish it today. I'm so sorry. She say she will ring you later about Consulate.'

Behind them he could hear gentle chanting from the temple. It felt like a door had opened, giving him a glimpse of something to explore on the other side. He wanted to go deeper into this other world before he left on Friday. He hesitated, aware Sunny had already been very generous with her time. 'I wonder if we could go to Du Fu's house tomorrow?'

'I work Wednesday.'

'After you finish?'

'I thought you out with German friends?'

Torin shook his head. Friedrich and Helmund would manage perfectly well without him at Octopussy. 'I'm free all evening.'

'Finish at four. Maybe meet at nearest metro?'

He smiled. 'That would be lovely, Sunny. You tell me where I need to go.'

'Easy to take metro from *Tài sheng nán lù*. I will text instructions. Only four kwai.'

Back in her bedroom she opened her laptop to discover that Zhao Han had sent the graphics. The blockage about the Chambers' report evaporated. She was clear about what she wanted to say, and the English translation came fluently. Before midnight she mailed it to Gloria and then fell into a deep sleep.

# Chapter Six

## Fenghuangshan Airfield:
## Thursday, September 20th 1942

It was early afternoon when the Tigers limped back to Fenghuangshan. Harry Winchester nursed his battered aircraft over the strip of woodland beyond the perimeter-track, after being cleared to land. He taxied to the hangar beside the operations-room. Already teams of mechanics were working on damaged planes, patching holes in the fuselages and wings, rearming the gun-turrets.

Harry flicked the engine-switch and watched the propeller whirr to a quivering halt. Wong Swee Wee, the senior mechanic, slid back the canopy and helped him climb onto the wing and down to the tarmac. Harry took a deep breath, grateful to be back on terra firma. The fresh breeze blowing from the Songtan mountains to the north was tinged with kerosene.

'Rudder barely working,' Harry pointed to the end of the fuselage, where a chunk of tail-fin had been shot away. 'Got some of the blighters though!' He held three fingers up so Bi Zhong could add it to the tally on the blackboard beside the hangar.

After inspecting each plane with Sergeant Wong, satisfying himself they would be airworthy tomorrow, Harry pushed open the door to the ops room. It was empty except for Major Walters standing at the far end beside the gas-burner. He was concentrating on the skillet in his left hand but looked up as the door banged shut. 'I've sent them to their bunks with a little present from Uncle Sam. Yours is the last.' He tossed the contents of the pan into the air and watched it flip.

Harry caught his reflection in the mirror beside the sink as he dropped his parachute over a chair. For a moment he hardly recognised the face. Green eyes sunk into their sockets. Brown hair pressed hard against his scalp, sticky with sweat, some longer strands glued to his forehead. Grime etched into the laughter-lines, mouth tight-lipped beneath the grey skin of his cheeks. He blinked his eyes, hoping to wash away the expression of meanness, but nothing changed. He turned from the glass.

'You've earned this, Harry. Brilliant sortie.' Douglass Walters ladled maple-syrup across the pancake, passing the plate to the young pilot slumped in the chair nearest the door. The American rubbed his chin and poured another large spoonful of batter into the reheated skillet. 'Twenty-three destroyed and eleven damaged, with only one aircraft lost on our side. Xu Wen is safe though. He managed to find a phone in a village. A farmer is bringing him back on a bullock-cart.' Dougie chuckled, allowing the words to trip out like a jazz sonata. 'Classy form of transport. Probably arrive tomorrow night if he's lucky. I asked if I should give the cart-driver a couple of greenbacks, but Xu Wen said it was more than the man could earn in a month, and a bag of rice would be enough. However, we need word to get around we appreciate farmers looking after our pilots. Not like the reception they gave the Japs who bailed out. Rather quick with their pitchforks.'

He tipped the fresh pancake onto another plate and sat beside Harry. 'How did you pull it off?'

Harry caught the sweet smell of the fried batter and raised his tired eyes to meet the American's, aware what he most wanted was sleep. He registered the hazel-brown irises behind the thick-rimmed spectacles, reminding him of Amy. He breathed in slowly. 'We nearly didn't Dougie.' He described how the escort of Zeros appeared at the last minute.

'You went for them first?'

Harry shook his head, cutting the waffle into slices. 'We split the attack. I knew the bombers would be sitting ducks first dive, and we'd be able to come round for a second run, if Lin could keep the Japs off our backs.' He lifted some pancake from his plate and chewed it slowly. 'I think two Nells must have simply exploded. I only counted seven going down and five heading back to Hubei, trailing smoke.' Pink mist sank from the ceiling and Harry stared at the naked light bulb above his head to prevent it engulfing him. He rubbed his eyes with the back of his hand to keep it at bay. 'We were short of ammo and fuel after the second dive. But I reckoned we could have a final pop at the eight bombers still on course for Chengdu. Then a second flight of Zeros appeared.' Harry was struggling to form sentences. 'They hadn't seen us though. God knows why. It was a turkey-shoot. Each of us nailed one on the first dive, which left four of the buggers intact.'

Harry scraped his fork across the plate, savouring the golden drops of sweetness. 'We pulled up to prepare for a second attack, but only Lin had ammo left. The rest of us were sitting-ducks. If we ran for home, they would catch us, so I gave the order to climb to Angels Eight, as if were reforming to attack. When we turned to drop down on the remaining Zeros, they were full bore towards Hubei.' Harry's eyes followed the American as he took his plate back to the stove. 'We were lucky, but it can't have been great for Chengdu that some Nells get through.'

Dougie looked up from the skillet. 'None made it, Harry.' He explained he'd received the radio message and was about to scramble B flight, when he learnt that Colonel Scott had already ordered up fighters from Shuangliu, 'They took out the rest of the Japs as they reached the outskirts. Not a bomb reached the city. Free Sichuan radio has been full of what the Tigers achieved today. It has given such a boost to morale. You deserve another waffle! Being British, a mug of tea as well, I imagine?'

Harry smiled weakly. 'Sorry, Dougie. One frigging sortie and I'm more shagged-out than the station bike.'

'First action for nine months.' Dougie flipped the pancake. 'Not surprised you're knackered. Adrenalin is an amazing drug, but it drains away quickly when the fighting ends. Your body will get used to combat again though. Things are going to get pretty busy by all accounts. Tojo's boys want to crush the Chinese resistance.'

The American turned back to his gas-ring and Harry watched him preventing the mixture from sticking to the base of the pan. The closely-shaved hair across the scalp and thick neck, combined with the roundness of his chin to give his face a resemblance to Humpty Dumpty; a moustache above his full lips twirled and crimped into a fine point at either end. It reminded Harry of the dressing-up games his sister Lydia played with her male doll. Immaculately adorned in lederhosen, it was a gift from an uncle who'd run against Jesse James in the 1936 Olympics.

Lydia had a range of stick-on moustaches she swapped around according to her mood, from the Hitler smudge above the lip, to the coiffured coils of Groucho Marx.

Harry noticed the polished buttons on his tunic pressing against a bulging midriff, as Douglass scraped the waffle. He'd heard that Major Walters had once been a fighter pilot, but it was hard to get a sense of this from his current shape. He was breathing heavily, just moving around the stove. How had he let himself go? Perhaps Yanks didn't care that much about fitness for combat.

Harry studied the American, trying to work out how old he was. Early thirties? As his eyes dropped below his neckline, he registered the right arm of Dougie's tunic was neatly-folded and pinned against the shoulder. The sleeve hung emptily from the epaulette. He was stirring the mixture in the skillet and flipping pancakes with one hand. Dougie looked up to see Harry staring at his arm.

'Not noticed before?' Dougie tilted the handle so the pancake slid onto Harry's plate. 'It's the reason I'm now flying desks.'

'Rotten show old boy. What happened?'

'Came off worse in a dogfight. In January I was one of a hundred Yanks recruited to knock the crap out of the Japs in Burma. We were the original Flying Tigers.' Dougie described how he'd flown into Mingaladon airfield close to Rangoon, a month after Pearl Harbour. Initially they'd managed to keep the Japs at bay, but once Singapore had fallen, the enemy redeployed hundreds of planes to bases in Thailand. Rangoon fell at the end of February, and the Tigers and their RAF allies were pressed into a ground-attack role to support the retreating Commonwealth troops.

Harry could hear Dougie talking from another room. It was the voice of a jazz singer, resonant with melody and laughter. A very different part of America to General Chennault. Dougie's words rolled into the room like the beating of kettle drums.

'Relentless advance... pilots outnumbered...

'Air Force to India... Tigers to China...

'Jap bridge at Salween... threatening Kunming...

'Tigers fight back... intent on destroying...'

The news was leaving Ghent.

*"Good speed!" cried the watch, as the gate-bolts undrew;*
*'Speed!' echoed the wall to us galloping through*
*Behind shut the postern, the lights sank to rest,*
*And into the midnight we galloped abreast.'*

'It was then it happened.' Through the swirling mist Harry watched Dougie pick up the last slice of pancake from his plate and spread it with syrup. 'As I pulled out of a diving attack on three Zeros, something whacked my back and the bloody instrument-panel exploded in front of me. I had no power and limited aileron. I couldn't prevent the plane drifting into a spiral. It twisted upside down and I dropped out of my straps through the half-open canopy. I barely managed to pull the chute before hitting the jungle.'

Dougie had emerged from a coma to discover the bullets that destroyed the instrument-panel had also shredded his right arm, which meant amputation. The surgeons couldn't remove the shrapnel from his head because of the risk to his brain, so he'd struggled with failing eyesight in one eye. After discharge from hospital in Kunming, he was taken off combat-duties, but insisted on retraining as an air-traffic controller.

'I'm now a rather different shape to the fit guy with twenty-twenty vision who helped stop the threat of a Japanese invasion. Bald and fat with failing eyesight. Not a pretty picture.' Dougie rubbed his left hand over his bulging midriff. 'But at least I'm alive and can do something to get back at the bastards that did this. I was assigned to Fenghuangshan at the beginning of September, the day after my twenty-first birthday. You arrived with the squadron three days later.'

Harry registered the silence in the room and opened his eyes, aware he'd been listening through a thick fog. He took a gulp of tea and replaced the mug on the wooden table next to the empty plate. He was struggling to focus on the face next to him. 'Christ, Dougie, you're the same age as me.' Harry ran his fingers over his smooth cheeks. 'I thought you were an old hand.'

'I thought you were too, when I heard your war record. Ten kills and a DFC.' Dougie sat beside the pilot. His left hand massaged the shoulder above his empty sleeve. 'How did you get involved? When I heard a Brit was taking over the squadron, I thought there must surely be some Yankee pilots available from Burma.'

'Pure chance Dougie, like everything else in this ruddy war.' Harry rubbed his eyes with the knuckles of his right hand. It eased the murmuring in his ears. 'After twelve months of flying Blenheims on patrols against the Luftwaffe along the south coast, I was taken off combat-ops and ordered to ferry Beaufighters from Bristol to

Cairo, with my navigator.'

His fingers played with his ear lobe, recalling how they'd both thought it meant the end of active service. After a few days leave in Cairo, they were flown back to England in the bomb-bay of a Liberator, lying like sardines with other aircrew on similar missions. Then it was back to the aircraft factory at Bristol to repeat the process. They'd done it four times, without incident.

'On the fifth trip in early April, instead of beating off flies and mosquitoes under canvas in the desert, we were given rooms on a house-boat up the Nile, commandeered from Thomas Cook. We never discovered what we'd done to deserve the upgrade, but we didn't complain, especially as my navigator got a dose of Cairo tummy and was running to the karzi every few minutes. Next day his temperature shot up, so I took him to the British Infirmary. Turned out to be Nile fever, which developed into encephalitis. He's still there, poor sod.'

Harry related how he'd returned to the houseboat, wondering whether the Penguins in the Ministry would leave him alone till Archie was better, or whether he'd be re-crewed with another navigator. He described meeting an American General trying to sort a delivery of planes to China. 'Rangoon had fallen to the Japs and he couldn't work out how to get his aircraft into China.'

'Hang on, fella.' Dougie was frowning. 'Was this guy called Chennault?'

Harry nodded.

'*Claire* Chennault? The legend? The man who created the Flying Tigers and is now in charge of the China Air Task Force?'

'The very same.'

Dougie whistled. 'You sure know how to mix with the right people.'

'Not really, I'm just capable of getting shredded and keeping my wits about me. It's a skill honed in pubs around airfields in the south of England during 1941.' Harry stood to refill his glass from the sink. He passed Dougie a tumbler of water and sat again. 'I didn't know any of that Flying Tigers stuff, just that this Yankee General wanted to fly over the Himalayas from India, but people were telling him it couldn't be done. By midnight, we'd had a skinful. I bet I could get one of his planes into China.'

'What did you stake?'

'Pack of cards.'

'A deck of Jacks for a Warhawk? Pull the other one, buddy.'

Harry grinned and tapped his breast pocket. 'I always carry them. Lots of waiting in ops rooms doing sweet Fanny Adams. They're not ordinary cards though.' He explained about Javier and the art work. 'I've won loads of money at poker—but not because of the paintings. People hang on to the Hearts as long as possible.'

Dougie raised his eyebrows. 'I hear that's one way to get Chennault on side. What did he bet in return?'

'Honeymoon on the Nile.'

'You must have won then, if you're standing here!'

'Yet to happen, old boy, because I was posted here.' Harry pursed his lips. 'He wrote to the King though, because of what happened after I reached India. The base at Dinjin was in a right mess, coping with the collapse of the Allied resistance in Burma. However, there was a plan afoot by your kinsmen to shift eight thousand gallons of aviation fuel to Kunming across the Himalayas in a couple of Dakotas. All very hush-hush.' His green eyes looked directly at the air traffic controller. 'Chennault had told the Yanks at Dinjin about the bet to fly a Warhawk into Kunming, so I was asked to join the fuel ferry as fighter escort, together with Robert Scott.'

Dougie's eyes widened. 'Same Scotty who is in charge of our fighter group?'

Harry smiled. 'Right man in right place at right time. We took off on eighth of April. It's only five hundred miles, so the distance didn't seem a problem. Scotty and I kept a respectful distance from the flying grenades we were escorting.'

'Jeez, Harry, I was still patrolling the Salween river in April. You must have flown right over me!' Dougie reached for a bottle of Jack Daniels from a cupboard above the sink and poured generous dollops into two glasses.

Harry swallowed a large mouthful. 'The first part was a doddle, going over the top of Burma. The crunch came at the Santsung range, where turbulence was horrendous. We were tossed about like leaves in a tornado. But once we passed the source of the Mekong, it went quiet and it was literally downhill to Kunming. I got a phone connection to Cairo and was put through to Chennault himself. He was having dinner with Keith Park. I arrived back in the UK to receive an invitation to the Palace for the first of June. That's where the DFC came from. Next morning, I was told I was being sent back to China. Special request from Chennault. I'd learnt Archie was likely to be hospitalised for several months, so I didn't protest.'

'And the cards?'

Harry unbuttoned the flap of his flying suit. 'Chennault handed them over when I met him at Kunming airport at the end of June.' He laid out the deck in its four suits. 'See what I mean about the Hearts?' His finger stroked the Queen and he glanced up to see the American staring at him strangely.

'Did you ever find out what the fuel was for?'

'There was talk of having a go at Japan itself. This was four months after Pearl Harbour and you Yanks were still mighty angry.'

'Friggin hell, Harry, you sure mix it with history.' Dougie picked up the bamboo-cane and turned towards the map. He pointed at the patch of blue sea beyond the east coast of China. 'You're talking about the Doolittle raid, for Christ's sake. A squadron of Mitchells took off from the USS Hornet to bomb Tokyo on eighteenth of April. The plan was to return over the Yellow Sea and then cross-country to Kunming. The eight thousand gallons of kerosene were to get em back over the Hump.'

Dougie rubbed his shoulder as he related the saga. It had been a military disaster; the planes had already been in the air twelve hours by the time they reached the Chinese coast. Every bomber crashed and some crews who came down in Japanese occupied-territory were executed as war criminals. One plane even ended up in Vladivostok. Dougie tapped the stick above the Korean peninsula, shaking his head. 'We're still waiting for the Soviets to release the crew. I gather Chennault was furious that he'd not been told, because he'd have organised safe landing-fields as they came in over the coast. But the top brass still managed to turn it into a huge morale-boost for folks back home, showing us Yanks could hit the enemy heartland.'

The American placed the bamboo-cane on the table and reached for his glass. 'The Japs reacted like hornets who'd had their nest attacked. They took revenge on Chinese civilians for having sheltered the crews. Towns like Nancheng were burned to the ground. Chennault reckoned they killed two hundred and fifty thousand men, women and children.'

'A quarter of a million lives as reprisal for a single bombing raid?' Harry closed his eyes, forcing down despair. 'I had no sodding idea. Two weeks later, I was on my way back to Blighty.'

'And two weeks later I lost this bugger.' The American massaged the joint beneath the empty sleeve. 'Before I met you, I'd been told you'd resisted pressure from Chennault to put new pilots on the front line. I didn't believe it; everyone knows the big boss doesn't take "no" for an answer.'

Harry emptied his tumbler and held it out for Dougie, thinking back to the meeting in Chennault's office shortly after he'd arrived from England. The previous day a thousand civilians had been asphyxiated during a bombing-raid on a hillside-tunnel close to the Yangtze. The General had wanted the squadron airborne next day.

Harry ran his fingers through his brown hair, recalling the tense conversation with the granite-jawed American, chewing his cheroot. He had quietly repeated the mantra that raw crew quickly become dead meat, and flying replacement pilots or aircraft over the Hump from India was not a priority for the Allies, after the Japanese advances in the Pacific. If Chennault wanted victory, the young squadron-commander had to be sure all pilots were combat-ready. 'With only seventy-eight serviceable planes in the whole of his Fighter Group, against seven-hundred Japanese aircraft, I told him he just needed to do the sums. Simple bloody arithmetic.'

'I bet Chennault loved hearing that from a Brit speaking with his mouth full of plums. I'm surprised he didn't send you packing on the next plane over the Himalayas.'

'We both knew he owed me one.' Harry smiled, humming the words from 'Let's Call the Whole thing Off'. 'You like tom-eight-o and I like tom-art-o. You say nee-ther and I say nigh-ther. I say *Him*-a-lay-as and you say Him-*arlyas*...'

'Sod off limey. You Brits hold your bum-cheeks so tight, it's a wonder you can ever fart.'

'Important skill if you're ever in the presence of the King—or you're on a date.' Harry smiled at the American. 'Not a lot of opportunity for that round here, although I hear Chennault is planning to fly some girls in from Delhi as a Thanksgiving present.'

Dougie nodded. 'His rationale is that it will save on medical bills for clap. But I can't get excited by the idea. The fact is...' He stopped mid-sentence as if searching for the words. '...I'm not holding my breath.' He put down his glass and looked straight at Harry. 'November is a long way off and his boss will have to approve it. In the meantime, if we get a lull in attacks, I can show you a place in town that caters for all tastes. The real thing buddy, better than flying solo with your playing cards.'

# Chapter Seven

## Du Fu's Cottage, Chengdu: Wednesday May 15th 2019

Sunny came up the escalator at Sichuan Hospital to see Torin studying the map beside the ticket barrier.

He turned as she called his name. 'This metro is huge Sunny. Is it really only eight years since the very first line opened? In the UK we'd still be arguing about planning issues. You know how to get things done. Security impressive too.'

He pointed at the two police-officers standing beside the baggage scanner. 'I'm wondering why those are not on the London underground, but maybe the numbers of people would make it unworkable? Expensive I guess, two guards on each machine at every tube entrance.'

'Here people glad for police. We know about London bombings. Not want in China.'

From the exit, Chen Xi walked along the pavement underneath the First Ring Road. 'Maybe fifteen minutes to Dù Fǔ park. Could get taxi, but walk more interesting.'

Opposite the entrance to the Museum of Kiln Ruins, Chen Xi turned right onto the driveway for the Academy of Medical Sciences. 'I know short cut because my friend work here.' She pointed to a bridge across the Modi river. 'That will take us onto Qinghua Road, and then Dù Fǔ gate.'

As they entered Huanhuaxi Park, the city noise retreated. They strolled through the bamboo glades between meandering waterways, smelling the rich moistness rising from the still waters, tranquillity seeping into them.

The track opened into a clearing, revealing a thatched house beside the lake. Torin's eyes widened, recalling a childhood image. His father's car breasted the crest of a small hill beside a white church, and they were looking down at a cluster of oak-beamed buildings. 'It's like a Scandinavian farmhouse. The Vikings criss-crossed timbers to hold the reeds in place, just like those.' Torin indicated the straw rolls along the ridge. 'Can we go inside?'

'Yes, I bought tickets already.' Chen Xi showed her phone to the attendant, dressed in a cheongsam, embroidered with chrysanthemums. The woman glanced at Torin and there was an exchange with Sunny. She smiled and let them through the gate.

'She ask if I am interpreter for you.' Sunny led the way up the stone incline, and they stepped over the solid, wood threshold into the shaded interior. It was furnished in the way Du Fu had lived more than a thousand years ago—a bed with a sleeping roll, a desk, a cooking area, and a blanket on the floor for meditation and prayer.

'Did he live alone?'

'I think so,' said Sunny. 'He had wife and children but not always with him. Whole story is in museum next door, but this gives an important date.' She pointed to a brown sign inscribed with Chinese characters. 'He was here five years, escaping war and famines. 760-765.' She pronounced the numbers carefully. 'He died in 770, but over a thousand poems are still read today.'

Torin pursed his lips. 'England was just coming out of

the Dark Ages. Our first poet was a farm worker, and only nine lines of one poem survive. He died not long before Du Fu was born.'

'What was his name?'

'Caedmon the cowherd.' Torin frowned, trying to remember what his English teacher had said about the illiterate poet from Whitby, who'd recited songs to the Abbess.

In the museum shop Torin chose a translation of Du Fu's poems, and two woodcuts of paintings. 'For my sister and grandmother,' he explained. 'Neither of them has ever been to China. Gran is too old, and my sister is in New Zealand.'

Sunny looked puzzled. 'Yesterday, you said two brothers also. Are you not buying them presents?'

Torin shook his head. 'Both dead.'

'Sorry to hear. I didn't know.'

He pressed his lips together. 'It was fifteen years ago.'

'What happened?' The question slipped out.

Torin was conscious of her brown eyes looking straight at him. 'Boxing Day Tsunami. We were on holiday in Thailand.' He hesitated. 'Was it in the news in China?'

Sunny nodded, recalling the images on television in her last year at primary school. The family in the apartment above had flown to Phuket. They were all on the beach when the waves came, except the mother, who had gone shopping for *dòu shā bāo*, the sweet bean-buns the family liked for breakfast. Sunny remembered returning from school one afternoon and finding her own mother in the kitchen, with her arms around Mrs. Deng. She had never seen an adult crying before, gulping for breath as she wailed, like a pig having its throat cut.

For weeks she noticed the quietness above. Instead of television, music, voices calling, feet running across the floor, or doors banging, there was just the occasional padding of slippers. The silence of a cemetery. One day Sunny met Mrs. Deng in the lift and noticed tears welling in her eyes, as the woman looked at her. It happened again the following afternoon when they were queuing for noodles in the small *chāo shì* on the ground floor. After that, if Sunny saw Mrs. Deng waiting for the lift, she would take the stairs, even though their flat was on the twelfth floor. She made sure the woman never saw her again. Eventually Mrs. Deng went to live with her sister on the other side of Chengdu.

'My brothers were a lot older and I wasn't as close to them as my sister.'

'But she okay?'

'Emily and I had gone to take photos of the sunrise, so were on higher ground, when the waves struck. I was hit by a falling tree. Gashed my neck.' Torin touched the scar. 'My sister managed to get me to hospital. I was unconscious for several days. They never found our parents or brothers.'

In the silence, Sunny felt the rawness of loss across years and beyond words. Mister Torin looked different to the poised presenter she'd watched at the *Pitch Perfect* conference. She wanted to reach out to him, but was hesitant about intruding on private grief. She turned away to pay. The elderly shop-assistant was retying the strawberry-red scarf around her head. Wisps of white hair curled out from the thin cotton as she wound it in a loose bow under her chin. Her brown skin was etched, like the bark of an old oak.

She talked rapidly to Sunny while she wrapped the package, glancing at Torin and smiling. 'She also ask if I translator. Says if you like poems we should take road to south gate by Huanhua stream. Poetry Avenue has three hundred statues of Chinese poets.'

As they walked past the plinths, Chen Xi read the inscriptions. It was mostly dates of births and deaths, with famous lines from their poems.

*'Everything has beauty, but not everyone sees it.'*

*'Study the past if you would define the future.'*

*'Before you embark on a journey of revenge, dig two graves.'*

Sunny frowned. 'To be honest, I never heard of these poets. But words enchanting. Some are friends of Dù Fǔ.'

They walked from the exit of the park onto the bridge over the river. The sun was low in the sky, hovering like a balloon above a line of skyscraper blocks beyond the Second Ring Road. She noticed Torin dragging his left foot again. 'Was that also tsunami?'

Torin shook his head. 'Much more recent. Paragliding. I twisted my ankle, landing on a rock.'

Sunny's eyes widened. 'You mean jumping off mountains with parachute?'

'More running off, than jumping; or just being lifted by the wind.' Torin explained about thermals and described how one of his quiz team had encouraged him to try it. Graham had a mate who ran a flying-school in Shropshire, which meant days on Long Mynd or Corndon, followed by evenings in the Green Man. He didn't add that it had been the perfect balm to the raw wound of separation from Kat.

Torin glanced at his watch, remembering that Graham had said he'd phone to tell him if a trip was planned for the coming weekend.

'You need to return to hotel?' Sunny wondered if he was meeting his German friends after all.

'I'm not in any hurry. Maybe we could find somewhere to have food?'

She hesitated. While waiting for the presents to be wrapped, she'd seen a message from Gloria on her phone, asking for changes to the report. She ought to go home and work on it. 'I know a place you might like. Kathmandu. Next to river. Very close. Food from mountains.'

'Sounds intriguing.'

She led the way to the restaurant, zigzagging through back streets to avoid the traffic-filled main roads. Electric scooters whined in and out of the cyclists and pedestrians. From the front of Kathmandu, they saw the Jin Jiang river beyond the railings. On the far bank a fisherman was flicking a rod above the water.

'Will he catch anything?'

'Maybe. The river comes all the way from Dujiangyan.'

'Looks pretty muddy. Is it edible?'

'You get chance to try. They have fish on menu. See page four.'

Torin looked up from the glossy folder of photographs to see Sunny smiling behind her hand.

They ordered *momos* and *dal bhat tarkari*, and watched the dusk settle over the city beyond the river bank while sipping *raksi*. She asked him about his job and Torin explained how he had become involved with *Pitch Perfect* after his degree at LSE. The company had been started by people from his course three years previously, with support from the university's entrepreneur fund.

'The concept would work with almost any company in the public or private sector. Every organisation can use a heightened profile that cascades into the inbox of potential users. We think we're a jump ahead of our rivals, but it's very competitive.'

'China UK Ventures very interested to help.' She told him about *Lucky Banana* and the million kuai for marketing. 'We hope you want to work with us.'

'That's down to the board, Sunny. I'm not senior enough to make that decision; but I've already emailed my recommendation.'

'You come to Chengdu again?'

'Maybe.' He looked at her, wanting to say something more positive. 'Some of the board were hesitant about funding this trip, so they will need to see clear outcomes.'

Sunny tried to push away the feeling that it mattered. He was from England and she was Chinese. Their lives were in two very different cultures. She watched a young couple walking hand in hand along the path beside the river. The man's white shirt gleamed under the street lighting. They stopped to look at the water, heads pressed close, black hair brushing together. A child crying in one of the apartments mingled with the chirping of crickets beside the river.

'Do you want anything else?' Beyond the railings the fisherman was unscrewing the segments of his rod. She remembered the *Yā cháng*. 'Not tried muddy fish yet.'

'Next time?' Torin smiled and glanced at his watch. 'You've been the perfect host Sunny, but I think I should head back to the hotel. I need to prepare for the Chamber of Commerce conference tomorrow.'

Sunny stared at him. 'I thought you were meeting British Consulate in Chongqing?'

'Cancelled—something to do with Brexit. Gloria suggested I came to the British Chambers instead.'

Frowning, Sunny recalled the phone call to Gloria outside Wen Shu monastery, the rough stone against her back as her boss asked her to tell Torin she would call him later. She'd had to go home to finish the report. Had there been another arrangement with Gloria she'd not known about? Of course, Torin should go to the Chambers meeting, which was all about developing new business in Chengdu. But why hadn't Gloria mentioned it when she'd asked her to manage things in the office on Thursday? Was something going on? Did that explain why Torin had been in such a hurry to go back to his hotel after they'd seen the pandas?

Everyone in the office knew Gloria had not seen her husband for over a year since he'd moved to Shanghai. He hadn't even returned for the spring festival. Qi Qi thought Gloria's husband was seeing another woman. If he had a girlfriend in Shanghai, he wouldn't be coming back to Chengdu any time soon. Gloria was free to do what she wanted. Sunny breathed deeply, trying to push away the tightness in her stomach.

'Will you be there?' he asked.

'Gloria is speaking, so I don't need to go as well. I gave her report yesterday.' Sunny was aware her voice was clipped. Would Gloria be wearing the cheongsam again?

Torin could see the river reflected in her eyes. 'I'm sorry

about that. I was hoping I'd see you again.'

'But you leave next day?' She pressed her lips together.

'Yes, Air China to Heathrow. Check out after breakfast on Friday.'

On the back seat of the Didi, Sunny was conscious of the looming farewell. The taxi would drop him outside the St. Regis and she'd be driven alone to her parents' house. Unless he asked her into the hotel, it was goodbye. Not *zài jiàn*.

He stood beside the open window of the taxi, looking down at her. The glass doors to the hotel entrance rotated slowly behind him, flashing the reflection of the plaza lights opposite.

He leant forward. 'Thank you for showing me Chengdu. I will treasure the memories.' He kissed her on the cheek, then stepped back from the car as it pulled away.

The driver slowed at the approach to the barrier. The attendant pressed a button to lift the arm and the car accelerated up the ramp. She turned her head to see Torin disappear through the revolving doors.

# Chapter Eight

## Chengdu:
## Thursday 25th November 1942

'Raise a glass to Hirohito.' Lin Xiaobin staggered unsteadily to his feet and poured a generous shot of *baijiu* into his glass. 'To his divine majesty, forty-one today.' The shrill voice cut across the hubbub.

Harry lifted his eyes from his own drink. 'I thought you hated the Emperor?'

'Sure do,' slurred the pilot.

'So why celebrate his birthday?'

'Two reasons.' Lin Xiaobin hiccoughed and swayed, splashing Dougie's shoulder. 'Firstly, it has given us a day off. His glorious warriors would have their testicles rammed down their throats if they didn't honour his special day.' He emptied the glass and reached for the bottle to refill his tumbler. 'Secondly, it brings him one year closer to his death.'

Harry looked round the room, lit by a string of red, candle lanterns hanging from metal hooks driven into the ceiling joists. The six tables along the wall were occupied by men from the Fenguangshan base. Most were in battledress, although a few had pulled out civilian clothes from the depths of their lockers.

A flight had been stood down since early afternoon, when the pilots and ground crew from B flight emerged from their billets, hungover and bedraggled from their previous night's celebrations. Enemy attacks had trailed off over the weekend, and there was little likelihood of bombing raids on a sacred day in the Japanese calendar. Harry and Dougie reckoned it was safe to allow the men a night out in Chengdu on two separate shifts. If anything happened, half of the squadron was still on standby.

Dougie had commandeered two trucks to ferry everyone into Chengdu. Having heard about B flight's antics, the men were determined to outdo their colleagues. After a crawl through a series of bars recommended by Zhou Zi Qiang, who knew the backstreets of his hometown, they'd ended up in Fu Zhe Ji's smoke-filled saloon, along a narrow alley.

'Lái ba!' screeched Lin Xiaobin, urging the crews to their feet, reaching for a chopstick as a baton. Harry recognised the familiar notes of 'Happy Birthday to You' swelling in volume, and found himself humming along. Lin Xiaobin slowed the chorus as they approached the final line, rising to a crescendo with 'Huángdì shēngrì kuàilè'. He lifted his tumbler high and threw it on the floor. 'Húndàn huángdì. Bastard Emperor.' Shards of glass splintered across the room to cheering.

A large man, dressed in a black lóng páo, embroidered with golden dragons, appeared with a young woman in tow. On the lined face, long threads of moustache trailed either side of the taut lips. The man barked an order at his companion, who bent to sweep up the broken glass. His eyes took in the prostrate figure of Lin Xiaobin, snoring loudly, with his pigtail trailing in spilt beer. 'Báijiǔ always sort men from boys.' The rasping voice was tinged with disdain. He glanced from Harry to Dougie. 'You want bang-bang? I bring you girls.'

'We're in the queue, Mister Fu.' Major Walters gestured along the line of carousing men, where each table was emptying in rotation. 'Two more to go, then it's our turn.'

'No need queue.' Fu's smile revealed two gold teeth in his lower set. 'You top men. Deserve best girls.' He rubbed his hands. 'You like special? I have high-class girls across road.'

'How special?' asked Dougie.

Mister Fu stroked the strands of his moustache. 'Special as you want. They do anything. You tell me. I arrange. Tell me. Tell me.'

Dougie looked around. 'I ain't shouting it out in front of the others. Come here Mister Fu.' The bar-owner pulled up a chair beside Dougie. As the American whispered in his ear, Fu Zhe Ji's eyes widened. 'You brave Yankee friend. Me sort.' He turned to Harry. 'You like extra special too? Bendy girls?'

Harry shook his head, wondering what Dougie had asked for. A well-thumbed copy of the Kama Sutra had been lying around the ops room for weeks. 'No thanks Mister Fu. Spoken for already.'

'Not matter. Girls here understand arrangement. Chinese man many wives. You need be leader, so your men feel okay. Some also married.'

Harry rubbed his earlobe between his fingertips, unsure how to handle the situation. An image of Amy in the upstairs room of the Angel danced at the edge of his vision. It was another world. 'Just an ordinary girl, Mister Fu. As long as she smiles.' A frown creased his forehead. What difference did it make if she was grumpy as hell?

'All girls enjoy work. Paid well. Very clean.' He stood,

smoothing the creases from his *lóng páo*. 'I bring them here and they take across street, not upstairs. Own room each. No sharing. You have long time.'

Fu Zhe Ji named a price and Dougie passed across a wad of notes. 'There's a couple of extra dollars there from Uncle Sam—one for each girl. See they get it, Mister Fu.'

Gold teeth flashed in the flickering light from the lantern. 'You bet, sir. Fifteen minutes.'

The two men were left alone. Harry wiped his forehead. 'Dougie, I'm not sure I'll manage this.'

'I've had a skinful too. Plus I'm bloody unfit.' The American patted his rounded stomach. 'But it's been a long time since the real thing. Remember I promised you this, when we were discussing Chennault's plans to fly girls over the Hump?'

Harry snorted. 'They'd not be in much state for bang-bang after that experience.'

Dougie smiled. 'I heard he's now looking for dames in Guilin. If he can bring them here by train, the top brass won't need to know.'

'I thought Chennault *was* the top brass. Doesn't he call the shots in China?'

'Not completely. The high command in Washington don't really trust Chennault. General Stillwell's above him, with one day seniority. Deliberate decision by Roosevelt, because Stillwell is a stickler for rules.'

Harry rolled his eyes. 'Bloody desk-wallahs and rules. They lose touch with the real world as soon as they get scrambled egg on their caps.' He gestured along the row of the tables. 'These men are putting their lives on the line, Dougie. You know yourself, each time you open the throttle, you wonder if it's your day for the chop.'

A fortnight ago, he'd seen Wei Shanzheng's plane spiral to the ground on the outskirts of Chengdu. Two days later Zhou Ziqiang had exploded in an inferno of mutual annihilation, with a burning Zero that maintained its unwavering collision course. Before the last aircraft taxied to a halt in front of the hangar, their bunks had been cleared, ready for replacement pilots from Kunming.

They were the first fatalities for three weeks. Harry closed his eyes, recalling the briefing the morning after Zhou had bought it. He surveyed the sea of faces, knowing the young pilot wouldn't be the last to die in combat. Defending Chengdu was only the end of the beginning of the wider battle to liberate China. More aircraft destroyed, more letters to anguished families, more young pilots to nurse pre-combat jitters, more hatred sown in the hearts of those who witnessed the obliteration of friends.

Against the backdrop of the map of China, showing the line of the stalled Japanese advance, Harry talked about the plan for a night out at Mister Fu's.

'Most of them are still boys. If it helps with morale, I'm all for breaking a few rules.'

Harry was aware the air-traffic controller was speaking. He opened his eyes. 'With regard to rules, Dougie, I need to talk with you about Tuesday's op. You'd set off for Kunming by the time we landed.'

'You mean the dog-fight over Sui Ning? I would have stayed to see you land, but thought it time Tang Shuo had a bash at talking pilots down on his own. Didn't you nail eight Japs?'

'Impressive tally, Dougie, but there was an incident with

Captain Lin.' Harry pointed at the prostrate figure.

'He muscled in on your target?' Dougie nudged Harry in the ribs. 'Come on bud, you know he wants to be top of the leader board. Ten kills and rising.'

'Actually, he saved my life, Dougie. I owe him one for being a perfect wingman.'

'So what's the big deal?'

'What he did next.' Harry took a long drink. 'Xiaobin had clobbered the bastard on my tail. As I opened the throttle to rejoin the dogfight, I saw the Jap leap from the blazing plane and pull his 'chute. Then I noticed a Warhawk turn in a wide arc several hundred feet below. I recognised Lin's markings as his plane straightened up towards the parachute.'

Harry closed his eyes, watching himself press the transmit button. 'Yellow leader, break right, break right.' His voice tailed away, as he registered the flashes from the Warhawk's cannons and saw the Japanese airman twitch like a marionette, before the head fell onto his chest. Seconds later the plane was past the pilot and climbing into the dark-blue sky. The white canopy of silk sank towards the brown earth that stretched to the edge of the mountains.

'I watched the parachute crumple beside the body.'

'Captain Lin is not a stickler for the Geneva convention,' observed Dougie.

'Quite.' Harry raised his hand to order more drinks.

'Did anyone else see it happen?'

'Probably not, because we'd dropped below the main dogfight. The other pilots will have had their hands full.' His eyes narrowed. 'Is that significant, Dougie?'

'Maybe. The pilots take their cue from Xiaobin when you're not around. Have you said anything?'

'Haven't had a chance. He had to divert to Kwanghan with engine trouble and wait for spare parts from Kunming. He only flew back to Fenghuangshan this afternoon. But it was cold-blooded murder, Dougie. I watched him execute a fellow pilot.'

'The Jap's prospects wouldn't have been brilliant when he hit the ground.'

Harry frowned. 'Maybe a twisted ankle or broken leg?'

'I've said it before, but you don't take it in.' Dougie's tone was gently chiding. 'How do you think farmers with pitchforks treat someone they judge guilty of killing their relatives in Chengdu? Have you wondered why we don't have POW camps for Japanese aircrew?'

'That's not the point.'

'Isn't it?' Dougie emptied his glass. 'Either way, it's the same outcome. You could say Xiaobin did him a favour.'

Harry rolled his eyes. Was Dougie being deliberately obtuse? Surely, he could see the battle between good and evil raging across the globe? The Allies had to win, to preserve civilisation for the next generation. But if they discarded chivalry in the process, the victors would be too tarnished to reconstruct a decent world. He knew about King Pyrrhus of Greece. Men dying in the most horrible ways, and the scars of what survivors witnessed, would take a lifetime to heal.

Harry looked at the American. 'Shouldn't we treat defeated enemies honourably, if we have the chance? Otherwise, we're no better than barbarian hordes.'

Before Dougie could respond, Mister Fu appeared with

two girls, dressed in thigh-length house-coats, tied loosely at the waist. The taller girl stood behind Dougie's chair, caressing his neck. She had a jutting jaw, and rouged cheeks, and her skin was a different shade to her companion, whose face seemed almost white in comparison. As she reached over Dougie's head for the drink offered by Mister Fu, Harry noticed that the tiny hairs on her arm were darker and longer than the other girl, whose arms rested on his own shoulders. He'd heard Lin Xiaobin talk about people from Mongolia, as if they were a different race. The girl said something to her boss, and he patted her bottom approvingly. 'Zhang Xin Yi say she is very pleased to meet brave pilots. She yours Mister American. Very bendy.'

Harry looked at the other girl, smaller and slimmer. Her deep-brown eyes gave nothing away as she sipped her drink, while stroking his neck with her free hand. Long, black hair caressed her shoulders, resting against the open vee of her silk robe. Her face reminded him of the Queen of Hearts.

The girls finished their drinks and Mister Fu smiled. '*Zǒu ba*. We cross road.' They followed him into the narrow alley. Decorated red and yellow lanterns hung from the overhanging eaves beneath thatched-rooves. Smoke from braziers curled into the still air, carrying the smell of charcoal and frying *baozi*. From the upper floor of a house, a woman sang to the plucked strings of a *gǔzhēng*. Haunting words echoed along the darkened street.

The two airmen were walking behind the girls. 'Don't get me wrong, Harry.' Douglass spoke softly. 'I agree Lin needs confronting. It's a different world out here, though, and we should be careful. Some of the stories about what the Japs did to Chinese soldiers in Burma are pretty shocking. They were none too gentle with Yanks or Brits, but their treatment of Asian prisoners was simply cruel.' He rubbed the empty sleeve beneath his shoulder. 'Maybe we can speak to Xiaobin after Saturday's briefing. Chennault is joining us. He's meeting with the Generalissimo in Chongqing on Sunday and calling at aerodromes in Twenty Third Fighter Group on the way. We're last on his list on Saturday.'

Harry was still digesting this information when they entered the house opposite and climbed the stairs. The girl with long, black hair pushed open a door from the corridor, and she took his hand. A narrow bed almost filled the tiny space. Above it a window was open to let in fresh air, but the room was humid and dank. A single, red bulb hung from the ceiling, shrouding the bedroom in an eerie luminescence.

Harry caught his reflection in the mirror at the end of the bed. The face was worn and old. Were those eyes sinking deeper, or was the light stronger than last time he'd seen himself? When had he last shaved? Strands of brown hair touched the collar of his shirt. Time for a trim at Zheng's, in the village with the bamboo partridges.

Harry swallowed a large mouthful of water, grimacing as the cold liquid touched a nerve in the back of his mouth. Something else that needed attention.

He sat on the bed, feeling the mattress sag beneath. It smelt strongly of sweat.

The girl was standing in front. She untied the cord and let her robe drop to the floor. Harry looked at the naked body, lifting his eyes from the triangle of dark hair, across her flat abdomen and the small breasts with their button nipples, to her expressionless face.

She returned his gaze. There was a long silence. The girl smiled and took his hand, pressing it against her chest, before sliding it down over her stomach to the top of her thighs.

'You feel. Then fuck.' Her voice was quiet, devoid of emotion. She dropped to her knees, unbuttoning his trousers. Harry lay back. When he opened his eyes, the girl's face was pressed against him, black hair rising and falling across her cheeks as she moved her head up and down, like seaweed billowing out and back with the ebb and flow of the sea, caressing the rocks.

He sat up and lifted her head, registering the moist, open mouth and puzzlement in her brown eyes.

'Not good? Want fuck?'

Harry looked at the girl kneeling. She could be his sister, squatting beside her sandcastle on Mablethorpe beach. 'You're very pretty. *Piàoliang*' He wasn't sure she'd understood. '*Hĕn piàoliang*.' He stressed the adjective, trying to convey the meaning with his eyes. 'But I can't do this.'

'You feel *piàoliang?* I do more.' Harry thought he saw a faint smile crease her lips. She moved onto the bed, straddling his waist with her thighs. She sank, pressing her breasts against his chest. Her warm lips brushed his cheek and he smelt the sweetness of *báijiŭ* on her breath.

Harry lifted her upright as gently as he could and moved to create a space beside him on the bed. His arms folded around her.

# Chapter Nine

## St. Regis Hotel, Chengdu:
## Wednesday night May 15th 2019.

Torin watched the taxi drive into the darkness, then took the lift to the sixth floor and signed into the leisure centre. He lay, floating in the warm water of the outside pool, looking at the lights in the looming high-rise office-blocks, counting the floors to the top of the tallest building. Were forty-five storeys more than the HSBC building in Canary Wharf?

A full moon hung between two skyscrapers, a giant, round lantern, held by invisible threads from the towers. At the top of the building to the left, a lit window was half-open. Torin saw a person's silhouette against the yellow light. He imagined it moving forward onto the ledge and diving into the pool, like the tombstoners at Durdle Door the previous summer.

He swam several lengths on his back, watching the giant orb drift behind the right-hand tower till the last sliver of luminescence dissolved. He removed his bathing cap and went inside to warm in the sauna. Eucalyptus oil was heavy in the hot, humid air of the cabin. Torin pressed his back against the burning wood, thinking about the week's events.

Following the meal with Sunny, he'd assumed the invitation to the panda sanctuary had been a gesture of hospitality on behalf of CUV. He'd gone along as much out of politeness, as from interest in the animals. Although the hot-pot evening had ended on a sour note, he'd found himself drawn to the poised young woman with her thoughtful observations. There was a sincerity in how she spoke and a centredness that intrigued him. In the café at the Panda base, when they were sharing photos, he'd been struck by her hazel eyes from beneath the straw hat with its red ribbon. Tiny laughter lines creased the smoothness of her cheeks and revealed her white teeth when she smiled. She had a measured way of speaking English, and a delightful way of covering her mouth with her fingertips when she ate.

He'd been tempted by her invitation to go to the Narrow Alleys, which he'd read about on Chengdu Unchained. But he'd felt the familiar warning-signs, and knew he needed to get back to the hotel quickly. From his taxi, he'd watched Sunny walk to her bus stop.

The experience of Wen Shu monastery and Du Fu's cottage had touched something; he'd found himself in a snowscape globe, with shaken flakes of memory swirling.

After splitting with Kat two years ago, and the disastrous night with Louise, he'd become reconciled to living alone. There had been the occasional fling at a party or conference, but he'd been careful to drop the blinds quickly. Sex was one thing, romance very different—off-limits. He'd enjoyed it being like that. No commitments, no demands, and no responsibilities, except to himself—and his grandmother, of course. Graham's invitation to take up paragliding offered the perfect outlet. In the air, searching for elusive thermals to take him to cloud base, he was on his own, with attention focused on finding the invisible uplift. On the ground, the company was mostly male and lubricated by large quantities of real ale.

He had wanted to invite Sunny into the hotel for a drink, to bask for longer in the pool of these ancient wisdoms. But he'd felt nervous, in case she thought he was trying it on, so he'd remained silent. There was bound to be a boyfriend.

Back in his room, he picked up *In a House of Lies* from the bedside table and followed Inspector Rebus through the twisting wynds of Edinburgh, trying to immerse in the story. Images from the week flickered across the pages, interrupting his concentration. Sunny's face through the window of the taxi. He had stepped away towards the isolation of the lobby, watching the car drive towards the exit barrier.

Torin put the novel on the table and opened his phone to check his departure time. The cursor on the Air China website highlighted a flight to Heathrow on Monday, asking if he wanted to hold the option of changing his ticket.

Why not stay a few more days? Sunny had mentioned an intriguing place called Jin Sha. There was no reason to say anything about his situation. Would Sunny want to meet again though? He recalled the way she'd looked at him when they'd said goodbye. Alchemy of emotions was restless territory.

He lifted Ian Rankin and turned the page to a new chapter, pushing away the loneliness that mocked him silently from the empty bed.

The digital clock on the television screen showed 1.13 when he reached for his phone. The offer to change the date lit up again. His finger hovered above the accept icon.

Torin looked across the city skyline. A green light flashed from a descending plane, as it turned onto the flight path to land. He pressed the screen, and confirmation dropped into his email box.

He lay back against his pillow, checking the details, then texted Sunny so she'd have the message when she woke. A smiling emoji pinged back. Without thinking he touched call, and heard two rings before her familiar voice answered.

'Still awake?'

'Finishing some work. You?'

'Can't sleep.' He wanted to tell her why. 'You saw my message?'

'I will talk with Gloria and let you know in morning.' He guessed she was speaking softly, not to wake her parents.

Silence hung heavy. He was intruding into her personal space. 'Sorry for calling so late.'

He thought he heard her laugh. 'It's okay, but I should complete work now.'

'Of course, Sunny. I just wanted to—' He hesitated.

'Wanted to what?'

'Hear the voice behind the emoji.' He tried to make it matter of fact.

'Maybe I send you a recording of me teaching Chinese words? You remember the five ways of saying "*ma*"?'

Torin smiled at the memory. After she ended the call, he fell asleep quickly.

By the time he woke, there was a message from Sunny, with instructions to meet at the bus station next morning for a day-trip to Pingle.

Torin finished his reports for *Pitch Perfect*, then took a taxi to join the Chambers of Commerce conference in the afternoon. In the evening he returned to the rooftop leisure-centre and another thirty lengths of the open-air pool.

This time there was another occupant in the sauna, who looked up as Torin opened the door and talked without prompting. The defending champion for the Chengdu international squash tournament was nursing a sore head from an unwise choice of vodka the previous night.

He wanted to tell Torin he'd won the final in three straight games the previous year, trouncing his opponent from Pakistan. But this year none of his family had come to watch, although his manager was due to fly in on Sunday, just before the tournament started. He was thinking he'd throw the match mid-week, so he could head back to South Africa.

Torin closed his eyes, not wanting to engage with the rising tide of lonesomeness from the other side of the sauna. He shifted his weight on the hot planks, mulling over the information he'd gleaned about Pingle from Chengdu Unchained, wondering if the Giant Banyans would turn out to be a disappointment, like the time he'd visited the oldest tree in Britain.

He'd hiked from Pitlochry along the southern edge of Loch Tummel to Balnairn, from where he'd taken the General Wade track to Keltneyburn and then on to Fortingall village. He'd expected a massive bole of yew. Instead, he'd found a cluster of small trees, rising out of an area marked out by wooden pegs, where it was claimed a single tree had once stood with a girth of over fifty feet in the eighteenth century.

When he opened his eyes, the squash player had gone. Torin showered and took the lift to his room. He slept deeply and woke early for the taxi he'd booked to the north bus station.

Sunny and Torin sat together on the wooden-seats, watching the driver of Number 68 weave through the crush of taxis at the exit to the terminal. The illuminated digital clock beside his head registered 08.31.

Above the honking of car horns, they could hear the shouts of street vendors. A smell of frying dough mingled with exhaust fumes. Sunny pushed up the window beside her head. 'We open again when left city.'

The bus accelerated onto the highway and dust clouds fell like brown pillows of breath. They were soon driving across farmland. As Torin leant over to pull the window down, she caught the scent of his aftershave. The back of her neck tingled and she was grateful for the cooling breeze on her cheeks. She produced the bag of fruit she'd bought while waiting at the bus station—plastic boxes with black grapes and slices of melon, plus two bananas. 'Here *shui*.' Sunny broke the seal of a water bottle and handed him the container.

'How was Chambers reception?' She wondered if Gloria had worn her *cheong sam*.

Torin grinned. 'Your report was on display at the registration desk.'

'*Riding the Dragon in Sichuan?*' her pencilled eyebrows arched in surprise.

'Complete with the by-line *CUV's offer to British businesses*. Properly bound with some great pictures, showing your successes with UK companies. Lu Chen Xi in large letters on the front. Gloria highlighted it in her presentation.'

The bus hit a pothole and they were thrown in the air. She grabbed Torin's arm to stop her falling to the floor. 'When I back home after leaving you at hotel, Gloria phoned to talk about my report. She said everything good, but still need some changes. That why I still awake when you message me. After we speak, I send Gloria finished report and also ask her about today. See her reply.'

Torin stared at the screen of Chinese characters.

我刚刚阅读了您的修订报告。 太好了 我明天早上将在会议开始之前将其打印出来。 这次您辛苦了，所以和托林先生见面，希望与牛熊证建立合作关系

'Sorry, I press translate.' Sunny touched the phone and swiped up. '*I just read your revised report. It is excellent. I will print it out tomorrow morning before the meeting starts. You have worked hard this time, so meet with Mr. Torin on Friday and establish our co-operation with Pitch Perfect.*'

'After Gloria said this, I think about other places to see in Chengdu—Jinli, Wide and Narrow Alleys, Jin Sha museum, Sichuan Opera, but I could see how much you liked Du Fu house and I remember Pingle Guzhen.'

Sunny had been to the ancient town once before when she was thirteen, without her parents knowing. If they'd discovered that she'd taken a bus far away into the Sichuan countryside, instead of spending the day with Huang Guo at the park by their house, it would have been awful. Even now she didn't want to think about what her mother might have done.

It was Wang Laoshi who had given her the idea.

At school they had been studying the poetry of Chengdu writers. Her teacher had put *Pingle Ancient Town Lover* by Yang Ran on the blackboard.

Chen Xi didn't know what 榕树 was until her teacher showed them a photo of the ancient trees, and told them they were planted hundreds of years before Du Fu was born. Wang Laoshi had written out some of the poem in English.

'*Reflection of ancient banyan trees across the Baimo River*
*Float to the old lamp that has been gone for many years*
*That's the dream I've been looking for*
*Like the eyes of a lover I've been obsessed with for years*
*Ah, Pingle Ancient Town*
*I'd love to meet you barefoot*
*Stepping on the wet slate road, close to you*
*Rainbow ancient bridge curved*
*In the rain is imprinted with classical tranquillity*
*I would like to open my heart to you*
*Tell your remarkable ancient stories*'

The thought of stepping over wet slates onto a rainbow bridge with a barefoot friend, and looking down into the reflections of gnarled banyans across the Baimo River, sounded mysterious and magical.

She planned to visit with her friend one Saturday when there was no school. Wang Yu Ling was working late every night at her mahjong parlour, so she gave her daughter two kuai each morning to buy breakfast on her way to school. Chen Xi saved half every day. It took two months before they had enough for the bus fare to Pingle.

She told her mother it was Huang Guo's birthday and they were going to the park to meet friends. Maybe they would take a rowing boat onto the lake with a picnic. She would come home after dinner.

Before anyone was awake in her house, she crept out to meet her friend at *Chǎ diàn zǐ* station. The two girls found the green bus to Pingle and climbed the steps, hopping from foot to foot as they waited for the woman in front to buy her ticket. The driver smiled, as Chen Xi handed over their money. 'Visiting relatives?'

'*Nǎi nai.*' Chen Xi invented a fictitious grandmother. 'She lives in Pingle whole life.'

'In the old town?' asked the driver.

Chen Xi nodded, hoping he didn't ask for an address.

Although it was just forty kilometres from Chengdu, it took two hours to reach Pingle on the potholed roads. Chen Xi had never been on such a long journey without her family, and she felt grown-up as she sat next to her friend, listening to the two women behind talking about their families, and watching the countryside change from the dusty-grey of concrete building-sites to the richly-varied green-shades of cabbage, rice, lotus and bamboo on the small farms.

The two girls walked round the small alleys, excited to escape Chengdu. With some of the change from the bus-ticket, they bought two garlands of chrysanthemum flowers, woven by an old lady squatting beneath a *gǔ róng* tree. She pressed them on their heads as if she was crowning two young princesses. Chen Xi noted the admiring glances of passersby. They stood on the Leshan bridge, looking at the reflections of the line of ancient trees in the river.

Below them a teacher appeared leading a class of school-children in uniform along the river bank. Chen Xi wondered why they were in school on a Saturday. Maybe they were making up for the spring holiday earlier in the month? The teacher asked the children to stand in silence in front of the trunk of the oldest tree, explaining it had been put in the ground in the early days of the Tang Dynasty.

'If this *gǔ róng shù* could talk, its stories would go back more than one thousand years, before the time of the famous poet Du Fu.' Her words floated up to the two girls leaning over the stone parapet.'He may even have sat in its shade to write some of his poems when it was still a young tree, only two hundred and fifty years old. Imagine being young at that age?' Chen Xi watched the teacher's brown eyes scan the expectant faces of the children.'You are only seven years old but already you have many stories to tell your friends about things you've done in Pingle. This *gǔ róng* has lived two hundred times longer than you. Can you imagine what it has seen over all those years, and what it might say if you asked it to tell a story?'

The fifty-one children held hands as they wrapped themselves in three intertwined circles around the bole of the gnarled tree, those on the inside rubbing their shirts against the whorls of the bark. One of the teaching assistants took a photograph. Chen Xi heard the teacher say they would make a copy for the children to give their parents.

When the children left, Chen Xi and Huang Guo

descended the steps to stand underneath the tree. She looked up at the thick, brown arms that reached above her head to the blue sky, and shivered despite the heat of the day. Would the tree remember her touching its trunk, together with the thousands of other children who had stroked the bark, polishing it to the same sheen she could see on their dining table at home after her mum had rubbed it hard?

She thought about the teacher's question. How would the tree select a story to tell? Imagine fifteen hundred years of three hundred and sixty-five days, with more than twenty stories each day. She couldn't calculate the exact figure, but knew it was a very big number. Probably millions. How would the spirit of the tree recall each one?

As well as the *gǔ róng shù*, Sunny remembered the ancient wooden-houses that opened into the alleys and courtyards beside the river, with the street stalls selling cooked cobs of sweetcorn or spiced, fried potatoes, smoke curling lazily from the metal pots. She and Huang Guo had watched the old men playing mah-jong at a rickety, bamboo table on the pavement, banging the tiles on the wooden surface as they discarded from the wall, shouting with excitement if they scooped the moon from the bottom of the sea. Pingle had felt mysterious and alive at the same time.

She thought Torin might find it interesting because he'd seemed to enjoy Wen Shu monastery and Huanhuaxi Park. But she also knew it was about more than looking at old trees or buildings. She wanted to show him silent spaces between the sights, smells and sounds of China, her home.

She'd messaged Huang Guo on WeChat, telling her what she was planning. She thought her friend would find it amusing that she was going back to Pingle to see the ancient Banyans. The reply had surprised her. *'Be careful. Waiguoren only after one thing.'*

She'd messaged back. *'Same as Chinese men. Remember Wang Yi?'*

*'Húndàn,'* came the instant response. She'd replied with the Girl Power emoji, to reassure Huang Guo she knew what she was doing.

Sunny took a mouthful of water, tilting her head back to drain the last drops from the bottle, thinking how she'd ended it with Wang Yi, when she'd discovered his deceit. As she dabbed the corners of her mouth with a tissue, she noticed Torin smiling.

*'Zěn me le?* Something on my face?' She lifted both her hands to cover her mouth.

'Nothing at all.' His eyes levelled with her own. 'I'm just pleased we could do this.'

It was half-past ten when the bus drew up on the tarmac in Pingle. They walked from the bus station along Yingbin street to the archway of the Ancient Post Road where the carved, white lettering on the brown sign described its historical significance. Sunny explained how Pingle had been a staging post on the Southern Silk Road during the Qin and Han dynasties, over two thousand years ago.

They turned under the next archway, which formed the entrance to the ancient town, and zigzagged along the narrow alleys between the lines of traditional houses with their ornately-tiled rooves, decorated with blue stones that led down to the riverbank. Carved wooden-doors of the shop-fronts opened directly onto the streets, with living accommodation behind the jutting balconies above. Streamers of triple red-lanterns hung from the eaves.

The Millenary banyan tree was exactly as she remembered, its bronze plaque describing its age and girth. It was impossible to encircle the giant trunk with their hands, so they strolled along till they found a younger tree around which they could just get their fingers to touch. When a group of children came running up, they pulled away from the tree.

They continued along Changqing Street, passing old wharves squeezed between two-storey houses that followed the Baimo River, and then crossed over the Leshan Bridge, whose seven, ancient stone-arches linked the two halves of Pingle Town. Beneath Jianxian Tower there were clusters of people in front of stalls selling cobs of sweetcorn and fried potatoes. The tangy scent of charcoal mingled with a mouth-watering smell of roasting corn, as blue smoke curled gently up in the still air. Sunny bought a small bag of fries, dotted with chilli powder and oyster sauce, to share with Torin, and they walked along the western bank of the river, till they came to a cluster of traditional stilt-houses.

A pontoon jutted into the river, with a dozen boats tied against it. Beside the bank, in the shade of a willow tree, a group of women squatted round a bubbling pot of noodles, balanced on top of a small brazier. One stood as they approached. '*Nǐ men yào zuò chuán ma?*'

'*Shì de.*' Sunny nodded her assent. 'The woman is asking if we want to sit on a boat.' She negotiated the price and they clambered onto the raft. Under the afternoon sun they sat back on the wooden seat, watching the woman dig her pole into the river-bed to urge the boat upstream. Skilfully she made progress against the current and they watched the town disappear behind the curve of the river. Around the bend, water buffalos were wallowing in the shallows, and a group of children were playing upstream from the animals, where the water was rippling over small rocks.

Sunny let the warmth of the sun caress her eyelids, listening to the children's laughter float across the wide arc of the river, mingling with the birdsong from the trees on the bank.

She smelt charcoal again and opened her eyes. The boat passed a tiny pontoon on which a makeshift restaurant sold food. The driver deftly manoeuvred the raft alongside. They stepped onto the wooden boards, eyeing up the food on sticks. Sunny negotiated a selection of vegetables to go with the skewered fish, and they dangled their feet in the warm water as they ate lunch, watching the tiny fish nibbling the tips of their toes.

'These like doctor fish in spa. Pay lots of money for eating skins.'

When they'd finished the food, Sunny gathered up the discarded bamboo-sticks and empty spring-water bottles, and handed them over to the cook. They returned to the raft and allowed the current to carry them back to their starting point, sipping the green tea the driver offered them in small, porcelain bowls.

Sunny glanced at her phone. 'We still have four hours. Do you like climbing mountain?' Sunny saw Torin glance at her sandals. 'Not really climbing-climbing. Chinese say *pá shān*, which mean walk up mountain.'

'Like hiking?'

'It's called Jinhua Mountain trail? They say one hour. We take *sān lún* to start and pay driver to wait. Go straight to bus station after.' They sat in the back of the electric three-wheeler, weaving in and out of the pedestrians and bicycles on the small road to the beginning of the mountain trail.

'*We are all duty bound to keep the forest away from fire*', declared the white lettering in the framed sign at the entrance to the national park, with the English translation printed below the Chinese characters. Underneath, screwed to a rock, was a smaller sign, '*Balmy grass is so green, Careful step is so sweet*'.

The track wound through the forest, shaded by the thick canopy of overhanging trees. As the path climbed upwards, stone steps had been bedded into the red earth, and post- and rail- fencing ensured walkers couldn't stray. Other signs greeted them at resting points.

'*Money is a temporary benefit, environment is an immortal capital*'.

'*Feel by heart, communicate by love*'.

After twenty minutes of climbing, the track flattened and they rounded a bend to see a rope-bridge span a deep gorge. An uneven set of wooden boards formed the walkway between sets of railings. The waist-high barrier was supported by metal uprights, bound onto the twin arches of rusting cables that traversed the whole gorge. The rickety-looking structure was just wide enough to let two people pass, if they turned sideways and shuffled forward.

Sunny and Torin stood together on the loose planks in the middle of the bridge, looking down at the foaming torrent three hundred feet below. Miniature rainbows danced beside the wet rocks. 'This is like picture books of old China when I was child,' whispered Sunny, clutching the handrail, as the bridge swayed in the gentle breeze.

The boards juddered as two walkers stepped on the far end, and vibrations from their movement started to create oscillations in the planking beneath their feet. Sunny turned and walked quickly towards the stanchions at the far end, holding tightly onto Torin's hand. From the safety of the concrete base, they watched the other hikers nervously stepping across the slats, and then they turned to take the track to the small temple beyond the bridge.

An old man in a black robe ushered them into a shaded room, where a ten-foot-high squatting figure dominated the space. The smell of incense was heavy in the air. Torin read the wording beneath the title.

'*Dunhuang Buddha Statue was carved in the early Northern Wei Dynasty (386-493 AD). The original Buddha statue with the height of 0.92 meters, is located in No.259 grotto of Mogao Grottoes, Dunhuang City, Gansu Province. The Buddha statue in lotus position which has fine lines and wears tender smile on his face is called as the Oriental Mona Lisa. It is representative work of Dunhuang Buddhist sculptures. The copy here is 3.21 meters high.*'

The monk brought some tea on a tray. Time stood still. Eventually Sunny looked at Torin. 'We must go. Bus waiting.'

Back at the *sān lún* park, their driver had gone and the cluster of three-wheelers had evaporated, with just one solitary vehicle left in the gathering dusk. Sunny spoke with the driver, then crossed the road to where Torin was sitting on the kerb side.

'She waiting for other people who paid.' Her voice was flat. 'Ours gone.'

'Why?'

'I don't know. Maybe had other offer. We pay forty kwai already, so no need to wait for us. I'm very sorry.'

'It's okay Sunny, we'll walk.' He could see the lights of Pingle in the distance. 'It's not far.'

'But we miss the bus.'

'What time does it leave?'

'Six. Already nearly five and half. Maybe we stop a car.'

They set off on the road, but there was little traffic and only two trucks, weighed down with bricks, and a fully-laden family car passed them in the hour it took to reach the outskirts of Pingle. The bus station was deserted. Sunny tasted dust in her mouth. The day had soured. She could feel tears pricking the corners of her eyes.

'I don't have to be back tonight,' Torin said softly. 'Perhaps we can find somewhere to stay?'

Sunny hesitated. Did he know what accommodation would be like in Pingle? 'This old town. Village really. No smart hotels. Maybe private rooms.'

They crossed Leshan bridge and followed the cobbled pavement next to the river. One of the houses had an illuminated sign in English: 'Free room'. Sunny led them into the porch and spoke with the woman who appeared. *'Nǐmen yǒu zhu ma?'*

The owner nodded and replied quickly, tugging at Sunny's blouse. *'Lái kàn kan.'*

138

Sunny struggled to understand the dialect. 'I think she want us to look, but there is only one room. This her family house, not hostel.'

'*Lái kàn kan.*' The woman was insistent. 'American? Okay?'

'*Wǒ men xū yào liǎng gè fáng jiān xiè xiè.*' Sunny turned back towards the pavement. She could see Torin was confused. 'I tell her we need two rooms. Not together. Let's look somewhere else. Week day, so should be possible.'

Further along the street was another lit sign. Inside, a girl showed them two bedrooms, linked by a balcony facing the river. Sunny sensed Torin's hesitation. 'Sorry. Probably not so nice as your hotel room. But this hostel is owned by young couple. They just opened. Shower room along corridor. Small bar downstairs. Very cosy I think.'

'It's lovely,' he said. 'But we didn't bring anything. Do they have towels? I don't want to upset anyone by running back to my bedroom from the shower with no clothes on.'

Sunny could feel herself blushing. She spoke to the girl who nodded her head. 'She have towels. Also toothbrushes and soap.'

'Perfect.' Torin smiled. 'Shall we find some food and then we can sleep. If you're as tired as me, we'll be out like a light.'

They walked round the darkened streets, lit by strings of glowing, red lanterns, till they found a small restaurant in one of the tiny alleys close to the line of banyan trees. They ate barbecued vegetables and strips of shredded pork, then climbed steps onto the Leshan Bridge. Leaning against the parapet, looking upstream, the flickering lights of the town were reflected in the rippling water. A glowing lotus flower glided underneath them. Sunny looked along the bank. Beside the Millenary *gǔ róng* she could see a man offering tea-lights to passers-by.

They descended the steps and approached the candle-seller. On a low table beside him, a box contained dozens of red and yellow petals curved into the shape of a lotus flower. Torin pressed the tea-light into the holder in the middle of the petals and they both leaned forwards to place the container on the surface of the river. It spun gently round a few times in the tiny eddy at the water's edge, before the current caught the flower and pulled it from the bank, into the main flow of the river.

'Now we wish.' Sunny closed her eyes, lips parted as she mouthed a silent prayer. When she opened them, their lotus had joined another in the middle of the river. The two flowers drifted through the arch of the bridge, to join the procession of bobbing lights floating downstream. 'I'm sorry if you miss St. Regis.'

'I'm not at all sorry Sunny. I can't think of anywhere else I'd rather be—with you.' His voice dropped to a whisper as he breathed the last two words.

She turned to look into his blue eyes and her fingers reached up to touch his neck.

Then they were kissing, and kissing, and kissing, breathless and giddy, fingers curling and uncurling. She could feel the bark of the Banyan against her back. Would this be one of the tales the ancient tree would store for the future. Her head was spinning. 'Let's go back.'

They flew like birds over the old bridge, through the open door of her room, to land on the soft bed, fingers still curled together.

# Chapter Ten

## Fenghuangshan Airfield, Chengdu: Saturday 27th November 1942

Through the open door of the operations room Harry saw two mechanics, heads under an engine cowling. Dusk settled over the airfield and the rasping cicadas mingled with voices from the ground crew. A light breeze from the south carried the familiar smell of aeroplane fuel.

'I wanna congratulate you guys.' Claire Chennault's grey eyes scanned expectant faces in the operations room as he drew deeply on the cigar clamped between his lips. 'Since the beginnin of September this squadron has flown fifty-five missions.' His voice boomed the statistics as he chalked the numbers on the blackboard. Twenty Third Fighter Group had engaged the Japanese air force three or four times a week, flying several times some days. One hundred and seventy-six bombers and two hundred and fifteen fighters had been shot down, with the loss of eighteen Warhawks.

His lips curled in a smile. 'That's a remarkable kill rate, fellas. If you can do the math, it means that, for each plane lost, we have taken out more than twenty of Tojo's.'

There was a ripple of applause and Chennault's gnarled face cracked into a broad grin, the laughter-lines on his tanned cheeks further creasing the weather-beaten skin. In the yellow light from the naked bulbs hanging from the ceiling, he looked older than Harry remembered. Grey threads wove through the thinning hair above the prominent forehead, and his tall figure slightly stooped. Harry's thoughts drifted back to the first meeting on the SS Sudan. How had it ended with the sun-tanned legs?

The confident Louisianan drawl continued to declaim the terror-bombing of Chongqing and Chengdu, intended to destroy civilian morale and force Chiang Kai-shek to break from the Allies. Chennault was unequivocal. The Japs were hoping to persuade the General to join Wang Jinwei and Pu Yi—puppet collaborators in Nanjing and Manchuria—and help Tojo take on the Soviet Union to ease the pressure on Axis forces in Stalingrad.

Harry watched Chennault turn to the map of China behind him and reach for the pointer. Was the old man going to give the same geography lesson he'd witnessed in Cairo? Would he spell out the end-game: Japan in control of the Far East and India a shared prize for the Nazis?

The pointer swept in an arc, hitting the map as he marked the build-up of troops along the Japanese front line. 'Their plan was to capture Xi'an and attack Chengdu from the north east. At the same time, other troops would move through Wanxian, takin Chongqing in a pincer from the east. That way they'd cut off any chance of the Kuomintang retreatin to Kunming.'

Chennault rested the stick against the wall and faced the seated pilots, chewing the end of his cigar. 'If they'd gained air supremacy over Sichuan, this invasion would've happened. The Chinese armies couldn't have stopped it, because they're still regroupin and rearmin after the retreat from Burma. Sichuan would now be under enemy occupation and Kunming would have fallen, allowing the friggin Japs to move another quarter of a million troops through Burma to attack the Allied forces in India.'

Harry watched Chennault's steely eyes scan the pilots' faces as Lin Xiaobin translated. The silence that followed was broken by the steady drip, drip, drip from the tap above the porcelain sink.

Chennault breathed in, his barrel chest pressing against the polished buttons of his tunic. 'We've not been in combat for six days. No enemy aircraft have entered Sichuan airspace since Monday. Some of you even had time to shave before your little escapade into Chengdu. I gather Mister Fu's girls gave you a warm reception. Our way of sayin thank you.' Through the clapping and cheering, Harry thought about the upstairs room off the narrow alley.

Chennault picked up the bamboo cane and rapped the other map on the wall. 'I 'preciate many of you ain't ever seen the sea, but there's another punch-up happenin on the other side of your great country. The Japs have suffered huge losses here.' The stick swung across the Pacific Ocean. The General rattled off a list of names—Guadacanal, Tassafaronga, Rennel. Solomon Islands—explaining that US soldiers were advancing north, forcing Tojo to withdraw troops from China. At the same time Mao's soldiers were harrying him from his base by the Great Wall. Chennault pointed at Yan'an, where Communist guerrilla attacks were compelling the enemy to maintain large clusters of troops in Shanxi, Hebei and Shandong. He tapped the bamboo on each province, then turned to survey the seated airmen.

'I realise this is a lot to take in, and your job is simply to shoot down as many enemy planes as possible. But you've saved Chengdu from the same fate as Nanjing, and screwed the Japanese plan to invade India.' Chennault paused, scanning the youthful faces. 'But the bastards will try again in the Spring, if they manage to hold the line in the Pacific.'

He took a deep breath, stroking his bristled jaw. 'This victory maybe temporary therefore, but it remains a victory. When the history of the Second World War is written, the Chinese struggle to save Chengdu and Chongqing will stand alongside other great battles around the globe, as one of the war's definin moments.' Chennault drew himself straight, his presence filling the room. 'In years to come your children and grandchildren will celebrate what you have achieved, and you should be proud of that achievement. This goddam war is a long way from being finished, but today sees the end of the beginnin, which will result in victory for the Chinese people.'

Lin Xiaobin was struggling to keep up with the translation, as Chennault's oratory reached a crescendo, but the aircrew sensed the message, even before the final words. Xu Wen rose to his feet to applaud, the spring on his chair folding the seat shut. Moments later he was joined by pilots on either side. The seats clacked in chorus, reverberating round the ops room, and all thirty pilots were on their feet, clapping and cheering.

Chennault raised his hand for quiet. 'When I first came to China in 1937 and created the Flying Tigers, all our pilots were Yanks. That was the case throughout the Burma campaign till we started trainin Chinese pilots at Kunming earlier this year. Lookin round, it's clear we've been pretty darned successful.' He glanced at Harry. 'When

I took a wager with this crazy Limey in a Cairo bar in April, I had no idea I'd scoop the friggin jackpot. Not only did he have the balls to fly a Warhawk over the Hump, but he bet me he could have a squadron of Chinese pilots combat-ready in three months. He's the dogs bollocks because you fellas are all top guns. Recognisin this achievement, Generalissimo Chiang has asked me to award Squadron Leader Winchester the Order of the Cloud and Banner.'

Harry smelt the stale cigarettes on Chennault's breath as the medal was pinned on his chest, to yet more clapping and cheering. He watched the General wait for silence, shifting his weight from one foot to the other, wondering how he was going to finesse the difficult hand he was about to play. Harry listened to the explanation about his postponed wedding and felt the surge of anxiety in the room at the announcement that a berth was booked for him on the pleasure cruise over the Hump in a fortnight, with the chance of being reunited with his navigator en route to the UK.

'Harry is familiar with the bomb bay of a Liberator, so I hope he takes his special pack of playin cards to while away the time. If you boys don't know what the hell I'm talkin about, I'm sure he'll show you the dames in the bar. Before we head there though, there's one last thing.' Chennault's eyes raked across the lines of men, trying to drag them from the undercurrent of unease. 'What marks out a great leader is the extent to which he prepares someone else to take over when he's gone. In a front-line squadron that question is specially important. Harry will be hugely missed when he leaves us in two weeks' time, but there is no doubt his successor as squadron commander will be equally effective. In acknowledgin this, the Generalissimo has asked me to also award the Order of the Cloud and Banner to Captain Lin—whose tally of kills is just one Zero behind Harry.'

The pilots were whistling and shouting. From somewhere came the first words of 'Sān mín zhǔyi', and the anthem was taken up by the room. Through the open door, Harry heard the ground crew joining in. He glanced at Dougie, nodding in admiration for the way the General had played his cards. And not a Queen of Hearts in sight!

As the last note faded, Chennault surveyed the pilots. 'You fellas make "Three Principles for the People" sound almost as good as "The Star-Spangled Banner". Drinks on me, boys.' He led the way into the darkness.

As the pilots filed out, Harry touched Lin Xiaobin's shoulder. 'Can you give us a few minutes?'

Dougie closed the door. The whoops of the aircrew could be heard, as the shutters came up in the mess-room. He indicated for the young pilot to sit. He looked from Harry to Dougie and back to his boss.

'Congratulations on your medal, Captain Lin. Your flying ability and leadership have been remarkable and the men regard you as a hero. In addition, I owe my life to you. You have watched my back every sortie, most recently last Friday over Sui Ning.'

Lin Xiaobin's face remained impassive. He knew English well enough to know there was something else coming.

'But you killed an unarmed pilot who had parachuted out of his plane. This is against the rules of war.'

'Which rules, Commander Winchester?'

Harry frowned. 'The Geneva Convention. It protects prisoners of war.'

'He was no prisoner of war.'

Harry's eyes narrowed. 'He would have been if he'd landed alive.'

'He was Japanese. This Geneva Convention does not apply.' The voice was empty of expression.

Harry opened his mouth to challenge the assertion, but Lin Xiaobin spoke first. 'He was a murderer. I was dispensing justice.' The tone was matter of fact.

'He was only guilty of being a fighter-pilot, like yourself.'

Lin Xiaobin's unwavering eyes looked straight at Harry. 'Commander Winchester, there is no such thing as an innocent Japanese.'

Harry shook his head. 'You killed a defenceless man.'

Lin Xiaobin's nostrils flared as he spat his response across the space between the two men. 'Commander, you don't understand what we have suffered since the Japanese invaded in 1937. You think "The War" started in September 1939 when Germany invaded Poland, or...' He hesitated, his brown eyes glancing at Dougie. 'Or when the Japanese bombed Pearl Harbour.' The young pilot stood and walked towards the map hanging on the wall, his pigtail swinging against his back. 'For Chinese people this war has been going for years.' He grabbed the bamboo stick and pointed to the north east of China. 'The Japanese invaded Manchuria in 1931, and their aggression didn't stop there. Have you any idea what it has been like living under these bastards for ten years?'

147

Harry said nothing, registering the smouldering anger in Lin's eyes.

'My family was trapped in Nanjing when the city fell in December 1937.' The eyes flickered towards Douglass. 'That was exactly four years before you Yanks raised a finger to help us. Chiang Kai-shek's army was forced to abandon Nanjing, retreating west towards Sichuan, leaving four-hundred-thousand people unprotected in our capital city.' Every word was enunciated clearly, as Lin Xiaobin swung the stick from the eastern seaboard south of Beiping towards the west of China.

He turned from the map to look straight at Harry. There was an emptiness of expression, which felt more deadly than rage. 'I was fourteen years old in 1937. My parents persuaded a German consulate employee to smuggle me and my twin sister, Lin Mei Li, on the last train out of Nanjing, pretending we were his adopted children. Germany and Japan were already allies, and the Japanese had agreed to this final evacuation of European refugees before they closed the railway line.'

Lin Xiaobin was staring at something beyond the blackness of the window as he described what happened. The normally shrill voice dropped in pitch. He'd been sitting in a compartment with three German families. Four boys younger than Xiaobin, his sister, and six adults squashed into a space for eight people. The train whistled and they heard the engine building steam ready to leave. A group of Japanese soldiers burst through the dividing link from the next carriage. They staggered along the corridor, pulling open the door to each compartment. When they reached Xiaobin's, one of them stood in the entrance shouting to his friends as he pointed at Mei Li. She buried her face into Herr Klein's jacket, but the soldier grabbed her arm and dragged her into the corridor.

Herr Klein stood up to protest, holding out his Nazi party card, but they pushed him down into his seat, ordering him to stay silent or he'd be arrested as a spy. Through the window Xiaobin saw his sister bundled onto the platform. She was kicking and screaming, till one of the soldiers wrapped a strip of parcel tape across her mouth. The five soldiers carried her wriggling body towards the station waiting-room. He struggled to free himself from Herr Klein's arms, but the adolescent boy was no match for the solid German. Seconds later, the train jolted on its journey to sanctuary.

Lin Xiaobin placed the stick carefully on the desk and faced the two westerners. 'The last image I have of Mei Li is her expression as the door slammed shut.' His eyes clouded. 'That was five years ago. I have heard nothing from my sister or my parents since then. Nothing at all. But we know from a few people who managed to escape Nanjing that more than a hundred thousand civilians were killed in the orgy of rape and looting that followed the fall of the city. The killings went on for weeks, sanctioned by the Emperor. All Japanese soldiers took part. There were no dissenters. Think of the most horrible ways to die and you will be reliving what happened to unarmed men, women and children in Nanjing, whose only crime was to be living there when the Imperial Japanese Army occupied the city.

'In bed at night, when I close my eyes, I see Mei Li after the door closed. What do you think five drunken men, who've been away from their homes for years, might do to a fourteen-year-old girl with masking tape over her mouth?'

Harry heard the tap dripping into the sink. He noticed the smoothness of Lin Xiaobin's cheeks had hardened beneath the narrow blackness of his eyes. He registered how each syllable came from the depths of the young pilot's chest, propelled across the empty space of the briefing room. With his flared nostrils, there was a congruence of breathing, expression, and words. Xiaobin had found his voice.

'The words defenceless and innocent applied to Lin Mei Li. But certainly not to her captors or the rest of the subhuman race to which they belong. This is why I would execute every Japanese soldier between here and Tokyo. No surrender accepted, no mercy given, Commander Winchester.' Lin Xiaobin paused, looking directly at Harry as his hand brushed over his shaved head and tugged the long plume of black hair that hung down his back. 'I have vowed not to cut my queue till the last Japanese soldier is erased from Chinese soil. Every morning it reminds me my main task is to take revenge for what happened to Mei Li. My only regret is that a quick death was too good for the pilot. Burning alive in his cockpit would have been better.'

In the darkness facing him, Harry was aware of the unfathomable emptiness driving the fury. He was conscious of his own eyes misting over.

Slowly he reached forward and rested his hand on Lin Xiaobin's shoulder. The nineteen-year-old pilot flinched, drawing himself up to his full height to shrug off the gesture. A leaden silence stretched between them.

# Chapter Eleven

## Pingle to Tianquan:
## Saturday May 18th 2020

Chen Xi stood beside the waterfall, listening to the rivulets trickling over rocks and overhanging ferns before splashing into the pool. Early morning sunlight danced through the trees, creating dissolving diamonds in the water. A bird call floated in the still air: *coo oo... coo oo... coo oo.*

She opened her eyes with a surge of panic, as she saw a doorway and white walls in a configuration she didn't recognise. This wasn't her bedroom in Chengdu, with the wooden headboard pushed against the window. There was no dressing-gown on the door, no family photograph pinned to the wall. Instead, there was a fisherman poling his boat in front of the Karst mountains at Yangshuo. She started to sit up. Then she felt the warmth beside her and lay back on the white cotton, listening to the shower running along the corridor and the hoopoo calling through half-open shutters.

Sunny studied his face. Beneath the curling locks of blonde hair, the eyebrows arched above the bridge of his nose. She noticed the stubble above the curve of his lips, softened by the dappled light from the window.

She gently lifted the sheet aside so she could step from the bed. She wrapped a towel around her and pushed open the shutters, watching the river through the gaps in the fence at the end of the courtyard. Already bamboo rafts plied between the bridges. A barge laden with watermelons drifted downstream, a black cormorant motionless on its prow, head angled towards the surface, watching for movements beneath the surface. She blinked and the bird dived, disappearing below the brown ripples, surfacing seconds later with a flash of silver between its beak as it flapped to the bank.

Sunny felt a hand on her waist. She turned to see Torin smiling up from the pillow.

'Still early.'

Her towel fell to the floor.

By the time they went downstairs to the small restaurant there was no one else eating breakfast, but the steamed buns, dumplings and vegetables were warm in their metal tureens. Sunny placed two glasses of fermented milk beside their plates. 'There will be buses to Chengdu this morning.'

Torin was cutting a watermelon into slices and scraping the black seeds to one side of the red flesh. 'Do we need to go back?'

She frowned. 'I thought you must be in Chengdu?'

Torin rubbed his neck. 'I have no more meetings. I don't need to be there till tomorrow night. My flight is Monday.'

'Maybe we could see more in Pingle?'

He hesitated. 'I think you said your home town was near here?'

'Tianquan?'

'Is that where you grew up?'

'Yes, the farm that I tell about.'

'Might it be possible to visit?'

'My grandparents are not there this weekend. Only my great-grandfather.'

'Would he mind us coming?'

'I'm sure he be very pleased. But it is quite far.'

Torin passed her a plate with slices of the melon. 'You talked a lot about your home village. I don't mind if it's a long way.'

Their knees touched under the table.

They walked to the bus station to discover there was a coach for Tianquan at midday. It meant changing at Ya'an, on the crossroads of the Yakang Expressway to Tibet.

'When we get there, we still need to walk five kilometres. It's small and mud road. No buses.' Sunny felt his fingers tighten around hers as they meandered back through the alleyways to the river bank, not minding the hour wait for the bus. She was seeing the ancient town through new eyes. Yesterday, she was a tourist guide. Today, part of the poem.

*'I would like to open my heart to you*
*Tell your remarkable ancient stories'*

In the embracing shade of the *gu rong*, an old woman threaded garlands of flowers from a basket of blooms. She smiled as they approached, lifting the fresh lattice of peonies. She gently pressed the coronal onto Sunny's black hair, whispering in her ear.

Torin reached in his pocket for some coins. 'What is she saying?'

'Nothing. Just speak about beauty of day.' Sunny felt her cheeks redden as she stepped away from the tree, wondering whether this was another story the ancient tree would remember.

It was four o'clock in the afternoon when the bus pulled up on the bridge in Longwei village on the outskirts of

Tianquan. Sunny noticed the passengers watching as they stepped down from the bus. She knew they'd be speculating what a young woman was doing with a *wàiguó rén*. She smiled, content. '*Zài jiàn*,' she called to the driver, who waved and crashed the bus into gear, before pulling away in a cloud of dust.

'Tianquan that way.' Sunny pointed to the right of the flyover, where the road snaked down the valley between bamboo-clad hills. 'A lot of fighting there in war—see sign.'

She watched Torin study the laminated board, with its story of the assault by three thousand Kuomintang soldiers on the tiny garrison of one hundred People's Liberation Army troops in 1950.

'I thought the Communists took over in 1949.'

'Yes, it is seventieth birthday of National Day soon. Big celebrations planned in Chengdu for October.'

She could see Torin frowning. 'But it says this battle took place during a week in February 1950?'

Sunny looked at the board. '*Cheng Zhiwu, the Kuomintang party commander, collude with the head of Tianquan army of three thousand bandits led by Li Yuanheng, to attack Zhang Xiaoliang and his garrison of one hundred soldiers of Peoples Liberation Army during Spring festival. Cheng lost and fled into mountains, where he was captured a year later. Zhang Xiaoliang was appointed Mayor of Xa'an city till he retired in 1980.*' She turned from the sign. 'I think some rebels fight on after Chairman Mao victory.

'How many years did the fighting continue?' asked Torin.

Sunny shrugged. She'd never found history interesting. She knew about National Day when Mao Zedong had declared the creation of the People's Republic of China at exactly 3.00 o'clock Beijing Time on 1 October 1949 from the top of Tiananmen Gate. Her teacher had insisted the class copy out and learn his speech.

She recited it in her head, realising she'd never really thought about the actual words. It was like a mantra, sounds rising and falling in pitch with the rhythm. *Chiang Kai-shek Kuomintang government betrayed the fatherland… People's Liberation Army, backed by the whole nation, has been fighting heroically… eventually wiped out the reactionary troops… and the majority of the people in the country have been liberated.'*

She remembered Huang Guo talking about her grandfather, who had been part of the army sent to liberate Tibet. He'd stayed for five years before returning to Chengdu with an artificial leg, but he'd not wanted to talk about what had happened.

'It was a very long time ago and I not alive then. Now China all one country.' She wondered if he was going to ask more questions about the war, so she started to walk along the highway. 'Beside that house we turn off.' She pointed towards a red building with a line of banana trees shielding it from the traffic.

Torin noticed huge bricks of clay forming the walls of a large courtyard, either side of the entrance. Beyond the gateway was the house, with piles of drying maize on a canvas sheet to one side and assorted farm implements on the other. Chickens clucked and pecked across the dusty ground.

'Traditional Chinese house.' Sunny explained this was common in the countryside and how Chengdu had looked

155

before buildings were cleared for the forest of high-rise apartments. 'Can still see these houses in some cities, like Du Fu cottage in Chengdu. Also my home in Dazhentou.'

There was no signpost on the track up a gently sloping hill to the left, but Sunny didn't hesitate. She had walked from her home to the school near Tianquan every day for nine years, until moving to Chengdu to start high school. The road was wide enough for a vehicle to navigate the loose bed of stones, but the only traffic that passed were women carrying panniers laden with vegetables and fruit for the market in the valley.

The lane curved through a landscape of small, cultivated fields and wooded plantations of bamboo and eucalyptus. Tiny streams criss-crossed the terraced-landscape, feeding rows of lotus fruit and rice plants, before running into troughs for the buffalos, grazing freely on the slopes. In some paddocks, drying rice-stooks were clumped together, awaiting collection before the rains arrived to refresh the earth and restart the cycle.

Several times they came to a cluster of houses, where their trail divided, but Sunny maintained her pace. She responded to greetings from faces she recognised. After forty minutes they came round a corner into a settlement. A small building stood beside the track, its blue and white awning pulled across the front to shield the interior from sunlight.

'This shop in Jian Jiwan village is closest to our house. Come have a look?'

She lifted aside the plastic curtain. The shelves nearest the entrance were stacked to the ceiling with ironmongery; next were kitchen utensils and crockery. In the shaded coolness at the far end, tubs of pot noodles, crisps, packets of nuts, seeds and dried fruit jostled for space with bottles of water, cans of drinks, and a shelf of medicines. 'You like sunflower seeds and pistachios? Some water? Or maybe beer?'

'*Wáng pó pó, zài bù zài?*' Sunny called out, and a woman wrapped in an embroidered shawl appeared from the end of the shop. Dark-brown eyes sparkled behind her spectacles, and her smile deepened the creases on her lined face. She reached out to Sunny, drawing her close and kissing her cheeks. Sunny took hold of the gnarled hands. 'This is Mrs. Wang. Know her since I able to walk. Like a grandmother to me, so I call her *po po*.'

Mrs. Wang placed the various packets in a plastic carrier and reached behind for two bottles that she added to the bag. As she took the money from Sunny, the old woman pointed at Torin. '*Nǐ de nán péng yǒu ma?*' Her grin revealed a row of cracked teeth.

Sunny hesitated, knowing why the old woman was asking about boyfriends. Mrs. Wang's mother had started to bind her daughter's feet after she was born, and was stopped by missionaries who gave her money. But the young girl was then ugly to men, because of her big feet, so she was in her twenties before a marriage could be arranged with an older farmer, more interested in the dowry than the girl's looks. Sunny knew Mrs. Wang was worried she would soon be too old to get a husband. She chose her words carefully, relieved to see the old woman nodding.

Sunny turned to Torin. 'She ask about you.'

'You gave a long answer.'

'I talk about Confucius. He say *"Isn't it a delight should friends visit from afar"*, and I explain you are going to UK on Monday.'

Outside the shop, the sun was sinking into the fold of hills to the west. They continued along the dusty track as it wound along the contours.

'Not far now.' Sunny could hear Torin's breathing becoming laboured. His foot was dragging more than usual. 'Next bend.'

The wall of red bricks encircling the house was similar to the dwelling on the main road. Mounds of maize dried in the courtyard. A thick tarpaulin covered a huge stack of firewood.

'No chickens?'

'Last time I came we had five. Maybe great-grandfather closed them.' She surveyed the compound. 'Look. They are in the garden over there. I show you round later, but first we see if great-grandfather is home. He usually plays mah-jong with friends in afternoons, but I send message, so he will be waiting here.'

She took Torin's arm and walked across to the entrance of the farmhouse. A heavy wooden door was set into a wide frame with ornate carvings on the lighter wood. Red Chinese characters were engraved into the stone lintel.

'This about luck and long life.' Sunny turned the handle. As the door swung open, they heard a chair squeak in the entrance hall. The old man pressed his hand on the bamboo arm-rest, trying to lift himself upright.

Torin watched Sunny walk across to take hold of her great-grandfather's hand and help him to his feet. Despite his slight frame and curved back, he exuded authority. He was dressed in a dark suit with an open-necked, collarless-shirt. A flat cap with a hammer and sickle insignia pressed down on the shock of white hair above his broad forehead. His tanned face was weathered by decades of working the soil.

'*Xi Xi, huí lái lā.*' He smiled at Sunny, as he touched her cheek.

'*Zǔfù. Zhè shì wǒ yīng guó de péngyou. Zhuān mén lái kàn nǐ de.*'

The old man nodded as she spoke. He reached out his arm to Torin, who gently pressed his fingers around the trembling hand.

'He is my *zǔfù*, my great-grandfather. I tell him you're my friend, come from UK to see him. He is very happy.'

'*Nǐ hǎo.*' Torin remained holding the old man's hand, looking directly into his eyes, registering the curious milky-sheen clouding the brown of his irises. The black of his eyebrows contrasted with his hair. Yellowing teeth suggested he was a smoker for many years. He spoke quietly, rubbing his eyes with his left hand, looking at Sunny to translate.

'He sorry not able see you properly, because he broke glasses yesterday. Trod on them in the chicken shed.'

*Zǔfù* steadied against Torin's hand as he shuffled to the large living room. '*Jìn lái zuò xià.*'

'He say sit down. Do you want water or tea?' Sunny lifted paper cups from underneath the television table in the corner.

*Zǔfù* pulled out two packets from his coat pocket and passed them to Torin. '*Chī, chī.*'

Sunny watched Torin open the paper bags. 'Sunflower

seeds and peanuts. We have snacks before dinner.' She reached for a bowl, placing it on a small table. 'For the shells.'

Torin cracked open the kernels and offered a handful of the hazel-brown nuts to the old man. He settled into the armchair, grateful for the cup of tea Sunny handed him. He could hear birdsong through the open window. From another part of the farmhouse a clock chimed. He closed his eyes, counting the distant strokes, listening to the flow of conversation, aware of Sunny's voice fading away.

'Grandfather is going to close up the chickens.' Sunny's hand pressed his shoulder. 'He ask if you like to see the farm?'

'Sorry.' Torin rubbed his eyes. 'I must have nodded off.'

'Not matter. It good for me to talk with *Zǔfù*. We not usually alone. He already old when I born, so I know he is very wise. Sometimes he sees things differently to my parents. I can talk to him quite open.'

Torin followed Sunny out. The leaves on the distant trees were aflame, bathing the farm in an orange glow. They helped the old man pen the chickens beside the row of pig sties, then Sunny took Torin on a tour of the farmstead, starting in the large courtyard that looked over the rows of carefully-tended vegetables.

'This where we wash clothes in old days.' Sunny pointed at a stone table in the corner of the yard, beside the steps down to the kitchen-garden. A scrubbing board lay next to the earthenware bowl and pitcher. 'Do hair there as well. Not so fun in winter.'

They descended the wooden steps to the terraced allotment. 'Here grandfather grow everything for food—

cabbages, carrots, spinach, onions, potatoes, whatever want to eat.'

'I have a friend in London who grows vegetables near where we live. It is the same size as this. He says there is enough space to feed his family.'

They walked along the path between the rows of vegetables to the end of the garden, where a retaining wall dropped to a piece of open ground with a small lake. A line of bushes ran along the length of the wall, drawing heat from the rough stones.

Torin could see red berries dotted among the lush, green leaves. 'Looks like tomatoes.'

Sunny checked her phone. 'English name is wolf berry. Not sure why. It not howl at night. Also called goji berry, but that because Chinese say *gǒuqǐ*. Maybe we just make it easier for foreigners.'

'I've seen goji berries in health food shops. Supposed to be very good for you.'

'There is a story about a village in China where everyone more than hundred years old. They drink water from well surrounded by *gǒuqǐ* bushes. Ripe fruit fall into water and keep them healthy. One man even two hundred and fifty years.'

'Sounds like we should be eating them every day.'

'Many people do here.' Sunny knelt to pluck a berry from the top of the bush, passing it to Torin.

He bit into the succulent fruit and wiped his chin. 'Amazing taste. Sweet and sour rolled together.'

Sunny laughed. 'Traditional Chinese food.'

'It's like a mixture of tomato and cranberry. I've never had anything like it.'

'We buy dried goji in Chengdu, when get back.'

They sat on the stone wall, feet brushing the upper branches of the *gǒuǐ* bushes, looking across the lake ringed by eucalyptus. 'Beyond those trees, more fields. Rented to other farmer who keeps cows. Maybe twenty hectares. My parents had bigger farm, but sold land to pay for school and university.'

'How long have your family lived here?'

'Not sure, but my great-grandfather born here, so family own it for more than a hundred years. Maybe two hundred years? Sometime in Qing dynasty. When I lived here fifteen years ago, we don't have electricity. In the night we use oil lamp, but it still dark.' Sunny glanced up the steps at the courtyard. 'Our toilet was beside the pigs at that time. Very smelly.' She described going out at night, scared to trip in the dark and drown in pig poo.

'My family only rebuild our house five years ago and put toilet inside. Before that you probably don't even want to sleep here.' She took hold of Torin's hand and rested her head on his shoulder. She could sit there forever, watching circling birds lower into their nests, hearing the distant bleat of a goat, smelling water trickle over the rocks that fed into the small lake. Through it all was the warmth of his neck and the gentle pulse. She brushed her lips along the raised purple of his scar, tasting the faint trace of salt. 'Thank you for coming.'

She felt his fingers tighten around hers. 'This is a very special place, Sunny. How often do you return?'

'Maybe several times a year. Always for Spring festival, when the whole family come. That why we rebuild. It common now, when people make money in the city, spend it to make family farmhouse bigger and better. Where we sat with *Zǔfù* is the original farmhouse from Qing time. My number two and three dad made a large living room with wood fire, next to the dining room and kitchen. Still two bedrooms in the old house. I show you.'

Sunny kept hold of his hand as they climbed back up the steps to the courtyard, past the pig sties and the chicken shed, to the main entrance of the farmhouse.

They stood in front of the wood-burning stove. Sunny pointed to the two doors that led off the beamed room. 'That way to kitchen and dining room. Also, food store for rice, millet, and everything else we grow. Other way to bathroom and old bedrooms—my grandparents in one, because everyone see them as boss of farm, and me next door in room I always slept when child. The rest of bedrooms, including my great-grandfather, in new building behind, with extra kitchen, toilet and bathroom, and space for washing and storing. It also has living room, but not so big as here. We want whole family to be able to be cosy together.'

'It's beautiful, Sunny.' Torin surveyed the spliced timbers beneath the insulation under the curved tiles. 'Can I see your room?'

Sunny lifted the latch. A small bed was pushed against the casement window that looked onto the pile of maize in the courtyard. 'My grandparents are away in Chengdu, so I'm alone in this building tonight. You sleep in new building, same as Great-grandfather. I make up bed later.' She smiled at Torin's expression. 'We just be careful he not disturbed.'

Sunny led the way back to the living room. 'I can hear

163

*Zŭfù* in kitchen. You sit drink beer while I go to help.'

Torin settled in an armchair that scooped up his whole body. As Sunny reached out with the glass, he pulled her gently to him. She sat on his lap, resting her head against his cheek, conscious of the synchronised rising and falling of their chests. The clock chimed seven. 'I need to go. We together later.' She kissed him and stood.

Fifteen minutes later they were sitting round the wooden table in the kitchen. Sunny expertly lifted noodles into the small bowls. 'It feels like time stop in this room'.

Torin looked at the blackened timbers arching above. 'Has your great-grandfather always lived here?'

The old man listened as Sunny translated then turned to Torin. '*Wŏ zài zhè lĭ shēng huó le yī bèi zi.*'

'His whole life.' Sunny paused, resting her chopsticks on her bowl. 'Except when my great-grandfather was fighting Japanese'

'You mean the Second World War?'

'I think so.' Sunny turned her head to ask. '*Zŭfù, Nĭ dă zhàng shí. Shì bù shì dì èr cì shì jiè dà zhàn yā?*'

The old man slowly put down his chopsticks and pushed the bowl from the edge of the table. '*Shì de yā, dōu guò le duō nián le.*' His eyes fixed on Torin as he talked, pausing frequently to allow Sunny to translate.

When news of the Japanese attacks had reached his village, Lu Zhe Ming joined the Chinese Army. For him there was no choice. He was not prepared to see his country fall under foreign occupation, so he responded to Chiang Kai-shek's call to arms in the only way he could— by walking to Chengdu to enlist with his friend.

The first part of his war was fought in Hubei province.

Then they were sent on trucks to Burma in the spring of 1942. The journey from Kunming had taken four days. They bounced along mud-tracks that would become impassable once the monsoons started. There was little explanation from their officers, who just said their Allies needed help.

Then the young recruits marched along jungle tracks for three more days, till they met retreating groups of tired and desperate British soldiers. These were some of their Allies, and many more were surrounded by the advancing Japanese. The only way to escape was over a bridge, which the Japanese were fighting to take.

His commanding officer had spent time in America before the war started, and so could speak enough English to communicate by radio with the senior British officer in charge of the men holding the bridge. He learnt there were many Japanese troops dug in between his troops and the river. Lu Zhe Ming's platoon was ordered to fight their way through the jungle at night till they reached the bridge.

As Sunny translated each part of *Zufu's* story, Torin was struck by the clarity with which the old man recalled events of over seventy years ago. He thought about his own grandmother's reluctance to talk about the war. He knew she'd arrived as a refugee from Sweden and married an air-raid warden, who was killed in the Blitz. But whereas Granny Mette was evasive in her response to questions, Lu Zhe Ming needed little prompting.

The Chinese soldiers pushed back the encircling Japanese to create an arc through which exhausted British soldiers could escape. Using Burmese villagers who knew the terrain, the message about the open bridgehead was relayed to Allied troops hiding from Japanese patrols. The order was to retreat immediately, as the bridge defenders could only hold it for one more day.

'How many soldiers escaped?'

'*Qī qiān* '

'Seven thousand? In less than twenty-four hours? How old was your great-grandfather when he did this?'

The old man laughed, revealing rows of stained teeth.

'Seventeenth birthday next day.'

# Chapter Twelve

## Fenghuangshan Airfield
## Friday December 3rd 1942

The respite in bombing continued after Chennault's visit, giving the ground-crew time to repair and refit the Warhawks.

In the remaining days before his departure, Harry used the breathing-space to ensure the pilots were rested. Dougie organised a rota so each person could have extended time off, while keeping half the squadron on standby in the ops room. Any pilot leaving the base had to register a contact phone number of someone who would find him in case of emergency, and have arrangements in place to ferry him back to the airfield within an hour. Those with families close had taken the opportunity to meet them; others had continued to enjoy what limited nightlife was available in a city pulverised by four years of bombing.

They'd been back to Mister Fu's bar twice more, where the same two girls had led them across the charcoal-scented street to the upstairs rooms.

When Li Ya Fei started to untie the cord of her peignoir, Harry took both hands, and gently pulled her beside him on the crumpled bed. They spent the allotted hour exchanging words for parts of the body, with Ya Fei giggling as he struggled to copy her pronunciation. Finally, she lay back against the pillow, her left hand pressing the silk hem between her legs, her right hand brushing his cheek. He turned his head to see her eyes glisten in the light from the naked bulb.

The next time he ordered drinks and snacks from the bar, and she taught him the names of the different foods while they ate. Then they lay on the bed, listening to stallholders calling in the street below, and a woman's voice accompanying the plucked strings of the *gǔzhēng*. Ya Fei's hand closed over his and she pressed her body against him. He could feel her warmth through the thin material and shifted awkwardly on the bed to conceal his own arousal.

As the last note faded into silence, Ya Fei sat up. *'Tiān é.'* Her outstretched arms rose and fell like the wings of a large bird. *'Tiān é,'* she repeated, smiling as the silk material slipped from her shoulders. Harry looked up from the pillow, wishing he could break through the barrier of language. He reached up, and she allowed his hands to caress her body. He watched her eyes close and her breathing quicken through parted lips. Gently she pushed him back against the pillow and kissed him. When he left, he pressed the bundle of bank notes from his weekly pay into her hand, tasting the salt on her cheeks. He knew it was the last time.

The following morning, after the daily briefing with the aircrew, Harry and Douglass walked to the hangar to inspect the aircraft. A full complement of thirty Warhawks was lined up ready for action. Two Zeros were being worked on in the repair bay.

'Stroke of genius getting your hands on these,' observed Harry.

Douglass had been invited to accompany General Chennault on his visit to Kuomintang headquarters in

Chongqing. He'd learnt about a mission to steal aircraft from one of the Japanese front-line bases in Hubei province. Under cover of darkness, US special forces had secured a defensive cordon around two hangars. By the time the Japanese counterattacked, the Americans had evaporated into the countryside, and fourteen Chinese pilots had taken-off for Sichuan, with a squadron of fully-armed Zeros. Chennault's idea was to simply change the wing-markings and add them to his complement of fighter planes.

The armourers had run into difficulties though, because of the calibre of the cannons. Once they'd used up what was in the planes, there'd be no way of continuing to deploy them against the enemy, unless the special forces launched another ground-assault in Hubei to steal ammunition. But the logistics of carrying ammo back to Sichuan overland was insurmountable.

Dougie suggested they distribute the Zeros between each of the seven airfields around Chengdu so they could simulate dog-fights to teach novice pilots how to out-manoeuvre the nimble fighters. Chennault had supported this idea; it meant they could keep the Japanese markings, then deploy the aircraft against any renewed bombing campaign. Until the ammo in the guns ran out, they could come up behind an escort of Zero fighters, and blast them from the sky before unsuspecting Japanese pilots worked out what was happening.

'Just need to make sure no one gets trigger-happy during training!' Dougie's deep voice sounded a warning. 'Jap ammo is precious. We're trying to locate any Zeros we've shot down, to see if we can salvage unused shells.'

After talking with Wong Swee about deactivating the firing mechanisms, the two men walked out of the large hangar into the morning sunshine. Half a mile away, on the far side of the airfield, Harry saw a squad of soldiers drilling in front of a cluster of Nissen huts. 'Who's that lot, Dougie?'

'Remnants of the Chinese Expeditionary force from Burma. Chennault asked the station commander to allocate space at Fenghuangshan. Those huts have been empty since we arrived, so it seemed a good idea. They marched in yesterday. Chiang Kai-shek has restructured this half of his army with new recruits, and reckons the safest place for them to train is where there is defence against airborne attack. So he's using all the airfields around Chengdu, plus Bai Shi Yi and Jiu Long Po near Chongqing.'

'What's he planning?'

'Uniting his army under one command. At the moment the other half is over to the west in India, with Burma and a million Japs in between. He'd like to sort that little problem, so he can focus on the Japs to the east—from where the bastards keep sending their bombers.'

'How come half his army ended up in India?'

Dougie frowned, stroking the ends of his moustache. 'Maybe a quick history lesson would be helpful, Harry? Lying on my back in Kunming for two months, I did a lot of reading.'

'I haven't wanted to read anything apart from weather reports and the set of Agatha Christies I bought from England.'

'She the dame that writes murder stories?'

Harry nodded. 'My progression from Biggles. My jolly old English master would have a head fit, if he knew. His diet for us boys was Faulkner, Orwell, Huxley and most of all Forster. Though Agatha Christie had loads in the top one hundred, she was frowned on as lightweight.'

'They the ones with the Belgian detective?'

'Yes, or an old biddy called Miss Marple, although the one I'm reading just now doesn't have either of them. It's about a group of people isolated on an island. Killed off one at a time, and those still alive know the murderer is amongst them.'

'When you go back, I'll swap it for what I'm reading.'

Harry nodded. 'Sounds good. I'll leave the whole set. But you were going to tell me about the Generalissimo's army. Doesn't he need all his troops here to push the Japs back? Having large numbers in India sounds bonkers.'

'I could explain while we walk over to check everything's okay with the new arrivals?' Dougie pointed to the other side of the airfield.

Harry could feel the sun on his neck as he fell into step beside Douglass, who described events in Burma. When Rangoon fell in early March, the British Army had retreated northwards, thinking they could hold a defensive line from Prome on the Irrawaddy river in the west, to Toungoo on the Sittaung River in the east, where they had additional support from the Chinese Expeditionary Force sent from Yunnan.

The British Army in the west of Burma was forced back up the Irrawaddy towards Mandalay. They tried to hold the oil fields at Yenangyaung, but the Japanese surrounded them. Surrender seemed inevitable until Chiang Kai-shek ordered one of his generals, Sun Li Jen, to lead a thousand Chinese troops from the centre of Burma to relieve them.

A skylark lifted from a patch of grass, carrying its song high above their heads. Harry watched the fluttering wings rise into the cloudless sky till it dissolved in the haze of blue.

'General Sun was up against an army ten times the size and he couldn't deploy heavy weapons because of the jungle. But they still managed to beat back the Japanese at Yenangyaung, and enable the encircled Allied troops to escape north to Mandalay.'

Where the hell were these places? Harry could have done with Chennault's map. India to the West and China to the East. He closed his eyes, trying to recall the shape of the country into which he could fit the names. Moulmein, Rangoon, Prome, Irrawaddy, Toungoo, Sittaung, Yenangyaung, Mandalay. He knew he'd flown north of them all, high above Fort Hertz, at the point where Burma rose to meet the Himalayas.

An image formed of morning assembly in the library, surrounded by heavy tomes locked behind glass screens. A gowned master read from one of the leather-bound books, sonorous with the rhythm of the stanzas.

*By the old Moulmein Pagoda, lookin' eastward to the sea,*
*There's a Burma girl a-settin', and I know she thinks o' me;*
*For the wind is in the palm-trees, and the temple-bells they say:*
*'Come you back, you British soldier; come you back to Mandalay!'*
*Come you back to Mandalay,*
*Where the old Flotilla lay:*

*Can't you 'ear their paddles chunkin' from Rangoon to Mandalay?*
*On the road to Mandalay,*
*Where the flyin'-fishes play,*
*An' the dawn comes up like thunder outer China 'crost the Bay!'*

As a twelve-year-old, he was intrigued by the image of flying-fishes playing on a road. Harry imagined a creature like a dragon fly—round eyes scanning tarmac for oncoming cars.

Dougie's voice interrupted the thought. 'Soon after the battle at Yenangyaung, the Chinese armies suffered several defeats and the Japanese took Lashio on the Burma-China Road in the north-east. This meant they were in a position to move west and cut off the Allied forces at Mandalay. General Wavell gave the order to abandon Burma, and the British retreated towards India. They managed to make it to Imphal before the monsoon broke in May, but lost most of their equipment on the way.'

The American swatted a mosquito on his cheek and wiped the smear of bloodied insect against his tunic. 'That was bad enough, but what made it ten times worse was the Chinese army knew nothing about the order to retreat. They thought they were going to make a stand at Mandalay alongside you Brits. Once they realised what was happening, many of Sun Li-Jen's soldiers joined the retreat to India, while the rest tried to return to Yunnan to the east, through mountainous forests and over the Salween River.

'At least half the poor sods died—accident, starvation or disease—and the really unlucky ones were killed by the pursuing Japanese, not renowned for their chivalry. The

Chinese troops in those Nissen huts include survivors from that retreat.

'Sun Li-Jen's troops were luckier. They made it to Imphal in pretty good shape. And that's why half the Chinese army is in India.' Dougie stopped to gather his breath. 'Does that answer your question?'

Harry smiled. 'Trust a Yank to turn a one-liner into a fully-blown yarn.'

Dougie scratched the bite on his cheek as he looked at his friend. 'This war's not simple Harry. If you look at the map of China, it really doesn't make any sense for Chiang to have got involved in Burma. The main Japanese assault was from the east, and he needed to stop their advance. See here, buddy.' The American bent to pick up a stick, and scratched an outline of China in the dusty ground.

'China is a bit like a chicken, with its head looking towards the Pacific Ocean.' He prodded the top of his drawing. 'This part is occupied by Japan. We're in the butt of the bird, beneath the fluffy tail that is Tibet and Xinjiang, which the Soviets have taken.'

Dougie gathered small stones and knelt beside his drawing. 'It's like a game of checkers across Asia. The Japanese have taken all the squares on the right-hand side of the board.' He placed pebbles in the dust. 'They are now lining up their men to take the squares in the middle, so they can join up with the squares they already occupy in Burma on the left-hand side. Then they will be in a strong position to threaten the squares that make up India.' He dropped the remaining stones to the left of the chicken's rump.

'Chennault was correct when he said that the planned

assault on Chongqing and Chengdu has been put on hold. But the Japs won't give up. With the whole of South Asia under their control, they've been able to redeploy divisions from Malaya, Thailand and Vietnam into Hubei. If the Japs capture Chongqing and Chengdu, they can open more supply routes into Burma, and then they'll move on India.'

Dougie looked up at Harry, screwing his eyes against the glare from the sun. 'The Chinese are expecting this attack in the spring. Chiang needs support from the Allies if he's to stand any chance of holding them back. Us Yanks want him to stay in the war, because he's got half a million Jap troops bogged down in China, who would otherwise be fighting in the Pacific.'

Harry prodded the cluster of pebbles in Burma with his right foot. 'That still doesn't explain why he deployed Chinese troops here in the first place.'

'Simple deal, buddy. Support the Allies, and the USA will supply funds and weapons to keep the Kuomintang going. Chiang had no choice but to send his armies into Burma, even though he thought it was a doomed mission. After the Brits threw in the towel, he gave the order to retreat to Yunnan because he didn't want his best soldiers stuck in India. Which is precisely what happened of course, so he must be hugely pissed off.'

Dougie dabbed the beads of sweat on his forehead with his handkerchief. 'Chiang's in a hell of a position. The Allies are still weak and the Japs are boosted by the news from Europe. The German army has reached the outskirts of Stalingrad. Goebbels is claiming they will be in Moscow before Christmas, talking about installing a provisional government for the whole of Russia. The Nazis would then have a border with their Japanese allies.'

'Jesus, Dougie. Where will it end?' Harry sat down beside the American, fingering the pebbles.

'Christ knows. After El Alamein, you've got Hitler on the run in Africa. But if Russia falls, he can move troops back into Europe, so it might be wise to sort a peace deal before he has another bash at invading Britain. Not sure where that leaves China though. Chiang has the support of us Yanks, but there's this other guy in the frame, Mao Tse Tung, who Chennault mentioned the other day.' Dougie dragged his stick back towards the head of the bird. 'Mao leads the Eighth Route Army, engaged in guerrilla warfare against the Japanese from his bases here in Shaanxi and along the Yangtze. He has huge support from the civilian population. He's introduced land reforms that have created more equal ownership, so has been able to reinforce his battalions along the Great Wall with recruits from the villages.'

'What's his relationship with Chiang?'

Dougie hesitated. 'They're fighting a common enemy in a loose alliance, but there's some history between them. I was told they were buddies fifteen years ago till the Nanking incident, when Chiang blamed the Communists for the attacks on foreigners. No-one knows what really happened. Then there was something called the Long March, when Mao outwitted the Kuomintang army pursuing him, which has elevated him to the status of a hero in the eyes of his supporters.' He looked down at the shape he'd drawn. 'I'd bet my sweet butt if the Japs are ever removed from China, Chiang will have to do a deal with Mao, or they'll be at each other's throats. God knows who the Allies will back if that happened. Chiang's our man at the moment, and I know Chennault rates him, but not all the Yanks think he's the bees' knees.'

'Why's that?' Harry closed his eyes, savouring the sunshine on his eyelids. In a week's time this would be history. But he was still curious. China had wormed under his skin.

'Word is that a helluva lot of money has lined the pockets of the Kuomintang leaders. And Generalissimo Chiang is playing a dangerous game with Roosevelt. When I was in Chongqing with Chennault, I heard about Wendell Wilkie's visit in September. He's the guy who's angling to be next president of the USA. There's a story going round that Chiang's wife gave him some special favours, as a way of keeping the Yanks on board. But Wilkie is a Republican. If Roosevelt wins again, Chiang might not be such a shoe-in for leader of China.'

Harry sat up, hearing the familiar call of the bamboo partridge from the edge of the airfield. 'How do you know all this Dougie?'

'That last bit of info came from sitting next to Chennault on the plane to Chongqing. He's had the hots for Madame Chiang for years, but never dared make a move for fear of losing something precious to her bodyguard. They're under orders from the boss himself.'

'But the rest of the stuff—about Burma, India, Russia and this other chap, Mao.'

'Flying a desk since July has given me time to piece it all together.'

'But I've got time to do that too. I'm not flying every day.'

'Buddy, when I look at you after you've dragged yourself out of the cockpit, you're in no state to read anything more than *Up and Coming Girls*. I remember those days. You fly, you eat, you drink, you wank, you sleep. If you're really lucky, you shag at Mister Fu's.' Dougie rolled his brown eyes. 'I've been there too. But I'm also interested in asking questions. If it hadn't been for this goddam war, I'd have gone to university.'

Harry shook his head. 'I never thought about doing anything but joining up. It was all everyone talked about in my school after Dunkirk and Churchill's speech on the radio. When he said "we shall never surrender", I knew what I wanted to do. I'd have joined the Navy, but the recruiting office was closed for lunch, so I went next door.' His fingers played with the pebbles on the tail of the chicken. 'I'm fighting to defend King and Empire against the Nazi threat. I guess that's why we're involved in Burma.'

'Christ, Harry, I'm not doing this so you Brits can get your frigging Empire back. Fuck that for a crock of shit.' Dougie swept the pebbles aside with his hand. He was breathing hard as he looked directly at the young pilot. 'I know what it's like to be exploited—to be treated as second class. There are parts of my country I'm afraid to visit, because of my skin colour. Real fear, man. Heard of the Ku Klux Klan?'

'Only clans I know about are in Scotland.'

Dougie raised his eyes. 'Jeez, buddy, get real. In the state where Chennault comes from, I'd have been picking cotton on a frigging plantation eighty years ago, watched by a white dude with a gun. And the pay and rations weren't great shakes. Step out of line and you'd have your hide

178

whipped till you passed out from the pain or bled to death, whichever came first. The Klan are the descendants of those people. Favourite past-times include lynching black men after they've hacked off their dicks, and teaching their wives a lesson or two.'

Harry rested his hand on Dougie's shoulder. 'I'm really sorry old man, I didn't know about any of this stuff.'

'There's still time to learn, buddy.' Dougie looked across to the parade-ground, where the soldiers were heading for the hut that served as a dining-room. 'We can talk more later. Let's find the guy in charge.'

Dougie called out to the drill sergeant in his halting Mandarin. The man pointed to an office beside the dining hall. As they pushed open the door, Lin Xiaobin grinned up from an easy chair in the corner. 'It's okay, Commander Winchester. I'm not defecting to the army.' He introduced his cousin, explaining that Captain Lin Fu Chin was in charge of the regiment billeted in the Nissen huts. Xiaobin spoke quickly to his cousin in his high-pitched voice.

Harry heard his name mentioned. 'We thought we'd come and say hello to your men.'

Lin Xiaobin translated. 'Fu Chin says they'll appreciate that. It's nearly midday. He invites you for lunch.'

Harry looked at Dougie for approval. The American crimped the points of his moustache. 'Should be okay. I'll phone Tang Shuo, so he knows where we are—just in case the Japs decide it's time they sacrificed another twenty bombers!'

As they took their places at one of the long tables, Harry observed the soldiers queuing at the serving hatch with bowls and chopsticks. The room echoed with excited chatter. 'What's fired them up?'

'They're talking in Sichuanese, so not easy to understand.' Lin Xiaobin addressed the man opposite, who rested his chopsticks on the edge of his bowl as he replied. 'Mostly you two, Commander Winchester. They're intrigued by the Major's skin, and the colour of your hair.'

Harry stood to check his reflection in the glass at the serving hatch. 'I'd forgotten I bleached it for the cabaret.' At his farewell party two nights ago, he'd duetted with Dougie, performing 'Let's Call the Whole Thing Off' as Ginger Rogers and Fred Astaire. It had meant dunking his head in a bowl of peroxide to emulate the blonde heart-throb.

Harry recalled Li Ya Fei running her fingers through the flaxen spikes as they lay on the bed, listening to the *gǔzhēng*. 'It's going to surprise Amy, but it'll grow out soon enough.' He looked at the soldier, who was expertly flicking noodles into his mouth. It was hard to tell how old he was. His unlined forehead was that of a young boy, but an angry scar ran from the corner of his eye to the edge of his mouth. The brown eyes flickered up at Harry, who sensed he was looking into a deep well of experience. He turned to Xiaobin.

'We have heard how these soldiers helped rescue the British Army in Burma. Please tell them that we salute their bravery. Major Walters was shot down on the border, fighting to prevent the Japanese building a bridge over the Salween river. Chinese troops saved his life.'

The young soldier's face broke into a smile, revealing a line of cracked and broken teeth. He responded with a single sentence, pointing at the soldier sitting beside him, and then scooped the remaining noodles into his mouth.

Lin Xiaobin turned to Dougie. 'He and his friend crossed the Salween river to escape the Japanese.'

Dougie stroked his shaven scalp. 'We could have been there at the same time. How long was he in Burma?'

Lin Xiaobin listened as the man replied at length. At one point the soldier pushed his chair back, took a knife from the table and stabbed at the floor, repeating the movement and yelling. When he sat down, he was breathing quickly, eyes flicking between Harry and Dougie.

'That was a long answer.' Lin Xiaobin stroked the thin crescent of his moustache. 'Let me try and summarise. He was part of the Chinese Expeditionary Army that Chiang Kai-shek sent into Burma to help the British. One night he and three friends were ordered to crawl through the jungle towards the Japanese trenches. There were other Chinese patrols creeping on all fours in parallel, along a line that was about eight hundred yards wide. They got close enough to hear the soldiers talking in their dug-outs and waited, as instructed, for the whistle to attack. Then they lobbed their grenades.

'After the explosions, there was screaming from wounded men and they rushed forward with bayonets fixed. In the dark it was hard to tell who was alive or dead, so they stabbed anything that moved.' Lin Xiaobin fingered the discarded knife on the table. 'That was the point he stood up to demonstrate. He got the wound on his face that night and lost several teeth.'

Dougie pursed his lips. 'Not very different to a dogfight, except you never see the blood.'

Harry was silent, thinking about the pink mist.

'Many Japanese died that night,' continued Lin Xiaobin. 'The Chinese soldiers waited in the captured trenches till dawn. The next day was very hot and the jungle was steaming. Just sitting still, sweat oozed out, but they were ordered to move forward to engage the Japanese again. Birds screeched from the canopy in response to the gunfire below.

'There was more hand-to-hand combat; no one wasted energy taking prisoners. As they approached the Pin Chaung river they could hear British troops trying to clear an escape route through the Japanese lines. Night came and the fighting died down, but as soon as dawn broke, the Chinese troops advanced again until they reached the banks of the river, where British soldiers were battling to create a bridgehead.

'This man and his friend were ordered to take out Japanese snipers, who were shooting the Allied soldiers as they crossed the river. It was hard to spot the marksmen, high up in the jungle canopy, but every now and then a cheer would go up from the Chinese platoon as a body crashed down through the trees.' Lin Xiaobin took a long mouthful of water from his glass. 'Once the Allied troops had escaped the dragnet, the Chinese troops continued to press their attack against the Japanese. He says they celebrated a big victory at Yenangyaung.'

'What happened next?'

The soldier licked his lips and spat on the ground before responding. 'The Japanese sent reinforcements from Rangoon to take back the oil-fields, forcing the Chinese to retreat northwards, following the British troops. They kept up a rearguard action, believing they were going to join up with other British and Chinese army divisions from different parts of Burma, to halt the Japanese advance at Mandalay.'

'Why didn't that happen?'

Lin Xiaobin listened to another long speech from the soldier. 'Everyone was simply running from the Japanese They were sharing mud tracks with refugees and sick people, as well as British, Indian and Chinese soldiers. They realised there was no plan to create a defensive line, so the Chinese leaders discussed whether they should join the British retreat to Imphal, or head back to China.

'General Sun Li-Jen wanted to go with the British, but Chiang Kai-shek had ordered all Chinese troops to retreat to Yunnan. Because this was their homeland, the majority of troops set off north east from Mandalay. But the Burma-China road and other escape routes through the valleys were in Japanese hands, so the only way to reach Yunnan was over the mountains.

'Communications broke down and he ended up with a small platoon, struggling to find a track through the dense jungle. They were suffering from dysentery and malaria, barely able to manage a couple of miles each day. They had no medicines or food, apart from what they could find in the jungle. Occasionally, someone would shoot an animal or bird, but they were always afraid the gunshot would draw the Japanese towards them. All the Chinese soldiers knew what would happen if they were caught, so any sick or wounded comrades asked to be shot if they had to be abandoned.'

Harry's brows furrowed. 'Did he see this happen?'

The soldier put his finger to his temples. '*Sān. Sān.*' He

spat again on the dusty concrete.

Lin Xiaobin took a deep breath. 'He shot three comrades in this way. In the end it was just himself and his friend here, who survived from the original platoon of twelve soldiers. They had grown up together in a small village in Sichuan and been classmates in the same school. They reached the town of Wanting on the border between Burma and China, and stole a boat to cross the Salween river at night.

'Then they walked to Kunming and were reunited with the rest of his regiment. But not many made it. He says fifty thousand soldiers were lost in the retreat to Yunnan. It would have been better if they'd headed to Imphal.'

Dougie nodded. 'That's what I was showing you with the pebbles. There are now Chinese armies either side of Burma. The "X" force is based in India under Sun Li-Jen's command and the "Y" force is in China with Du Yuming, the general who led the retreat to Yunnan. This is why Chiang is so pissed; he wants his soldiers for the battle on the other side of China. But many of his best troop are actually being airlifted back to India over the Hump to join the "X" force. They aim to have a hundred thousand men ready to attack the Japanese next year, and reopen the road into Burma.'

Dougie rubbed the sleeve of his shoulder. 'At the same time Du Yuming is training his troops in Yunnan for an attack on Myitkyina from this side of Burma, to join up with Sun Li-jen and create a land corridor between India and China, so we don't need to rely on the Hump. This man's regiment will soon return to Kunming to prepare for an assault in the spring.'

Harry looked at the young soldier with his scarred cheek and broken teeth. What would it have been like struggling through thick jungle, hungry and exhausted, bitten by mosquitoes and leeches, in pain from a festering cheek-wound and broken teeth, with the fear of capture by the Japanese upmost in mind?

He reached across the table and shook hands with both men. 'I admire your bravery and wish you success when you return to the front line. I am flying back to my own country next week to continue the fight against Germany.' His eyes flicked between the two soldiers. 'I hope we meet again to celebrate an Allied victory.'

# Chapter Thirteen

## Dazhentou Farmhouse:
## Sunday May 19th 2019

Sunny opened her eyes to the familiar surroundings of her childhood bedroom: the books on the single shelf beside the door; a hat on the peg behind the door; posters of Chinese pop groups and Mao Zedong; map of China; framed certificates for Kung Fu achievements and membership of the young socialist group.

She realised she was alone, like she'd been throughout her childhood, waking in a house where hers the only voice of a generation, where thoughts and dreams and ideas had to be shared with her fantasy-friend Ma Yingsen. Her arm reached to where Torin had spent most of the night, before returning to the bedroom in the new building as it was getting light. She pulled up the duvet over her chin.

Through the unlatched window she heard voices speaking a mixture of Chinese and English. She raised her head to look through the gap in the curtains. Torin stood next to her great-grandfather at the far side of the courtyard, dressed in black boxers and a vest. The old man wore the collarless shirt from the night before, outside of his baggy trousers. The hammer and sickle on his cap badge flashed in the sun. He had his left hand on the side of a fence-post, holding a sledge hammer in his other hand, gesturing to Torin. Sunny caught the words. *'Nǐ néng chuí zhù zi ma? Nǐ néng chuí zhù zi ma?'* She saw Torin shake his head.

She swung her legs off the bed and pushed the window wide open. Chicken manure mingled with the scent of cut grass from the paddock beyond. '*Zǔfù* wants you hit posts,' she called. 'He mending fence round chickens.'

Torin looked across the yard. 'I went to the toilet and great-grandfather grabbed me as I was coming out. He wanted to show me something by the coop, but I'm not even dressed yet.'

Sunny's laughter rippled in the sunshine. 'Enough clothes for working. It will be warm today.' She exchanged words with the old man, who smiled and pressed his fingers against Torin's upper-arm muscles. 'If you hit posts, *Zǔfù* very grateful. He not have strength any more. Just end posts holding wire.'

She watched her great-grandfather steady the stake on the soft earth and incline his head to Torin. The hammer swept down in an arc. The thump on the post echoed from the hillside.

'*Zài cì… zài ci*,' repeated Lu Zhe Ming, encouraging Torin.

With each swing of the sledge-hammer, the stake shuddered, boring into the red earth.

Finally, Lu Zhe Ming let go. '*Zhēn bàng.*' His hand gripped Torin's upper arm, stroking the bicep. Even from twenty metres away, Sunny saw the sweat glistening on Torin's forehead.

'I make dumplings for when you finish.'

Quickly she showered and dressed, rummaging in the kitchen. Through the door to the farmyard the sledge-hammer banged and her great-grandfather chattered excitedly.

Her phone flashed with a message from Huang Guo. *'How was Pingle?'*

She sent a thumbs up emoji.

*'Want more detail. Did you?'*

*'What?'*

*'You know.'*

Sunny hesitated. Maybe WeChat wasn't the best way to discuss it.

*'I like him,'* she typed.

*'Does he feel same?'*

*'Think so.'*

*'Only think? What happened?'*

*'We share room.'*

*'You did it, then?'*

*'Yes.'*

*'Wow! Any good?'*

Sunny clicked the emoji of two champagne glasses. *'Talk later. Making dumplings.'*

The food was on the table when the men returned. Torin sat next to the old man on the bench. *'Jiǎo zi hěn hào chī. Hěn hào chī.'* Lu Zhe Ming smiled as he scooped dumplings into Torin's bowl. His left hand stroked Torin's forearm.

'He says you very strong.'

'Sometimes I lift weights at the gym, but I'm not fit like you with running—or your great-grandfather, in terms of stamina. He could have gone on for hours.'

'It is his life. He has been here since the war finished.'

'Against the Japanese you mean?'

*'Bùshì.'* Lu Zhe Ming shook his head as Sunny relayed

the question. His fingers touched the insignia on the front of his cap.

"He says it wasn't quite as simple as that," said Sunny. Between mouthfuls, she translated the continuation of *Zǔfù's story*.

After the battle to rescue the British Army, Lu Zhe Ming retreated with remnants of Chiang Kai-shek's expeditionary force to Kunming, helping to hold the line against the Japanese, while the Allies regrouped and built up their capability. The bombing of Chengdu lessened as the Chinese air force grew in strength, supported by the Americans and British.

Following the Japanese surrender in August 1945, celebrations were short-lived. The Nationalist and Communist truce didn't last. Chiang Kai-shek fought to maintain leadership of the country, but in 1949 the Kuomintang government flew from Chengdu to Taiwan. Lu Zhe Ming could see the way things were moving and shifted his support to the Communists, substituting the insignia of the People's Liberation Army for the white star of the Kuomintang on his cap badge.

His friend Zhong Chen was less fortunate. Unwilling to change sides, he was denounced as a traitor in 1949. Most of his farm was confiscated, and in public he had been forced to wear a hat clarifying he was a Kuomintang conspirator. Every journey to the shops was a gauntlet of opprobrium, worsened during the period of the Red Guards. On one occasion he was beaten to the ground and kicked unconscious by a gang of boys from the local school. Only Lu Zhe Ming's intervention saved his life.

'My great-grandfather says he was interrogated by the

local commissar, because he challenged the Guards.'

'Why did he take those risks?'

The old man's eyes flickered between Torin and Sunny.

'Great-grandfather say two reasons. First, they joined Chinese Army together in 1942 to defend country against Japanese invaders. Not know about Kuomintang or Communists. Never heard of Mao Zedong or Chiang Kai-shek. Just went to nearest recruitment office Second reason, more important. Friend saved life in Burma.'

Sunny listened, as Lu Zhe Ming took himself back to the leech-ridden jungle of south east Asia and the desperate journey from Mandalay across the border to Kunming. At one point his fingers jabbed the scar on the bridge of his nose. As the old man stopped talking, Torin saw his milky eyes misting. He looked at Sunny, who was crying. He reached out his hand.

'I will try to tell you.' She breathed deeply, and dabbed her eyes with a tissue. 'It is sad story.'

Lu Zhe Ming and Zhong Chen chose to return to China with six comrades from the battle at Yenangyaung. For a week they struggled through impenetrable jungle and cloying swamps, plagued by clouds of mosquitoes. Three men were badly wounded, their condition deteriorating till they were unable to walk. No one wanted to be taken prisoner. At that point they asked their comrades to finish them off. The remaining five soldiers marched for three more days without food.

In the early morning of the fourth day, steam rising from the overnight rains, they staggered into a clearing where a squad of Japanese soldiers held rifles ready. A hail of bullets felled everyone except Lu Zhe Ming and Zhong

Chen, who the Japanese pursued into the jungle. Lu Zhe Ming tripped on a root. With a twisted ankle, it wasn't long before the Japanese caught and dragged him back to the clearing, where he was tied to a tree.

They spat at him, beat him with sticks till he became unconscious. A bucket of water over his head brought him round, and one of the soldiers approached, a cigarette held between his fingers. He drew on the tobacco and exhaled, blowing the smoke in Lu Zhe Ming's face. He lifted the glowing stub till Lu Zhe Ming felt the heat on his eyelids. He twisted his neck, but the Japanese man gripped his jaw, forcing his head back against the trunk of the tree. The butt stabbed into the skin above the bridge of his nose, and he could smell burning flesh as the solider withdrew the cigarette for another puff.

The second time there was no doubt about the soldier's intentions, as the glowing end moved to the right of his nose. Lu Zhe Ming closed his eyes, tensing.

A shot rang and the hand holding the burning cigarette fell away. Lu Zhe Ming opened his eyes to see a body on the ground, blood and brains oozing from the space in the skull where his eyes had been. The other soldiers raised their hands.

Four shots followed in quick succession, then Zhong Chen was slicing at the rough creepers binding Lu Zhe Ming to the tree. Despite his twisted ankle and battered body, he found the strength to stumble through the undergrowth, and they kept moving until dusk, putting as much distance between them and the clearing.

Five days later they reached the Salween river.

Sunny turned to Torin, tears on her cheeks. 'When boys

beat Zhong Chen, my *zǔfù* tell them about bravery in Burma. Zhong Chen kept his house and wife and friends, like my great-grandfather who refuse call him traitor. In 1988, Deng Xiaoping gave pardon to Kuomintang soldiers for fighting Japanese. After forty years, Zhong Chen no longer need wear his cap.'

'Is he still alive?'

Lu Zhe Ming pointed towards the hills.

'Still on his farm,' said Sunny. 'Now ninety-five.' Sunny closed her fingers over the hand on her shoulder. 'And I carry his name into this century.'

# Chapter Fourteen

## Fenghuangshan airfield
## December 6th 1942

'I've got a present—something to while away the hours waiting for a plane to whisk your limey ass back to England.' Dougie's rich bass boomed across the small room. He pulled open the top drawer to his desk and passed a package wrapped in brown paper.

Harry studied the jacket of the book. Its sepia tones showed the sun beating on the furrows of a cultivated field. In the foreground a wooden plough waited to be yoked. 'Is this the book you mentioned the other day?'

'It was all part of my education in Kunming hospital. I look at the country quite differently now. I guess I'd grown up with all the usual stereotypes.'

Harry nodded. 'I remember my dad talking about coolie labourers building railway lines to supply trenches in France.' An image formed of his father, standing at the mantelpiece beside the coal fire in the front room. It must have been Easter; he was looking at painted eggs next to his father's large hand. Through the window he could see the yellow flowers on the forsythia hedge. It was early evening. A blackbird called from the yew tree in the garden. His father had switched on the wireless and was fiddling with the knob to reduce the crackling.

Harry's fingers brushed the cover of the book. 'The furrows remind me of the Japanese flag. Like rays of the rising sun.'

'Ain't ever noticed that. But it wouldn't surprise me. If you read the biographical notes, you'll see she spent time in Japan, when she had to flee from Nanking.'

'Isn't that where Lin Xiaobin comes from?'

Dougie nodded. 'Yes, now called Nanjing. Poor bloody city's been in the front line for decades. Pearl Buck was caught up in the punch-up that marked the end of the alliance between Chiang Kai-shek and the Communists.'

Harry watched his father glance at the clock above the mantelpiece. Six pips cut through the silence and then the announcer's voice. '*This is the News Bulletin from 2LO.*' A lump of coal shifted in the hearth and the fire sparkled. The six-year-old was more fascinated by the flames than the wireless. '*British Navy ships have been in action against the Chinese Army in Nanking. HMS Vindictive and a fleet of destroyers bombarded the city in retaliation for the attacks on the British consulate last night. The leader of the Chinese Army has promised the British and Americans there will be swift retribution dealt out to the deserters for their murderous behaviour.*'

His father sucked deeply on his pipe and then addressed the room, as much as the small boy warming his hands. What was it he'd said? That he always knew there'd be trouble after the Great War? In 1919 the Chinese had not been properly rewarded at Versailles by the Allies, who had allowed Japan to take over surrendered German concessions, like Qingdao.

'*The Good Earth* changed my thinking completely. Pearl Buck draws back a veil to reveal glimpses of the real China. It helped me understand the kinship that permeates everything in this country. And the morality.'

Harry's eyes followed the American, who lifted a bottle of Jack Daniels from a small cupboard above the desk. How was it possible a book could alter the way you saw things? Is that what his English teacher tried to help him understand, with the focus on Forster?

Dougie poured generous shots of the whiskey into two tumblers and passed one to Harry, indicating the water jug on the desk. 'Till I arrived in this country, the only Chinese name I'd ever heard was Confucius, and I thought he was living around the time of Shakespeare. Before coming to Fenghuangshan, I spent a few days in Chengdu, being shown round by an English-speaking guide that the Generalissimo found for me.'

The American sat, taking a large mouthful of amber liquid. 'I came to realise they have a history stretching back thousands of years.' Dougie described how his guide had taken him to a flood-prevention system built a couple of hundred years BC and still functioning, temples dating back over one millennia, and a cottage where an old poet had lived in the eighth century. 'Where I come from, we get excited if we come across a building that's a hundred years old. Apart from the oral history of the Red Indians, which palefaces like Custer did their best to obliterate, we have nothing that connects us with the distant past.'

He pointed at the book in Harry's hand. 'She doesn't talk about any of that stuff, but her characters feel a genuine connection with their ancestors and with the land—and the actions of people who lived several thousand years ago still influence how they think and live. You get a sense of where their values come from. And you realise that loyalty and respect are pillars of modern China.'

'We have our philosophers too though,' interjected Harry. 'And Christianity stretches back nearly two thousand years.'

Dougie snorted. 'And don't we hold ourselves as superior because of it. What gives us the right to send missionaries to every corner of the world? Have you seen it happening the other way round? Confucian missionaries working in rural England, or Louisiana where my family came from?' Dougie emptied his glass. 'Pearl Buck was the daughter of missionaries and came to question the morality herself. Anyway, let me know what you think of the book. If you like it, I'll send you the sequels.'

'There's more?'

'Jeez, Harry, she wrote dozens and is still writing. She won the Nobel Prize for Literature five years ago. Quite a dame.'

Harry tugged his earlobe, unsure Agatha Christie was a fair swap. He drained his glass, looking round the small office that doubled as Dougie's bedroom. The walls were covered with maps of Sichuan, including one of all the airbases. Above Dougie's desk on a pinboard between the maps were two photographs—one of a child beside an old woman in a wheelchair, and the other the face of a young man in US military uniform, eyes looking intently at the photographer. Harry could see a resemblance to Dougie in the first picture.

'Is that the great-grandmother you told me about?'

'Yes, Mary-Ellen James. In her apartment in Chicago shortly before she died. I carry it with me everywhere to remind me of my roots. She often talked about her own mother's memories of a village in Africa.'

'Blimey, Dougie; going back some. Your great-grandmother's mother?' Harry did a quick calculation on his fingers. 'You could be talking about the end of the eighteenth century.'

'I am, and you know what the main business was between there and America?'

'You mean—?' Harry hesitated.

'Too right man. Just think. I was ten when my great-grandmother died in 1930 at the age of eighty-seven. She'd been born in 1843. Her mother was a slave on a cotton plantation in Louisiana, having been captured as a young woman twenty years before. My great-grandmother passed on stories from her mother, about life in the village, before being transported across the Atlantic.'

Dougie looked intently at Harry. 'Can you imagine, bud? As a child I shared a house with a woman whose life story and memories connected to another continent a hundred and fifty years previously. Sometimes my great-grandmother talked as if *she* was the young woman in Gold Coast, living a simple farmer's life, before Europeans arrived. She reached back in time to help me glimpse the freedom her mother had briefly known. I learnt stuff at school, about the Civil War and abolition of slavery, but she was someone who'd lived it.'

'Was she still in Louisiana when she died?'

'Hell no, I'd never have made it into the airforce. The best I could have hoped for is shining boots on the street corner, or being a chauffeur for some rich, white dude. No siree. After abolition, she saved for a year and bought a train ticket to Chicago and took the first job she was offered—as a cleaner in a factory.' Dougie paused to empty his glass. 'She earned enough to make sure her daughter, my grandmother, went through school and found work in an office. By the time my mother was born, grandmother was running a typing-pool for a large law-firm in downtown Chicago. I grew up surrounded by aspiration and expectation, and she persuaded the head of the firm to sponsor my application to be a pilot. Without his backing I'd never have been allowed on the all-white parade-ground.'

Dougie mock saluted. 'I owe my great-grandmother everything, including my name. She met Frederick Douglass at a rally after she was liberated, and said she was so moved by his oration.' The American noticed Harry frowning. 'Escaped slave, became one of the leaders of the abolitionist movement in the USA.' Dougie described a formidable orator and articulate writer, whose autobiography became a bestseller. He wrote an open letter to his former slave-master, asking how he'd feel if Douglass had dragged away his daughter and treated her how he'd been treated himself? At the end he invited the slave master to stay in his own house, so he could show him how people ought to be treated. Dougie shook his head. 'How is that sort of forgiveness possible, Harry? By the time my grandmother met him, the Civil War had ended and he was arguing for black people to get the vote, and challenging segregation. "Us niggers need to be welcome everywhere" was one of his mantras.'

Harry shifted uncomfortably, thinking of the Agatha Christie cover.

'Shortly before she died, she told me, "learn how to get on with people and you'll be able to weave your way through life with one hand tied behind your back."' Dougie smiled. 'She was so right, except the arm's now tied at the front.' He twitched his shoulder muscle to lift the epaulette.

Harry stared at the naked bulb, thinking about his own family. His father fought at the Somme and Passchendaele, invalided back to England in 1917. His grandfather mined coal at Easington Colliery for fifty years. There were boilermakers and shipwrights in the dockyards at Stockton; bakers and wheelwrights in the Yorkshire dales. Behind the one-word descriptors there must be heroic stories to match Dougie's family? Being in the trenches or swinging a pick-axe at a narrow seam of coal, in a hot, dusty tunnel, was courageous. His grandmother died giving birth to their tenth child, and Grandfather coughed his way to an early death the year Harry was born. His only memory of them came from the sepia-tinted photo of the couple on their wedding day, above the mantelpiece in his parent's house in the East End—now buried in the rubble of Eric Street.

'Come on buddy, no point in saving this.' Dougie tilted the bottle of Jack Daniels to equalise the levels in the two glasses. 'You'll never get this back in the UK. Uncle Sam isn't going to allow precious space on the convoys for liquor, however good.'

Harry opened his eyes to focus on the pinboard behind Dougie's head. 'And the other photo?'

Dougie hesitated. 'That's Brian, who I trained with at West Point.'

'Pilot too?'

'Was. Past tense. We shared a room at Pearl Harbour. He managed to get his aircraft off the runway beside mine and we waded into the Japs together. But he didn't make it back to terra firma. I watched his plane spiralling into the Hawaiian sea.'

'You were good friends?'

Again, Dougie hesitated. 'Very close.'

Harry registered the check in the American's voice. 'You miss him?'

'Like fuck, Harry.' Dougie breathed in slowly, his fingers squeezing the collar of his jacket. 'More than anyone else in my whole life, including my great-grandmother.' The light from the bulb in the ceiling was reflected in the sheen that covered his pupils.

Harry reached for the bottle and split the remains between the empty glasses. 'This ruddy war has a lot to answer for. Every time I shoot down an enemy plane, I think two things almost simultaneously. The first is, thank God it's them not me. The second is, somewhere there will be grieving families.'

He looked through the open window at the menacing teeth of the Warhawks, just visible in the fading light. 'Legalised murder, isn't it? None of us doing our best to kill each other are anywhere close to the people who really deserve to die for starting it all. Xiaobin hates the Japanese because of what happened to his family, and I feel exactly the same about the Germans. But we're like gladiators in ancient Rome, forced to fight each other, when the real enemy is the Emperor and his court, watching the encounter from the ringside. You, me, Brian, Archie,

Xiaobin, we're just pawns on their ruddy chessboard.'

The American silently stared into his tumbler. Finally, he lifted his head to look at Harry. 'When I think about Brian, I try to tell myself that he died for a good cause—that he gave his life to make a difference—like the Bible says about Jesus dying on the cross so we might live.' The voice had softened, but retained its resonance; Harry struggled to catch the words. 'I used to believe that crap, when I went to the local church with my great-grandmother. But not now. My faith in religion died when I saw Brian's plane hit the water. His death didn't achieve anything, beyond an awful emptiness that aches inside when I wake every morning.'

'Sounds like a very special bloke.'

'More than special, Harry. I loved him you see.' Dougie turned his tear-streaked face to the British pilot. 'I can say this because you're leaving tomorrow, so it doesn't matter what you think. I need to tell someone though, to make it real, so that it's out there in the world, not just bottled up in my head.'

'You mean you were—' Harry recalled Mister Fu's question. '*Bendy girls for you too?*'

'Bent as a three-dollar bill. Bum bandits. Queer as a flying fuck!' Dougie spat the words. 'I prefer "the love that dare not speak its name". He was a white guy from New England—a Harvard graduate with a career destiny in law to die for, so we knew there was no future together. We had to be secretive because the military would have court-martialled both of us. Back in the USA, I'd have been strung up from the nearest tree.'

Dougie drained his tumbler, replacing the glass gently

on the desk. 'But we both reckoned war was coming, so we agreed to take each day as it came.' His voice trembled as he looked at Harry. 'I just feel torn apart at the way it ended, with no chance to say goodbye.'

Harry watched the shoulders shudder. He grasped Dougie's good arm, held it, thinking of the tally of planes etched on the fuselage of his Warhawk. Fourteen confirmed kills and a number of probables. Faceless, nameless men blasted into oblivion or forced to parachute onto the waiting pitchforks of farmers. Through the open window he heard an animal howl, maybe the solitary wolf spotted in the village at the edge of the airfield. It was like the wailing of a mother, wretched with the misery of sudden loss, triggered by the telegram ripped from its envelope. In villages and towns across Japan and China, as well as Europe and the dozens of other countries immersed in this battle for the soul of civilisation, hundreds of thousands of desolate, tormented parents and grandparents grieved their children.

Not to mention bereft lovers. Amy's face drifted into consciousness.

He'd managed to speak with her on a phoneline routed through the north of China and across the Soviet Union. They'd had to shout to hear each other, and the three-second delay added to the confusion. But she understood he was coming home. A new night-fighter squadron was being formed to protect bomber-streams over Germany, and he had been asked to lead it.

In the morning he'd be on the train to Kunming. A Dakota flight over the Hump was scheduled for the following day. Soldiers from the Chinese Army were being sent to boost Sun Li-jen's X Force. If there was room on the plane, he'd be at RAF Dinjin by nightfall, and then look for a way to reach Cairo. He'd heard Archie was convalescing.

Dougie's shoulders stopped heaving. 'Time for bed.' Harry half-carried the American to his bunk in the corner of the room. 'I'll say goodbye now; I'm off at first light.'

Dougie smiled weakly. 'Thanks for your friendship, Harry. Chennault was right to recruit you. Done a brilliant job—despite talking with a rod up your goddamed ass.'

'Team effort, Dougie. I couldn't have done any of it without you. Not just gathering intelligence about the Jap formations, and talking us down in piss-awful weather, but the personal support for all the pilots. You kept us going with your energy and humour—even if it has a Yankee twist. And your waffles really were something to die for.'

The American looked up from his pillow. 'You'll be travelling with some of the soldiers we met across the airfield.'

Harry nodded. 'What was the name of the man who stabbed the table with his knife?'

'Corporal Zhong, I think.'

Dougie was asleep before the door closed.

# Chapter Fifteen

## Dazhentou to Chengdu:
## Sunday afternoon 19th May 20th 2019

Torin and Sunny stood at the entrance-gate to the farmhouse in front of Lu Zhe Ming. Wisps of white hair curled from beneath the flat cap with its polished badge. He reached forward to wrap his sinewy arms around Chen Xi, who hugged him, whispering into his ear. Finally, he straightened and extended his hand to Torin. '*Zài jiàn.*'

'Please tell your great-grandfather it's been a privilege to meet him and fascinating to hear his stories.'

Lu Zhe Ming smiled as he listened to Sunny's translation. His response came rapidly.

'He say next time you come, he will ask army-friend to eat supper.'

'That would be a very special honour. And I promise to get fitter, so I can help with fencing.' Torin pressed his bicep.

The afternoon sun warmed their backs as they descended the hill to the main road. Mrs. Wang stood outside her shop. A wide straw-hat protected her face and she was wearing baggy, black trousers under a white cotton-tunic, embroidered with red dragons. '*Nǐ men zài yì qǐ ma? Nán péng yǒu bā?*' A quick interchange with Chen Xi triggered a cackling laugh. She stroked Torin's arm, as she held his left hand, looking directly into his eyes.

'She wants to know whether you now my boyfriend.'

'What did you say?'

Sunny smiled. 'That we had a cosy evening with my great-grandfather and you spent morning fencing chickens.'

Torin chuckled. 'Is diplomacy your middle name?'

'All Chinese children taught to be careful with words.'

Mrs. Wang passed Torin a plastic bag. He opened it to reveal two slices of yellow-green fruit. His nose wrinkled. 'Jesus, Sunny, that's hard to stomach.'

'Taste much better than smell. Close eyes and hold fingers on nose.'

Torin did as instructed and she broke off a piece and slipped it into his mouth. Mrs. Wang clapped approval as a smile creased his face. 'I see what you mean. It's a bit like walking past a sewage farm into a field of jasmine.'

'We call it *liú lián*. I think English word is durian. Most favourite fruit with Chinese people. We love it. Just not allowed on bus.'

'I can see why.' Torin passed the bag to Sunny. 'Maybe you finish it before we get to the main road! Thank Mrs. Wang for introducing me to its delights.'

The journey back to Chengdu was like watching a film in reverse. They changed buses in Pingle. The sun sank below the bamboo-covered hills behind them, and they fell asleep, waking only when the bus pulled into the terminal beside the Third Ring road. Sunny was aware of Torin's hand reaching for hers. 'Will you stay with me tonight?'

Her eyes were unwavering. 'I will text my mother. Say still at Pingle.'

Half an hour later Torin pressed the card against the lock and pushed the door open to the room in the St. Regis. Through the window beyond the desk Sunny could see the lights of the skyscrapers across the road. The pattern of lit-windows resembled 爱.

She placed her bag on the stand next to the television and looked round the room. A glass-screen looked directly onto the jacuzzi in the bathroom. Two white robes hung beside it. She watched Torin draw the curtains, closing the city from their private world. He turned and walked slowly towards her. She reached up to touch his scar, smiling at the expression in his blue eyes.

It was late morning once they'd bathed and showered, each soaping the other in a lather of discovery that had them laughing and kissing, before they finally dressed to go to Shuangliu airport. In the Didi they continued to make love with their fingers.

Once Torin had checked in his bags, Sunny suggested a snack. Neither of them had eaten any breakfast. They sat in the corner of the restaurant, lifting the little dumplings from the bowl. For a while neither spoke, as they concentrated on the food. The imminence of the parting lay over them like a cloud.

Finally, Sunny placed her chopsticks on her plate and her eyes met Torin's across the table. 'When will you be coming back to Chengdu?'

'If the orders come in, I am sure *Perfect Pitch* will want me to return to China,' he said. 'But there is not a plan yet.'

'Maybe I can visit you in UK?' She imagined standing beside the River Thames, whose curves and twists she'd followed on the map above her desk, walking hand-in-hand through the cobbled streets of the old city, watching the lights from the London Eye, seeing Buckingham Palace and Big Ben. The city of red double-deckers, black taxicabs, and Sherlock Holmes.

She felt a flutter and waited for him to indicate the next step. She could take time off in the summer or during the national holiday in October. She knew it was complicated to get a visa; it had taken Gloria six months and pages of information from the bank and her employer about her financial status—proving she would return to China at the end of her visit.

He hesitated. 'It could be a bit difficult though.'

Difficult? Sunny was conscious of a sick feeling in her stomach. She pushed away the half-eaten bowl of dumpling. 'Do you not want to see me again?' She wanted to hear him say he would be back as soon as he could, that the last days mattered to him more than anything.

'I do, Sunny, very much.' His voice softened and his hand closed over hers. 'It's been amazing. Utterly wonderful. Being with you has been such a fantastic experience.'

Her breathing quickened. Whatever he was about to say, she'd rather it evaporated into a void, unheard. She knew she should leave, but couldn't force herself to stand.

'The thing is...' Sunny knew what he was about to tell her. She had always known. It had been there in everything left unsaid since that first meeting at Plaza Tower. When she had talked about her life after college, she'd mentioned boyfriends and splitting up with Wang Yi. It was all in the past, history—and simply affirmation she was available for new adventures. But Torin had never said anything about girlfriends. He'd talked about his childhood, living with his grandmother, going to university, buying a flat, flying with his friends from the pub, and his passion for the job at *Pitch*

*Perfect.* But nothing about relationships. That should have alerted her. He didn't have girlfriends.

She stared at him, tears welling, fuelled by anger, embarrassment, jealousy, hurt, and disappointment. Seeping into it all was an emptiness—a void that suffocated hope. She pushed back her chair and watched herself leap down the escalator stairs, running through the terminal, dodging people with wheelie suitcases and duty-free bags, panting onto the concourse outside, where she gulped air like a stranded fish on a river bank.

'*Wǒ kě yǐ bāng nǐ ma?*' Chen Xi was aware of the female police-officer holding her to stop her falling, asking if she could help. Was she ill?

Chen Xi shook her head. '*Bù shì… Shì… Bù shì.*' She knew she wasn't making sense. 'Taxi please. Just get me a taxi. Out of here.' The police woman led her to the front of the queue and blew her whistle to attract a driver's attention.

Chen Xi stumbled behind the open door and fell onto the back seat of the green taxi. She choked out her address as the vehicle gathered pace.

# Part Two

If we don't know life, how can we know death?

孔夫子 Kǒnog Zǐ (Confucius)

# Chapter Sixteen

## RAF Swanton Morley, Norfolk: 1st January 1944

'Bravo Three Six to Control. Ready for take-off.' Harry repeated the call sign he'd used a thousand times. Behind him Archie was whispering through his final navigation-checks.

Harry's eyes searched the gloom beyond the nose of the Mosquito, making sure all the aircraft were in line. The string of white landing-lights shimmered like Christmas tree illuminations, reflected in the banks of snow cleared from the runway after the fresh fall earlier in the day. He glanced at his watch. ETD had been given as 21.00 hours to bring them into line with the Wellington bombers from Feltwell and Foulsham, that had started their lumbering journeys towards the Dutch coast an hour before.

Harry shifted his weight on the parachute and tightened the zipper of his flying-jacket. The freezing tendrils would worm through the woollen insulation as they flew over Germany, gnawing into the marrow of their bones by the end of the five-hour flight, with the Mosquito's propellors clawing their way back to sanctuary across the North Sea.

He flicked away the strand of tobacco from his bottom lip, savouring the cigarette's aftertaste. He'd shared a packet of Woodbines with the eight other crews beside their aeroplanes, waiting for orders to start their engines. Glowing fireflies danced around the group of airmen and

Harry was grateful for the twilight that allowed each man to take refuge in his thoughts.

Sergeant-Pilot Davis, the newest recruit to the squadron, sucked his cigarette some feet from the other crews. It was Frank's first sortie, having qualified the previous week after nine-months' training. At five-foot six he was the smallest pilot, but made up for it in flying ability. Harry had seen Frank execute low-level aerobatics that left those watching on the ground breathless. Harry moved across to stand beside the young flyer.

'You okay, son?' he asked softly. In the tiny light cast by the glowing butt, he observed a twitch in the boy's unlined cheeks. Were the Penguins in charge of recruitment still sending boys straight into combat before they'd started to shave?

The eighteen-year-old from Anglesey held the smoke in for a long time before exhaling slowly in Harry's direction. 'Just hope I don't make a hash of it, sir.' Apprehension was evident in his clipped speech. 'Suppose you're used to this?'

Harry breathed deeply, conscious of his own fear welling in response to Frank's admission, but he knew it didn't help to give expression to the jitters. That was the slippery slope to being relieved from operational flying and having 'Lacking Moral Fibre' stamped in your log book.

Could you ever get used to contemplating your last night on earth?

From the edges of his memory, three years and several lifetimes ago, Harry's squadron-commander loomed from the darkness beside the wing of his Blenheim as the nervous young pilot prepared to clamber up to the cockpit. 'First sortie is always a bit of a roller coaster, son. We all wonder if we're going to make it or if it's our turn for the chop. Stick close to me, keep your eyes peeled, and I'll see you back at base in one piece. Hunting is a fine sport and man-hunting-man is the finest sport of all.'

Harry put an arm round Frank's shoulder, unseen by the other crews. 'Truth is laddie, it gets worse each time. We're all scared, but we try not to show it.' He glanced at the crescent-moon peeking between a gap in the clouds, aware that in two hours the boy would be weaving through hostile skies above the Third Reich. 'Just remember your training, son. Never stop scanning from left to right; never relax for a moment; never make the mistake of thinking you're safe, till your wheels hit the runway. Do all that and keep Lady Luck on your lap, and I'll buy you a drink in the bar tomorrow night.'

The novice pilot smiled weakly, dropping his glowing butt on the ground, crushing the embers with the heel of his flying-boot.

Harry walked in silence beside his navigator towards their own plane, wrapping his scarf round his neck. Above the control-tower he noticed the cumulus thickening from the east, driven by winds off the North Sea and beyond from Germany and Poland and the thousands of miles of snow-clad land that reached to the edge of China. He glanced at the luminous dial of his watch. Right now, the first signs of dawn would just be visible around the edges of the wintry blanket folded over Fenghuangshan.

The two airmen stood underneath the wing of the Mosquito, looking up at the grey outline of the aircraft that loomed above them. 'Why is this ruddy war still not over, Archie?' The Allies had established a bridgehead in Italy at

Anzio, and there was talk of opening a second front in France, but the end was still nowhere in sight.

'Dunno Hal. Maybe Adolf and his gang know they'll be for the high jump if they call it quits.' Archie's languorous tones floated through the darkness. It was as if he had turned casualness into an art, but Harry knew this belied a forensic attention to detail that had saved their lives on many occasions. 'We've just got to keep up the pressure on the bastards.'

A gust shook the propellor above and Harry felt the chill on his cheek as he shifted the parachute on his shoulder. He was reluctant to admit he was ready to let go. He was tired of the war, of seeing empty beds where friends had slept, of writing letters to bereaved wives and girlfriends, of the ebb and flow of adrenalin, of training and retraining on the latest aircraft from the factory production lines at Filton and de Havilands. Tired of it all. As he climbed onto the wing to lower himself into the cockpit, his gloved hand touched the pocket of his flying-jacket and he felt the familiar rustle of paper folded round the pack of cards.

He waited for the ground crew to scrape the freshly-fallen snow from the leading edge of both wings, careful not to puncture the doped fabric stretched taut across the wooden frame. He glanced at the aircraft beside him, already cleared of snow. Frank Davis lifted his thumb above the rim of the canopy. His wheel-chocks were pulled clear and he taxied from the dispersal bay. Harry waited till the other planes had followed Frank before pulling the starter.

With cylinders firing evenly, Harry was conscious of

the adrenalin countering traces of New Year's Eve with the Yanks from Lakenheath. When the old man suggested Archie and he drive over to the American base near Mildenhall to give a talk about the squadron's operations, it seemed an opportunity to shoot a line about the superior qualities of the Royal Air Force.

In the briefing-room, they'd been confronted by forty aircrew, sporting brown leather-jackets and chewing gum like they'd stepped straight off a film-set. Earlier that day their squadron of Mustangs had been escorting Flying Fortresses to Berlin. With every crew safely back, the Yanks were much more interested in their Planters Punch than anything two fresh-faced Brits might have to tell them about doing the same journey in the dark. Daylight raids resulted in more pinpointed destruction, but this had to be weighed against higher casualties. Attrition rates meant it was unusual to complete a tour of thirty sorties.

As he looked round the room, Harry was aware that most of the men would be shot down before Easter. They knew the odds too, so were determined to make the most of Hogmanay. Harry couldn't recall the drive back to Swanton Morley across the fenland, but remembered playing 'Pin the bollock on Adolf' long after the strains of Auld Lang Syne had subsided. When their batman carried two steaming mugs into their bedroom and drew the curtains to reveal the wintry dawn, the pounding in his head suggested it had been a very good night.

Harry adjusted his goggles and massaged his temples. After three years of operational flying, surely they'd done their bit? Maybe he could ask Chalky to arrange some decent leave? Or perhaps they should just ease back a little on the throttle and let others take the lead? Trouble was, if you dropped your guard, the next stop was likely to be ruddy Valhalla, drinking in the mess reserved for dead heroes.

The intercom crackled. 'Control to Bravo Three Six. Hold in line. A flight rolling in turn.'

'Roger, Control. Bravo Three Six Holding.' The silhouettes of the other eight Mosquitoes queued ahead. Harry wanted to be sure everyone was safely airborne before releasing the brakes. He adjusted his goggles and his right hand dropped to the control-column.

'Control to Bravo Three Six. Clear for take-off.'

'Roger, Control. Bravo Three Six rolling.' As the aircraft moved forward Harry knew this was the cue for Archie to kiss the tiny pocket-compass kept threaded on a silver chain round his neck, before tucking it beneath his shirt collar. If all else failed they could rely on the luminous dial of the penny purchase from Woolworth's to show them the way back.

Harry eased both throttle-levers forward, his right foot pressing the rudder-bar to hold the nose straight. The landing-lights underneath the fuselage became a continuous stream and the tail lifted off the tarmac. Harry watched the airspeed-indicator pass one hundred and twenty.

'Okay. Archie. Off like a bomb.' With a final bump the Mosquito leapt clear of the ground, its propellors clawing through the frozen air. Harry held the aircraft steady for twenty seconds before pushing the joystick to the right. 'Bravo Three Six. Turning Zero Nine Five.'

'Roger. Good luck Three Six. You're all away.' The

controller's voice crackled in his ears and the runway-lights went out.

Beneath the Mosquito, a jigsaw of drainage canals glistened across the graveyard-grey earth. Darker smudges of woods dotted the fenland between the rhynes. Harry noticed the altimeter-needle wind past two thousand feet. Somewhere below, Amy would be studying the green luminescence of her radar-screen, directing the bombers across the North Sea from their bases in Lincolnshire.

'Turn One One Ten, Harry.' It was the first time Archie had spoken since they'd waved away the chocks. They were now in cloud and reliant on instruments.

The aircraft lurched right, smashing Harry's head against the perspex. The pilot blinked away his tears, trying to focus on the instrument-panel, conscious of an eerie quietness in his left ear. He wondered if the drum had burst, then noticed a rev counter had dropped to zero.

'We've lost a sodding engine.' Harry rammed the throttle-lever backwards and forwards to no avail. The plane was drifting into a spiral. He kicked the rudder-bar to straighten the nose.

'Glycol trailing port side!' A stream of liquid was visible to the navigator from his position behind the wing.

'Can't feather the damned thing.' Harry concentrated on the artificial horizon, struggling to keep the aircraft on an even keel, fighting the torque of the starboard engine's erratic surge. He didn't need the altimeter to tell him the plane was sinking. As they fell out of the cloud-layer his eyes tried to pierce the blackout below. They were too far from Swanton Morley, but there might be other airfields in range.

Harry pressed the intercom. 'Mayday, Mayday, Mayday. Bravo Three Six losing height. Port engine gone, starboard misfiring. Emergency landing. Jettisoning reserves.' Following the ingrained instructions from his training, he tugged the heavy levers to free the hundred-gallon fuel-tanks below each wing. The rate of descent slackened but didn't stop.

Behind him Archie released the cockpit-canopy and it banged against the tail-fin before falling away into the blackness. Icy air pierced their face-scarves. 'No visual on Swanton. Can we request runway-lights?'

'Too late Archie. Thirty seconds at most. Possible field to starboard. Okay for wheels up, if we skim the grass.' At three hundred feet Harry pulled the control-column to the right. His other hand nursed the throttle for the remaining engine, trying to reduce the rate of descent. It was the drill they'd practised dozens of times in flying-training, when the instructor cut the engines seconds after take-off. This time no one would restart the engine as they approached the tree-line. They were entering unmarked territory beyond the pages of the flight-manual.

The aircraft brushed a small copse, crossed a track and touched the ground at one hundred knots. It slid across snow-covered earth on its belly, like a metal tray on ice, with no way to slow the headlong rush towards the distant hedge. The fuselage bounced over a small hummock in the ploughed field and the tail broke away with a grinding crash. The amputated airframe turned on its axis, a pirouetting dancer with wings and propellors. Harry was aware the speed was slackening. Surely friction would work its magic before the boundary?

The plane slithered to walking pace and Harry pressed the release buckle of his seat harness, to be ready to leap from the cockpit. At least there would be less of a jump to the ground with no undercarriage. Without warning the nose of the aircraft dropped abruptly, and hit the bank of a ditch. Archie's seat was wrenched from its mountings, throwing him forward on top of the pilot, and pressing him into the corner of the cockpit.

The silence was broken by the steady drip, drip, drip of fuel from a ruptured tank.

'You okay, Archibald?' Harry's muffled voice came from the nose cone. He was wedged in by the radar equipment and Archie's seat. He could feel the navigator's long legs across his shoulders, pressing him down on to his parachute. He needed Archie to move so he could climb out.

'Yeah, but I can't budge.' The navigator was struggling to pull his foot back through the fabric of the plane.

Harry became aware of another sound above the dripping octane—the crackling of flames dancing along the wooden fuselage towards the fuel-tanks and the ammunition-belts.

'For Christ's sake Dumbo, shift your sodding arse.'

'Ruddy leg's wedged.'

Harry could feel Archie's thigh twisting against his neck, bruising the skin below his ear. 'You joking?'

'Wish I was, Harry.' Like a flattened rawlplug the top of the flying-boot had splayed against the outside skin of the fuselage. The more Archie tugged, the more it resisted.

Harry smelt smoke. 'I'll chop the bugger off.' As his free hand scrabbled round the crumpled cockpit, searching for the emergency-axe, he could hear Archie yell for help. 'Bloody nuts, man. Who's going to hear you a mile from the nearest track?'

Archie's hollering grew hoarser. It was suddenly simple. There was no escape and they were going to die any second.

'Sorry Dumbo. Should've seen the blasted ditch.' The muffled apology was just audible above snapping flames.

'At least you got us down in one piece,' came the quiet response.

Was it any consolation to know they could both die intact?

'Been a good run, Hal. Three years. Nineteen Huns. Whizzo show. We've had a lot of luck.'

Harry couldn't help smiling. Luck? A perfect landing only to die because his ruddy navigator's legs wrapped round his neck? His free hand brushed his sleeve pocket. 'Sorry, Amy,' he muttered, but he knew she'd find someone else. There were plenty of admirers back at Bylaugh Hall. Harry concentrated on his breathing, wondering how it would feel to have his body ripped apart in an instant. At least it might shift the weight of his sodding navigator. Images from Sichuan seeped into his consciousness. Was it only twelve months since he'd helped Dougie empty a bottle of Jack Daniels on his last night at Fenghuangshan?

General Chennault had made good on his promise to get Harry back to Blighty before Christmas. Having survived the Hump, he was flown onto Cairo and reunited with Archie, who had finally been discharged from hospital. He was in need of a few good steaks to fill the flying-suit that hung off his skeleton. After negotiating a couple of spaces in a bomb-bay to Gibraltar, they'd flown into RAF Lyneham on the twelfth of December.

Amy had come down to meet them in Archie's Ford Eight and driven back across the country roads past Oxford and Cambridge, and across the Fens to Swanton Morley rectory. God knows how she'd got together enough petrol coupons. The vicar had agreed to publish the banns the following day, and they'd booked the wedding for the first Saturday in 1943, four nights after seeing in the New Year.

Archie had been his best man, and Amy's sister the bridesmaid. His aunt and uncle had come up with his sister Lydia on the train, together with Archibald's parents, but travelling was difficult and most relatives were hesitant about making a return journey in the black-out. Chalky White, the station adjutant, had arranged a guard of honour in the church porch as they came out from the shaded aisle into the weak, winter sunshine.

After the wedding lunch in the anteroom of Swanton Morley mess, Archie and Chalky had rolled up the carpet to clear a space, and someone had brought in a phonograph with a pile of big-band records. They danced to Joe Loss and Harry Roy, and Amy duetted with Marjorie Kingsley on 'You Started Something'.

A voucher for a week on the SS Sudan had arrived in an envelope from Chennault, and Harry put it in the front of his log book, for some point in the future when he and Amy could fly to Cairo over a continent at peace. Meanwhile they enjoyed a brief honeymoon in Eastbourne with no swimming but plenty of time in the bedroom. On the last afternoon they walked along the pebbled beach of

Beachy Head and watched the Spitfires returning from France to their bases at Friston and Deanland. There was a strong sense that the RAF was gaining the upper hand, and it wouldn't be long before the Allies took the fight across the Channel.

After returning from Eastbourne, he and Archie had been assigned to lead the newly formed 188 squadron at Swanton Morley to protect the British bomber-streams hammering enemy heartlands. *Vincimus in tenebris.* They'd been true to the motto. In a year of operational flying the squadron had destroyed an impressive tally of Junkers 88s and Messerschmitt 110s. Sixty-eight German crews blasted from the night-sky, some extinguished instantaneously in the blazing inferno of an exploding plane. How many girlfriends and wives had mourned the results of the squadron's success?

And now it was their turn.

A strange calm settled over Harry. Whatever death was like, it was going to be warmer and more welcoming than the numbing pain in his feet and hands at twenty-thousand feet. He closed his eyes. Far away he could hear Archie yelling again and wanted to tell him not to bother. It was going to be all right. They were going somewhere very special.

In that instant his right hand closed over the axe-handle and he wrenched it free from its mountings. He ran his left hand along Archie's leg to where it disappeared through the fabric of the aeroplane. He might just be able to swing the axe in a limited arc.

'Don't chop my sodding foot off. Just whack the bloody boot.' It was Archie's final refrain.

Harry felt the weight shift from his shoulders. Archie's seat was no longer pressing into his back. His legs evaporated. Harry turned his neck. The navigator had gone to heaven. Now it was his turn. His seat shifted back. He could see the stars and feel the frozen air on his face. Hands grasped at his body, holding his arms, his shoulders, his waist, and the top of his thighs, lifting him upwards. Weightless, he waited for the angels to carry him through the clouds.

'Shift yourself my booty. Move your arse.' The angel had a local accent. Harry was on the wing and then the ground. He looked up to see orange tongues licking towards the fuel-tanks.

'Run, for Christ's sake. Run before it goes up.' He recognised the voice as his own.

The angels leapt forward. Harry realised his legs had seized. He watched the three figures fall into a ditch, then found his own feet starting to move. Left in front of right in front of left. Again and again. He rolled down the shallow slope, falling on top of his navigator, pressing him into the icy mud.

Thirty yards away the sky heaved into a ball of orange flame. Five-hundred gallons of kerosene erupted alongside the ammunition. The echo of the explosion rolled across the frozen earth, then faded to silence. Harry felt his shoulder twinge. After a few seconds he lifted his head above the rim of the ditch. Tiny curls of flame flickered into the night-sky, illuminating the skeletal corpse of the Mosquito.

He saw shapes moving to his right. Three faces appeared from the grey-black slime.

'Thank Christ you appeared.' Harry could feel his chest trembling as he moved to stand.

'Thank Percy sir, not the Good Lord.' The fenland vowels were reassuringly broad. 'If he'd not been after pheasants, we'd have been warming our feet at the farmhouse. We nabbed him just as your plane came over. I'm Clifford, this is Albert.'

Harry tried to shake hands, but realised his right arm was hanging limply down.

'Jeez, sir, you're bleeding rotten.'

Harry followed Clifford's gaze. Blood was pumping from a tear in the sheepskin-lined jacket just below the shoulder. 'Must have grazed it as I dived into the ditch.' He could feel the night spinning out of control as he fell backwards into the sludge.

# Chapter Seventeen

## Norwich Hospital:
## 2nd January 1944

Harry was swimming up from the bottom of a deep lake. Above the surface, images were refracted down into the green depths. There was a strong smell of antiseptic. Faces floated in and out of focus. He opened his eyes to see a man sitting in a chair beside the bed. The broken nose and Dumbo ears from Archie's days as a rugby player were reassuringly familiar.

'Christ Hal, you gave us quite a fright. Thank God you're still with us.'

'The crash?' Harry struggled to speak, his mouth full of wool. 'The plane?'

'Not a lot left. I found the piece that nearly took off your arm in the ditch.' Archie held up a jagged chunk of metal. 'Six inches to the right, it would have sliced your head off. Severed an artery. I reckon you had about a pint left by the time the blood-wagon arrived. Needed gallons to sort you out—more than we drank between us at Hogmanay.'

'The farmers?'

'Two and a poacher. Took a while to persuade old Clifford to drop charges against Percy. I said the King wouldn't give an Empire Medal to a convicted felon—so it was either all or nothing.'

'Medals?' Harry blinked.

'Christ, Harry, they deserve bloody knighthoods. Not

only did they pull me out and drag me into the ditch, but they ran back for you, even though the ammo had started to explode.'

Harry nodded. 'We owe them a lot.'

'Thought you'd say that, so I had these tankards engraved as a thank you.' Archie held up the silver pots. The burnished metal caught the low sunlight through the Victorian window of the hospital-ward.

'Bloody hell, Archie, how much?'

'Twenty quid.'

'Jeez.' There was a long silence. 'More than a month's pay.'

'Each,' added Archie.

'That's my anniversary weekend in Scotland down the drain. Ruddy Hell, Dumbo, you know we've been waiting to do it ever since Amy returned from Arisaig.'

'You may have to wait a while longer anyway, Hal.'

There was something in Archie's tone that made Harry lift his head from the pillow, despite the stabbing pain in his shoulder. The navigator was looking towards the sash-window, avoiding his eyes.

'What do you mean, "wait"? I'll be out in a jiffy. I can still climb aboard the night-sleeper to Fort William, even if fumbling in the dark is tricky. Can't let Amy down after all this time.'

'It's not you, Hal.'

The pilot caught a flicker of unease before Archie's gaze returned to the security of the window. Beyond the glass panes a solitary crow flapped across the leaden sky towards Swanton Morley. The sun was already low above the horizon, although it was not long past three o'clock. The rising chill inside Harry's chest felt worse than the penetrating pain fomented by the arctic skies over Germany.

'Tell me, Archie!' he insisted.

'Luftwaffe must have known Bylaugh Hall was directing the bombers. Blitzed the site the night we pranged. Radar didn't even pick em up, so no ack-ack defence. Destroyed two Nissen-huts in the grounds, where the radio teams worked at night. High-explosives. Nothing left.'

'You're joking?' Harry desperately searched the brown eyes for reassurance.

'Wish I was old man.' This time Archie didn't turn his head away. He was looking straight at Harry. 'She's dead, Hal. I'm so sorry.'

The world blurred as Harry tried to lift himself onto his side. But the effort was too much and he fell back on the pillow, conscious of the aching emptiness in his chest. He felt a tiny droplet trickling down his right cheek and brushed it away with his free hand. 'Sorry Archie. Poor show. Blubbing like a baby. Need to pull myself together.'

'No need to put on a face for me, old boy.'

'We never had a chance, Archie. Half a dozen weekends and a few phone calls in a whole year of marriage.' His chest was heaving. 'Next weekend we'd promised ourselves a fresh start. We were finally going to put the marriage thing first, and have a go at being husband and wife in that little place beyond the control-tower. Even talked about children.'

He could feel the raw misery welling up inside him. 'Fuck the Germans. Fuck Hitler. Fuck the Luftwaffe. Fuck the War. Fuck it all. Fuck. Fuck. Fuck.' Harry buried his face in the pillow, shoulders heaving, vaguely aware of a hand resting on the back of his neck, as he howled at the pain.

After Archie left, Harry reached for the envelope his friend had brought from Bylaugh Hall. One of Amy's fellow WAAFs found it in the drawer of her locker beside the bed. He unfolded the two sheets of paper. The top page contained the words he'd treasured as a talisman since they'd first met two years ago.

The second was a new verse.

*I love thee with a love I seemed to lose*
*With my lost saints, - I love thee with the breath,*
*Smiles, tears, of all my life! - and if God choose,*
*I shall but love thee better after death.*

Harry read and reread the words, trying to find solace in the final sentence. But it didn't work. He closed his eyes, willing the excruciating ache to ease. It was cruelly unfair to have everything snatched away. He allowed his thoughts to drift, hoping to find something in the memories that would fill the emptiness.

They had returned from their honeymoon in Eastbourne, having talked about renting a thatched-cottage from the farmer who supplied Swanton Morley's officers' mess with eggs. It had been empty for months, since the previous occupant, a retired labourer, had gone to live with his daughter in Norwich.

It hadn't happened though. Before they sorted the tenancy, Amy had been posted to Arisaig, despite protesting that she was newly-married. She was told that essential war-work over-ruled domestic arrangements. It was Special Operations, drawing on her skills as a radio operator, and he knew enough not to ask any more. If he ever ended up in the caring hands of the Gestapo, the less he knew, the better.

It was supposed to be a short assignment, but she was away for nine months. They wrote letters and spoke on the phone, although the line wasn't always that clear to Scotland, and there had been four weekends when they'd managed to arrange leave that coincided. But finding somewhere midway between Arisaig and Swanton Morley, and sorting train-connections that worked, had proved a challenge. Two of the weekends had ended up as a snatched, intense night in a shabby bedroom in Carlisle.

In the summer of 1943, with the diminishing hours of darkness limiting bombing raids, there were less demands on 188 squadron, and Harry managed to negotiate a block of ten days leave in the middle of June. They'd booked a small hotel in Scarborough, which Amy knew from her time growing up in the East Riding. An old school-friend was the manageress and promised her a good rate.

On the evening before his departure, Harry put his few clothes in a small suitcase, savouring the scent of the honeysuckle drifting through the open window, and a blackbird calling through the still air, when Archie's familiar ears appeared round the door. 'Phone in the adjutant's office, Harry. Think it's Amy.'

On a crackling line, with the volume fading at the end of long sentences, he listened to Amy explaining that she couldn't make it. There was a special exercise planned for the week and she had been ordered to stay in Arisaig. There was nothing she could do. In the background he heard the excited chatter of voices and presumed she was close to the mess bar. She repeated how sorry she was and breathed reassuring words of love down the crackling line.

He went to Scarborough anyway, hoping something might change for Amy. Her friend had reserved the bridal suite, with stunning views across the seafront. Harry lay in bed the first night, listening to the waves breaking on the shore below. It seemed like the perfect escape. When he phoned Arisaig next morning, he was told Sergeant Thorp was unavailable. He stayed one more night in the hotel before taking the train back to Norwich, changing at York and Peterborough. As dusk settled over the Fens, air raid sirens sounded from the city and the train pulled into a siding for safety. It was five o'clock in the morning before it puffed into Norwich, and midday before Archie turned up to ferry him back to Swanton Morley.

When they managed to meet in Gretna Green in September, they both acknowledged theirs was not much of a marriage. Amy promised to apply to rejoin her old team at Bylaugh Hall. Maybe the Penguins in Whitehall were touched by her plea to be with her husband. He met her at Norwich station on a freezing afternoon in November, and they spent a night at the *Maids Head*, before the RAF transport arrived in the morning to take them to their respective bases.

188 squadron was allowed to stand down over Christmas, so they went to Amy's parents in London for a night and then onto Eastbourne, where they rediscovered old haunts. It felt like they were beginning to reconnect.

Two nights ago, Archie had lent him his Ford Eight to drive Amy back to Bylaugh Hall after an evening at the *Angel*. Under the cover of the half-light in the late afternoon, a sympathetic mechanic had filled the car from the aircraft-bowser, after checking the station-adjutant was nowhere near dispersal. It had cost Harry three packets of Navy-Cut.

Outside the gates of the old house, they'd cuddled on the leather bench-seat, both wishing they had somewhere of their own to go back to. Fumbling with straps and belts either side of a gear stick wasn't romantic. They promised themselves leave for their anniversary, when they would revisit the thatched cottage before going to Scotland. Harry had been in touch with the farmer again and it was still empty.

Harry lifted the two sheets of paper off the blanket, and slowly read the words of the poem aloud, imagining Amy's fingers on the keyboard of the Remington, metal letter-heads clacking against the carriage, and her right hand shifting the white paper up the slide of the machine.

He closed his eyes, recalling the photograph she'd sent from Arisaig, which he'd kept with the poem in his flying-jacket. Wavy hair was pressed down by a flat cap, with the polished insignia of the RAF woven into its black headband. The shiny peak reached over her high forehead to the line of neatly-plucked brows. Her dark eyes looked deep into his own, willing him to respond to the hint of a smile that played around her lips.

She was his girl.

*For better, for worse, for richer, for poorer. Forsaking all others. For as long as we both shall live. Till death do us part.*

The marriage vows uttered in the shaded sanctuary of Swanton Morley church had charmed the congregation, captivating the small group of witnesses with the power of their quiet promises. It had been a magical moment. But now the spell was broken. Never again would he see that expression.

Harry felt his chest tighten and he allowed the white cotton to soak up his misery, grateful for the privacy of the room. It was as if the tears were washing something away, lifting the blackthorn barb from a wound, bearable hurt replacing pulsating agony.

When he finally lifted his head from the sodden pillow, it was dark beyond the window. The open fens towards Swanton Morley had gone. Instead, there was a man with a bandaged arm lying against the iron bedframe, clutching two sheets of paper. The aching pain still gnawed at his insides. He stared steadily at the half-prone figure with the tearful, green eyes, promising to carry on the fight for both of them.

# Chapter Eighteen

## Arisaig:
## April 10th 1944

The train jolted, waking Harry from his slumber. He opened his eyes to see a sign saying Crianlarich through the open window.

'Train divides here,' called the guard. 'Front coaches to Oban. Back coaches to Fort William. Ten-minute stop while we move engines around.'

Harry stepped onto the platform, breathing the chilled air. To the north the hills rose towards Ben Lomond. The long, golden chains on the laburnum trees beside the track fluttered in the gentle breeze. He pulled out his cigarette case, tapped the end against the silver lid and flicked the catch on his lighter. He drew the warm smoke into his lungs, savouring the sensation of lightness and calm. He watched a group of squaddies being drilled by their NCO at the end of the platform.

The whistle blew. 'Time to go ladies and gentlemen. The Fort William flyer will whisk you there in a couple of hours.'

The train puffed across Rannoch Moor, allowing Harry to drift back through the last four months. It had been a longer haul getting back to fitness than he'd thought. The arm had been half-severed below the shoulder, and required intensive physiotherapy, even after the surgeons worked their magic. In the two months in Norwich hospital, he saw many men wounded worse, including a tail-gunner carried through the ward in three separate pieces after a crash-landing without undercarriage, and a pilot whose face had suffered hundred-degree burns when his cockpit exploded.

Harry was sitting in the day-room, enjoying a cigarette and watching snowdrop heads bobbing in the February sunshine, when a nurse put her head round the door. 'Visitor, Wing Commander.'

'Thanks Rose.' Her smile reminded him of Amy.

The familiar Dumbo ears loomed. Harry reached out his arm. 'Just to show you that the medical-magicians have pulled off the five-card trick.'

Archie brought him up to date with squadron news. 'Windy' Gale and his navigator 'Bertie' Wooster had bought it the night before over Dortmund, 'Sticks' Leggitt had written off his plane, misjudging the end of the runway in thick fog, but the rest of the team were going strong. Frank Davis and his navigator had been put forward by Group Captain Avery for a DFC, after bringing down two Heinkels during the raid on Hamburg.

Despite the cheery chat, Harry could sense there was something else Archie wanted to tell him. He was avoiding eye-contact again, staring out the window. The smell of lavender polish was hanging in the air. He could hear the clattering of crockery in the kitchen next door. Harry took a deep breath. 'What is it, Dumbo?'

There was a silence. Finally, his friend looked at him. 'I've been reassigned, Hal.'

'Sounds painful, Archie. Get one of the nurses here to have a look at you.' He knew what his navigator meant.

'They reckon it'll be another two months before you're

fit, so I've been crewed with Larry.'

Harry had heard that Flying Officer Lazenby had lost his navigator when they had to ditch two weeks ago. The air-sea rescue boys had been scrambled as soon as they received the Mayday, but the coordinates weren't quite right. They wasted half an hour searching the wrong quadrant of the English Channel, till they saw Lazenby's last flare go up on the horizon. Both men were like ice cubes when they lifted them out of their dinghy. They managed to save Lazenby, but his navigator never regained consciousness.

Harry had known this moment was coming, ever since Avery had told him he couldn't expect to return to operational flying till after Easter. He rested his good hand on his navigator's arm. 'I'll be back soon enough Archie, so don't do anything daft in the meantime. I need you behind me when I next open the throttle. We're the old firm, after all.'

Two weeks later Laurence Lazenby and Archibald Standing were reported missing over Bremerhaven.

Once he was passed fit for ops at the beginning of April, Harry requested a transfer from 188 squadron.

In the interview with the station commander, he was clear why. 'You've had a new Wingco running the show for three months. He wouldn't want me snapping at his heels, or bumping him out.' He didn't add that he was reluctant to start over again with a new face in the back seat.

Clarence Avery took a cigarette from the pack on his desk and offered one to Harry. He'd earned a Military Cross on the Western Front and hadn't expected to be caught up in another worldwide conflict during his lifetime. But he knew the value of leadership to squadron morale. There was no way he could shoehorn Wing Commander Winchester back into 188. 'You're one of the best though, Harry. Charterhouse man, aren't you? We need you at the controls, downing Jerries. There are plenty of others around to do the desk-jobs.'

'I'm not asking to become a Penguin, sir.' Harry tugged his ear lobe. With the Allies advancing in Italy, there was talk of a second front opening in France and the War being over by Christmas. 'I'd like to put my night-fighting skills to good use while there's time.'

The station commander sat back, waiting for Harry to continue.

'Truth is, sir, I want to get back at the bastards who killed my wife We didn't have much of a marriage, because of this bloody war. But she was doing work that was important and she only came back from Arisaig to be with me. If she'd not done that, she'd still be alive. She didn't talk about her work there and I never asked, for obvious reasons, but she said she finally understood the meaning of bravery.'

'I think you know a bit about bravery as well, Harry.' Clarence Avery held up the citation his secretary had typed. 'Putting you and Archibald forward for a bar to your DFCs—for the Jerries you downed last year. In Archie's case it may be posthumous.' He placed the sheet on the desk. 'What are you after?'

'Transfer to 161 squadron, sir?'

'That's supposed to be top secret.' The Group Captain sucked on his cigarette, drawing the smoke deep into his lungs before exhaling slowly. 'Was this pillow-talk?'

Harry noticed the poster beyond the blue haze above Avery's head. Three officers from the respective armed services were yakking behind a sofa, on which a young woman with blonde hair reclined, breasts and lips provocatively highlighted. 'Keep Mum; she's not so dumb'. His eyes flicked back to the station-commander. 'It wasn't Amy, sir. I was in the control-tower here the night the Lysander landed.'

It was two days before the New Year's Eve shindig with the Yanks. The plane had diverted to Swanton Morley with engine trouble, hidden in a hangar the other side of the airfield. Avery made no mention of it at the morning briefing. However, as squadron commander, Harry insisted that the adjutant tell him what was going on. Chalky was reluctant to say anything, forcing Harry to pull rank. The Lysander had been to France on a Special Ops night-drop. Hush-hush stuff. Harry had heard Churchill's joint broadcast with General de Gaulle about supporting the Resistance.

'This was what Amy was involved with. I'll feel I'm keeping part of her alive, if that makes sense?'

Amery nodded. He understood about loss. The day before he'd received news from Italy that his brother, a major in the 18th Infantry Brigade, had been killed during the German counter-attack at Monte Cassino. 'I'll see what I can do. It's a very small squadron though, so not much chance of anything happening quickly.'

A week later Harry arrived at RAF Tempsford for conversion-training on the Lysander. They were suddenly a pilot short. No details were given and he didn't ask. The Lysander was different to anything he'd flown operationally. It took him back to initial-training with the Tiger Moth. Flat out, it could barely reach two hundred miles an hour. Harry could see why so many had been shot down by the Luftwaffe in the Allied retreat from Belgium.

But the Lysander could take off in less than two hundred yards and land on a postage-stamp. It was perfect for the makeshift strips constructed by the Resistance. With a stalling speed of sixty-five miles an hour, it was even possible to drop an agent in a padded-suit, without having to touch the ground.

After he'd logged the requisite fifty circuits and bumps at night, with a couple of landing-lights to guide him, the station commander called him into his office. Harry shut the Nissen hut door and turned to salute. It was the first time he'd met Group Captain Fielden in the flesh, but he knew his biography. Fielden had been the personal instructor to the young Prince of Wales when he'd acquired a Gipsy Moth in 1929. This had led to his appointment as Captain of the King's Flight in 1936. Although Edward's reign was short-lived, Fielden was known as a master of discretion, and continued in his role for the younger brother. Harry registered how immaculately Fielden was dressed. The four gold-stripes on the epaulettes and sleeves of his uniform glowed in the light from the window. His dark tie was knotted in a symmetrical Windsor, matching the colour of his neatly-trimmed pencil-moustache.

The Group Captain responded to Harry's salute and shook the young pilot's hand. 'Great work, Winchester. You've mastered the finer points of the Lizzie in less time than most. You're on board with 161, old boy. Congratulations. May not be a Malvern man, but we won't hold that against you.' The deep voice oozed the confidence of privilege. 'Before your first mission, it's important you do the SOE training. We expect our pilots to come back from each sortie, but you need to know about evade and escape, and all that stuff, just in case the Gestapo take a fancy.' He held out a brown envelope. 'Warrant to Arisaig tomorrow.'

Harry had to change trains at Fort William. As the connecting service puffed around the head of Loch Linnhe, he looked back through the bare branches of silver birch and alder to see fingers of white cloud clawing the summit of Ben Nevis. Crossing Glenfinnan Viaduct, he opened the window to study the curve of the concrete arches, marvelling at the engineering ingenuity that had bridged the River Finnan, half a century before.

At Arisaig he was met by a short, middle-aged man, dressed in combat-fatigues, who gripped his hand like an old mate. 'I'm Corporal Woolmore, but everyone calls me Fleecy.' His lopsided smile displayed two missing teeth. 'Chuck your bag in the back of the jeep, sir. Arisaig House is the other side of Druimindarroch, just over a mile away. We'll be there in two shakes of your wife's best friend.'

Harry concentrated to understand the broad accent and ascertained that Fleecy was from Clydeside. A welder by trade, he'd worked at the shipyard during the day and volunteered as air-raid warden at night, once the bombing started in the autumn of 1941. 'I was too old for front-line stuff, but I felt like I was doing my bit to get back at the Jerries. Then my gaffer heard about Arisaig House needing a handyman who could keep his gob shut, so he recommended me.'

They turned off the main road onto a track that wound

through a small wood, to the back of an imposing granite-grey building. Fleecy pulled onto the gravel forecourt and turned off the engine. 'Here y'are sir. Arisaig House. I hope your visit is productive. I believe you're here for two weeks, so it'll be me who drives you back to the station.'

Harry reached out his hand. 'Thanks for picking me up, Fleecy.'

'Nae bother, sir. It's all part of the service. I'll show you to your room and then I'll expect the old man will want a word.'

Stepping out of the vehicle, Harry looked up at the façade of the three-storey building. At the end of the line of dormer casement-windows, smoke spiralled from a large chimney on the East Wing. A thick-boughed wisteria was trained over the entrance, its creeper-like arms reaching up to the slate-tiled roof beneath the chimney-stack. Buds swelled on the criss-crossing stems beside the door. Harry noticed the downspout on the guttering was stamped 1864 on one side of the building, and 1937 on the other.

He followed the Corporal through the studded door at the side of the forecourt. A fire was burning in the hearth beyond the slate flagstones. 'Your room is on the top floor, sir. Sharing with one of the other officers.' Fleecy led the way up a spiral staircase behind the chimney. 'Like a secret passage, sir. Very appropriate for the work we do!' He opened the door to the bedroom. Low eaves wrapped around the small window. Harry pushed down the sash. Sunlight exposed the outline of an island a few miles off the coast.

'That's Eigg sir, with Rum behind. If your eyes are good

enough you can pick out Muck, off the south-western edge of Eigg.'

'Bonnie Prince Charlie country, isn't it?'

'Aye, sir. He embarked from the cove to the right of that outcrop. There's a cave above the foreshore with marks from the tallow candles he burnt, while waiting for the French frigate.' Fleecy related how the fugitive Prince had spent his final night anchored on the shore of Loch nan Uamh, gathering together the clansmen who would accompany into exile, before they set sail for Skye in the morning. 'Speed bonny boat, and all that.' He hummed the first line. 'Truth is sir, it was Muck on the stern nae Mull, but that wouldnae have made such a fine sounding line. Sad ending to a promising campaign, which all started further down the line at Glenfinnan. Did you see the monument beside the loch?'

'I was looking the other way.'

'Watch out on the way back. Kilted highlander on the very top. It's where he first landed on 19th August 1745.'

'Fleecy, you're a mine of information. You'll be telling me next what he had for his last supper.'

'Creels and black pudding, sir.'

Harry looked closely at the Corporal. Apart from a twitch of his lips, the expression was impassive.

'I'll leave you now, sir. Come down when you're ready. Nae hurry. The old man's office is beside the front entrance.'

Harry hung his suit in the small wardrobe beside the assortment of jackets and trousers of his roommate. He laid out his wash-things in the top drawer of his locker.

Downstairs, the office was empty, so he walked onto the forecourt. On top of the granite slabs, weathered wooden-chairs were scattered around a couple of large tables. Rhododendron bushes were coming into leaf beside the stone-mullioned sash-windows, through which he could see the tables in the oak-panelled room set for dinner. He strolled to the low wall at the end of the forecourt and discovered it was protecting a ten-foot drop to the sweep of lawn below, laid with croquet-hoops.

'Need to keep up standards. We have a match every Tuesday night. You'll be on the team of course.' A Scottish voice boomed behind him.

He turned to see a stockily-built man walk across from the house. His trimmed moustache matched the neat coiffure of hair, swept back from a high forehead. The bushy eyebrows framed penetrating, deep-brown eyes. He wore an open-necked, grey shirt above black trousers, held up with webbing. His right hand gripped the smooth handle of a large knife protruding from the leather-sheath in the belt. 'You must be Wing Commander Winchester. Welcome to Arisaig. I'm Major General Colin Gubbins.' His accent was different to Fleecy's, resonant with the soft burr of the islands. Harry could almost smell the heather-clad hills and hear the call of the curlew. He raised his arm in an instinctive salute.

'No need for ceremony, young man. Here we tend to be relaxed about ranks. It's not the amount of scrambled egg on your hat that matters, but what you know about unarmed combat, forgery, radio operating, sabotage and such like. My friends call me Gubby, but most people here refer to me as the old man, which is fair enough as I'm a relic of the Great War. Good journey?'

'Thank you, sir.'

'I'm told you're skilled at landing the Lizzie on a cricket-pitch and getting off unscathed. That's what we hope will happen every drop.' Gubby ran his hand across his thick head of hair. 'However, just in case you prang or catch a packet, you need a crash course in basic survival, morse code and how to cope with the Gestapo. We'll fill those gaps in your personal armoury and then you'll be ready to hack it. You've got a fortnight to learn what's going to help you, son.'

Harry felt the eyes bore through him, assessing his weak points. There was more to come.

'Two rules while you're here, old boy. First, no one asks people what they're being trained for. If you don't know, you can't tell. Only I know and I'm not leaving the country. I spent enough time filling my mouth with mud from the Somme last time round. Second, everyone can play hard if they work hard. It's fine to prop up the bar till late, or shag the socks of any bluebird who fancies you, but we start with a cross-country run at seven every morning. Hangover or fatigue is no excuse. Clear?'

'Perfectly, sir.' Harry registered the smile playing round the Major General's lips.

The fortnight passed quickly. A few lectures took place in the dining room, but most of the time was spent outside, acquiring skills under the supervision of instructors. He enjoyed the smalls-arm training from Captain Maxwell, whose family were from Kyle of Lochalsh, a boat-ride up the Sound of Sleat. Gavin was knowledgeable about local wildlife, and took a fiver off Harry with a bet he could show him a fox, badger, otter, deer and red squirrel in one evening. It was two in the morning before they spotted the black-and-white-striped animal grubbing for worms up the valley, but both men were on the starting-line for the cross-country run at dawn.

Once he began the unarmed-combat sessions with William Fairburn and Bill Sykes, Harry realised how unfit he was. The 'Heavenly Twins' had worked together as knife specialists in the Shanghai police-department before the war. They were also experts in boxing, wrestling, karate and aikido, and how to kill a man with bare hands. Looking at their exhausted trainees collapsed on the ground after an hour of being pummelled, they'd conclude with the sage instruction *just kick him in the balls, if he's still moving.*

Harry was surprised to meet several men from Czechoslovakia. Vaclav spoke English well enough to explain they were training to return to their homeland, to avenge the atrocities that followed the assassination of Reinhard Heydrich. He described how two Arisaig-trained operatives penetrated the armed protection surrounding the Obergruppenführer, as he drove through Prague's streets in his open-topped Mercedes. Vaclav showed him the small plaque in the garden commemorating Jan Kubiš and Jozef Gabčík's bravery; they had died in the subsequent shoot-out when German troops surrounded the church in Prague where they hid. 'The Nazis killed everyone in my village as reprisal. Only my cousin Alex escaped to join the partisan resistance. I will find him and fight till our last breath to free our country.' Harry wanted to know more, but remembered Gubby's warning.

On his last night General Gubbins raised a glass to Harry at dinner. 'We wish you well as you take the fight to the enemy. Although you've not completed the full whack of six weeks, we still think you deserve this. It was designed by the Heavenly Twins and is now part of the standard ration for all commandos.' He passed a package down the line of men and women at the table. Harry was surprised at the weight. He tore off the brown paper and held up a sheath with a dagger-handle protruding from the polished leather.

Later, in his room, Harry lay on his metal-framed bed studying the weapon. His room-mate looked up from the copy of *Health and Fitness*. 'Gubby must have taken a shine to you Harry. In the fifteen months I've been here, only full-course recruits have received one of those.' The Yorkshire accent reminded Harry of his aunt, in Skipton. Major Fox had been a congenial bedroom-companion for the fortnight, very willing to share his hand-rolled Karelia Blue cigarettes, and stash of magazines. Seconded from the Royal Signals, Freddie Fox was an expert in radio transmission and secret codes.

Harry passed the knife across and watched Freddie weigh it in his hand. 'Frightful weapon. I hope you never have to use it in anger. I guess it gives people confidence though, just having it on their belt.'

'You must have seen a lot of people pass through in your time here. Do you wonder what happens to them? Most don't merit a plaque in the garden.'

'Too true, old boy. But we never ask.' Freddie ran his fingers over the blade. 'I expect once the ruddy war is over, we'll discover all the stories. The Czechoslovaks were an exception, because it was front page news in the UK, and Gubby wanted us to share the achievement. When we heard the Gestapo had ordered the execution of everyone in Lidice and Lezaky as reprisals, it took the edge of our celebrations. But that's the evil we're up against and why our work is so important. I have a feeling the Dubcek boy will make quite a difference if we can reunite him with his cousin.' He handed the knife back to Harry and reached for his magazine.

'You married, Freddie?'

'Good God, no.' The slim fingers caressed the swimsuit of the cover girl. 'Not while there's a bloody war on. You?'

'Just for a year. She got the chop in January.' Harry realised it was four months to the day since the attack on Bylaugh Hall. Conscious of the blockage rising in his throat, he stood up to look out of the window. Across the Sound, the moon rose above the jagged outline of Eigg.

'So did my girlfriend. Rotten show, eh?'

'Had you been together long?' Harry stared at the flashes of silver on the surface of the sea, wondering if Amy had seen the ever-changing dance of luminescence visible from Arisaig House. He was aware Freddie was speaking, but only registered some of the words.

'Nine months… one of the instructors… kept it quiet… Gubby knew… never said anything… made sure no one else was billeted in the other bed… lovely girl… taught me a thing or two… posted south before Christmas… never said why… killed in air raid.'

Harry turned away from the window to see Freddie rummaging through his locker-drawer. 'I've held on to her photo, though I know we're not supposed to keep any records. God knows why, because this will be the last place on earth the Jerries will ever reach.'

The Major passed across a small piece of card. The black and white image showed a young woman leaning against an oak tree. Harry guessed it had been taken in the autumn, as the leaves were varying shades of grey. Her curly hair was swept back from her high forehead, held in place by a flat cap, with the RAF insignia woven into the headband. She was smiling at the camera.

His hand was shaking as he passed back the photograph.

# Chapter Nineteen

## France:
## May 30th 1944

The moon rose above the horizon as the Lysander passed over Rheims. Somewhere below was the cathedral his history teacher had waxed eloquently about, when they'd covered the Hundred Years War and Joan of Arc.

The drone of the Mercury engine was reassuringly steady and there was no sound from the passenger behind. The sooty face had hauled himself up the ladder, dressed in black jacket and trousers, almost invisible in the darkness shrouding the runway. There were no introductions. After a brief handshake, he climbed into the back seat and settled his canvas-bag on his lap, while the bowser topped up the tanks.

This was the ninth sortie for Harry. Previous flights followed the same pattern. Departing from RAF Tempsford at twilight, refuelling at Tangmere, flying for two hours to the allocated drop-zone, looking for flares marking the landing-strip, touching down and coming to a halt just long enough for the passenger to jump to the ground, then opening the throttle and rising above the line of trees for the solitary return-journey.

The destinations had all been very different, the last being the tiny village of Fontenoy-aux-Roses, south of Paris, so the biggest challenge was navigation. There was no Archie in the back seat to guide him through darkened skies. It was basic map and compass work on his knee-pad, reliant on moonlight to pick out significant landscape-features below. Rivers and railways were obvious waymarks, the former glistening in meandering curves, the latter tiny pencil-marks across the smudges of a mixed landscape of woodland and open fields. Intercom chat was not allowed. Better to know nothing about the passenger. There was simply the open, empty sky and the thrum of the pistons.

This time Harry also had a canvas-sack. From the weight and shape he knew it was firearms. There were rumours around the airbase about an impending invasion, and he guessed this was connected. Below, the railway track to Troyes cut through rolling hills that fed the River Marne, leading towards Dijon and the landing-strip at St. Columb des Eglises. He estimated five minutes to drop-off and alerted his passenger.

'Roger, pilot,' came the response from the back seat. 'Thanks for a smooth flight. Rocked me to sleep like a baby.' The only clue to identity was the broadened vowels of the Derbyshire Dales.

Harry checked the map with his flashlight. The white marker-line extended beyond the village to a small forest. The Lysander passed a cluster of houses, descending gently with the engine ticking over quietly. One minute to landing. Harry pulled back the canopy, senses sharpened by the rush of air. The plane was now over trees. Tiny pinpricks of light appeared in a clearing three hundred yards ahead. Torches were being waved. He zigzagged over the branches, the wheels touched the ground, bounced twice and the Lysander came to a halt. A strong scent of pine filled the cockpit from the warm summer-night.

French voices approached the plane. '*Vite! Vite!*'

Harry's passenger tossed his bag to the ground and leapt off the ladder, rolling over beside the canvas-sack. Harry lifted himself from his seat to pass his own bag to the outstretched hands. '*Merci beaucoup.*' A smile flashed in the darkness and disappeared beneath the wing of the plane. Harry looked round to check he was clear to roll. Tiny fireflies danced at the edge of the wood and snapping branches crackled from the trees.

'*Merde! Salauds!*' The man with the smile swung his machine gun in an arc towards the fireflies. Harry could hear screaming behind the wing as he opened the throttle. The Lysander gathered speed and small stones pattered along the fuselage.

'Come on Lizzie!' Harry rammed the throttle against its metal stop. When the indicator touched sixty, he eased back on the control-column and breathed as the plane lifted. Its wheels brushed the tree tops and he turned slowly to starboard, a helpless observer of the firefight that raged below. The forest disappeared behind the tailfin and he set a course of Three Five Zero that would see him crossing the channel just before three o'clock.

As Harry wriggled to adjust the parachute beneath him, he felt a stream of cold air at his feet and looked down. There was a gaping hole beside his right boot. The engine spluttered, coughed and caught again. His eyes darted to the fuel gauge. Starboard was showing empty with less than half in the port tank. He stared at the needle to see if there was any discernible movement to the left. It was holding steady.

His mind raced. There was enough fuel for about one

hundred and twenty miles. If he flew straight on, he might make it to Amiens, but there was no way of crossing the Channel. The Germans would be thick on the ground near any port. If he swung onto One Seven Zero he might reach the foothills of the Alps around Belfort, but not as far as Switzerland. He'd still have to hike to the border. At Arisaig they'd made it clear there was no chance of getting through the fence, so he'd simply experience the misery of being captured in sight of freedom.

Or he could try for Chiny. Arisaig had said Belgium was the best bet. There was huge hostility towards the Nazis, so a good chance of finding local support, despite the dangers to anyone who offered help to a British pilot. The Resistance had a network that led through France and over the Pyrenees into Spain, from where repatriation via Gibraltar was possible.

Amiens, Belfort or Chiny? Harry pushed the control-column to the right and settled on a bearing of Zero Two Zero that would bring him over the Belgian border in half an hour, if he nursed the Lysander at maximum cruising speed. Better to land with spare fuel in the tank than be forced into a crash landing in a field not of his choosing. In any case he needed enough to set fire to the plane.

The needle was close to empty when he passed the River Semois west of Chiny, so he calculated on flying towards Neufchateau and aiming for touchdown anywhere away from houses. The moon was still high in the sky as he settled on a field east of Herbeumont. Harry cut the engine and glided down. He jumped from the cockpit onto rows of young maize-plants.

He pulled his rucksack over his shoulder, reached for

the Arisaig knife and sliced a hole in the side of the tank, allowing petrol to run over the fabric of the fuselage. He clicked his lighter and seconds later the aircraft was an inferno. Harry ran towards the shelter of the wood to his right, which he remembered led to the outskirts of a small village, where a railway-line followed the curve of the River Semois.

Sitting on a fallen tree, Harry weighed his options. If it hadn't been for one sodding bullet rupturing his tank, he'd be safely tucked up in a warm bed at Tempsford, savouring the thought of bacon and eggs. He pushed the image away, aware that was the start of a slippery slope of loneliness and longing. The bullet could equally well have gone through his leg, rendering him unconscious from loss of blood.

The sky was lightening as he unpacked his rucksack. He looked at the small bag of clothes, knowing that if he changed, there was no going back. He would have to evade capture or risk being shot as a spy. The alternative was to stay in RAF uniform and hand himself into the local gendarmerie. He could still expect a rough time from the Gestapo, but at least he'd survive the rest of the war as a POW.

Maybe he should call it a day? It was a lifetime ago when he'd walked along The Strand, as a fresh-faced teenager, looking for the Navy recruiting office. 'Gone for a bite. Back in 10 minutes', said the sheet of paper stuck to the window with Sellotape. It was raining hard and he had no umbrella. Fortunately, the RAF office next door was open.

Images from the last four years ran through his mind.

Securing his coveted wings at Church Fenton had led to 29 squadron and the patrols along the South coast, followed by the jaunts to Cairo, where the biggest danger came from the food. Then Chennault and China and a whole other war, before being reunited with Archie in the bomb bay of the Liberator. After the wedding, he'd sent Xiaobin and Dougie a photo of Amy and himself exiting the church under the arch of swords. He wasn't surprised to have heard nothing back. Getting supplies over the Hump was more of a priority than letters. How many kills would Commander Lin have etched on the nose of his plane? Would Douglass have joined the Generalissimo's entourage? He'd heard the Japanese were being pushed back across China, after the Communists and Nationalists had joined forces.

And Amy? He pulled out her photo from his breast pocket. As he studied the expression on her face, in the greying light, he struggled to separate the feelings of loss from anger. He knew he was close to being engulfed by a desperate, furious sadness.

Harry lay on the mossy grass beside the horizontal trunk, the dawn-chorus gathering volume as the sun rose over the horizon. It felt surreal. England was barely a hundred miles away, yet out of reach. His reality was the middle of a wood in occupied Europe, surrounded by hostile forces. Maybe he could close his eyes, soak up the sunshine, finish his rations, then stroll into the village, ready to surrender. Lulled by the calling of distant wood-pigeons and the dappled warmth through the leaves, Harry fell into a deep sleep.

The sun was nearing its zenith when he woke, with a

stiff neck and a rancid taste in his mouth. Harry pulled out the water-bottle from his rucksack. He gulped the contents, grateful for the cleansing sensation on his teeth and the coolness in his stomach. His right hand massaged the back of his head to ease the tension. Amy's photo had fallen onto the grass, beside her crumpled poem. He unfolded the sheets. Her words reminded him of his English master, handing him a slim booklet on his final day at school. 'Try this when you get bored with Agatha Christie.' The name on the cover meant nothing, although Elliott had been his best friend in the lower fifth. When he'd first read the poems, shortly after joining up, he'd struggled to understand, but he'd taken it with him on the train to Arisaig, drawing comfort from some of the phrases. *What might have been is an abstraction... footfalls echo in the memory, down the passage which we did not take, towards the door we never opened... that which is only living can only die...*

Harry thought of his mother and father, wiped out in an instant by a random doodle-bug, Amy obliterated by high explosive, like the pink mist drifting across cloudless skies in China, and the endless series of letters he'd had to write to the grieving parents of downed aircrew. He recalled the vow he'd made in Norwich hospital. He couldn't give up now.

After devouring the emergency rations, he scratched a shallow hole with his knife to bury the uniform. Layers of moss were scraped from the fallen tree to cover the disturbed earth, then he walked to the far side of the wood, where a forester's track led to the small town. Surely any hue and cry for the pilot of the downed aircraft would have died by now? If there was nothing left of the plane, they may even have concluded he'd been burnt to a cinder.

As he came through the ornate arch of Herbeumont station, Harry was relieved to see no queue in front of the ticket office. The bearded clerk smiled. '*Oui?*' Harry showed his forged identity-card. In carefully prepared French, he asked for a ticket to Bruxelles and passed across a handful of francs.

'*D'accord.*' The brown eyes behind the metal grille narrowed. '*Un moment monsieur, s'il vous plaît.*' He said something to a woman who had appeared behind Harry and issued her with a ticket. Once she'd moved through to the platform, the clerk beckoned him forward again. '*Ici monsieur. A droite.*' He pointed at the door to the right, which opened into a small waiting-room. Harry did as instructed. He noticed there was another door at the far end. The ticket-clerk appeared and closed both doors, slamming the bolt behind Harry.

'I think you are the British flyer they are looking for, *non?*' He spoke quietly, in English.

Harry's eyes darted round the room. Could he make a run for it? Would he be able to overpower the ticket-clerk, without the commotion being heard? He thought of the Heavenly Twins and flexed his right hand, wondering if he could deliver the killer chop. The ticket-clerk remained by the door, watching him carefully. Harry knew he couldn't do it. This was an unarmed civilian not a Nazi storm-trooper. He nodded, resigned to the inevitable. There were worse things than seeing out the war in a POW camp. He might even be reunited with Archie, who he'd heard was in Stalag Luft III, somewhere in Poland.

The ticket-clerk put his finger to his lips. '*Silencieux monsieur.* No Bruxelles today. Germans look-out. Wait a few days and we move you. *Comprenez?*' The accent was strong, but Harry understood the advice he was being given.

'We?'

'There is a network, monsieur.'

'You mean—'

'I mean nothing, monsieur. Better you not know. We get you to Denmark. Meanwhile, go here. *Ici.*' He scribbled an address on a piece of paper. 'It's at edge of village on road to Nantes. Red house with roses over the fence. Ring bell. Tell the woman who answers that Pierre sent you for fruit. I will be there after work. Stay inside and do what she tells you. Go now. Don't stop on the way.'

The man slid back the bolt and opened the door. Harry walked quickly out of the station and took the road as instructed to the rose-covered house. Ten minutes later he was sharing a glass of cognac with a middle-aged woman in a russet headscarf, whose name was Marie. '*Ne parle pas Anglais, Seulement Francais ou Allemand.*' She spat into the sink behind her as she uttered the last word. Harry looked at her lined face and calloused hands, and tried to imagine living under German occupation.

Once his tumbler was empty, Marie showed him to a space in the attic, fitted out with a thin mattress and a couple of grey blankets. As he climbed the steps, she passed him a flash light. '*Attends ici. Tout seule. Très tranquille.*' She pressed a finger to her lips and closed the hatch, neatly concealed beneath a wide lampshade.

Beneath the rafters touching the edge of the floor, he

could see thin slivers of daylight. The twittering of swallows nesting in the straw of the eaves outside drifted into the tiny space, along with the clattering of a horse-drawn mowing-machine in a field nearby. Harry lay on the mattress. He needed to close his eyes for a few minutes. Cut grass mingled with the scent of roses, carrying him back to the tiny cottage near Swanton Morley.

He woke to voices below and struggled to orientate himself. From the hands on his watch he could see he'd slept for five hours. Should he open the hatch? With the help of the flashlight, he scrabbled for a catch, but realised the lock was outside. He lay back on the mattress, breathing slowly to calm the rising claustrophobia.

There was a tapping on the wood. *'Monsieur. Etes vous éveillé?'* The whispered words carried through the thin partitioning.

Harry was grateful for the light that flooded into the tiny space. He was encouraged down the small ladder into the kitchen, where the smell of a stew made him realise how hungry he was. The last food had been the three pieces of chocolate from his ration tin, before he left the sanctuary of the forest.

The ticket-clerk smiled, introducing himself as Pierre and his wife as Marie. He had changed from his blue uniform into an open-necked checked-shirt and brown twill-trousers. He looked about fifty, the same age as the woman stirring the pot on the stove. Round spectacles sat above the thick tangle of beard that covered his lower face. He shook Harry's hand warmly, before ushering him to a seat at the table. The pilot wolfed generous portion of stew in his bowl, breaking off chunks of rye-bread to dip into the thick gravy. Marie joined the two of them at the table, but said nothing.

In his accented English, Pierre outlined a plan. Harry needed to stay hidden for at least a week. The Gestapo knew the plane was part of a special operation, and were watching railway stations. Had he walked onto the platform, he would have been stopped; they were questioning every man boarding a train. Pierre smiled, explaining Harry would have betrayed himself the moment he spoke.

'Je suis désolé.' Harry shook his head with embarrassment. French was never his strong point at school.

'Pas de problème,' Pierre chuckled and spooned more stew into Harry's bowl, explaining that before the war his daughter had married an Englishman, who was never able to ask for a baguette without being given a slice of salami instead.

Between mouthfuls of red wine, Pierre assured him the Reseau de Résistance would help him escape. The usual route was the Comet Line through France and Spain, but this could take months. There was another way through Denmark. Harry didn't need to know details. The first stage would be in a week; Pierre would accompany him to the border at Aachen.

The days passed slowly. After a visit by the police the first evening, as they searched every house in the village, it was agreed Harry should stay put in the attic space during the day, only taking exercise when it was completely dark. To relieve the boredom, Marie gave him two books in English she found in the house. By torchlight, Harry read

Truby King's *Mothercraft* and a book of children's fairy tales, alternating the stories of *The Little Mermaid* and *The Emperor's New Clothes* with chapters on *Baby Care* and *Breast Feeding*. He had just finished *The Tin Soldier* when Pierre tapped on the access flap.

'We leave in half an hour. Come down for food first.' In the kitchen he showed Harry two printed tickets—the first to Aachen and the second to Flensburg. He had already studied the identity card that Harry had been given at Arisaig. '*C'est très bien.*' He passed over a beret. 'Better you look like a *fermier.*'

Marie put her arms around him, whispering in his ear '*Bon courage, bon courage.*'

He turned back to Pierre who was waiting by the door. 'Thank you so much. You have been very kind. I have just one question. Why do you take risks to help a foreigner?'

Pierre rested his hand on the door latch and looked directly at Harry. In his halting English he explained that their son had joined the army. He'd been shot at Eben Emael, defending the Belgian fort against the Nazis in May 1940. They held up the German advance so the Allies could reach Dunkirk. Their daughter had moved to Bristol before the war. Her house was destroyed by the Luftwaffe in November 1940. 'My wife and I have no love for Germans. In this way we fight back for our children.' His eyes misted over and Harry could see he was struggling with the memories. He said nothing but gripped Pierre's hand for a long time.

'*Allons, mon ami. Parlez maintenant français. Aujourd'hui c'est D day.*'

# Chapter Twenty

## Kirkenbjerg, Fyn, Denmark:
## June 7th 1944

Harry stepped off the train at Odense in the late afternoon to be met by a woman in blue dungarees. She was exactly as his minder from Flensburg described. Wisps of blonde hair strayed through the edges of her headscarf. The finely-chiselled face could be from a figure on the prow of a ship. She looked young enough to still be at school. Her eyes matched her aquamarine clothes.

He glanced back at the carriage-window for his travelling-companion, but the seat he'd occupied was empty. Further up the platform an inspector with a swastika armband surveyed disembarking passengers. Harry faced the woman and delivered the signal phrase about the weather. *'Det er godt vejr i dag.'*

*'Det bliver også godt vejr i morgen!'* She put her arms round his neck and kissed him, then muzzled his cheek, breathing words into his ear. 'Just respond. It will lower suspicions of that goon.' She kissed him again, the tip of her tongue touching his. It was a long time since anyone had done that. Harry closed his eyes. He was reluctant to let her draw away, but she took his hand. *'Kom med mig.'*

She led him across the high-arched concourse to the front of the station, where she unlocked two black bicycles. 'Just follow. We cycle for eight kilometres. I'm Lone by the way.' Harry wobbled behind her through the city's backstreets onto the west road to Bogense. They were soon pedalling through open countryside with little traffic on the road, apart from farm-carts pulled by shire horses. Harry followed Lone as she turned right onto Staerehusvej, and cycled along a maze of small roads to Kirkenbjerg, with its clusters of red-rooved houses.

At the end of the village, a track led to a small, thatched farmhouse. Cross struts of weathered-timber held the reeds on the roof. On the upper floor, tiny casement-windows peeped through combed eaves. Chickens scattered as gravel scrunched under their wheels. In front of the red-brick walls of the farmhouse, lilac and mock-orange jostled above the clumps of bluebells and wild garlic. Lone pushed the oak-door at the back of the small porch, beneath the chandeliers of hanging wisteria. It opened directly into the kitchen, where another young woman prepared food. She was identical to Lone, although dressed in a blouse and floral peasant-skirt. As she moved between the sink and cooker, the hem swirled round her knees.

'This is Birgitte. We are twins, but I was born ten minutes earlier, so am the wiser sister.' She prodded her twin playfully in the side with a wooden spoon.

'And this is *kartoffelfrikadeller*, typical Danish food of potatoes and onions. Lone may think she is wiser, but I am a better cook, especially when we can't get hold of meat.' Birgitte's English was as impeccable as her sister's.

Over supper Lone explained that they had spent time in England before the war, working on a dairy farm in the Cotswolds. 'Our holding is small and we only grow potatoes and other ground crops.' Lone pointed to fields through the window. 'Our grandparents farmed it till a few years ago and they had horses, cows, pigs, everything. But they are now too old, so moved to the small town of Søndersø, which is much less isolated.'

'What happened to your parents?' asked Harry, hesitantly. He was wondering if Lone had explained this and he'd not heard. He was aware how tired he felt.

'Died of influenza when we were two years old. Not the Spanish flu that killed so many after the War, but later in 1926. There were epidemics most years in Denmark.'

'You must miss them.'

Lone nodded. 'Of course, but we were both very young. Only two years old. We miss the dream but not their presence. Our grandparents became our parents—a bit older than other mothers and fathers at the village school. But very loving.'

Harry did a quick calculation and wondered how twenty-year-old girls in a rural backwater had become involved with the Danish resistance, but he recalled Gubby's words at Arisaig. '*If you don't know, you can't tell.*'

'Holger Danske tell us we are not supposed to talk about our private life,' said Birgitte, as if she had read his mind. 'But the War will be over soon enough. The Allies have consolidated the Normandy beachheads, and are advancing towards Caen. I bet they will be in Paris in a month.'

'The Nazis won't give up easily, Gitte,' interjected Lone. 'France may be liberated soon, but the fighting will stiffen as they approach the German border. The SS will defend the Fatherland till the bitter end. It could be years before the Allies reach Berlin. What if they dig in along the western front again?' She looked at Harry, whose eyes were glazing over. 'We will get you to Sweden, though. Tonight, you sleep, and tomorrow I start arrangements.'

In the morning, Harry woke to an empty house and a note from Lone. 'We are both at work, but will be back this afternoon. Don't go outside.'

Birgitte was the first to return, ringing her bell as she pedalled across the gravel-forecourt. After resting her bike against the side of the farmhouse, they sat on chairs in front of the porch, soaking up the summer sunshine. Harry could hear bees in the mock-orange shrubs that stretched out to touch the wisteria behind them.

Birgitte talked about work at a printing firm in Odense. It was by the river, close to the house Hans Christian Andersen had lived in when he wrote his fairytales. The Germans had occupied Denmark as she finished at the Gymnasium and enrolled at Ryslinge Folkehojskole to study Art. She would have continued into Aarhus University. But their grandparents were struggling with the farm, so she left Ryslinge and took a job at the printers, requiring an early start, and allowing her to finish at lunchtime. 'I've been there two years. Part of my work involves design, so I am able to use my artistic skills.'

'Does Lone work there as well?'

Birgitte chuckled. 'We are alike only in appearance and surname, Vestager. She is my opposite. At the printers I mostly work alone and here I love the silence, especially in the fields. Lone is happiest at parties. She works in an interior-design business, with forty other staff; it hums. We are typical extrovert and introvert twins. It's okay for the time being. But when the war finishes, we will move in different directions.' Birgitte broke a twig from the shrub above her head, its cluster of white petals protectively curving round bright-yellow stamens. 'Smell, Harry. Like the whole of summer in one bloom.'

Harry pressed the sprig to his nose. It was a year since he'd pushed aside the hanging bunches of flowers to insert the heavy key into the old lock of the cottage at Swanton Morley. He'd walked across the airfield before catching the train to Scarborough. The farmer promised to get the cottage in good shape if they wanted to move in. The rent would be a few shillings a month, just to cover maintenance, because he wanted to support the boys in blue. Harry had carried the key to Scarborough, intending to present it to Amy. On his return he handed it back to the farmer, who assured him the cottage would remain empty for him.

The days in the Danish farmhouse followed a repeating pattern. Both girls had gone by the time he woke, and he spent mornings doing odd jobs in the house, or around the enclosed farmyard, hidden. The Arisaig knife came in handy.

Birgitte was always first home in the afternoon and they spent hours sitting in sunshine, sharing thoughts and experiences. She talked about Julius, her boyfriend at Ryslinge, who had fled to Sweden the previous autumn when they were rounding up Danish Jews. 'I was so relieved he was safe, I didn't mind not seeing him at first. But I haven't heard anything since Christmas. Maybe he escaped to England. Maybe he met someone else. The hardest thing is not knowing. It's like he stopped caring.' She brushed the corner of her eye. 'Do you have someone waiting at home?'

Harry shook his head. 'Not any more.' He talked about Amy's death and Arisaig. He was aware it was the first time he had shared his grief, infused with a corrosive jealousy. He described the moment the smirking Freddie had showed him the photograph. 'I wanted to stick this knife into him.' Harry tapped the sheath. 'But I could see he was only interested in the girls in his magazine. Amy had simply been a diversion from his fantasy world.'

Birgitte touched his arm. 'But you have carried the feelings ever since. Always wondering whether it was a diversion for her too, unable to get an answer.'

'She chose to come back though. We were going to move in together. But I'm not sure if that was because she felt guilty, or whether she really wanted it.'

'I feel the same about Julius. I just don't know how he saw us.'

Harry felt Birgitte's fingers close over his. They sat in silence till they heard Lone's tyres on the gravel. Harry took his hand away, but the following day made sure to work close to the front of the house, listening for her bell.

Birgitte rested her bike against the farmhouse, her face flushed from the ride. She explained that Lone would be back later than usual. 'She goes for a meal with her work colleagues every Thursday. So it is just us two for *aftensmad*. I will make proper *frikadeller* this time. My boss, Jesper, killed a pig at the weekend, in preparation for Sankthansaften, and brought in joints to share. Our first meat for months, because the Germans take whatever is in the shops. We will enjoy it in the sunshine, but can I show you the old pigsty first?'

She giggled at his puzzled expression. 'My pet project.

Come.' They walked round the side of the farmyard to a low building Harry had not looked in before. Birgitte pushed the door open, but it was difficult to see anything in the dim light shining through the dusty casement. Birgitte flicked a switch and blue luminescence bathed the room.

Against the wall, filling the space from floor to ceiling, were four large cages. Harry peered through the gloom.

'Go closer,' encouraged Birgitte.

As his eyes adjusted, he saw a shape coiled round a branch. 'Snake?'

'Not just any old snake.' Birgitte opened the cage. She stretched her hand and clicked her teeth. The reptile uncoiled from the branch and slithered forwards, wrapping around her arm. She faced Harry. 'Meet my friend, King, the ball python.'

She explained how Odense Zoo had been looking for homes for animals once food supplies became difficult. Birgitte had really wanted parrots, but Lone had put her foot down, insisting she could only have something that could be kept away from the house. In the three other cages were rat snakes, a pair of anthill pythons, and a nest of desert scorpions.

'Take him. He's very friendly. They get their name because their defence strategy is to curl into a tight ball, with their head tucked in the middle, instead of biting.' Birgitte lifted the snake and draped its body over Harry's shoulders. Hesitantly he ran his finger along the mottled sandstone-blotches covering the black body. 'It's wonderfully smooth.'

'*Og smuk?* I often sit with King lying across me. Like

meditation.' Her hand stroked the back of the python, brushing against Harry's neck. He looked up from the snake to see her eyes in the semi-darkness.

They ate the *frikadeller* together in the sheltered courtyard, watching the swallows swooping around the eaves of the barn and talking about their hopes for when the war was finally over. Birgitte went inside to fetch another bottle of home-brewed ale from the cool larder under the stairs. Harry heard the click of a latch at the end of the house and turned to see a window being opened. The sound of a dance band floated across the courtyard. Birgitte reappeared, placing the beer on the small table and sat beside him. She rested her head on his shoulder and his fingers closed over hers. Harry lifted Birgitte to her feet and they swayed together with the beat of the music.

Harry breathed in the scents of midsummer, infused with the warmth from the blonde hair pressed against his shoulder. A solitary blackbird called from the upper branches of a beech tree at the corner of the farmyard. He took Birgitte's head in both hands, stroking her cheeks, staring into her blue eyes, aware of long buried feelings. Their lips touched.

A bicycle rang and Lone appeared round the side of the barn. Harry stepped back, reaching for his glass of beer, conscious of the burning in his cheeks. By the time Lone had set her bike on its stand, he was sitting on the seat in front of the porch.

Lone limped towards the bench-seat. 'Hurt my leg moving furniture in the warehouse, so thought I'd better come home instead of joining the team for dinner. Looks like you've both eaten. Any left?' Birgitte went inside to fetch the remains of the food she'd cooked for Harry, returning with a plate she banged down on the table.

Lone took a mouthful.' *Laekker mad.* I'd almost forgotten what real meat tasted like.' She smiled at Birgitte, as she massaged her ankle. 'I remembered grandfather's birthday. So I bought a present in Odense, thinking we could pedal over to Søndersø this evening. But I really can't cycle any further today.' She looked at her sister. '*Gider du tage derop på egen hånd*'?

'You want me to go there now?'

Lone lifted her eyes to the sun, disappearing behind the roof of the barn. 'It will be light for another hour.'

There was a brief exchange in Danish, then Birgitte retrieved her bicycle from the barn and pushed it across the farmyard to where Lone and Harry sat. The dance band was still playing. 'Save me the waltz,' she said, looking directly at Harry.

Harry and Lone watched her pedal off into the evening. Lone rubbed cream into the skin around her Achilles tendon. 'My leg feels better already. Some gentle exercise might be helpful. Shall we walk beside the brook? The honeysuckle bushes will be in full bloom. At this time, we're unlikely to see anyone, but if we do, I'll say you're my cousin from Svendborg.'

The sun sank through trees to the west as they followed the footpath along the tiny stream. Lone talked about growing up on the farm, leaving school to work at the design company; being recruited by Holger Danske to help repatriate Allied airmen. 'We are a pretty safe house, being so far from Odense. Who would suspect two young girls of such work?'

The stream opened into a small lake and they followed the footpath to the far side. A crescent of moon hung beneath its mirror-like surface, in contrast to the barred red and orange embers glowing on the horizon. They stood on the bank, watching the bats in their erratic flight. There was a splash as a fish rose to take an insect, breaking the surface and creating an ever-widening circle of ripples.

Lone took his hand and pulled him towards her. Harry was reminded of their first meeting on the platform and wondered if she was still playing a part. He stiffened, thinking about Birgitte, but Lone was insistent. 'Let's go home.' She kept tight hold on his hand as they walked back along the bank. Just before they reached the footpath, she stopped and pressed a finger to her lips. 'Come this way.'

Carefully she led him along a reed-covered culvert, which looped round to the back of the farmhouse.

'What was that?' he whispered.

'Didn't you see the man fishing? Aage owns the farm next door. I don't trust him at all, So creepy. His wife died a year ago and he is always trying to persuade Birgitte or me to go out with him. Or into bed more likely.'

'You can hardly blame him,' said Harry. 'With two unattached girls so close. I'd be sorely tempted if I was Aage.'

Lone looked directly at him for a moment. 'Shall we sit out here and enjoy the moonlight a while? It's still warm.'

Harry nodded. He wanted to listen for Birgitte returning.

Lone went into the house and came out carrying a bottle and two glasses. 'Last year we made apple wine from the windfalls. "*Meget velsmagende*". Very tasty.' She raised her glass. 'To victory over the Germans.'

'And the Japanese.' It was eighteen months since Fenghuangshan. A lifetime.

'Birgitte told me you'd been in China. What was it like?'

Harry hesitated, recalling the earlier conversation with Birgitte. He'd talked to her about Douglass and Xiaobin and the friendships forged through the fighting; meeting the soldiers from Burma and glimpsing the sacrifice of boys the same age; encountering Ya Fei and being reminded of his sister; his growing awareness of the dimensions of a war that was truly worldwide.

He didn't want to share any of this with Lone, so he described the challenge faced by the Chinese military and the defence of Chengdu. It was matter of fact but she listened attentively, refilling their glasses at intervals.

The moon disappeared behind the barn. 'Sorry, need a jimmy riddle.' Harry stood up and walked unsteadily to the privy beside the pigsty. On the way back he stumbled on the grass. Lone grinned. 'Bit much to drink?'

Harry looked confused. 'I've only had a couple of glasses. I was expecting Birgitte back by now, but think I need to lie down.'

Lone frowned. 'I guess you didn't hear what she said to me as she was setting off, about staying the night in Søndersø. Birgitte won't cycle back in the dark.' She took Harry's hand and led him upstairs. He lay on his bed and shut his eyes, but the room span. He opened them, aware of Lone stroking his head. The only light came from the tiny dormer window, but he could see she was half-dressed.

'No, Lone,' he protested.

'Don't you find me attractive?'

'Of course,' muttered Harry, conscious the room was threatening to spin again. 'It's not that.'

Lone moved closer. 'I know you feel something for Birgitte, and that's fine. You and she can pick up again tomorrow, when she finishes work. But she's not here and I want you. It's been a long time since Julius.'

He turned to her as she kissed him hungrily and nuzzled his cheek. 'That feels good,' she murmured. 'I've wanted to do that ever since we met at the station, but Birgitte has always been around. The ankle seemed a good way to sort things.'

Harry was aware of Lone tugging his clothes. He closed his eyes.

When he woke, the sun was already above the line of the window. He guessed it was mid-morning. The house was quiet, apart from the sound of swallows nesting in the eaves of the thatch. On the table in the kitchen was a note from Lone, beneath a small bottle. 'Try these for *tømmermænd*.' He rubbed his pounding forehead and swallowed three of the tablets, trying to recall what had happened in the night.

By early afternoon he felt better, and sat outside waiting for Birgitte.

The two girls arrived together, having met on the road from Odense. It seemed Birgitte had been given extra work at the printers, which had made her late.

'We came past Ole's farm and his wife Helga asked if we could go there this evening,' explained Lone. 'Ole has pulled a muscle in his back, and she needs the cows milked and wood chopped.' She looked at Harry. 'Will you help us?'

'Of course,' replied Harry. 'As long as you think it's okay for me to be seen.'

'We will say you're our cousin from Svendvorg.'

After preparing food, Birgitte announced she was going for a walk. She needed to think about some things at work. She presumed Harry and Lone could manage Ole's jobs. Birgitte laced her boots and set off towards the lake. Harry hurried after her and caught up at the footpath beside the small brook.

'Is everything okay?'

'What do you think?' She stared levelly back.

'I'm really sorry it didn't work out last night.'

'I'd like to believe you, Harry.'

'But you went to your grandparents.'

'What else could I do? Lone had brought the present. But I don't trust my sister. Amazing how her ankle seems fine today.'

Harry looked towards the farmhouse. Lone was watching them. 'Can we talk when you get back?'

'It'll be late. I'm going to Tastrup to see a friend.'

'I'll be awake in my room.'

'Sure?

Harry registered the doubt in her voice. 'Quite sure,' he said. 'I'll be waiting.'

After working through the woodpile at Ole's farm, Harry went to lie down in his room. He watched the long twilight slowly darken through the window, listening for Birgitte's return.

He woke with a start at the click of his door-latch. 'Is it you?' he whispered.

'Yes,' replied Lone. 'I can't sleep.'

Despite the darkness it was clear what she wanted. He sat up in bed. 'Lone, I'm sorry about last night. It shouldn't have happened.'

'But you enjoyed it? Be honest.' Her voice was soft, purring.

'Of course,' he said. 'But it's not—' he hesitated, thinking how to explain his feelings.

'For God's sake Harry. Don't be such an idiot,' she said impatiently. 'Holger Danske say you'll be gone in less than a week, and we will probably never meet again.' She lay next to him, talking about her feelings, the loneliness of living in a village in a country at war, the longing for adventure and excitement. She stopped. hearing footsteps on the gravel.

'Birgitte?' he whispered.

'Doesn't sound like her.' Lone pulled on her clothes and hurried downstairs. Harry followed. The kitchen door was wide open and there were two pairs of boots on the mat. 'Birgitte's not come in. Hers have got red laces.' Lone called her sister's name into the darkness, but there was no answer. 'Maybe we imagined it?'

'I promised I'd stay awake till she came home,' said Harry.

Lone looked at him. 'Please yourself, but you know where I am. Birgitte is quite likely to stay the night in Tastrup.'

The sky was lightening before Harry fell into a deep sleep. By the time he came downstairs the house was empty.

The next day followed a similar pattern. Birgitte returned home with Lone. After they'd eaten supper, she tied her boots and set off for a walk across the fields behind Aage's house. She didn't say anything to Harry about why she'd not come to his room the night before.

Harry helped Lone on Ole's farm again, and they returned to the farmhouse in the gathering dusk. There was no sign of Birgitte. He wondered if she'd gone to Tastrup.

This time he didn't protest after Lone lifted the latch on his door.

At the end of his third week in the farmhouse, Harry was listening to music in the sitting room, when he heard bike tyres crunching gravel. He walked into the kitchen to see Lone standing in the doorway, her outline framed by sunlight. She wore the same blue dungarees as at Odense station. Her long hair was tied back from her reddened face in a pony-tail.

'I have cycled straight from the harbour. There is a boat to Sweden tomorrow.' Lone paused to catch her breath. 'It leaves at midnight. You will be in Göteborg by dawn.'

She kicked off her clogs and stepped across the threshold. Her words continued to tumble out as she explained they needed to dye his hair to make him look more Danish, and gather up the documents he needed. Birgitte had used equipment at her printers to make identity papers and a permit for Sweden. He would be their brother, Ejgil Vestager, a welder at the shipyard in Odense, with an old school friend in Göteborg, who he always visited at midsummer festival.

'We don't have much time. Today is Sankt Hans evening and there will be bonfires and parties across Fyn. Birgitte and I need to go to our parent's house in Søndersø, so you will be alone this evening.' Her fingers touched the zipper beneath the neck of the cotton overalls, and a smile played around her lips. 'But I will try not to be late back.' She moved closer to Harry and put her hands around his neck, pulling him towards her.

They were still kissing when they heard Birgitte's bell. Lone stepped away, before her sister appeared in the doorway. She explained the situation and went upstairs to change out of her dungarees. By the time she came down, Birgitte was towelling Harry's hair. He was kneeling in front of her with his hands on her waist.

Unseen, Lone watched Birgitte's lips brush across his forehead and noticed the expression in Harry's eyes. Angrily, she pressed her weight hard on the final board of the wooden stairs and the two heads moved apart. 'It makes you look like a Viking." Her lips barely parted as she uttered the words. "Maybe you should keep it that way when you return to England.'

Harry stood up and studied his reflection in the mirror above the mantelpiece. 'It's been blonde once before.' He described the cabaret with Dougie at Fenghuangshan. Another life.

Lone sniffed the air. '*Er der kaffe?*'

'*Vaersgo!*' Birgitte splashed the brown liquid into a cup and passed it to her twin, who savoured the smell.

'The real stuff. So different to the ersatz liquid at work. How do you manage this?'

'A little flirtation can be rewarding—as you know.'

'Careful you don't get carried away,' taunted Lone.

Harry saw Birgitte's head flick up. Her eyes blazed. '*Skal jeg tage ved laere af min storesøster? Du ser ud til at være gået hele vejen!*

'*Og hvad så?*' The disdain in Lone's voice cut through the room. '*Jeg ville have lidt sjov, og han var tilgængelig.*'

'*Ikke engang den mulighed kunne du modstå,*' retorted Birgitte. '*Også selvom det betyder, at du måtte skubbe mig til side.*'

Harry could hear the censure in Birgitte's tone. Although he couldn't understand a word of what was being said, he knew it had something to do with him. He stepped between the two girls. 'Why so much anger? You two will be together long after I've gone tomorrow.'

Birgitte's eyes were unwavering as she looked at Harry. 'I'm angry because of what she did.' Her voice was strong and steady.

'Trouble with you sister is that you were too slow off the mark—as always,' snapped Lone. 'Tomorrow never comes, you know.'

'It's not just about sex, Lone.' Birgitte's tone was quietly commanding. 'There's something called a relationship, a meeting of minds, a connection between soulmates, something special that is more than simply fucking. But you've never understood that, have you?' Her voice remained deadly calm. 'For you, it's about getting inside the pants of every eligible male who comes within a mile of our house. Julius was just the start. You're worse than a bitch on heat.'

Lone's mouth twisted with rage. 'Screw you sister. You don't have a clue. I'll bet a million kroner you'll still be a miserable old maid when you're a hundred, like Great Auntie Dorthe.'

Harry's eyes flicked from Lone to Birgitte, taking in the

anger and jealousy. 'I'm sorry.' It sounded lame, but he meant it. 'I don't deserve your friendship, especially after you've done so much.'

'You have no idea what I've done for you Harry,' said Birgitte, tears welling into her eyes. 'Maybe one day you'll understand.' She pushed past him and ran outside.

There was silence in the kitchen. It was Lone who spoke first. 'I'd better go to her. She'll calm down. She always does. It will be okay by the time we get back from Søndersø.'

Ten minutes later Harry watched the two sisters wheel their bikes onto the track to the village, and followed their heads above the top of the hedge as they pedalled towards the Søndersø road. Lone had told him it would take them about an hour. 'Sankthansaften sometimes goes on till midnight, so don't wait up.'

Harry tossed restlessly in the small room, wondering about the argument and ashamed at what had happened. He should have sent Lone away, after she'd helped him into bed the night Birgitte cycled to Søndersø. She was right though. Life was too short and it had been a long time since Amy. It might have been different if he could have talked with Birgitte, to find out why she'd not come to his room. It didn't make sense. Perhaps there was a boyfriend in Tastrup? As he struggled to understand, the sounds of the night faded. He had only been asleep for a few minutes, when the door creaked and a familiar shape crept under the blanket. The sky was cloudy with no moon, so it was dark in the bedroom but he didn't need a light to guide him. He knew it was the last time, and the finality made it more intense.

When he woke, the bed was empty. Once he'd washed and appeared downstairs, Lone was brewing coffee on the stove, dressed in her night-clothes, a housecoat across her bare shoulders. Birgitte had already left. The door to the garden was open and he heard skylarks. There was a strong smell of pig manure.

Harry wrinkled his nose. 'I thought you didn't keep animals.'

'Aage is spreading fertilizer on his fields.' She took his hand and looked into his eyes. 'I'm sorry you are going, especially after last night.'

There was a knock on the door. Lone pulled away. 'That'll be Birgitte. Coming back for something. She's always forgetting her key.' Angrily, she swung the door open.

'*Gud*,' gasped Lone. '*Den fanden til Aage!*'

'What is it?' Harry pushed back his chair and moved towards the doorway. He stared at the two policemen standing on the stone step. The taller one was holding a gun and the shorter had his right hand on his holster. Beyond the two men, a prison-van stood on the gravel yard, with its back door open.

'*Følg med, englænder!*' barked the man with the Mauser, gesticulating at Harry, who raised his hands above his head and stepped into the yard. The gun prodded him in the back and he stumbled towards the van. Behind he could hear Lone screaming and cursing. He turned to see the other man grab her by the hair and drag her across the gravel, scraping her bare knees on the sharp stones. She was kicking and punching.

Harry watched Lone break free and run into the house.

'*Skide luder*,' cursed the man and pulled out his revolver, as she appeared in the doorway with a pistol in her right hand. There was a simultaneous crack of gunfire and Lone sank down, blood oozing through the front of her nightdress. The policeman ran across, pushed the barrel against her forehead and pulled the trigger.

Harry was handcuffed and bundled into the back of the van. He fell forward, banging his chin on the metal floor. The bolt slammed shut. He dragged himself round to the tiny air-slit in the back door. He could see Lone lying across the doorstep, with one arm outstretched. Her nightdress had rucked up her thighs, exposing her grazed knees. Her blue eyes were staring straight at him. Harry tried calling her name, but all that came out was a strangled groan.

The van bounced round the corner and the farmhouse disappeared behind the hedge.

# Part Three

Countless words
count less
than the silent balance
between yin and yang

老 子 Lao Zi, *Tao Te Ching*

# Chapter Twenty-one

## Chengdu to Li Jiang:
## Saturday 12th September 2019

Through the window of the carriage, they could see the Salween river snaking through the gorge, where the railway line followed the twists and turns of the fast-moving current. Pinpricks of light appeared as the gathering dusk settled like a blanket over the clusters of houses close to the water's edge. The clacking beat of the wheels increased in tempo.

'We have climbed Yunnan plateau. Downhill all way to Kunming.' Sunny spoke softly, smiling at Torin's reflection.

'*Xū yào lái fèn tào cān ma?*'

Sunny turned from the window to see a white-jacketed steward standing next to their table. She was pushing a trolley of food. '*Mei nu* say do we want set meal. I find out dishes. *Yǒu xiē shén me ne?*' Her eyes flashed as she engaged the women in conversation.

Torin listened carefully, but the only word he understood was *mǐfàn*.

Sunny faced him. 'They have choice of two set meals. First is egg fried with tomato, and pork with green pepper and cabbage. Second is *gōng bǎojī dǐng*—chicken fried with vegetables, and *dòufu*.'

'And rice?'

'It all come with *mǐfàn*. This is China.'

Torin glanced at the trolley and back at Sunny. 'Let's have both, then we can share.'

The waiter flashed a gold-toothed smile and Torin helped her position the various plates onto the tablecloth.

Sunny surveyed the trolley for drinks. '*Nǐ yǒu píjiǔ ma?*'

'*Xuě huā hé Qīng dǎo, nín yào nǎ zhǒng?*'

'*Xuě huā píjiǔ.*' She smiled at Torin. 'I order Snow beer for you rather than Qingdao, since we going to land of Leopard, even if he hiding.'

'What for you?'

'*Xuěhuā* for me too. Not allowed to drink alone on train. Bad luck.' Sunny looked along the dining car. Only one table was empty, with a sign: '*Wèi yuángōng bǎoliú*'. 'That reserved for cooks. They join when made last meals.'

Sunny peeled the plastic wrapper from the chopsticks, and they dipped them in and out of the bowls, as they talked.

'When do we get in tomorrow morning?' asked Torin.

'Arrive Kunming six o-clock.' She covered her mouth with her hand. 'The bus leaves near station at eight half. Maybe eat breakfast if train correct. Never sure whether problem with time. Not like Bullet—straight across Yunnan on new track away from river.' She sliced the air above her head with the side of her hand. 'Three hundred and fifty kilometres an hour Possible come in six hours, instead of eighteen. I think too quick. We are last of slow-train travellers.'

Torin pressed his nose against the window through which he could see the grey, rippling luminescence curving between the black hillsides. 'Mysterious and magical. It reminds me of *Murder on the Orient Express*.'

Her eyes flashed. 'Hope not happen tonight.'

He pushed his spectacles onto the bridge of his nose.

'Depends on who takes the top bunks after that couple left at Ganluo.'

'When I went to bathroom earlier, I heard someone saying two people missed our train. Maybe they are from our compartment. Could be just us.' Her knee brushed against his jeans, registering the responding pressure. 'Have you finished?'

Torin surveyed the plates. A few shreds of cabbage lay at the edge of one plate. 'That was perfect. How do you say delicious? *Hǎo chī?*'

'*Hěn hǎo chī* if really good.'

'*Hěn hěn hǎo chī* then.'

Sunny smiled. 'I think in English I say, "*the pleasure is all mine*", but I don't want pleasure on my own. It is for both.'

His fingers closed over her hand on the white, cotton table-cloth. 'Thank you.'

She said nothing, but her brown eyes were unwavering as she met his gaze.

'I'm not talking about the food,' he added.

'I know,' she said quietly. 'We see. Just hope at moment. I'm happy to do this trip with you. Wishing luck.'

'In that case we need another beer. Strengthen our good fortune.'

Sunny caught the eye of the cook, who was clearing plates from the table behind. '*Má fán zài gěi wǒ mén liǎng píng pí jiǔ?*'

'*Hái shì yào dòng de ma?*'

'*Shì de, xiè xiè.*' She looked across the table. 'You prefer chilled?' She raised the bottle and tilted her neck to take a mouthful of the amber liquid. She placed it back on the table and noticed he was smiling. 'What is matter?'

'Nothing. Nothing at all. You look very lovely, that's all. Sorry, if I'm staring too much.'

'I think we need go back to our compartment. If empty we can stare as much as want.' Sunny felt a mixture of emotions. This would be their first time alone since he'd arrived at Shuangliu airport on the morning flight.

She'd waited on the edge of the crush of people in the arrivals' hall, so he wouldn't miss her in the crowd. He'd come through with another westerner, a young woman with a blonde pony-tail, laughing. A friend? Or the sister he'd talked about? Sunny tried to suppress her disappointment that he was accompanied.

She waved her red scarf above her head, not wanting to call out. Finally, he spotted her. They kissed awkwardly on the cheeks. He explained Martha had been sitting beside him on the plane. Could they give her a lift into town? The person meeting her was stuck in traffic.

Sunny found the thirty-minute journey an agony of impatience, trying to follow the thread of the fast-paced interchange between the two westerners in the back seat, frustrated that her English was not quick enough to join the small talk. She wanted to know how he was feeling.

They dropped Martha at her hotel and Sunny gave instructions to the North Train station. She wasn't sure if she should stay sitting in the front seat, but the taxi moved off before she could do anything, so she talked to Torin through the arch of the headrest. She could see he was tired from the overnight flight, so she avoided the question she most wanted to ask. She would wait till they were on their own.

But then came the interminable queues at the station,

having their tickets and identities checked, suitcases scanned by security, and finally, joining the snaking line of passengers waiting to board train 2145 to Kunming.

The two top bunks in their compartment were already occupied by a middle-aged couple, travelling to see their daughter in Ganluo. The woman wanted to try out her English on the young westerner below, cackling every time she repeated the name Eddie Redmayne, which further inhibited conversation. It had been a relief when the couple had clambered down as their station was announced, but then it was time to go to the restaurant car.

As Sunny looked along the dining car, she could see the cook smiling at her. She stood, holding the beer-bottles in her left hand. It had already been ten hours since she'd watched Torin enter the arrivals' hall. She clasped his hand and they swayed between the tables, aware of the eyes that followed them into the connecting link between the carriages. She slid open the door to their compartment, glancing up at the two top-bunks. Both beds were empty. She dropped the catch on the door and pulled Torin onto the narrow bed.

Dawn was breaking as the loudspeaker announced Kunming station in ten minutes. Sunny shifted her head on the pillow and lifted the blind to look through the window. A thick mist enveloped the city's outskirts. Beyond the bamboo trees lining the track, she could just make out ghostly silhouettes of the nearest buildings.

She looked at the body squashed against the wall, face towards her with his eyes closed. They had slept huddled and entwined. She pressed her lips to his forehead. 'Time to wake, we nearly at Kunming.'

His eyelids flickered and opened. As recognition floated to the surface of his consciousness, Torin smiled and reached for her hand, drawing it under the thin duvet. His feet curled round hers, pulling her closer.

'Not now. We must climb down. Attendant come to clean soon.'

He swung his legs over her warm body and reached for his trousers. 'I must pee before we get off.' He smiled to read '*No using when stabling*' on the toilet door, thinking this would make a good tag for Great Western Railways, then joined the line of people in the washroom next door. He splashed water on his forehead and quickly rubbed some toothpaste round his mouth with his finger, before rinsing it into the cracked basin.

Sunny was dressed and ready when he returned to the compartment, with everything packed in their rucksacks. Her black hair was tied with two red bows.

'Not washing?'

'Did early when you asleep.'

'Both fresh then.' He pressed his lips against her cheek, smelling the scent from the wet wipes. The train jolted to a halt and they stood with arms around each other's waist, until the attendant knocked on the door, telling them to disembark.

Outside the station-concourse, the city-traffic was already busy. 'Bus over there.' Sunny pointed to the terminus across the road. 'But we go for food first.'

*Sān lúns* and electric scooters were weaving around the pedestrians on the dedicated strip of tarmac beside the main thoroughfare, so she turned down a side-street. Workmen were pruning the trees growing through the pavement. Against the brightness of the early morning sun that blazed along the length of the street, silhouettes of black trunks stretched above the mounds of cut branches.

'Try to have it ready for October festival, so can hang lanterns.'

People were already at work in the shops that sprawled onto the pavement. A mechanic was stripping forks from an electric bike, crouched across the black, oil-soaked concrete, while inside the makeshift foundry, sparks were flying from the angle-grinder being wielded by a teenage boy, to construct a set of railings for the balcony above. A fruit-seller laid out trays of apples, bananas, oranges and pears, while behind the shutters of the massage-parlour next door a woman was stripping the sheets off reclining couches, ready for the men who would soon arrive.

A dog sniffed around the mound of discarded vegetables from the stall, watched by an old woman in a red jacket, sweeping the pavement, with bowed legs and skin etched deep from decades of weathering.

They passed a restaurant where a man mopped the floor, as his partner wiped tables and lifted chairs from the stack ready for new customers. Two men squatted on their heels in the entrance, huddled over a bowl of noodles. The air was laced with the smell of fried oils.

'How about here? I ask if they have *mán tou* or *dòu shā bāo* with milk or yoghourt—steamed buns with sweet fillings.'

The owner's smile revealed his chipped teeth. He waved his arms for them to come in. 'He says he do something in honour because we from Chengdu, where daughter lives. He asks if I know her. Maybe not aware how big city is.'

They sat at a table next to the noodle-eaters, watching the street come to life. The distant blaring of car-horns merged with voices from televisions behind closed shutters, dogs barking in upper rooms, and the clacking of tiles from an early morning mah-jong game in the parlour next door.

Across the road, two women prepared their street-stall of barbeque-sticks. slicing the array of aubergine, lotus fruits, courgettes, potato, bamboo, and okra on one tray, with strips of chicken, pork, beef, ham, bacon, sausages and small fish on another.

'If I watch, get hungry.'

'I'm hungry already.'

Sunny looked at him. 'Last night not enough food?'

He smiled. 'Last night is why I'm hungry.' It had been long after midnight before they'd fallen asleep on their shared mattress, reluctant to let go of the moment, yet overcome with a wonderful tiredness.

The food arrived on a tray with two soup bowls and a couple of glasses of milky liquid. The owner gave a careful explanation of each plate. Sunny tipped the rice noodles and vegetables into the soup bowls, before adding spices. She mixed everything and pushed one towards Torin. 'Try. His daughter says very good. Hope you like.'

Torin swallowed a mouthful from the glass. 'And this?'

'Peanut milk. Also good.'

On the bus to Li Jiang they sat behind an elderly couple with two canaries in a wire-cage. Despite the trilling of the song-birds, they were both asleep soon after leaving Kunming. Occasionally they were jolted awake at the stops, but quickly fell back into slumber, reassured by the other's presence.

It was mid-afternoon when the bus pulled into the terminal at Li Jiang.

They shouldered their rucksacks and set off along the Nankou road. towards the entrance of the old town beside Zhongyi market. The traffic-noise faded as they followed a winding street up past rows of houses, with streams criss-crossing a cobbled walkway. Running water mingled with singing from speakers that hung below the eaves of ancient buildings.

She checked her phone. 'This way.' A narrow alley opened onto a track that led steeply uphill. 'Here.' She pointed to an archway with carved panelled-doors.'*Hao Ke Long Ya Deng* guesthouse. *Hào kè* means enjoying having guests. It also means welcome.'

Inside the shaded office, she collected a room-key and led the way onto a balconied second-floor. From the entrance to their bedroom they looked across the interlocking rooftops that covered the area of Li Jiang's ancient town. Lines of weathered roof-tiles cascaded from the curved ridges with their pointed eaves. Here and there a tree pierced the canopy of rooves, breaking through to the daylight above and stretching its branches across the grey-brown mantle.

Torin stared at the rooftop panorama. 'You wouldn't guess there is a maze of waterways concealed beneath, with people shopping, eating and walking beside the invisible streams. It just seems like a hugger-mugger collection of houses.'

'Hugger-mugger?'

'One on top of the other. No spaces. Crowded.'

She shook her head. 'This not crowded. Next week is *Zhōng Qiū Jié*, our mid-autumn festival, where we eat special Chinese moon cake.' Sunny showed him a picture on her phone. 'Lots of hugger-mugging then. We lucky here this week.' She pushed open the door to the bedroom. A large double bed with a carved wooden headboard filled the space. She placed her rucksack on the stand beside the television and turned towards him. 'We see doctor tomorrow, so we can do anything you want today.'

By the time he'd slipped the rucksack-straps from his shoulders, she was lying across the bed, pulling her green jumper over her head.

# Chapter Twenty-two:

## Li Jiang to Baisha:
## Sunday 13th September 2019

The autumn sun was already high as they walked from the ancient town onto Longquan Road, looking for Qiangwei Boulevard to the north. They had woken late and taken breakfast in the small courtyard, under the shade of a banana tree in the corner, its purple pods swelling to reveal the green fruit inside. The appointment with Doctor Ho was fixed for four o'clock, so Sunny had planned for them to walk to Baisha.

The road curled round the suburb of Wenang and then straightened north. There was little traffic and layers of red earth filled ruts in the tarmac. The dusty track took them past large farmhouses, reminding Torin of the walk to Sunny's family home at Dahzentou. The walls of baked, red bricks stretched solidly, supporting curved wooden-eaves and tiled-rooves. Inside each courtyard, yellow mounds of maize husks were piled against high walls. Chickens pecked the dusty ground. Beside farmhouses, where waterways circled fields, stooks of drying rice-straw were arranged in neat lines, awaiting collection before autumn rains.

A few miles to their left, the ground rose sharply to the mountain above Banjieyang, and the vegetation of bamboo and banana clumps gave way to low, thorn-like bushes, better suited for the arid hillside. Torin saw a zigzag track etched into the red-brown earth leading to the summit, and wondered if they might try a hike next day. For the moment it was enough to be walking beside Sunny on a beautiful morning. Baisha was six miles away and they were in no hurry.

'Who are we seeing?' He reached for her hand.

She squeezed his fingers, noticing he was no longer dragging his left foot. 'Maybe Doctor Ho's son, but could be another doctor. Father Ho Shixiu died a year ago. He why I know Baisha. When I was little girl, my grandfather see him. That time he not famous. But then BBC interviewed him.'

'You mean the Monty Python actor?' Torin recalled the reference on the clinic's website before he'd left London.

Sunny frowned. 'I don't know his name. I only heard BBC. But yes, after Monty, a lot of people came to see him. Doctor Ho like a super-star here, and made Jade Dragon Snow Mountain Herbal Medicine Clinic famous round the world.

'Why did your grandfather come?'

'Huge bubbles on his legs and neck. I remember telling him very smelly. Maybe I shouldn't say that to old person, but anyway Doctor Ho treated him.'

'Bubbles? You mean boils?' Torin wrinkled his nose. 'Not pleasant.'

'I don't know that word,' Sunny frowned. 'But maybe Doctor Ho will make you better too, just like the magic he did with my grandfather.'

'It will have to be very strong magic, Sunny.'

She pulled him towards her, pressing her lips against his cheek. They stood close in the middle of the road, oblivious to everything but the rise and fall of their breathing. A moped honked and they stepped to the edge to avoid the cloud of red dust drifting towards them in the light breeze. A woman with a headscarf was squeezed in front of the driver, holding a small child balanced on the handlebars. Behind the driver a teenage girl was squatting on the panniers, arms tight round her father's waist.

'Doctor Ho always said optimism is best medicine, so we hope.' Her fingers touched the purple scar on his neck. 'We strongly, strongly hope. I'm sure this can help, especially with all my love to add.'

Torin looked into her eyes, not knowing how he could convey the gratitude he felt for the way she'd managed to penetrate his protective shell.

That morning at Shuangliu airport, when he'd watched her run down the escalator and out to the concourse, had been one of the lowest moments in his life. He'd wanted to chase after Sunny, to halt her flight, to hold her close and explain everything, but he'd been too afraid of hurting her. It was rather ironic, given the final image of her anguished face, glancing up from the bottom of the escalator before she fled the departure hall.

In the months after he'd returned to London, he thought about her so often he feared he was becoming obsessed. His first waking thought, as he emerged from sleep into the consciousness of a new day, was about Sunny. Sometimes the image was their first meeting in the conference room at Plaza; or dipping chopsticks into the hot-pot bowl to retrieve the quail egg; holding a strip of bamboo to the panda; looking at him across the small table at Kathmandu; or talking to Mrs. Yang on the track to her family farmhouse. Often it was seeing her outlined against the sunshine streaming through the window of the small bedroom in Pingle. But the memories were quickly dampened by the dark cloud of separation.

After three months and summer had grown dusty and heavy in the air of the city, he knew he had to offer her some sort of explanation, if only to ease the pressure from the wraiths in his head, but he couldn't bring himself to phone. One Friday evening after work, he sat down to write to Sunny. His fingers hesitated and stumbled over the keyboard. He produced text and deleted text, whole paragraphs were constructed and erased, but he kept going till the dawn chorus outside his flat told him it was time to stop. He went for a walk along the Regents Canal towpath to Limehouse, where only an occasional runner disturbed the early-morning calm, and returned to read what he'd written.

*Dear Sunny,*

*I am so sorry for the way we parted at the airport. I was very clumsy. You deserved better and you certainly deserve an explanation.*

*The thing is I have a serious condition which can't be cured.*

*I get seizures without much warning and they often result in blackouts. It started after the tsunami. Although they managed to stitch up the wound to my head, there was some damage to the brain, which the MRI scan revealed. I have ECG tests every six months and they show an irregular pattern of brainwaves. The doctors think it's a kind of epilepsy. A few years ago they had to remove a swelling in my neck, which they thought might be putting pressure on the brain, but*

296

*it doesn't seem to have helped.*

*I take medicine to try and calm the brain. Sometimes I get a little warning, and I can go somewhere safe. It happened the day we went to the Panda centre, which was why I had to return to the hotel rather suddenly, instead of doing something with you in the afternoon.*

*Most of the time I can lead a normal life, apart from not being able to drive. But the blackouts are becoming more common—maybe once a month these days, when it used to be just two or three times a year.*

*It will keep getting worse, and I will become increasingly incapacitated, which makes a relationship impossible, and I should have been more honest with you.*

*I didn't expect to get involved, but I was so enjoying being with you I couldn't stop. That week was very precious, but I realise it came at the expense of your own happiness. That was very selfish and I am so very sorry Sunny.*

*I hope you meet someone who can make you truly happy. You deserve this, because you are a very special person.*

*With love*
*Torin*

He dithered over the text, amending and editing. He tried a shortened version, but that seemed too curt. A second attempt described his fears and his feelings about the epilepsy, and decided that was inappropriate. A third variant was matter of fact and made no mention of his feelings, but that seemed too brutal.

In the end he reverted to the original. He wondered whether to send it as an attachment, or have it simply as the text of the email. He pasted it as a new message, but it didn't look quite right, typing luchenxi@cuv.china.com into the address box. He hesitated at the subject line. '*Hello from London*' seemed a bit too light-hearted. '*An explanation for having led you up the garden path and back again*' might be more accurate, but not succinct. What he'd written just needed to be read as it was, without topping and tailing.

He dithered for ages and then realised he could simply send it in the post. A letter might just make the last collection at midday, if he was quick. He printed it off and signed it. He hesitated whether to add kisses at the end but decided against. He rummaged through the stationery on his desk for an envelope, addressed it to the CUV office in Chengdu and took it to the post office in Mile End high street, where he paid an extra £18 to have it tracked. The counter clerk assured him it would be in China by Monday, but then would depend on the local postal-service. Torin watched the woman place it in the special-delivery bag, then walked back to his flat along the towpath.

He counted the days, reckoning he might receive a response by the following weekend.

Nothing came and he tried to console himself this was good; it meant she had moved on. A fortnight passed and he registered that Sunny was no longer in his head every waking minute. It was possible to pay attention to something else. He didn't need a reply.

Three weeks after he'd posted the letter, Torin accepted an invitation to join the old team for Friday's quiz night in the *Wentworth Arms*. It felt good to just talk and drink with friends and be able to laugh over communal mistakes, as they won the wooden spoon and the bag of cheese and onion. It was nearly midnight when he arrived back at his flat. He had just put out the bedside-light when his phone pinged.

'*I received your letter last night. I want to talk to you. Do you have time?*'

Torin glanced at his watch. It was seven in the morning in Chengdu.

'*Awake already?*' he messaged back.

'*Zzzzzzz … texting in sleep.*' There was an emoji of a body lying in bed. '*Do you have Skype?*'

'*Yes.*'

'*One minute. I call you.*'

Torin's screen lit up, showing Sunny's face in front of her poster of FanxyRed. His chest tightened and he resisted the urge to press his fingers to the screen.

'*Nǐ hǎo ma?*' It felt strange to utter the greeting again.

'*Wǒ hěn hǎo. Nǐ ne?*'

He floundered to respond, but her smile was encouraging. 'Just say "*Wǒ yě hěn hǎo*."'

'*Wǒ yě hěn hǎo,*' he repeated. 'Sort of.'

'You mean you are sick?'

'Just very tired. It often happens at the end of a week.'

'How is *Pitch Perfect*?'

'Going well. Lots of orders from Chengdu.'

'Yes, I heard some big companies chosen you. Also, *Lucky Banana*.'

'Thanks to the work you and Gloria put into the conference.'

'That's our job.'

There was a silence. He could see Sunny waiting for him to speak.

'I'm sorry the letter took three weeks.' He was aware it was a stupid statement.

'Need to put my phone number. It stayed in post office for a long time, because address all in English.'

'I'm sorry, Sunny.' He was repeating himself, but didn't know what else to say.

'It is four months since you left Chengdu. I been waiting to hear from you.' Sunny struggled to control her anger. Nothing her friends had said in the days after returning from the airport had dampened the fierce flames of rejection and humiliation. She had cried herself to sleep many nights, unable to erase images of Torin. Training for the Chengdu marathon helped a bit, and she reckoned she might be close to a finishing time of three and a half hours. She spent time at Dazhentou with *Zufu*, soaking up the sounds and smells of the farm, allowing herself to be rocked gently in his cradle of unwavering acceptance. Her boxing coach had shown her some deep-meditation techniques, silencing the noise of her thoughts a while, and steering her into a short-lived sanctuary. *'There is always a positive reason for every behaviour, but it isn't always easy to see it. Have patience.'*

She breathed deeply, fixing her eyes on the man eight thousand miles away. 'I hope for text or email. Finally, I received a letter. We not send letters in China for a long time.' She recalled reaching for the special knife on her desk that she'd been given as a New Year's gift by Gloria, and slitting open the envelope. Her trembling hands had unfolded the sheet of blue paper. She'd taken it into the rest-room to read, and re-read and read again until she knew it by heart—almost as well as the poetry she had learnt to recite in school.

'Why didn't you tell me when together?' Her voice steadied. 'We could have talked. I understand illness. My cousin sick from leukaemia. My uncle unable to walk because of blocked lungs. I know about disease. Why did you stay silent? It like you punishing me for your illness. But not my fault. Why you do it?'

Torin blinked at the screen. He recalled the miserable ending to his relationship with Kat. They'd lived together for three years. There'd been the occasional blank 'episode', but she'd said it made no difference. The talk had been of marriage and children and buying a house. But one night, after a few drinks with friends, he'd walked home alone and blacked out by the canal. Kat had received a visit from the police at three in the morning, saying Torin was in intensive care with hypothermia. Following that she was anxious every time he was late home without telling her; they often argued. It became rancorous. It was a relief when they separated, although he had missed her terribly for a long time.

Six months after splitting with Kat, he got together with Louise at the Christmas office-party, and it was the first thing he told her when they woke in his flat. Within ten minutes Louise had gathered her clothes and left, explaining she couldn't cope with another doomed relationship. Her previous boyfriend had been paralysed from a skiing-accident.

That was when he decided long-term involvements were off-limits. Paragliding with Graham and his friends was a good substitute. He kept quiet about his condition, knowing that his mates would insist he packed it in. If something happened in the air, it would be just too bad. It would end soon enough anyway, if the medics were right about the prognosis.

'I didn't mean to hurt you, Sunny.'

'How can you not hurt if you spend time with someone without care? I not a dream you can just wake to forget.'

'Of course I cared Sunny. It was beautiful.' He paused. 'But there is no future for us.'

There was a long silence. Both of them were staring at their screens, searching for a way through the sadness.

'Thank you for sharing this.' Sunny spoke quietly, her words spinning a fragile, gossamer thread of connectivity across the time zones. 'I understand you are scared. But you know you can trust me. Maybe I can help. Be your friend.'

There was another long silence. She dabbed her eyes with a tissue.

'The doctors say it will get worse.' Torin was trying to keep his voice steady. 'When it becomes more frequent and more obvious, it will affect the kind of work I can manage, as well as daily living. Probably stop me from flying, as I'll be refused insurance.' He told her about falling in the canal. 'I nearly died.'

'We all die. Only sure thing about living. Just not know when.'

'Uncertainty doesn't offer much reassurance though.'

'Tell me what happens,' she said softly.

She listened as he described the symptoms. He could see her writing on a notepad. When she'd finished, she pushed the paper to one side and looked at the screen. 'Are you coming to Chengdu for *Pitch Perfect?*'

'The company needs someone to go, because of the orders. I suggested Marcus, my deputy.'

'Why don't you come? I know a Chinese doctor maybe help. It's worth trying.'

'There is no cure, Sunny. We must be realistic.'

'I *am* realistic. We each make and decide our own life. You need to be optimism.'

Two weeks later he had arrived at Shuangliu airport.

In that fortnight Sunny had time to do her own thinking. She'd messaged Huang Guo straight away to tell her.

'*You mad?*'

'*What do you mean?*'

'*After what happened with Wang Yi.*'

'*Splitting up?*'

'*Deceit. Remember?*'

Wang Yi had encouraged her to do modelling work for a phone company in Chengdu. She'd been hesitant, but it only involved an occasional weekend and the money was good. After the fifth shoot, the photographer asked if she'd be interested in other work for a magazine. Maybe a few sexy poses? She turned it down, but Wang Yi was strangely insistent. He offered to be at the shoot. Crazy not to do it, he said. Make more money in one session than a month at your company. He promised he'd stop the shoot if it was getting out of hand, so she agreed. It had been okay at first, just face shots and a profile. Then the photographer wanted her to take off her tee shirt. Wang Yi assured her it was okay. She'd felt uneasy, but he was insistent, so she slipped the cotton V-neck over her head and stood facing the photographer. Lift your chest higher, he'd instructed. As she arched her back, she felt fingers slide up the curve of her spine and slip the catch of her bra in a practiced movement. She turned to see Wang Yi's laughing face, as she covered herself with her arms. The photographer was also grinning. Earn more with boobs showing. Even more if you go all the way.

Wang Yi grabbed her hands, dragging them down to her sides, so she was exposed to the camera that was clicking away. Swiftly, she kicked Wang Yi in the crutch and swung her fist at the photographer, knocking the camera from his hands. The sound of breaking glass gave some satisfaction as she gathered her clothes. She turned the handle of the door and glanced back to see the photographer holding his head. 'Stop her, or no cut.' Wang Yi was moaning on the floor, both hands clutching his groin. She slammed the door. Later she discovered that Wang Yi had also been paid a 'management' fee by the phone company. She deleted his details and never answered his calls. A month later he moved to Shanghai.

It was early afternoon when Torin and Sunny reached the outskirts of Baisha Village. The single track, that crossed the flat plain past the farmsteads, opened into two parallel streets lined with traditional houses. A cluster of bicycles was parked in the shade of the jacaranda trees. People walked along the thoroughfare of grey-brown, interlocking slabs of stone, beside the gully for the rainwater run-off, with steps across to the shopfronts.

He noticed a few western faces as they walked the length of the street, but the village was a different world to the tourist attraction of Li Jiang. They strolled past a shop with Batik fabric drying in the sun; another selling embroidered shirts and dresses; a man sitting on a small, wooden horse, beating sheets of copper into bowls; and a group of women squatting on steps in front of baskets of vegetables, resting their backs against the wooden-panelling of the house. The eldest called a greeting as the couple walked past.

'She wishes good luck.'

'It sounded like another language?'

'You're right. Different dialect. Here Naxi. One of minority groups in China. *Hànzú* is most people, like me, but some places, like Yunnan are different. You remember the woman we saw at Wenshu Monastery?'

'With the blue jacket and headscarf?'

'Yes, special colours of Naxi. Been here a thousand years. I think language have symbols like you see on Egypt stones.'

'Hieroglyphics?'

'If that means picture-symbols.'

On the main street they hesitated in front of the Impression Baisha Café. The menu was written on a large whiteboard, beside glazed panels that formed the entrance to the shaded courtyard of the restaurant.

'Let's try Yak. Special Naxi dish.'

The food arrived on a sizzling plate, chunks of meat sitting on a bed of fried potatoes, tomatoes, onions and peppers, with a spicy sauce.

'*Mǐfàn?*'

Torin nodded. 'That's one Chinese word I do know.' He watched Sunny spoon rice onto his plate.

'Are minority languages protected?'

'Protected? How?'

'Encouraged. In UK we have Welsh in one part of the country. Also Gaelic in some areas of Scotland. But a hundred years ago, the languages almost disappeared. Teachers forbidden to use them in school. Sometimes children were beaten if they didn't speak English.'

'I don't know if it's protected, but I'm sure they not beaten. It's more of a choice by people themselves what language they want to speak. Many young people move to city, like Chengdu, and use Mandarin for government job, like teacher, or police. And then people slowly forget how to speak Naxi.'

After lunch they strolled around the village. Torin was fascinated by its timelessness. The heat was evaporating from the day when they approached the entrance to the clinic. The hand-painted, wooden-sign said *Jade Dragon Snow Mountain Herbal Medicine Clinic* in black letters between two, red crosses.

Torin read out the words pinned on the front door.

*'We work hard for the world and the future. All for one and one for all. Benevolence in medical practice. We use Chinese techniques and medicines as well as herbal medicines to treat everything from everyday ailments to complex, difficult diseases. Real therapeutic results due to comprehensive understanding and a dialectic approach.*

*To achieve successful treatment, patients must be confident in their own cure, optimistic in attitude, conduct their own lives rationally, improve their knowledge of public health, and apply both western and Chinese medicine where appropriate. Life and disease co-exist, each moving in tandem. Optimism is the best medicine. Avoid smoking and drinking. Eat simply, live simply, but above all be optimistic.*

*I wish you peace and good health.'*

The reception-area was laid out like a museum, with photos of celebrities, framed accolades and quotations jostling for space on the walls. Book shelves gushed with literature, and several texts were suspended by string from the high ceiling. They stood in front of a life-sized photograph of a man in a buttoned-up white coat over a blue fleece, zipped to the open neck. A white, wispy goatee-beard covered his Adam's apple and brushed against his lips, which were pressed tightly on a face lined with experience. A black beanie was pushed over his forehead and dark, penetrating eyes stared intently at the photographer.

'This was my father.' They turned to see an old man in a white coat behind them. He bore a striking resemblance to the photograph. 'He died last year. I have the privilege of carrying on the work of his clinic. You must be Mister Cameron from London? Your appointment is with Doctor Zhang. He is a graduate from the school of Chinese medicine in Xi'an.'

They were ushered into a side room, where a middle-aged man with a long, grey beard sat on a wooden chair. His eyes were closed and he seemed to be meditating. On the wall were illustrated diagrams showing various dimensions of the human body: skeleton, muscles, blood system, lymph network, and *qi* pressure points. On the shelves, buckets labelled with Chinese characters jostled for space between measuring cylinders, weighing scales and books.

Behind the door, a four-foot wide-framed embroidery hung on the wall, showing an oarsman poling a traditional wooden-raft towards a cluster of houses, each with steps down to the surface of the water.

The old man opened his eyes and reached out his hand. 'Good afternoon. I am Doctor Zhang.' The English was measured. 'Have you come far?'

'Only from Li Jiang today.' Torin smiled. 'But Chengdu yesterday, which is where Chen Xi lives. And before that from London.'

'A long journey then. Is this consultation the reason for your visit to China?'

Torin was surprised at the question. 'Yes,' he said, then glanced at Sunny. 'Well, not entirely.'

The old man smiled. 'I can feel your presence overlapping, and that itself is a good thing. You carry optimism between you.'

'We read that on your sign outside.'

'That was Doctor Ho. But we all believe it. A lot of Chinese medicine relies on attitude of mind. Tell me why you have come.'

'My head.' Torin touched the raised, purple weal on his neck, and talked about the epilepsy and the ensuing treatment.

The doctor rested his hand on Torin's knee. 'I am sorry. I was not very clear. Tell me about the journey that led you here.'

Torin frowned. 'Am I not explaining what has happened?'

'You are giving me the facts, which are important, of course. But I am more interested in the *thinking* that brought you to Baisha. Why have you come here instead of the operating theatre at the Royal Marsden? I spent time there in my training, so I know it is good. They can do wonderful things for the brain.'

Torin hesitated. The answer seemed simple. Because of Sunny. Is that what the doctor wanted to hear?

Unbidden, the memory of the first discussion with his GP eight years ago rose up. He had gone because he'd fallen off his bike in front of a bus. Fortunately, the driver stopped in time. It was then they'd diagnosed the epilepsy. The subsequent six-monthly ECG tests and the yearly MRI showed the damage was worsening. He had done his research and knew the trajectory of the worst-case scenarios. But it was all very slow, and the doctor explained he could well live into his seventies or eighties, as long as he was careful.

Then four years ago he'd been referred to the Marsden because of the swelling in his neck. Lymphoedema was diagnosed. The cyst was removed, but separating from Kat and the night with Louise after the office party were all part of a predictable journey. He had come away from his last consultation at the Marsden in March, resigned to the fact that he was not in sufficient working-order to be anyone's husband.

But then he'd met Sunny.

He explained all this to Doctor Zhang.

'Were you lonely as a child?'

'Not really. Like most children I wondered at times if I'd been adopted, when it seemed I was the odd one out. But I was close to my sister. Generally, we got on okay— more so when my parents died.'

'Was that recently?'

Torin shook his head. 'No. Fifteen years ago. I was still at school.'

'What happened.'

'Boxing Day tsunami. It was their retirement holiday. My mother had always wanted to visit Thailand and they spent a month in Chiang Mai and Bangkok before going to a resort on Phuket for Christmas. My elder brothers and my sister and I flew out to join them for a week of surfing and swimming around the islands. They were walking along the beach when the waves hit. My sister and I were on higher ground, so we survived.' His voice faltered, as he recalled the huge ridge of water sweeping across the bay.

'Very sad.' Doctor Zhang waited for Torin to continue.

'Their bodies were never found. It is some consolation knowing they were all together, but not a good way to die. I was fifteen and my sister seventeen, so we moved in with our grandmother in London till we finished school. Our house in Forres was sold and the money held in trust. My sister struggled at school, so we actually finished A levels in the same year. I went to the London School of Economics and Emily moved to New Zealand with her boyfriend, who had been studying in the same sixth form. They both enrolled in Otago University.'

Doctor Zhang looked thoughtful. 'So, you've been on your own since then?'

'Not exactly. When I was at university, I stayed with my grandmother a lot, especially during vacations. After graduating, I used my share of our parents' estate to buy an apartment in London, and moved from Gran's house, but we still keep in close contact. She's ninety-five next birthday and beginning to slow a bit, so I go to her house at least once a week.'

'Is she your father's mother?'

'Mother's mother. Scandinavian. Came to England from Sweden at the end of the war. A lot of close friends had died and she wanted a fresh start somewhere new. She was very young and I think she had relations in London. That's where she met my grandfather, who was working as an air-raid protection warden.'

He thought about Granny Mette, living alone in her mews house in Kensington. His grandfather had been killed trying to save a family from a building hit by an incendiary bomb. But Mette would only have been in her early twenties when that happened. He'd seen a photograph, taken on a farm in the Cotswolds, not long after the war ended. Standing between two men in RAF uniform, laughing at the camera, blonde hair curving onto her shoulders. Torin looked at the girl sitting beside him, thinking Mette would have been five years younger than Sunny when the war finished.

He wondered why she'd not become involved with anyone else. It wasn't like she'd lived as a recluse. Her house always hummed, accommodating undergraduate students from the local college in spare rooms, hosting visiting artists whose work she exhibited at her gallery, not to mention the friends he and Emily brought back.

As he talked about the apparent contradictions, it seemed a long way from Baisha village and the consultation with the expert in Chinese medicine. 'I'm not sure what this has to do with anything?'

'Everything connects,' replied Doctor Zhang. 'The

challenge is to understand how.' He pressed his fingers to the scar on Torin's neck, then ran his palms over Torin's bare back, before taking both his hands. He closed his eyes in silent prayer. There was a long silence in the room, broken only by the cheeping of the chit-chats darting in and out of the eaves above.

Doctor Zhang opened his eyes. 'I will make up some medicines this evening. Can you come back tomorrow?'

Torin hesitated, but Sunny intervened. 'Can do. When?'

'The clinic opens at ten o'clock, so any time after that.'

'*Shí diǎn yī kè,*' said Sunny. 'That give a quarter of hour of calmness.' They stepped over the sill, into the warm sunshine.

'Are you okay about walking back again tomorrow?' asked Torin.

'Maybe stay here. What do you think?'

'In Baisha?'

'Yes, looks like there's a lot rooms. I saw one next to Inspiration Café? Biguiyan Inn. Let's go and see.'

They followed the owner up a spiral staircase to what seemed like a hayloft above a stable. Through the eaves they could see daylight. The room was simply furnished with a metal-framed, double bed and wardrobe; in the corner a washstand and a pitcher of water.

'She says restroom downstairs and they keep light in corridor.'

'How much?'

'One hundred kuai.'

'Each?'

'Both.'

Torin paid the money and they went outside. Sunny

looked up and down the wide street. 'What do you like to do?'

'At the entrance to the village, I saw a sign saying School of Naxi Art. Might be interesting to visit?'

Sunny led the way through the backstreets of the village, checking once with a young woman carrying two vegetable-laden linen-bags. They walked beneath the archway of the school into a courtyard where six girls worked at desks, with different pieces of embroidery. One stood to greet them, hands pressed as she bowed. Her cropped hair was twisted into two bunches, tied with a black bow that hung over each ear. An embroidered, white blouse was tucked into her short, grey skirt. When she smiled, the eyes in her round, tanned face almost closed as the lids pressed together. Torin guessed she was fifteen or sixteen years old.

She introduced herself as Ngy Wen and took them on a brief tour of the school, explaining how the government was paying for the school to preserve Naxi embroidery-skills, which were nearly lost during the Cultural Revolution when such activities were banned.

In the small shop next door, where the mounted art-work was displayed, they recognised the picture they'd seen in Doctor Zhang's consulting room. 'Maybe take three or four weeks to do each one.'

'This is very important part of Naxi culture,' explained Ngy Wen. 'Also dancing, singing and music. Tomorrow night is concert in Li Jiang, with many Naxi performers. Maybe you come? I will be one dancer.'

'Have you been here long?'

Ngy Wen frowned. 'Over three years. We didn't have

313

much education in my village near mountains. I help with farm work, but the money no good. We have three children, not enough food for everyone. I came here twenty-five years old.'

Dusk was settling over the quiet streets of Baisha, as they strolled back to their accommodation. Chen Xi took his hand. 'What you think of the doctor?'

'To be honest, Sunny, it was a bit of a mystery. I wasn't sure why he was asking some questions—like about my parents.'

'He is Taoist.' She explained about *yin* and *yang* and beliefs about balance and counter-balance. 'That is why he say "everything connects". I am glad we here, Torin. Feels good.'

Outside the Biguiyan Inn, two women had set up a barbeque-stall. One turned sticks over the glowing charcoal, the other served food to customers waiting patiently in a line. On the vegetable-platter Torin recognised slices of lotus fruit between strips of potato, bamboo and aubergine.

'Would you like something to eat?'

She shook her head and smiled. 'I'm not hungry after Yak. Prefer to go inside.'

# Chapter Twenty-three:

## Baisha:
## Monday 14th September 2019

Doctor Zhang offered them tea and they sat in the shaded courtyard at the back of the clinic, watching the dappled sunshine dance across terracotta paving-slabs.

The doctor lifted the small, porcelain cup to his nose. 'This is from Mount Emei. Very good in the morning, releases positive energy.' He took a sip and carefully replaced the cup on the saucer. 'Your case is very interesting and challenging. I have made some medicine for you and it may be helpful if I explain my thinking.'

Torin sat forward. He breathed deeply, trying to control rising anxiety.

'After you left last night, I sat here for a long time, troubled by what you had told me. You are a young man with a condition that usually affects people who are older. Some might say you are just unlucky, but I think luck is not entirely random. I remember reading something your famous Prime Minister Winston Churchill wrote: *"Life is a whole and luck is a whole and no part of it can be separated from the rest."*'

'*Audentes Fortuna iuvat.*' The words of the Latin proverb drifted into Torin's mind. Was it fortune favours the bold, or the strong, or the brave? He couldn't remember. Maybe it was all three?

'So yes, it is unusual and unfortunate to have this condition so young, but you have experienced great trauma, and the shock to your system of your parents' death is bound to have affected you.'

They listened as Doctor Zhang described how western medicine concentrated on the blood system and the connections between the heart and other organs. 'Since the time of Leonardo da Vinci, doctors and surgeons have had a good understanding of the physical structure of muscles and bones, and the way these are nourished and nurtured by the flow of blood.'

He pointed at one of the wall-charts, explaining how some Chinese physicians had focused their interest on the lymph system, which operated like a parallel railway-track to the blood system, with some overlapping stations that allowed transfer between the two networks. 'Similar to the way metro-systems have interchanges.' He described how lymph replenishes the blood with red blood-cells and white blood-cells, playing an important role in maintaining the body's immunities. 'Lymphoedema is an over accumulation of fluid. The Chinese term is *tán yǐn*. *Tán* refers to thickened fluids and *Yǐn* to thin fluids and together they are pathological, warning us that something is not right.'

He touched Torin's neck. 'Although you have had the cyst removed, it doesn't seem to have affected the epilepsy. But we know conditions of the brain can be difficult to address. There are no magic potions that guarantee success. All we can do is try and support the body in developing its own response.' He took a sip from his cup. 'Are you following me?'

Torin nodded, sensing Doctor Zhang knew exactly where he was going, as he listened to him talking about a man called Gong Tingxian. It was like a Wikipedia entry, with dates and medical terms embedded in the tale of the old Chinese physician from the Ming Dynasty, who had developed herbal therapies for treating lymphoedema conditions. After curing the favourite concubine of the King of Lu, who suffered from severe abdominal pains, he was appointed physician at the Imperial Medical Academy. It was 1593 and he was seventy-one years old. Gong lived another twenty-six years and was a prolific writer. 'He described his treatments in his book *Wànbìng Huíchūn,* which translates as "Restoration of Health", because *huí* means return and *chūn* refers to Spring. His favoured herbs included magnolia bark, liquorice, ginger, citrus and cardamom, as well as less well-known plants like hoelen, atractylodes, pinellia, arisaema, saussurea and cyperus.'

Doctor Zhang glanced across at Sunny, catching her eye to draw her into the explanation. 'Last night I looked through Doctor Gong's writings—we have many of his books in our library here—and I meditated at length when I woke this morning, confident my mind will have been working on this while I was asleep.

'It led me to make up several medicines for you to try.' He pointed to three jars beside the table. 'The instructions are written in English and Chinese. Each has a different way of encouraging the lymph system and supporting the body. You will experience more *qi*—the vital life energy force, which flows through us all. This will strengthen your body's ability to challenge. But we are talking about enhancing capacity, not guaranteeing victory.' He paused, brown eyes looking straight at Torin. 'I cannot promise this will cure you. I cannot even say whether there is a good

317

chance or a small chance. It is not possible to give percentage probabilities. In any case that would not help you, as each individual is very different. If I say to a patient that there is only one per cent chance of recovery, it is quite possible for him to be that one person in a hundred. Does this make sense?'

Torin noticed the pressure of Sunny's fingers. 'I am very grateful for your time and effort.'

The doctor smiled, rubbing his beard. 'You are lucky to have met each other.'

Spontaneously, Torin and Sunny reached across the table, each holding one of Doctor Zhang's hands. Torin registered the vitality in the wiry fingers and the electricity passing through them. For several minutes no one spoke. The call of a distant pigeon and snuffling of a piglet next door only strengthened the power of the silence in the small courtyard.

Torin felt a calmness fill his body. Finally, a cockerel broke the spell, crowing loudly from a chicken-coop. After a final, gentle squeeze, their hands dropped to their sides. They left the doctor sitting beneath the banana tree.

The two young people were silent a long time on the walk back to Li Jiang. As they came past the farmhouse, where the herd of pigs had run out in front of them, Sunny reached for his hand. 'What are you thinking, Torin?'

'How lucky that I met you, Sunny.'

'Same for me.'

'This is not going to be a quick fix. You heard the doctor. The medicine may help, but equally it may make no difference.'

'We both know that. We also know optimism

important, as well as medicine. I optimistic.'

He pulled her close, feeling the warmth of her body beneath the embroidered blouse she'd bought in Baisha. They could hear a bamboo partridge calling beyond the baked, red bricks of the farmhouse. *Ki-ko-kua... ki-ko-kua... ki-ko-kua...*

# Chapter Twenty-four:

## Shuangliu airport:
## 22nd September 2019

Having checked-in Torin's suitcase, they sat in the airport restaurant, sharing bowls of dumplings.

'Very different to when here in Spring.' She smiled. 'I finish food this time.'

'I'm sorry Sunny. It was so stupid.'

'No need be sorry. Part of journey.'

It was a week since they had flown back from Li Jiang, checking Torin in to the St. Regis Hotel, four hours after leaving their room with the balcony that looked across the rooftops.

The first evening in Chengdu they met with Sunny's parents at a small restaurant near her home. Torin had sat awkwardly beside her father, frustrated by his inability to communicate anything but the most basic pleasantries. Sunny had to act as translator the whole evening.

After the meal Torin produced his bank card, only to find that Lu Tian Yi had already paid the bill. He looked helplessly at Sunny.

'You our guest. My family is very happy meet you,' she said simply.

The four of them stood on the pavement outside the restaurant. Torin shook hands with mother and father and looked at Sunny. 'Shall I see you tomorrow?'

She hesitated, her finger brushing her lower lip. 'I was going to come with you tonight.'

Torin glanced at Wang Yun Ling and Lu Tian Yi, who were smiling impassively at the interchange. 'Is that okay with your parents?'

She smiled at his confusion. 'Yes, of course. They know we are together. I'm not a little girl anymore. They want me to have a boyfriend for so long, especially now I am twenty-six. You only in Chengdu a few days. I'm not missing you while here.' Her voice quietened as she looked directly at Torin. 'Plenty of time for sadness when gone.'

Every morning they breakfasted in the dining-room of the hotel, having found a quiet corner surrounded by trickling water features, where they could be unobserved. Sunny took the metro to China UK Ventures, while Torin met representatives from each of the companies who wanted to work with *Pitch Perfect*. One evening they went to a restaurant with Huang Guo and Lin Ting and their respective boyfriends, and another with Gloria and colleagues from CUV.

Between these times there were evenings alone—at the Sichuan Opera, followed by a meal at the top of the 339 TV Tower, and at Kathmandu, where they ate at the same table as before.

Every night they took the lift to their bedroom in the St. Regis, making the most of the jacuzzi pool and cotton bath-robes.

They knew the magic wouldn't last forever. But this time they also knew Sunny would not be leaping down the escalator, desperate to get away. They had booked a flight for her to come to London in January, just before the start of Chinese New Year. Torin had already emailed his boss with a request for several weeks leave from *Pitch Perfect*.

'It will be the middle of winter. Maybe very cold.'

'I don't care if freezing. In fact, I want see snows in London. We can throw balls and get white together.' She was determined they do the London sights. And meet his grandmother. She liked the sound of Granny Mette. Torin's description of her reminded Sunny of *Zǔfù*.

On their last evening they agreed to have a farewell meal with Sunny's parents. They strolled from the St. Regis hotel to the restaurant Lu Tian Yi had chosen in the Narrow Alley. It was late afternoon and the September sun warmed their necks. as they walked hand-in-hand along small backstreets parallel to Zhong Fu Road, joining Tianfu square at the northeast corner. Torin looked back at the busy pavements beside the main road, recalling the day he'd emerged from the metro beneath the towering statue of Chairman Mao. Was it really only five months?

Sunny led the way along Shaocheng Road and through the entrance to People's Park. The calm of the still water in the lush beds of lotus flowers soaked up the hum of the city beyond the trees. As they walked through the tea-house in the central pavilion, with its bamboo roof and carved dragon-gargoyles, they passed a man bending over a woman. Her head was resting on the wooden table, left cheek pressed against the circular glass-top. Grey tresses splayed across the table and her brown eyes were wide open.

The man was wearing the robes of a monk, with his hair tied into a top-knot, skewered by a thin stick of blackened bamboo. He lowered a brass rod into the canal of her right ear. The woman flinched, and the monk paused, then rotated the polished, metal stave by rubbing his hands backwards and forward. The woman's lips moved, as if she was chanting a prayer.

Torin saw a set of gleaming sticks protruding from a leather pouch, buckled to the monk's waist. It looked like a quiver of arrows, without the fletchling of feathers. He turned to Sunny, curious to understand.

'Removing wax,' she explained. 'Hope not cough.' Her hand pointed to an archway at the end of the path. 'We go along Xiao Nan street and then we there.'

They crossed a road beside hoardings, which looked like a set of protective barriers for excavation work. A picture of the skeleton of a shattered house caught Torin's eye.

'What is this?'

'Maybe building work for new metro line?'

'This is something about war.' Torin pointed at the adjacent board, with images of aircraft diving towards the roofline of a city. 'And this next photo?' The blurred black and white picture showed a huddle of men, women and children in a doorway, wide eyes looking up at the sky.

Sunny was silent as she digested the Chinese. 'This where people hide from bombs. Also writing in English.' She pointed to an information-panel set into the wall beside the hoardings. Ornately-carved tiles, with fierce face-masks etched into the interlinked coils, provided a protective overhang against the rain.

Torin read the wording beneath the Chinese characters. *Site of Air-Raid Shelter in Anti-Japanese War Period. This was used by Chinese civilians to escape the indiscriminate bombing from Japanese Mitsubishi and Nagasaki aircraft during the War of Resistance against Japanese Aggression*

*1937-1945. The city of Chengdu underwent six years of attacks by the Imperial Japanese Air Force from November 8, 1938, to December 18, 1944.'*

He frowned. 'I had no idea Chinese cities were bombed like in Britain. In school we learnt about the Allied battles against the Nazis, and we knew there had been fighting in Singapore and Burma. People still talk about the Second World War as if it's part of our collective memory. It's not only old people who were alive then, like my grandmother. War films like *Dunkirk* and *Saving Private Ryan* are watched by everyone.'

'We also see British and American movies. Subtitles help us learn English, even black films like *Dambusters.*'

'But nearly every story is about fighting Germans.' Torin scratched his head. 'Maybe one or two are in the Far East, like *Bridge over the River Kwai*. But I've never seen a film showing Chinese soldiers fighting the Japanese.'

'All children learn about War of Resistance. We taught about horrible things Japanese do in Nanjing and other cities. Thirty million Chinese people killed.'

Torin's eyes widened. 'Do you mean thousands? Thirty million is like half the population of England.'

'I know difference between million and thousand.' Sunny ran her hand through her long, black hair, letting the strands slide through her fingers. 'It is why many Chinese people not like Japan. But it all long time ago. We should continue to restaurant.'

A cry carried across the street. They looked up from the notice-board to see an old man walking towards them. He was wearing a red jacket, buttoned tight to the collar.

'*Zǔfù!*

Lu Zhe Ming smiled as he kissed Sunny's cheek. Then he turned to Torin and his expression changed. He pointed at Torin's face with a trembling hand and jabbed the board behind. '*Guǐ, Guǐ, Guǐ.*' His spectacles slipped down his nose.

Sunny raised her voice, shrilly insistent, and the old man stepped back, shaking his head and muttering. The hammer and sickle insignia on his cap flashed in the afternoon sunlight.

'What's wrong? Doesn't he recognise me?' asked Torin.

'He imagine things.'

'Has something scared him?'

'I tell you later,' she spoke quietly but firmly.

'Did he come by bus from Dazhentou?'

Sunny shook her head. 'Too far. My father went and picked him up. I think he gone to park the car.'

Lu Tian Yi had booked a private room in Fu Li's, so they could all sit around one table. Torin was introduced to the relatives he'd not met, including Wang Yu Ling's parents and her two sisters living in Chengdu, as well as two of Lu Tian Yi's brothers. Torin was placed on the right of the father, with Sunny beside him. Great-grandfather, who was sitting next to Sunny, leant across and squeezed Torin's biceps. '*Niánqīng zhēn hǎo, xiǎohuǒzi hěn qiángzhuàng.*'

Sunny laughed. '*Zǔfù* say it's good to be a young, strong boy. He wants you to help him with the farm again.'

'Tell him I would be delighted, but I'm leaving tomorrow. I will go back next time.'

Torin watched the old man's face crease into a grin, as he listened to Sunny and then responded.

'*Zǔfù* believe your promise. He will be waiting.'

Torin took Lu Zhe Ming's hand. '*Zài jiàn.*'

'You speak Chinese perfect. Now he certain you meet again.'

'Can you ask him about the air-raid shelter?'

Sunny turned back to her great-grandfather. There was a long exchange. Lu Zhe Ming pointed at Torin, '*Ta kàn qǐlái yīyàng. Tài xiàng le.*'

'*Tài xiàng le?*' Sunny repeated the statement, shaking her head in disagreement.

'*Duì duì duì.*' Great-grandfather nodded vigorously.

'*Ganbei!*' Lu Tian Yi had poured a generous shot of baijiu into Torin's tumbler and stood to clink glasses, before walking round the table to share a toast with his brothers.

Sunny nudged Torin. 'Do the same as my father. *Gānbēi* with them.'

'What about *Zǔfù*??'

'He also man. *Gānbēi* him too.'

'I mean what did he say about the shelter?'

'I'll explain when we go back to the hotel.' Sunny hesitated. 'He tell me to look at the photos on the wall beside restroom over there.' She was frowning as she pointed to the corridor that led to the toilets. 'He not making sense. That happened with my great-grandmother. She lose mind altogether.' Her face brightened, as her father approached their side of the table with a raised glass of baijiu. 'Anyway, important you *gānbēi* with men.'

'And the women?'

'*Gānbēi* everyone if you can stay standing. It polite. But you don't have to empty the glass every time.' She smiled. 'I don't want you drunk tonight.'

Now they stood beside the security gate, unwilling to let go. Torin sensed something was not right. 'Is anything the matter?' he asked quietly.

She shook her head. 'It okay, Torin. Just need to stay optimistic.'

'You're not worrying I'll change my mind?'

She laughed. 'I hope not. I have booked my flight tickets. If you can't meet me, I'll look for Sherlock Holmes.' Two nights before, they'd watched Benedict Cumberbatch give the speech at Watson's wedding.

'I'll be counting the days.'

She handed him a brown envelope with his name written on the front. 'Small present. Please only open on the plane. Keep in your pocket for now.'

They kissed again and Torin showed his passport and boarding card to the security guard.

As he disappeared behind the glass screen, Sunny was relieved he hadn't asked any more questions about her great-grandfather.

On the aircraft Torin took the envelope from his pocket. Inside was a sheet of paper and a tiny red envelope, the size of the greeting cards Granny Mette attached to presents at Christmas. He unfolded the paper and realised it was the first time he's seen anything hand-written by Sunny. The letters were clearly formed, and gently sloping to the right.

*'After you talked to me from London, I went to Wenshu monastery next day. I bought incense at the temple, and I pray you will come back to Chengdu. I pray I will see you again. I pray you will get better. The time we had together was short but is the most beautiful time I ever had. Very special. I bought*

*you this to keep you safe. We call it hùshēnfú. I think English means protective amulet. It is my blessing to you. May God be with you all time. I love you.'*

He lifted the flap of the red envelope, and a laminated triangle of card fell onto his lap. Torin studied the three red characters on the yellow background.

# Part Four

Study the past if you would define the future
孔夫子 Kǒng Zǐ (Confucius)

# Chapter Twenty-five

## Shell Hus, Copenhagen:
## June 25th 1944

Through the air vent at the back of the prison-van Harry worked out they were driving east. At Nyborg the vehicle queued to board a ferry, then bumped and clattered onto the metal-deck of the ship. Bolts were slid back, handcuffs unlocked and replaced, with his hands in front, and he was allowed up on deck. The policemen stood either side of him at the handrail.

A woman walking past said something in Danish to the taller guard, who shrugged. She reached in her bag and handed Harry a sausage wrapped in a thick wedge of bread, then hurried away before he had a chance to thank her. He lifted his manacled hands to his face, smelling the meat. He wolfed the sandwich, watching the red-roofed buildings on Funen disappear into the summer-haze. It was a beautiful day. The sun was high in a magenta-blue sky. Seagulls wheeled and dived above the ship as it steamed across Storebaelt, passing an island midway to Sjaelland.

Harry closed his eyes, feeling the sun soothing his skin as he breathed in the fresh air laced with salt and the smell of seaweed. He was back on Brighton beach, hearing wooden struts of deck-chairs clicking into slots, waves breaking over the shingle, and pebbles rustling against each other, as the sea dragged them beneath the pier. He tasted the first lick of an ice cream and smelt doughnuts frying, beside the stall selling candy floss, whisked from pink sugar.

He opened his eyes and looked into the grey water, foaming past the prow of the ship as it cut through the placid sea. He thought about jumping, but there was no chance he could swim for long with his wrists bound. In any case the June sunshine would only have warmed a few inches of the sea's surface. Still, drowning might be better than what awaited him. Arisaig had made it clear the Gestapo were tough with Special Operations personnel. He had declined the offer of a poison-capsule in a tooth-cavity, not wanting to tempt Lady Luck. Harry studied the coastline around Korsør, weighing his chances of flailing his way onto the sand-bars.

As if the guards could read his mind, he was ushered below deck and shoved back into the vehicle. Through the vent he watched the van bounce up the ramp onto the dockside and along the highway towards København. The sun was still high when it stopped again. Harry was bundled from the mobile prison onto a wide, cobbled road. He looked up to see a seven-storey building with barred windows on one side of the street. On the other, in a mustard-coloured house with a red-tiled roof, he heard children singing.

'*Til skrivning din tilståelse*,' grunted the guard, prodding him towards the dark, wooden door with his revolver. Harry was taken inside, up three flights and along narrow corridors, then pushed into a small room. He turned to see the two men had drawn their truncheons. There was no window, with the only light from a naked bulb in the ceiling.

'We want the names of people who hide you. Also information about mission.' The taller man with a wispy, blonde moustache, patted the head of the smooth rubber-club against the palm of his gloved hand. He spoke English with a strong accent.

'I am Wing Commander Harold Winchester, Royal Air Force. Number 81452369. I am a prisoner of war and demand to be treated according to the Geneva convention.'

The guard smiled, revealing a missing tooth. 'We want names. Information. You speak. We listen. Or else.' The truncheon tapped his leather glove.

Harry tried to empty his eyes of expression. His mouth felt dry. 'I am a British prisoner of war,' he forced the words through clenched lips.

The first blow knocked him to his knees. Harry lifted his hands to protect his face. A heavy boot crashed on his cheek, knocking him against the wall. He crumpled, curling into a foetal-position as instructed at Arisaig. Truncheons fell on his back and head, and steel-tipped boots cracked into his ribs and solar plexus.

At one point he was sick, throwing up the remains of the sausage. There was a pause in the beating and the men laughed while he retched. Then the taller man reached down to drag his face across the vomit-streaked boards. The stench was awful. The beating and screaming started again and he focused on protecting his face and stomach, till the room slipped sideways and blackness overwhelmed him.

At the grating of bolts being drawn back, he woke to see the same two men standing in the entrance to his cell. He was lying on a wooden frame. A stinking, metal-bucket was the only other piece of furniture. Daylight showed through the tiny barred-window above his head. He had no way of telling what time it was. His mouth felt foul from the vomit and he could taste blood caking his lips as he moved his tongue across his teeth, measuring the damage.

'Kom med os.'

Harry indicated he needed to relieve himself in the bucket, and his handcuffs were removed for as long as necessary. As he limped along the corridor Harry could barely see through his swollen, right eye, his front teeth ached from the truncheon blows, and there was a singing in his left ear. A door at the end of the passageway was opened to reveal a single, wooden chair in front of a desk. On the other side sat a flaxen-haired young man in uniform, with a neatly-ironed shirt-collar and black tie visible above the line of gleaming buttons on his jacket, with its SS epaulettes sewn on the shoulders. The brown ridge of the collar pressed gently against his prominent Adam's apple. The face was round, like a baby, with a carefully trimmed straw smudge above his upper lip. Neatly coiffured hair, firm, flawless skin and tanned complexion. A picture of youthful health and fitness.

Harry was forced onto the chair and his hands and feet were manacled to the arms and legs. The uniformed-man waved both guards away, closing the door behind them. 'The handcuffs are for your own safety,' the smooth voice spoke quietly, lips stretched in a smile. The English was polished. 'We don't want you tempted to attack me or try to escape, because you know what our warders can do. They are waiting in the adjacent room in case I need them.' He pointed at the intercom on his desk.

The piercing blue eyes surveyed Harry's face. 'A bit bruised I see. Some of my people are—how shall we say?' he paused. 'Over-zealous perhaps? They enjoy their work and can get carried away. We are not happy with the cooperation of the Danish police, so are recruiting men into our own *Hifspolizei*, who we know we can trust. Knud and his brother Steen were whipped by their father for being stupid when they were small boys, so enjoy the opportunity to take revenge. They are sometimes a bit too enthusiastic and we end up with dead prisoners, which is not a good outcome, so I try to rein them in. They mostly stop before that point. Their father was correct though, about them being mentally defective.'

The Gestapo officer reached for a silver box on his desk and flipped the lid to reveal a neat line of white cigarettes. His manicured fingers stroked the rippling surface. 'Would you like one? I can recommend the flavour. The best the Red Cross provide—too good for the prisoners they are intended for.'

He noted Harry's silence. 'Please yourself. I hope you don't mind if I do.' He flicked the catch on the lighter and inhaled deeply, blowing a cloud of smoke towards Harry who coughed and turned his head.

The officer pulled open his desk-drawer and drew out a folded paper and Amy's photo .

'*Deine Freundin?* Your girlfriend?'

'Wife.'

'*Eine schöne Frau.* You must miss her.'

'She is dead. Luftwaffe raid.'

'I am sorry to hear that, but it happens in war of course.' The thin-lipped smile lacked warmth. He replaced the photograph in his drawer. 'I will keep her memory safe.' The ice-blue eyes fixed on Harry. *'Es ist sehr einfach.* Very simple. We want to know about your mission and how you arrived at the farmhouse in Kirkenbjerg. Who helped you on the way? What was the route? Simple questions.'

'I am Wing Commander Harold Winchester. Number 81452369.' Harry struggled to press his lips together and could hear himself mumbling the consonants.

The officer clicked his tongue. 'Don't waste my time repeating your identity card details.' The eyes narrowed. 'Perhaps I should have introduced myself. I am Oberführer Adolf Heydrich, reception manager at Shell Hus hotel. My patience is limited, because there are other guests waiting to meet me. I am not willing to play games, much as you public-school boys like to do that. Your identity card shows you with dark hair, but I am looking at a man with blonde hair. Only people trying to hide something would change their appearance. We can shoot you as a spy—or you can answer my questions.'

Harry repeated his rank, name and number.

Heydrich shook his head. 'So very British, *und so dumm.*' His lips tightened as he pressed the intercom. *'Führt ihn ab.'*

Knud and Steen appeared in the doorway. Harry was dragged along the corridor to an empty room. He was pushed face down on the floor, his arms and legs pinioned by leather-straps screwed into the wooden planks. He could only lift his head and shoulders a few inches. He braced for the blows on his back, pressing his face to the floor and closing his eyes to steady his breathing.

There was a scraping of metal by his right ear. Harry

turned his head to see Knud's boot pushing an electric-fire across the floor. Another fire was placed to his left. A switch clicked and he could feel the bar radiating heat, as the glow changed from a dull red to a whitened orange. His cheeks sweated and he tried to drag his head back into his shoulders. A foot on his neck held him down.

'Who helped? What was the route?' Oberführer Heydrich had come into the room. Harry could see the polished toe-caps of black boots close to his face.

Harry remembered gripping Pierre's hand at Amiens station. He couldn't let him down. Not for anything. He groaned his own name and number. There was a double click and the intensity of the heat increased. His skin stung and blistered.

'Who helped you?' Heydrich spat above his singeing ear.

Harry heard screams roar across the bare floor as he tossed his head from side to side. The fires were pushed closer. He forced his face hard against the wooden boards, flattening his nose and cheeks away from the fierce heat. An acrid stench of burning hair filled his nostrils. A tidal flame rolled across his scalp, licking it clean. Above the screaming he heard laughter.

A bucket of water was tossed over him and he passed out.

Harry came to in his cell, prostrate on the wooden slats, conscious of the stinging in his cheeks, blistered and raw. If he moved his lips, shooting pain bored through his nose deep into his skull. His hands were handcuffed behind his back, so he was unable to touch his head. From the tingling across his scalp he guessed there was nothing left. The sky was darkening through the window and he wondered if he'd be left alone till morning.

It felt like he'd only been asleep minutes when the cell door opened and Knud appeared. '*Kom igen.*' Harry was bundled upstairs into Heydrich's interrogation room. The Gestapo officer was enjoying another cigarette. He tapped the ash into a white bowl beside the silver box and blew on the end of the smouldering tobacco, lifting the cigarette towards Harry's face, as if to offer him a puff. 'We find these make good persuaders, when pressed even closer. Maybe you have enjoyed enough heat for a June day.' His smile lacked humour.

'Everyone cracks in the end, so I would advise you to talk sooner rather than later. It will save your body being completely destroyed.' Heydrich pointed to a small, wooden box with a leather strap and a handle on the desk. 'Do you know what this is?'

The young pilot shook his head, an involuntary gesture.

'A clever way of giving a manicure. *Deine Hand kommt hier rein, so.*' Heydrich pushed his fingers into the tight space. 'This strap holds it firm, so you can't pull away. The vice at the end fixes it tightly to a table. The handle has a curved hook on the end. As you pull downwards, it gouges into the nail and draws it forward. Ouch!' Heydrich removed his fingers and lowered the handle as a demonstration. 'Ingenious, eh? I think the original design came from the Spanish Inquisition.' Harry felt a dryness in his throat, his face-muscles tensing.

'We will give you time to think, before we apply this,' continued Heydrich. 'We have another prisoner next door who is reluctant to talk. Knud will try it out on him first.

That may help loosen his tongue—and yours.'

Knud lifted the contraption from Heydrich's desk and closed the door behind him. For a few minutes there was silence in the office, apart from Heydrich quietly smoking another cigarette. A moan came through the wall followed by a rising cry of 'nej, nej, nej' and then screaming. Harry tried to blot out the torrent of animal-howls that screeched through the partitioning, mixed with crying and pleading. Then there was silence.

'Knud will do one more, to reinforce the point.'

Harry felt his body sweat as the moaning resumed next door. He closed his eyes, desperately holding on to the image of Pierre.

When the yelling had subsided to sobbing, Heydrich stubbed his cigarette into the bowl, alongside the other discarded butts. 'It is well into the evening and I don't usually work so late at the office, especially on a Sunday. My wife will be wondering if anything has happened.' His fingers brushed the neatly-combed, blonde hair and down the nape of his neck. 'We will not do any more now. I will give you the rest of the night to think. Maybe tomorrow you will be ready to talk. If not, we will apply the gentle persuader. If necessary, we will repeat it every day till the weekend.'

Heydrich stood and reached for his greatcoat. He paused in the doorway, looking back at Harry, bound to his chair. The blue eyes were devoid of emotion. 'Of course, you have another hand as well—and then there's your feet.'

Harry lay on the bare planks, unable to sleep. He could feel despair closing in.

Arisaig had been clear about the inevitable breaking-point. Holding out long enough for warning messages to circulate was the only victory that mattered. The first forty-eight hours were crucial. Who was there to warn though? They'd killed Lone, and her sister would be captured by now. Surely Birgitte would have much more valuable information about Holger Danske than him? There was the man who had accompanied him from Flensburg to Odense, but he'd never asked his name, and presumed the black moustache and beard was a disguise.

There was only Pierre and Marie, in the farmhouse in Herbeumont, quietly and bravely resisting the occupation of their homeland. How could he betray them to save himself? Could he conjure up Jacques in a different village from another part of Belgium. Or somewhere in France. The Gestapo would check and come back to him when it produced no result. But that would buy time.

It would be worse if they discovered a link to the SOE, but the Lysander had burned to a skeleton, destroying the maps of the landing field. The only incriminating evidence was the knife with its telltale crest, but the policeman who'd shot Lone had pocketed it before he was pushed into the van. Surely, he wouldn't have handed such a valuable prize to Heydrich? Could he just claim to have been shot down while protecting bombers? It might so easily have happened that way.

Harry looked up at the window and could see two, tiny stars twinkling in the midsummer sky. Were they the lovers Perseus and Andromeda, destined to orbit at a distance from each other for eternity? Like himself and Amy? He stared at the stars, drawing comfort from the distant lights. Amy's presence filtered through the bars.

She could have been sent into France herself and would have been given the same pep talk at Arisaig. What would she advise him to do?

He thought back to their first meeting at Swanton Morley on Hallowe'en in 1941. Amy had been with a group of WAAFs, celebrating a friend's birthday in the snug of the *Angel*. They were part of the radar team at Bylaugh Hall. He'd gone with chaps from the squadron, after they'd been stood down two days. Jimmy Lincoln, the landlord, had seen action with the Royal Flying Corps in France, and was always pleased to welcome girls and boys in blue. Jimmy claimed a family's connection to Abraham Lincoln, and a framed photograph of the President hung above the fireplace, signed by one of his descendants.

Squeezing from the crush at the bar, Harry had spilled beer over Amy's skirt, going down on his knees to lick the froth off the rough, woollen material. Looking up, he'd seen her amber eyes laughing, and knew he wanted to walk out with her.

Four weeks later, in the hotel on Aldeburgh sea-front, after signing in as Mr. and Mrs. Smith, with Amy wearing a curtain ring on Archie's advice, they fumbled through the preliminaries. A few months before, a WAAF girl had taken him back to her small flat in Dereham after a mess-dance. Her house-mates had conveniently gone for the weekend and Doris was eager to be his teacher. So, he wasn't a complete novice—not that Amy seemed inexperienced either. They were relieved when they finally made it. The first time was not that good, but they persevered. By the end of the weekend, there was an intensity that made it difficult to break away and return to their respective billets.

At Christmas they travelled down to London to meet her parents, which felt like an official 'coming out'. Back in East Anglia, at the start of the new year, it was public knowledge they were an item, and saw each other whenever possible. It was tricky though; the Luftwaffe had increased its efforts to bomb industrial production, so they were at work most nights—him in the air and Amy in front of her radar screen. With Jimmy's help they made the most of free moments.

Early in February, Archie and he were assigned to ferry Beaufighters from Lyneham to Cairo. His home shifted to the officers' mess on the edge of the Cotswolds. He was allowed a few days leave between each jaunt, so borrowed Archie's Ford Eight, cashed their petrol coupons, and set off on the five-hour drive to Swanton Morley. Snatched evenings with Amy in *The Angel* simply fuelled the longing. Harry's breathless proposal the night before his fifth sortie was met by an equally heartfelt response, and they clutched the possibility that marriage might mean the Air Ministry would allow them to be together. That flight ended with Archie on a drip in a Cairo hospital and the bet with Chennault.

The Chinese posting had delayed wedding-plans, but they finally clinched it in All Saints Church in January 1943, fourteen months after that first encounter. If only they'd moved to the cottage beside the airfield, it might all have been very different. But they'd put it off, because he'd been immersed in shaping the new squadron, and then Amy was assigned to Arisaig. Had she really objected to the posting? Or had she gone because he'd not been there for her? Despite the warm welcome at the *Angel*, whenever leave coincided, he found it difficult to switch off from the pressure to maintain effective protection for the bomber streams. He was sleeping badly, waking tired every morning, and reliant on strong coffee and Prozac to see him through each flight.

They'd argued about silly things: how she wore her hair, and pronounced words differently, or the way he left the bathroom. He was relieved when she left for Arisaig at the end of February. Nine months later, she returned, saying she wanted to sort things. But during those months apart he'd become increasingly irritable, not helped by the solitary journey to Scarborough. They both knew there was a limit to how much operational-flying people could handle, before crews turned away from targets, terrified at seeing comrades destroyed by flak or enemy-aircraft. As they sat in the Ford Eight outside Bylaugh Hall, just after Christmas, Harry acknowledged he'd been on active-service long enough. He resolved to put in for a desk job when Chalky White returned from leave.

If it hadn't been for that doomed flight on New Year's Day, they would have spent the spring together in the thatched cottage, and begun to imagine a future beyond the end of the war. *If only, if only, if only…* the refrain echoed in his head as he watched Andromeda slip out of view, leaving Perseus orbiting alone in the blackness of space.

# Chapter Twenty-six

## Zhijiang:
## June 26th 1944

'Time to start, fellas. Thanks for makin sure you had your beauty sleep before rockin up. I know it's only six o'clock, but I like to see well-scrubbed faces on full alert.' The gravelly voice reverberated round the ops room, and the General glanced at a young man in the front row stifling a yawn.

He patted the embarrassed pilot on the shoulder. 'Don't mind me, son. Yawnin's good for two reasons. Firstly, it reassures me you're alive, and secondly it means you want to stay that way, because your lungs have worked out your brain needs oxygen.' He turned on his heel and walked to the line of windows looking out on the airstrip. Grey skies were lightening to the east. 'Let's have some mountain-air to freshen us up.' He lifted the catch of the nearest window and swung it open, repeating the action with the other four windows. The pilots nearest the wall shivered at the blast of cold air. 'It'll soon heat up, once the sun hits the tarmac. If you feel frostbite comin on, cuddle your buddy. Don't think you'll be put on a charge as a shirt-lifter. We're here to fight a war, not fanny around with inhibitions.' General Chennault moved back to the centre of the room. 'Talkin of which, I've come to an arrangement at Wang's bar in town. Use that from now on for horizontal exercise. I've flown some Judys in from Guilin. They've been checked for clap. We can't afford to have any of you in the sickbay because your crutch is on fire.'

There was a snigger from the middle row; Chennault's eyes flicked towards its source. 'Buddy here obviously knows what I'm talkin about. Serious stuff fellas. Look after your jocks and you'll stand a better chance of keepin your mind on the main task.' His steely eyes scanned the seated aircrew. 'And what is the main task?'

No one spoke. Men shifted uncomfortably on their chairs, avoiding eye contact.

'Main task, fellas?' Chennault's jaw jutted forward. 'Don't be shy. What we here for? Anyone got a clue?'

A hand raised at the back.

'Well, son?'

'To win the War, sir?' The voice was hesitant, expecting a rebuke.

Chennault's leathery face cracked into a grin. 'Too right. Thank God, someone's on the ball. Free beer for you tonight, fella. We've been tryin to do this for seven years, and just when we thought we might be gettin there, what do the fuckin Japs do but throw half a million soldiers into carvin out a supply route from the south. They call it Operation Ichi-Go, which means Number One, so gives you a clue about its importance to the bastards. That's why I've called this briefin.' He reached for the billiard-cue on the table and turned to the map of central China behind him. 'Four weeks ago, we lost this city in Henan province.' The stick pointed to Luoyang. 'Last week we lost Changsha, which had been defended by three hundred thousand Chinese troops.' The cue whacked against the canvas several inches below. 'Since then, the Japanese armies under General Okamura have been advancin on

Hengyang.' The stick moved down the map, marking the route of the Japanese armies. 'Not a large city, but strategically important.'

The deep voice boomed out an explanation for the men listening. The Beijing-Guangzhou and Hunan-Guangxi railways intersected at Hengyang, so victory for the Japs meant they could link up with their armies in Indo China. Hengyang was also the gateway to south-west China. They could move on to Guilin and push west through Guizhou to take Chongqing from the south.

Chennault took a deep breath, drawing himself up to his full six foot two, as he scratched the stubble on his chin. 'I can see men here who were involved in the battle to save Chongqing and Chengdu. We succeeded, thank God, and there have been very few bombin raids since the end of last year. We know what victory looks like and, more importantly, so do the Chinese civilians we protected. But the friggin Japs haven't given up.'

Chennault spelt out the situation. Under the command of Fang Xianjue, the Chinese Tenth Army had established a defensive shield around Hengyang with trenches, pillboxes, and bunkers. Soldiers had dragged up rocks and earth to build twenty-five feet cliffs to protect the city, with machine gun posts commanding the ridge. General Fang had also ordered the evacuation of the civilian population, the day before the Japanese fire-bombed the city.

'The Chinese soldiers are up against an army five times their size, so they need all the help we can give em.' Chennault explained he'd requested the return of the Chinese divisions that had been unwisely sent into Burma to support the Allies in retaking the overland road to India.

'Two days ago, anti-tank guns and other heavy artillery reached Hengyang from Kunming, and two squadrons of Warhawks arrived here last night, under the command of Colonel Lin.' Chennault pointed to the pilot in the front row. 'Once his planes are refuelled, he'll lead them to Hengyang and take full command of fighter operations to defend the city.'

The battle plan would see Liberators and Mitchells continuing to bomb supply lines from Nanjing, as well as destroying factories engaged in war production in the Japanese homeland. 'This is an all-out battle, fellas. As the young man said at the start, our task is to win this fuckin war. We are going to throw everything we can into savin Hengyang. We've got plenty of daylight, so kick tires at seven, and wrap up when it gets dark. If you've got the energy to visit dames at Mister Wang's in between, good luck, but I want you ready to roll at dawn every day. We'll show the bastards what itchin to go really means. Any questions?'

No one raised a hand. The crews knew the score.

'Action stations in half an hour. Good luck.' Chennault glanced at Colonel Lin. 'I'm headin for the can son, then we'll talk? Back in two shakes.' He followed the pilots from the briefing room. Those in the first attack-wave were already striding to their aircraft. The remaining pilots ambled to the mess.

'Great to know you'll be leading the air defence of Hengyang.'

Lin Xiaobin spun round at the familiar drawl. 'Major Walters!'

'Now Lieutenant Colonel, like yourself.' Douglass

pointed at the silver leaf on his epaulette. 'Liaison and logistics. Link between US command and General Chiang.'

'Still at Chongqing?' Lin Xiaobin recalled Douglass being posted to join the American team at Chiang Kai-shek's headquarters, shortly after he'd taken over from Harry.

Douglass shook his head, explaining how Chennault had asked him to take responsibility for logistics on the eastern front. Zhijiang was the largest Allied airfield in China, and Chennault was using is for airborne reconnaissance, as well as the base for the Flying Tigers and bomber squadrons attacking Japan.

'You're here then?'

'I have a desk in the command-centre with Chennault.' Dougie stroked his shoulder. 'But most of the job is visiting other airfields to monitor operational-capacity, and make the case for more support from General Stillwell.'

Lin Xiaobin ran his finger across the sliver of a black moustache, shifting his weight from one foot to the other. 'I hear there are difficulties between the Americans and General Chiang?'

Douglass shook his head. 'Not this side of the country. He and Chennault are pretty much in tune. The problem is in Burma, with Stillwell. Trying to respond to his demands for support there, while holding the front line here, has been difficult. There are only so many troops to go round.'

'Jeez man, you hit the nail on its friggin head.' Chennault had returned and was listening to the conversation. The exasperation was clear, as he described

Stilwell's efforts to open the overland route between India and China. 'He's a complete asshole. Flyin supplies over the Hump is clearly workin. Jap fighters can't penetrate that far, so the only enemy is the weather, but our pilots have learnt how to hack that. If Stillwell persists in opening the Ledo Road, the Japs will bomb it next day and make it impassable.'

Chennault was blunt in his assessment of his boss, dismissing the venture as a vanity project driven by Stillwell's obsession to get even for losing Burma two years before. 'The worst thing is that the old tossbag persuaded Roosevelt to threaten to cut supplies to Chiang, unless he sent troops to Burma. Fifteen friggin divisions were relocated to Mitikyana two weeks ago. No wonder the Japs are kickin butts this side of the country.'

Chennault glanced at the open door to the airfield and flicked it shut with the tip of his boot. 'I didn't say anything to the boys, but I'm not sure we'll hold Hengyang. Although General Fang has built impressive fortifications, the odds are stacked against him. Nineteen thousand Chinese soldiers against one hundred thousand Nips. I wasn't a great student at school, but even I can do the fuckin math.' His grey eyes fixed on Colonel Lin. 'Do what you can at Hengyang, son. Having one of our ace pilots leading the air defence will boost morale. But if it gets sticky, pull back here. No heroics. If Hengyang goes, Guilin will follow and I don't want us giftin precious Warhawks to the soddin Japs.' Chennault glanced at his watch. 'I must leave you guys. Weekly treat of a phone briefin with Stilwell at eight, and I need to prepare my pitch to the stupid bugger.'

The two men were left alone. The call of a partridge floated through the open window.

'Reminds me of Fenghuangshan,' said Dougie.

Xiaobin nodded. 'Lots of bamboo partridge in Hunan. Far from any large city.'

Douglass walked to the window. Mist was rising from the warming runway. Beyond the perimeter of the airfield, he could see a ridge of karst mountains, bamboo-clad peaks pushing through the puffy blanket of clouds. 'One day, travellers are going to come here in their thousands to see this amazing scenery. America can boast the Rockies and the Grand Canyon, but you have even more beautiful sights in your country, Xiaobin.'

'If only it was our country.' Commander Lin was studying the map, running his finger from Zhijiang towards the coast. 'I long to see my home town again.'

'Me too.' Douglass sounded wistful. 'Three and a half years since Pearl Harbour. Feels like a huge chunk of my life. But now the Allies have landed in France, the war in Europe might end soon. If Hitler agrees a peace deal, resources could be channelled this way.'

Lin Xiaobin turned to face Douglass. 'But the Bushido code means they'll never surrender. They'll fight to the last man. This war will go on for many more years. We've seen how they are defending the Mariana islands. Every inch they relinquish is soaked in blood. Think what will happen if the Americans try to land troops on their homeland.'

'You're right Xiaobin.' Douglass tapped the cue against the south-eastern corner of Japan. Any invasion here would make Normandy beaches look like a walk in the park.' He stepped from the window, lowering his voice.

'Last time I was in Chongqing, there was talk of the Americans building a super-bomb with the power to destroy whole cities.'

Xiaobin stroked the long tail of hair at the back of his neck, 'I have such fantasies too. I look at the weapons being loaded onto the Liberators and think, what if we had a plane large enough to carry something ten times the size? That would make the bastards stop and think.'

'Live in hope. buddy. One of Harry's mottos.'

'Have you heard from him?'

'A couple of months ago a letter arrived from a cousin of mine, flying Mustangs in the UK. He was at a New Year's Eve party, where Harry and his navigator were guests of honour. Sounds like he's still going strong.'

'He was a good pilot.'

'And a great leader, Xiaobin. What he achieved with seventy-four squadron was impressive.'

'His combat strategy worked.' Xiaobin stared levelly at the American. 'He was wrong about prisoners.'

Douglass rubbed his shoulder. 'Lucky there were no more incidents before either of us left Fenghuangshan.'

'My men agree with me.' The young pilot stroked his queue. 'Your job is logistics, so you know guarding prisoners is a drain on resources. It takes precious manpower away from front-line action. Completely pointless.'

Douglass shook his head. 'We have to respect international agreements on treatment of captured pilots, or we are no better than savages. They are mostly innocent kids, whose only crime is fighting on the wrong side.'

'*Húshuō.*' Xiaobin's anger exploded. 'Millions of

Chinese civilians have been killed by these animals you call kids. This evil has to be totally eliminated.' He lifted his clenched fists. 'If I ever run out of ammunition, I will use these as weapons, even if the enemy is fully armed. Strangling the life out of a Japanese soldier with my dying breath would be a good way to go.'

# Chapter Twenty-seven

## Shell Hus, Copenhagen: June 26th 1944

Harry awoke to see swallows dart across the thin strip of azure blue and the sound of incessant activity beyond the bars. It took moments before the awful awareness of the day ahead pushed through the fog of sleep. He sat up, bracing for the rasping of the rusting bolt.

The chattering and gurgling of the birds took him back to his room in the officers' mess at Church Fenton, beneath the eaves of the ivy-clad, brick building. After the batman had delivered the early-morning tea, he would lie in bed replaying the training flights of the previous day, working out how to correct mistakes. It was a grey November afternoon in 1940 when he'd taxied the Blenheim into dispersal, after the concluding sortie that merited the coveted wings. The corporal mechanic pulled back the canopy to tell him he was wanted in the adjutant's office.

Harry grinned as he knocked on the door, knowing Squadron Leader Armitage would be holding a balloon to launch at his face before they decamped to the bar. But there was no whoosh of air. Instead, a grim-faced adjutant relayed news that his parents had been killed in the previous night's blitz on London. Direct hit on Eric Street. House destroyed.

The smouldering urge for revenge had carried him through the years of fighting, every flight an opportunity for retribution against the forces that had unleashed the war, each downed German plane one less killing-machine available to the Nazi murderers.

He breathed deeply, strengthening his resolve. He'd be damned if he'd allow the Gestapo to best him. He sensed Heydrich knew it was no normal flight, and would stop at nothing. Denying him information for at least a week would be a victory of sorts. Harry could feel his anger rising, fuelled by the aches in his back and the stinging from his swollen eye.

Heydrich was immaculately dressed again, with a symmetrical Windsor knot in the black tie. 'Sorry to keep you waiting, but there has been rather a queue. I hope you are going to be reasonable and tell us why you were flying from England, where you were shot down and who helped you. It is very simple.'

'I am Wing Commander Harry Winchester, a British pilot, and I demand to be treated as a prisoner of war according to the Geneva Convention.'

'You were caught in civilian clothes with bleached hair like a true Aryan. You look nothing like the photograph on your identity card, especially now you've experienced our depilation techniques.' Heydrich brushed his hand across his own neat parting. 'As you know, the Geneva Convention does not apply to spies. In any case this is Gestapo headquarters in occupied Denmark, not a public courtroom in Switzerland. No one knows you are here and no one cares. More importantly, since we have a school next door, we have soundproofed our rooms, so no one can hear you either.' He pressed his face close to Harry's ear. 'For the last time Wing Commander, are you going to give me answers?'

Harry stared back at the Oberführer. He forced his cracked and swollen lips together and spat at the tanned face. Heydrich wiped the spittle from his cheek, before flicking the switch of the intercom. Harry was dragged to the adjoining room and strapped to a chair, with his hand forced into the blood-stained contraption. Knud pulled the lever slowly towards him.

The pain was excruciating and he could hear animal-howls reverberate on the walls of the small room. He was on the edge of unconsciousness, the pain easing, when Knud gave the handle a final jerk, and searing agony rammed through his body, threatening to explode his head and burst his brain. He cried out till his throat hoarsened.

Finally, Knud released his grip and Harry fell back into the chair, gasping, shattered by the throbbing in his hand. He was aware of Heydrich's face pressed close to his own. 'Are you ready to talk?'

Harry saw Amy standing beside Pierre in the doorway. He opened his mouth, but only saliva dribbled out and down his chin. All he could manage was an anguished shake.

Heydrich sighed. 'Everyone breaks. It is only a matter of time. Why are you allowing yourself to be mutilated?' He purred the words. 'What is it you are hiding?' He turned to Knud. 'One more I think.'

Harry remembered the promise of one nail a day and opened his mouth, but only managed a low groan, as his hand was clamped into the wooden machine.

By the end of the week every nail on his right hand had been dragged out. Only the time of the torture differed. On Tuesday Harry had waited all day for the bolt to be drawn back, watching the sky lighten and darken, counting the anguished minutes. It had been after dark when Knud appeared. On Thursday he was still in a pain-wracked sleep when it happened at dawn.

On Friday afternoon Knud handcuffed him once again to the chair in Heydrich's office. From the calendar on the desk he could see it was his twenty-second birthday.

'Let me see Knud's handiwork.' Heydrich held the mutilated hand in his gloved palm. 'Do you really want us to continue? We are patient, you know? We can also break the fingers.' He clamped Harry's hand to the desk with his left fist, and pushed the middle finger towards the vertical with his other arm. Harry screwed up his eyes.

'A name. That's all we want to start with.'

Harry opened his eyes and looked at the officer, with his neat tie and ironed shirt. 'Okay. It's Jacques. Jacques. Jacques.' He repeated the name with weary conviction.

Heydrich let go of the finger and spoke into the intercom. A young woman came into the room with a notepad and drew a chair beside the officer. Harry caught the scent of her perfume as she brushed her hand over the seat. Another world.

Harry described how he'd been escorting the bomber stream on a raid over Germany, when he'd been shot down by a Heinkel. He had baled-out of the doomed Mosquito.

'Where is your navigator?'

'Killed by cannon-fire, I think. There was no answer behind when I broke open the canopy. We were in a tight spiral with seconds left. The plane crashed and burst into flames near a wood.'

'Tell me about your mission. I want details of the

Mosquito and its interception-equipment, I want to know the strategy of bomber-command, and the number of fighter-aircraft deployed as escorts. Everything.' The smooth voice was insistent.

The woman dutifully scribed Harry's answers. He wasn't giving Heydrich anything that couldn't be accessed from German military intelligence.

'And what about the man called Jacques, who arranged your escape to Denmark?'

Harry held the image of Pierre in his head as he described a man with contrasting features. He thought he worked in a food-processing factory in Amiens.

'And where did Jacques leave you?'

'Flensburg.'

'Who met you there.'

Harry didn't hesitate. He recalled Lone's words as she opened the kitchen door. 'Aage, the farmer next door. He took me to Kirkenbjerg.'

The interrogation lasted two hours. Finally, Heydrich sat back, a genuine smile on his lips. 'Isn't it good to cooperate? Just remind me of what you said about Jacques?'

Harry repeated the previous description word for word, relieved to see the girl leaf back through her pad and point at her earlier notes. '*Das ist richtig.*'

He was returned to his cell. Many days and nights passed with no interruptions, apart from the jailer banging the tray of food on the ground each morning and evening. To keep track of time, he scratched a mark every day in the roughcast concrete beneath the window.

There were sixteen lines above his head, when he was woken early and taken to Heydrich's office. 'We have obtained your war record. You are a highly-decorated pilot, responsible for the deaths of many young Luftwaffe pilots. An experienced killer it seems.'

'It is war.'

'Ah yes, it is war.' Oberführer Heydrich leant forward, looking straight at Harry. 'One of my relatives was assassinated in Prague by experienced killers two years ago. The work of men linked to the British SOE network. It is why I like to get my hands on special agents. I particularly enjoy it if their deaths are very slow and very painful.' Heydrich's blue eyes were unemotional. 'What is strange about your story is that we have no record of any bombing raid on the thirtieth of May. German cities were spared that night. However, we have evidence of two flights into France delivering spies for the Resistance.' Heydrich's lips tightened. 'Not you by any chance?'

Harry kept his eyes steady and unblinking. 'I may have muddled dates. It is many weeks since I was shot down. I just know it was two nights before the full moon. You have my war record, so you can see I am a night-fighter pilot. Why would the British waste my expertise on courier work?'

'Why indeed?' Heydrich smoothed his hair. 'We clearly have more research to do.'

Harry was in his cell for three more weeks. The hours and minutes dragged between the times he forced himself to exercise. The only consolation was that boredom was infinitely better than beatings, and his wounds were healing. The stiffness in his back eased, and milky-white crescent-moons were pushing beneath the cuticles of his right hand. Through the missing pane of the barred-window, he could smell autumn approach.

The calendar on Heydrich's desk said Monday September 4th, when he was next handcuffed into the familiar chair. He accepted the proffered cigarette and Heydrich undid the manacle on his right hand.

'It is very mysterious Wing Commander. We have not been able to find Aage Christiansen. No one has seen him since the day you were captured. It is particularly strange, because we planned for him to lead the Odense *Hifspolizei*, once we remove the Danish police who cannot be trusted. If he is a member of Holger Danske as you say, it seems he has two faces. He was supposed to arrest the sister when she returned from work, but she has disappeared as well. We think they must have escaped together.'

'Quite possibly.' Harry's face was expressionless. 'Lone told me Aage was after Birgitte.'

'He may have caught her then.' Heydrich looked thoughtful. 'It seems he was a keen photographer, with many pictures of the two girls, taken through the windows of the farmhouse at night.' The Oberführer tapped his cigarette on the ash tray. 'But he was also very interested in young children—three- and four-year olds in particular. And we found evidence he was doing more than just taking photographs—manacles and whips and gags in his bedroom. When we catch him, we will shoot him as a pervert. It will save a space on the transport to a concentration camp with the rest of the Danish collaborators.' Heydrich drew deeply on his cigarette, before exhaling a sequence of smoke-rings above his head. 'What do you know about the other sister, Birgitte Vestager?'

'Not a lot,' Harry shook his head, 'She was at work all day. I spent more time with Lone, the one involved with Holger Danske. She could have given you useful information.'

'Except that our stupidly-enthusiastic Knud shot her.' Heydrich demonstrated his humourless smile and sat back in his upholstered chair. 'It has been good to talk with you Wing Commander. I don't have so many opportunities to practice my English these days. I went to Malvern you see, and enjoyed a great deal about your country. If only the Generals had not advised the Führer to pause at Dunkirk, I could be sitting in an office in Whitehall and sending our children to my old school—or maybe even to Eton.'

Harry listened to Heydrich's explication of the *Sonderfahndungliste*, wondering if the man was completely mad. Was it possible that he had helped a senior Brigadeführer make a list of three thousand people to be rounded up and shot after the invasion, including Churchill? Would Chamberlain and Mosley have collaborated with Hitler's plan to reinstate King Edward and his mistress?

'I met them when they visited the Führer in 1937.' Heydrich smiled. 'Lovely couple; very supportive of our plans to sort your Jewish problem. Such a pity it didn't happen.' He pulled a package from his drawer. 'There is just one other thing I want to ask, now we are being open with each other.' Harry recognised the playing-cards. 'These pictures are very interesting. I would like to hear more about them.'

Harry said nothing, wishing he'd buried them in the wood at Herbeumont.

'Come on Wing Commander,' Heydrich oozed encouragement. 'I have accepted your tale about the thirtieth of May. The report has been filed with my superiors and stamped satisfactory. It is no longer any concern to me whether it is the truth, as I will be moving to Berlin very soon. There are a few vacancies following the little upset with the Führer.'

Harry frowned. What the hell was Heydrich talking about?

'You wouldn't know about that, of course, because we don't have wireless in our hotel rooms.' Heydrich lit another cigarette, before recounting von Stauffenberg's assassination attempt. 'Now a rather dead Colonel of course, but not before the Gestapo gently encouraged him to give us names. Some were very senior, like Field Marshal Rommel, so there are now opportunities at the highest level. I have been promoted to Obergruppenführer and will be working in the Reichstag, close to the Führer himself.'

Heydrich laid the cards in four rows of suits. 'I know a little about art. While the Hearts are diverting and stimulating, I think it is this suit that is particularly arresting.' His finger jabbed the Diamonds. 'I will return the photo and letter, if you can explain.'

Harry hesitated. Could he negotiate? Heydrich seemed capable of civilised conversation. He took a final drag from his cigarette and stubbed the butt into the white bowl, conscious of the steely eyes watching. 'You are right about there being a story.'

'I want to hear it, Wing Commander. Preferably without having to make use of the little persuader.'

361

Heydrich pointed to the blood-stained contraption.

'No need, if you will do one thing.'

'You are not in a strong bargaining-position, Wing Commander.'

'I would like to join other POWs in Stalag Luft Three.'

Heydrich frowned. 'That is simply not possible. I have been gentle with you, because I have a soft spot for Charterhouse boys.' He mentioned the spirited defence of the King's trophy at the Public School's Cup Final at the Oval in 1937. 'Unfortunately, though, my superiors learnt that a commando knife was removed from you at Kirkenbjerg. There can be only one explanation, so I have orders to finish the job before leaving for Berlin.' The voice was devoid of emotion as he explained that Harry would either be shot in the execution-yard of the Shell Hus next morning, or transported to a concentration-camp. 'Since you are not Jewish or Russian, you may survive a few months, but the outcome will be the same in the end, I'm afraid. Perhaps there is something else I can do for you?'

'Let me write a letter?'

Heydrich nodded slowly, digesting the request. 'A final letter seems reasonable. Who to though? Your wife is dead and I presume you have no children?'

'The family of my navigator.'

'The man who died the night you were shot down? Whose body we've never found?'

Harry ignored the sarcasm. 'His mum was like a mother to me, after my own parents were killed in the Blitz.'

Obergruppenführer Heydrich stroked his tiny moustache. 'At Malvern I always admired the British sentimentality, so I feel inclined to agree. But you must, of course, say nothing about the wonderful hospitality in the Shell Hus. I will destroy it if there is any mention, Wing Commander.'

'It will be personal thoughts.'

'Just so. And what about these?' Heydrich pointed again at the Diamonds and sat back in his chair while Harry described the provenance. His eyes widened at the mention of the artist's name.

'Very interesting indeed. You British like to shake on a deal.' Heydrich stretched across the desk and grasped the bloodstained hand that had held the cigarette. The young pilot winced. 'I am so sorry. Thoughtless of me to forget your injury.' He gathered the playing cards. 'They will enable me to buy my way out of any little difficulties, if the Allies get too close to Berlin. There are escape-routes for those who can afford it.'

Heydrich pushed the photo and the letter into the stained pocket of Harry's shirt. 'Knud will give you writing-paper this evening, but we have to decide your next move. I just need you to tell me what you prefer, before I ask Knud to unlock your hotel room. If you choose the execution yard, I can always arrange for you to join your compatriot on my desk. We can maintain a connection.' Heydrich, smiled, gesturing at the white bowl, now full of discarded butts. His finger rested on the intercom button. 'It is entirely your choice, Wing Commander.'

# Chapter Twenty-eight

## Dachau:
## September 3rd 1944

It was dark when the train stopped. Harry sensed the nervousness among the men beside him, fuelling his own panic. He heard steam escape the engine's boiler, then shouting along the line of wagons.

'*Raus! Raus!*'

Dogs barked as metal bolts crashed back against their stays and the wooden doors of the cattle-truck were pulled open.

Harry gulped in the fresh air. For a moment it took away the gnawing emptiness in his stomach from two days without food or water, crushed together with forty men using the floor as an open toilet. The rancid stench of the soiled wagon rolled over him and he retched, aching to fill his belly. He was pushed by the men behind and fell onto the platform, scraping his knees on the rough concrete.

'*Raus! Raus!*' The snarling face of a rottweiler snapped at his ankle, held back by the leash from a guard, grasping a whip in his other hand. The tip cracked on Harry's neck as he tried to stand, muscles stiff from two days unable to move or stretch. He heard a scream echo from the blacked-out building opposite. The whip slashed at his back and the anguished cry came again, desperate with pain.

He staggered to his feet before another blow fell, and hurried to join the line of men forming at the end of the platform. In the flashlights from the guards, he caught a glimpse of the station-name. Dachau Bhf.

'*Links! Rechts! Marsch, ihr Schweine! Marsch! Links! Rechts!*'

A rifle cracked at the end of the platform, a man screamed, and the column roused itself into formation and moved onto the road beside the station.

Careful not to look up, Harry's eyes darted left and right, trying to make sense of the location. The column turned right to go through a tunnel under the railway-line. Beside the shuffling caterpillar of haunted faces, he could hear water rippling, and caught a sliver of luminescence. It reminded him how thirsty he was. He wanted to dive in and drink his fill till his stomach burst. He closed his eyes, trying to force the thought away.

In front, a man stumbled and fell. The column swept over him, trampling feet bouncing him forward like a large football.

'*Steh auf! Steh auf! Du Abschaum. Steh auf!*' Harry heard the guard yell for the man to move. There was a shot, and a splash as something heavy hit the water. Harry didn't turn.

The men lumbered along the darkened streets and across open countryside. Two watch-towers loomed, with heavy, metal gates set into the stone columns, topped by barbed wire. They were ordered to halt. A column of ten men marched from the prison, carrying shovels and pick axes over their shoulders. As the work-party passed Harry, the man in front raised his head. In the arc-light from the tower, Harry caught a glimpse of expressionless eyes, sunk into hollowed sockets. Yellow skin hung from empty cheek-bones. Trousers flapped above stick legs protruding from a pair of wooden clogs. The walking skeleton shuffled past and Harry closed his eyes to shut out the future.

'*Arbeit Mach Frei*.' Harry muttered the words formed by the wrought-iron letters on the open gate, before they were herded across the courtyard into the *Jourhaus*.

They were ordered to strip and pile their soiled clothes in a corner, together with possessions. Harry wondered whether to retrieve the photo from his shirt pocket, when he saw a guard approach a man clutching a small locket. An order barked out and the man shook his head. The guard ripped off the gold chain, drawing blood from the prisoner's neck. Tears were running down the man's cheeks as he reached out, pleading to hang on to the keepsake. The guard lifted the butt of his rifle and smashed it into the prisoner's face. He collapsed on the floor and the guard swung his boot hard into his groin. Harry moved past the pile of clothes without a glance.

The prisoners were driven through a communal shower, before having their hair roughly shaved by a team of men in prison garb. Stinging carbolic disinfectant was swabbed over bleeding scalps and the men formed in a naked line to collect uniforms. Ill-fitting, striped jackets and trousers were given out, with a pair of wooden clogs, a bowl and a spoon.

The forty men in the group were ordered outside onto open ground in front of a large pond. '*Lauft! Schweine! Lauft.*' A snarling doberman snapped at the legs of any prisoner who didn't run quickly enough. The men stumbled round the edge of the pond, forced on by the bull-whips of the guards. Harry lost count of the times they circled the water. A man in front was gulping air into his lungs. He fell and the blundering prisoners behind cursed as they tripped on the body.

'Halt!' The shuffling pantomime came to rest, men gasping.

Two guards approached the fallen body. 'Raus, du Abschaum!' The man lifted his head, pleading for water. The men put down their whips and grasped the limbs of the prisoner, swinging him into the pond. His face appeared above the surface, arms flailing as he tried to reach the bank.

'Da hast du Wasser, du Drecksau! Schwimm! Schwimm!'

The prisoner tried to grasp the rocks at the edge, but the guard kicked him in the face, forcing him back into the pond. He staggered to his feet, metres from the bank, slimy water swirling round his waist, eyes darting round the group of men.

The prisoners stood in silence, watching the guards taunt the shivering wretch, flicking their whips whenever he approached the edge. Half an hour passed before the man was finally allowed back onto dry land. He stood close to Harry, sodden clothes dripping onto the muddy ground, teeth chattering.

The men were ordered to approach the barrack-blocks at the edge of the parade-ground. Assigned to hut number four, they stumbled through the doorway. Lines of bunk-beds stretched the length of the block, rising from floor to ceiling, three levels high. Even through the gloom it was clear every bunk was occupied.

'Raus, du Schwein,' bellowed a guard.

Groaning men made space in the narrow bunks so new arrivals could squeeze in, lying head-to-toe like sardines.

Harry found his shoulders wedged between the feet of two men, face pressed against the stinking, wooden boards. There was an angry exchange at the far end of the hut, and the guard moved along with his flashlight. His whip cracked and an animal howl reverberated, quickly subsiding into a whimper. Men controlled their breathing.

The guard slammed the door and the barrack-room settled again. Harry guessed it was midnight. Despite the stench of rotting flesh beside his face, he fell into an exhausted sleep.

A whistle shattered the silence, sending shards of despair through the emerging consciousness in the barrack room. Bodies stirred and groaned, some forcing their eyes to remain closed to blank out the anticipation of another day. Men sat up, coughing and swearing. Legs appeared from upper bunks, clogs slipped on to coarsened feet. The queue for the toilet lengthened, with curses for any man who sat longer than absolutely necessary.

'Essen.'

Harry clutched his bowl and followed two gaunt men from his bunk through the doorway of the barrack, across the open space beside the pond, to a building where a line of prisoners shuffled past a table with huge metal-cauldrons. A ladle of liquid-porridge sloshed into his bowl, and he was given a wedge of coarse, brown bread. He wolfed the bread and gulped the gruel, licking the bowl clean, looking around to see if there was a chance of seconds, but the queue was already lengthening beyond the cauldrons.

He watched his bunk-mates finish their food and followed them onto the parade-ground. To the east a thin sliver of light appeared beyond strands of barbed-wire stretched between the watch-towers. Against grey clouds on the horizon, he could see the silhouette of a helmeted soldier cradling a machine-gun, as he surveyed the prisoners stumbling across uneven ground.

Two guards appeared with clipboards. Numbers were shouted and inmates answered quickly, until there was a long silence, punctuated by raised voices and aggressive barking. The men stood in rows while a guard searched the blocks. It took a quarter of an hour to establish that the missing prisoner had died in the night. Two men were detailed to carry the body to the crematorium. There were three more such silences and each time the barracks had to be thoroughly searched.

As the roll-call continued, the sky lightened and Harry saw thousands of striped uniforms standing on the parade-ground, some swaying with the effort to remain upright. In front a man sank to the ground, clutching his stomach. A guard approached.

'Steh auf!' The boot swung forward kicking the man in the face. Harry watched the prisoner's outstretched arms trying to push himself to a squat. For a moment it seemed he might succeed, then his head fell back to the ground, groaning.

'Steh auf!' The guard drew his revolver from its holster, and the click as he cocked the trigger could be heard across the hushed space.

'Abschaum. Auf jetzt!' There was no response. Harry closed his eyes. The crack of the gun echoed from the buildings beyond the parade-ground. He heard another barked order and opened his eyes to see two prisoners dragging the corpse across the muddy ground. A clog dropped off one of its feet as the body bounced over rutted earth.

Harry was ordered to join a work-party in a quarry outside the main prison. The job was to break boulders into small stones and transport them in a cart to a railway-siding, where they were loaded onto a wagon. The finger-nails on his right hand had partly grown back, so he had some protection from the rough edges, but mostly he scrabbled at the rocks with his left hand. Because of the emaciated state of his co-workers, even one muscular wrist was enough to match their work-rate. There were ten men for each cart. From the sunken faces of the other prisoners in his group, he guessed he was the only new arrival. He understood quickly from a whispered 'shh' in response to a question, that they had to labour in silence. He had only wanted to know if they worked all day without a break.

The question was answered by the blowing of a whistle when the sun was at its zenith. The men were marched back to the kitchen-block, where watery soup and a wedge of bread was handed out during a brief respite, before the guards ordered them to work again. Harry watched the autumn-sun sink between strands of barbed wire around the quarry-compound and twilight settle over exhausted prisoners. It was dark when they returned to the barrack-block, lights along the electrified fence twinkling like Christmas decorations.

Supper was more soup. Harry witnessed an argument between the prisoner ladling out the meagre portions and a recipient, pleading for more. A guard strode across and knocked the dish from the prisoner's hand with his rifle-butt. The metal container clattered on the floor and slivers of potato and turnip splattered across the dusty concrete. The prisoner dropped to his knees, trying to scrape the pieces with his spoon and cram them into his mouth before the SS man intervened again. Jabbing the barrel of his rifle at the scrabbling figure, he called over his fellow-warders to watch the entertainment, while he crushed chunks of food under the heel of his boot. With a final kick, which lifted the prisoner from the serving-table, the jailer turned to scan the queue waiting to be served. Heads were bowed to avoid eye-contact.

In the hut, before the light was switched off, there was finally a chance to ask questions of his bedmates. They were both Polish, arrested in their home-town in the early hours of New Year's day for breaking curfew.

'Is every day like today?' Harry managed to get Tomasz to understand with the help of the few words of German he'd picked up from the Shell Hus.

'Ja Ja. Immer suppe. Morgens, mittags and abends. Suppe mit Brot. Sonntag speziel…' The man paused, a smile spreading across yellowed teeth. 'Zehr speziel. Suppe mit Brot.' He lay back, laughing at his joke.

Harry tried again to explain he meant the daily work-schedule, breaking rocks.

'Ja Ja. Steine brechen. Arbeit halb sieben bis eins. Mittagessen. Arbeit halb zwei bis sieben. Schlafen neun. Namensprufung bei sechs jeder morgen. Winter sieben. Fauler morgen!' Again Tomasz chuckled, but Harry struggled to find solace in knowing that roll-call in winter was at seven o'clock.

He looked at Tomasz's emaciated face; skin like

parchment beneath his hollowed-out eyes. The cracked smile revealed broken teeth. Was that just a result of eight months in the camp? In another eight, it would be spring in England. News had filtered through the cells in Copenhagen that Paris had been liberated in August and the Allies were closing in on Brussels. There was talk of the war being over by Christmas. Surely, he could survive a few months, and be back in Blighty to see wisteria blossoming in the garden of the *Angel*?

But winter would come soon. Although it felt warm enough, with the accumulated, foetid exhalations from eight-hundred bodies packed into three layers of sleeping-spaces, he'd not seen a stove. Early autumn was mild in Bavaria, but the ill-fitting boards of the walls would be poor insulation against arctic-winds whistling down from Siberia.

Harry surveyed the barrack-room. The only decoration came from hundreds of metal bowls, hanging on hooks fixed to the wooden-frames supporting the bunks. From conversation with Tomasz, he understood most of the occupants of Block Four were Poles, with a small number from Czechoslovakia, Romania and Hungary. Tomasz was adamant there were no Russians. They were housed separately, so the guards could torment them away from other prisoners.

The grey mass of bodies snored continually, heaving, turning and coughing. Delirious men called for help. Silent, ghost-thin shapes rose from their wooden slats to go to the toilet, climbing over bodies, who cursed as their own space was disturbed. The air grew heavy and foul with the stench of urine and disease, mixing with carbolic and the staleness of men who had not washed for a week. Breathing became difficult.

Harry pulled the thin blanket tightly around him, trying to push aside the thought that Dachau had been his choice.

# Chapter Twenty-nine

## Dachau:
## April 26th 1945

Harry's eyes glanced at the lettering on the metal gate. *ARBEIT MACHT FREI.* Had eight months of hard labour earned him the right to freedom? He looked behind at the line of emaciated men standing beside the *Jourhaus*. Heads were bowed, awaiting the order to move. Was this his last day in the stinking cesspool of Dachau? He shivered, concentrating on the stripes of the ragged shirt in front, trying to prevent memories surfacing.

The routine of that first morning had repeated daily, with quarry work blistering his hands and rubbing the ends of his fingers raw above the regrowing nails. Tomasz had taken him under his wing, ensuring he made no mistakes to incur the wrath of the bored and watchful guards, such as sitting when waiting for the cart to return, or warming his hands in his pockets. In return he had taken the lead in lifting heavier stones onto the cart, enabling the group to meet their daily target and avoid a whipping. Despite the treatment in the Shell Hus, his muscles still had residual strength.

Food became an obsession, and the queuing for soup a moment to relish. Tomasz had not been totally accurate, because the evening meal sometimes included a tiny piece of cheese or a square of meat. But there was never enough. Harry woke with hunger gnawing at his insides, sucking sustenance from his flesh. The watery slops did little to soothe the pains. He was still ravenous after licking the bowl spotless.

Once, a cook slipped in additional potatoes and he savoured every scrap, including the bitter skins, but even that left his stomach aching. During the day the pangs never ceased. He learnt from Tomasz to drink his fill from the water-tap whenever he had the chance, which fooled the stomach for a few minutes.

Evenings offered the only opportunity to talk, but the exhausted men in the barrack-block just wanted sleep, the only escape from their living-hell. Harry noticed Tomasz prayed every night, before resting his head on the makeshift pillow he'd created, by wrapping his cap over his eating bowl. He wondered how anyone could find solace in a God that had abandoned humanity, but he respected Tomasz's need for silence.

In the snatched conversations before tiredness overwhelmed them, he learnt Tomasz and his friend Stefan had left school at fifteen to train as electricians. They worked for a local company in Malkina, which became close to the border with Russia in 1941. The Nazis had forced the company to work on a massive construction-project, which required a generating-unit to supply electricity to a would-be training-camp for soldiers fighting on the Eastern front.

After completing the project, they were retained by the German army to maintain uninterrupted electricity to their facilities, despite the blackouts caused by fuel-shortages or enemy-action. Although the pay was a pittance, Tomasz had little choice; there was no other work and he had twin girls to feed, having married a girl from his school the previous year. He and Stefan discovered the food-store that supplied the Abwehr, and a friend helped make a replica key to one of the huts. Under cover of darkness, they made frequent sorties for boxes of food, some of which they traded on the black market for precious Reichsmarks.

This worked well for two years, but one night they were intercepted by two SS soldiers returning from the brothel. Fortunately, Tomasz and Stefan were empty-handed or they'd have been shot. Their explanation of visiting girlfriends was accepted by the horny guards, who sniggered as Tomasz demonstrated what they'd been up to. However, there were rewards for soldiers catching local Polish people breaking curfew, so the Germans marched them to the military-barracks.

Next morning, after a short hearing in front of an Abwehr officer, they were sentenced to five years hard-labour in Germany. Tomasz managed a few snatched minutes with his wife on the platform at Malkina, before the guards pushed him and Stefan into the truck and slammed the door. As their train pulled out, he watched another draw into the station, carrying passengers for the training-camp at Treblinka.

Despite the gloom of the hut, Harry could see Tomasz's sunken eyes misting as he recounted. He felt the thin body tremble, and raged in silence at his own helplessness.

Later, as he was sinking into sleep, he was aware of Tomasz shaking his shoulder. 'Essen' whispered the Pole, pushing something into Harry's hand. It was the stump of a sausage. Harry could feel saliva ooze into his mouth at the smell of cooked pork. He chewed it carefully, savouring each bite, letting his taste-buds extract the full flavour from the grams of gristly meat.

'*Dziękuję,*' he whispered.

Tomasz smiled at Harry's attempt to speak Polish. '*Warum bist du hier? Kasernenblock zwanzig Britisch.*'

Had he heard Tomasz correctly? Harry asked him to repeat the block-number. His mood lifted at the thought there might be other English prisoners in the camp. After roll-call next evening, he walked along the line of barracks, shuffling to avoid attracting attention. In the twilight, ghostly shadows flitted between blocks.

Two men sat in the entrance of Block Twenty, hunched over a chunk of bread. They had the same cadaverous look as Tomasz and Stefan.

'British?' asked Harry quietly.

The taller prisoner shook his head. '*Pas Anglais.*' He called out behind him in French and a man, wearing a black peaked-cap, looked up from a huddle of bodies squatting inside the open door. There was a brief interchange and he stood and came to the entrance. He was taller than Harry. The outline of a once-large frame was evident beneath the buttoned-up jacket,

'We heard someone else from Blighty had recently arrived.' The refined vowels carried Harry straight back to the common room at Charterhouse. The man extended his hand. 'I'm Brian. Welcome to Dachau. Sorry we weren't around to greet you properly.'

Harry sank against the striped jacket, grateful for the arms that wrapped round his battered body. He could feel himself shake. He dragged his grimy shirtsleeve across his damp cheeks, embarrassed by the uncontrolled emotion.

Harry learnt that Block Twenty contained other British prisoners, captured on Special Operations work.

'You as well?' grunted Brian.

Harry gave a brief account of his intercepted mission.

'There's more security-leaks in the network than a ruddy sieve.' Brian lifted his cap, scratching his shaved scalp. 'Some of our people must be double-agents. Rotten show old boy. You're lucky to be alive. The Gestapo aren't renowned for their hospitality to Resistance operatives.'

In response, Harry lifted his right hand. The crescent-moons were half-way to the tips of the red-raw fingers.

'Bastards. After the rubber truncheons, I had the electric-shock treatment. Not a great experience either. Keeps you on your toes though.' He laughed at his weak joke, scanning the line of barrack-blocks for guards. 'Better head back to your hut, old boy. Keep your pecker up. We'll see what we can do.'

They arranged to meet again the following night, when Brian introduced him to the other British prisoners. Pat, Tom and Bob had also been involved in clandestine operations in France. John, the fifth man, had been married to a Frenchwoman in Paris when the Germans occupied the city. He'd helped the Resistance, until he was betrayed by the concierge. All five worked in the infirmary as orderlies.

'We need to get you transferred.' Pat seemed confident this could be sorted. 'Be patient and keep your head down.' Shorter than the other British prisoners, he was dressed in a black jacket over a zip-up sweater-vest, in contrast to the striped coats and trousers of other men in the block. He brought Harry up to date with news of the Allied advances across France and Belgium, gleaned from snatches of conversations between guards and information from recent arrivals. Beneath a prominent nose, he displayed a broad grin, as he laced his explanation with humorous asides. With his cap pushed back above the high forehead, he looked like a French onion-seller. But he had an air of quiet authority and Harry guessed he was the leader of the group.

Later, he discovered, from a conversation with Brian, Pat had run an underground network from Toulouse, helping Allied airmen and soldiers escape back to Britain through Spain and Gibraltar. For two years from April 1941 until his betrayal to the Gestapo in March 1943, over six-hundred service-men crossed the Pyrenees and returned to England. Fluent in French and German, and understanding some Polish and Russian, he was a key link in communications between different groups of prisoners in the camp, and eavesdropping on conversations between guards, which might reveal plans for certain prisoners.

Next morning, as he assembled with his group at the *Jourhaus*, Harry saw a door open to the prison-block behind the kitchen-complex. Four women marched out accompanied by three guards and the Lagerkommandant. These were the first female prisoners he'd seen and there was something about them that made him think they were British. Was it the way they walked and held themselves? Where were they going? One was Asian in appearance, her tanned, smooth cheeks contrasting with the lighter complexion of the three others. He registered the brown eyes, full lips; she approached, looking forwards, head held high.

'Rule Britannia.' Harry called, without thinking, and the woman glanced at Harry. A smile flickered briefly and then the woman had passed, moving to the iron gates. One of the guards broke away and smashed his rifle-butt against Harry's face, knocking him to the ground. The warder kicked him in the ribs and hurried back to join the women. Harry lay on his side, panting, watching the group march through the metal gates and along the track towards the crematorium. That flicker of a smile was consolation for the pain in his ribs. As his work-detail trudged along the track to the quarry, he heard shots ring out in the still autumn air. A flock of starlings took flight from the thick beech-trees, chattering into the blue sky.

That evening Brian told him that four female agents had been executed. He had trained with one at Arisaig, Noor Inayat Khan. The unusual name sounded familiar. Harry lay thinking about it in his bunk and woke before dawn, remembering Amy had talked about an Indian princess. She couldn't understand why someone who espoused Gandhi's beliefs in non-violence had joined the SOE, but she'd been impressed by her commitment to learning wireless transmission.

Two weeks later, Harry was moved into Block Twenty with the other British prisoners, and instructed to join the team of orderlies in the infirmary. Under Pat's watchful eye, he was shown how to treat patients, wash bodies and carry corpses. There were aspirins and a small amount of iodine, with limited ways of sterilising needles used to lance carbuncles and boils.

For several months he undertook this work, which was less physically strenuous than the quarry, but more emotionally draining, because of the mounting tally of deaths. Christmas passed and news of Allied bridgeheads across the Rhine filtered into the camp. Snow swirled in the air around the barrack-blocks, freezing the drinking water in each block.

And then typhus arrived.

Red, spotty rashes appeared on emaciated bodies, men staggered into the infirmary with temperatures of forty degrees, sweat pouring from their bodies. Those affected became delirious, lying soiled in their own faeces, unable to move. Mostly they died; occasionally they recovered.

It was not uncommon for fifty bodies to be carried out each morning, Harry and Brian had the job of wheeling the cart piled high with corpses along the track beside the electrified fence between the Mirador guard-towers. At the crematorium they heaved the bodies onto the concrete floor, where prisoners shovelled them into the ovens, under the watch of SS guards.

Eventually Harry caught typhus himself. Dark red blotches marked his skin and he could feel the sores erupt round his teeth. His head was dizzy and his pulse beat in his temples as his temperature soared, despite the freezing winds that howled through Dachau. He staggered in a daze to the infirmary and lay sweating on the soiled mattress beside another prisoner, delirious with agony from a lanced carbuncle the size of a football, exposing a huge, bloody cavity. The man's constant moaning was only interrupted by the occasional scream as the pain bit deep into his body. Unable to lift himself to the toilet, he fouled the bed where he lay, and the stench filled Harry's nostrils. In the morning his stiff body was lifted onto the cart for the crematorium and the space taken by another sick prisoner.

Through it all Harry was determined not to let a rat-borne bacteria succeed where the Luftwaffe and the Imperial Japanese air force failed. He would see the guards held accountable for everything he'd witnessed. For two more days, he clung to the pulse in his weakened body, while another prisoner oozed his life away on the stinking bed beside him. On the third day his temperature dropped and next morning he was upright and treating other sick patients. Anything was better than sharing a bed with a rotting corpse.

Despite the deaths from typhus, the population of Dachau increased, with trainloads of new arrivals each day, as other camps were emptied ahead of the Allied advances. Starving and exhausted men carried stories of days incarcerated in cattle-trucks, without food or water, surviving by lying on top of the corpses beneath. Whole convoys perished because trains had been delayed by attacking Allied-aircraft, diverted to sidings for several nights, till a replacement locomotive could be found.

One evening in early March, Pat called the British group together. He had been elected President of the International Prisoners' Committee, which had secured a small number of guns and ammunition by bribing a female SS guard, hoping this would buy her protection when the camp was liberated. Pat explained how they were preparing to take control of the camp when the Americans approached. 'We need to time it right. We cannot beat an army of SS guards with four pistols.' He pushed his cap towards the back of his head and scratched the thinning hairline. 'We know that the Germans plan to kill all inmates to conceal evidence. Groups of men will be marched from here into the woods and shot. Each day a list will be published of men selected to parade at the *Jourhaus* the following morning.'

There was a long silence as the prisoners digested this information. When Pat spoke again his tone was determined. 'We can fight back by swapping numbers in the infirmary.'

Over the next two weeks Harry observed a macabre drama, in which the identity of prisoners, whose pulses had finally stopped, were given to those earmarked for the marches. Russians, Poles, Czechs, French and a myriad of other nationalities on the list were carried into the infirmary to take the vacated bed-spaces, and walk out later with the numbers of the dead prisoners whose identity they had assumed.

Finally, the SS guards realised something was interfering with their ability to execute their orders effectively. A more rigorous head-count was initiated in the infirmary. By then Pat estimated five-thousand prisoners had been saved. Among the British orderlies there was a grim satisfaction at having duped the enemy.

As March turned to April, aeroplanes appeared overhead, and distant gunfire could be heard. Rumours were rife about the Allies approach, but trains continued to arrive at Dachau from other parts of Germany, and death marches set off from the main gate each day. Within the camp, organization was breaking down. Outside work details had halted and men were confined to barracks. In the infirmary the death-toll was still rising. Bodies were carried to the crematorium each morning, and corpses shovelled into ovens that had already disposed of tens of thousands of prisoners. The supply of firewood ran low and bodies stacked in the yard outside the furnaces.

Harry was scrubbing down the infirmary floor one morning, when a man was brought in with blotched skin and soaring temperature. The emaciated face, its sunken cheeks and hollowed eyes, still bore some resemblance to Tomasz. He treated him as best he could, drawing on the limited supply of precious aspirins and bathing his head frequently with cold water. Finally, the temperature dropped. Tomasz opened his eyes. He clutched Harry's hand.

'You'll be okay, Tomasz. Here you are safe.' The gunfire from the approaching Americans sounded close. 'The war will be over soon. You will see your wife and children.'

The hoary eyes glistened. '*Nein, nein, nein.*' Tomasz whispered that his name was on the list. '*Vielleicht morgen. Vielleicht am nächsten Tag.*'

In his bunk that night, pressed between bodies either side, Harry couldn't sleep. Having survived fifteen months at Dachau, it was unbelievably brutal Tomasz should be shot in cold blood with liberation in earshot. He imagined the faces of his wife and children, desperate for the return of a husband and father to end the misery of Nazi occupation. He found himself thinking about Wang, the peasant-farmer, and his wife O-Lan in the book Douglass had given him. Driven from their home by famine, they had fought to avoid destitution, determined to secure a future for their children. O-lan's stoical loyalty, and the bonds of family and kinship, had given them strength to make the journey back from the abyss.

He wondered about Lin Xiaobin and Douglass. Little news about the war in the east had filtered into the camp, although two weeks ago a captured French resistance fighter, who had spent time in Vietnam, relayed that the Americans were island hopping towards Japan, having secured Iwo Jima after a bloody battle. But the advance was slow and there was talk of the Pacific war lasting several more years.

Harry thought about his own war. Following Churchill's appeal to patriotism after Dunkirk, the talk in the sixth-form common-room was all about Britain standing alone against the tyranny that had devastated Europe. He'd walked into the recruiting office in the Strand, determined to join the fight to vanquish the forces of evil, and create a new world-order where respect for every individual prevailed. The death of his parents in the November Blitz had sharpened his resolve.

That determination had given him an edge. Discovering he had some flying-skill was a huge uplift, and the partnership with Archie had seen them become one of the Royal Air Force's ace crews, before they were even old enough to vote. And then he'd learnt the enemy was also the Japanese, and there had been a second war, with different comrades and codes.

Through it all, Amy and Archie had been the lynchpins in his journey from Aircraftsman Second-class to Wing Commander Winchester, with an impressive tally of downed German and Japanese planes. If life was about making a difference, he'd had an impact. Scores of wives, girlfriends and mothers would have cursed the unknown assailant that robbed them of their loved one. Orphaned children would have wailed at the news they would never see their father again. Seeds of revenge would have been sown deep in the hearts of those affected.

On his bunk, Harry scratched lice gnawing at his yellowing skin, conscious of a body aged with experience beyond its years. He would be twenty-three in two months' time, the same age as Tomasz, who had two children already. He recalled the conversations with Amy that had concluded with her saying, *'when the war's over.'* But after they'd pushed open the door to the cottage at the edge of the airfield and glimpsed the possibility of another way of living, they had agreed to stop taking precautions and let nature takes it course.

It may well have happened on that last night together. The explosive intensity had surprised them both, and they'd curled round each other on the leather covering for a long time. When they'd finally climbed over to the front seats and Harry had pressed the button, whirring the engine to life, Amy stretched her arms around him. *'I think we may have started something.'*

But the incendiaries that landed in the grounds had put an end to any beginning. Once again, Harry was looking up from his hospital bed at the Dumbo ears of his navigator, watching the crow flying towards the wintery sunset.

*'Luftwaffe must have known Bylaugh Hall was directing the bombers. Blitzed the site the night we pranged. Radar didn't even pick em up, so no ack-ack defence. Destroyed two Nissen-huts in the grounds where the radio teams worked at night. High-explosives. Nothing left.'*

Why hadn't Archie seen the enemy-aircraft on his tube, as they took off? There had been cumulus, but it was mostly a clear night, as they'd climbed from Swanton Morley and turned above Lybaugh. Why no tell-tale glow from intruders' exhausts? He'd not seen any other aircraft, apart from the familiar outline of the Mosquitoes ahead.

Why would radar have failed to pick up the Luftwaffe? That was Amy's job after all. Somewhere below their plane, she would have been studying the green luminescence of her screen, directing the Allied bombers across the North Sea from their bases in Lincolnshire. Surely she would have spotted a rogue blip?

Harry was conscious of a sick-feeling rising in his stomach, of understanding something that he didn't want to recognise, knowledge he'd rather not possess, a truth Archie had carefully masked. Hundred-gallon drop-tanks wouldn't show up on anyone's radar. But they'd make a hell of a mess when they hit the ground. He could feel himself being dragged down into a bog-dark blackness of despair, in which he was utterly alone.

In the morning he was at the infirmary before dawn. The night-orderly made no comment as Harry entered, simply pointed to the numbers chalked on the wooden board, listing those in the sick-bay required to march. Tomasz was asleep, sharing the foul mattress with two other comatose prisoners. His breathing was normal and the skin had regained its usual colour. Harry reached for the block of chalk. Half an hour later he was standing on the parade-ground for roll-call, watching the guard who held the plank of wood. Hearing his number, he joined the group of Polish prisoners lining in front of the *Jourhaus*.

Stefan's eyes widened with surprise. '*Gdzie Tomasz?*'

Harry pressed his fingertips to his lips, praying Stefan would remain silent. When the last number had been called, Harry risked lifting his eyes to glance behind. Hundreds of emaciated men were standing in-line with heads bowed. Away to the left on the parade-ground, a tattered multitude stood watching in silence.

'*Marsch, ihr Schweine!*' The guard by the gate cracked his bull-whip and loosened the leash of his doberman, who snapped at the closest men. The shambling column shuffled across stony ground in an assortment of footware, some with strips of cloth tied round planks of wood fashioned into crude clogs, others with patched boots, cracked at the toes, and a larger number now barefoot, toes suppurating from untreated frostbite and oozing puss.

They passed under the entrance-gate with the great-crested Eagle spreading its wings over the swastika. Harry brushed against Stefan and allowed a smile to form inside his lips. It felt good to have beaten the bastards again.

'*Links, rechts.*' The dogs barked and snarled, forcing stragglers into line as the ragged line stumbled towards the woods beyond the crematorium.

The steel trellis-gate banged shut behind them, loosening flecks of black paint from the rusting ironwork above. *Arbeit Macht Frei.*

# Chapter Thirty

## Nanjing:
## September 8th 1945

Sunlight flashed on the wings of the Black Widows. The formation banked left to begin their descent. The Dakota in the centre of the hexagon of fighter planes looked like a Queen bee surrounded by her protective swarm. Beneath, the city emerged from the haze, resembling the remains of an archaeological excavation. Along the wharves beside the Yangtze, surviving walls of apartment blocks and concrete pillars that had once supported bridges, cast long shadows across the rubble of flattened houses, inter-crossed with the grey lines of former roads.

As the flight straightened to approach the runway, Colonel Lin ordered the fighters to veer away, allowing the transport plane to touch down unencumbered. 'Yellow Leader on final approach.'

'Control to Yellow Leader. Clear to land.' A familiar mid-west accent crackled over the intercom.

How on earth had Douglass positioned himself in the tower? It was a year since they'd parted at Hengyang, hours before the airfield was overrun by the Japanese Army. He allowed the Dakota to sink gently towards the runway. It bounced twice and settled, and he pulled back on the throttle to slow the plane to a walking pace, swinging to the left to line up in front of the corrugated-iron hut serving as a terminal-building. He cut the engines and the propellors quivered to a halt.

Colonel Xiaobin opened the cabin door behind, surveying the uniformed men, struck by the adornment of gold braid. He bowed to the three-star general in the front seat. 'We have arrived exactly on time, sir. The fighters will land shortly and crews will remain on standby.'

General He Yingqin unbuckled his belt and stood. 'Thank you, Colonel. I believe we will be met by General Wu, controller of Jiangsu province, and there will be members of the Chinese Army in attendance. However, I would like to maintain protection from our air force, and would be grateful if you could accompany us personally during this visit.'

He outlined the schedule. After a tour of Nanjing to witness the devastation caused by eight years of occupation, they would meet General Okamura, the Japanese commander, to agree surrender details for next day's ceremony. Although a formal signing had already taken place, with General MacArthur on USS Missouri in Tokyo Bay, this would be the official surrender on Chinese soil. The world's press was expected.

General He surveyed the assemblage of gold braid. 'It will set out the arrangements by which our victorious army takes back control of the different regions of China.'

Lin Xiaobin was hoping he'd have time to go to the control tower, but the cars were lined on the tarmac as the generals descended the steps. He instructed his co-pilot, Fu Zheji, to organise billets for the eight fighter crews and ensure an armed contingent was on duty at the Military Academy, by the time they met with the Japanese generals at three o'clock.

'We have no guns, though.' Fu Zheji frowned.

'Find some.' Colonel Lin was blunt. 'You have full authority to requisition weapons. If necessary, invoke the Generalissimo. It is important we muster a personal bodyguard for General He. Although Emperor Hirohito has agreed the surrender terms, not all Japanese soldiers will set aside the Bushido code. Some will prefer a warrior's death to the dishonour of capitulation.'

Xiaobin sat in the back of the commandeered car, as the convoy of vehicles negotiated rubble-strewn roads. At ground level, the devastation presented a different picture. Along the river there was considerable bomb-damage, where the Chinese air force had tried to prevent supplies being landed to prop up Wang Jinwei's regime. But other areas had been left unscathed and many buildings were intact, although the city was cloaked in a covering of dust that hung in the air at every stop.

The convoy passed through a suburb, where Lin Xiaobin recognised the familiar shape of the water tower that had been a landmark when walking to school as a young boy.

He turned to the officer beside him. 'Can we stop for a moment, sir?'

General Zhang nodded. 'Of course, but don't be long. The past is another country.' He understood what Colonel Lin needed to do.

Xiaobin stepped across the debris of what had been a courtyard garden around a farmhouse. A solitary banana tree and hibiscus bush had survived the choking weeds growing through the rubble. The posts of a chicken coop were still in place, although the wire had gone. The walls of the building were mostly undamaged, but the roof had collapsed into what had been the communal room, with brambles clawing round the broken tiles.

He kicked the front door and the hinges squealed as it swung open. In the hallway a makeshift shelter had been constructed with plastic sheeting. A grimy mattress lay on the beaten earth. Several tin cans contained stubs of candles. There was a strong smell of urine, he guessed was a fox, as the brambles had already straggled across most of the mattress. He called out, but the hollowness of the echo mocked him. Lin Xiaobin turned and spotted a small, white arm in the rubble. He reached down and pulled out a panda bear. It was missing an eye and the shavings showed through the broken stitching of its stomach. Mei Li's favourite bear. He climbed into the car, clutching the grimy toy.

At the Military Academy, Fu Zheji had secured rifles for the squad of pilots, who formed a guard of honour for General He as he mounted the steps.

In the huge auditorium Lin Xiaobin and Fu Zheji sat to one side, watching the Japanese delegation take their seats at the large table in the centre of the room, across from the Chinese military. Around the room, a line of soldiers stood watching impassively. Although they were close enough to hear what was being said, Lin Xiaobin couldn't understand a word. General He was laughing as he shook the hand of one of the Japanese generals.

Xiaobin turned to Captain Fu. 'Are they all speaking Japanese?' His disbelief was evident.

'Many of the Chinese generals trained at the Imperial Japanese Army Academy in Tokyo. General He and General Okamura were there at the same time. They are sharing stories about their instructors.'

'How do you know Japanese?'

'My father was in the embassy in Tokyo, so I went to school there four years before the war.' Fu Zheji explained the men were discussing the shape of the table for the official surrender ceremony. The Chinese leaders had wanted a round table, so the Japanese delegation would be seen as equals, but the Americans had over-ruled this.

'General He is apologising to General Okamura for subjecting him to such an embarrassing arrangement.'

'But we are the victors?' Colonel Lin ran his fingers through his black hair, straightening the queue down his back.

'The Generalissimo needs Japanese troops to remain in control of many areas of China, until the Army can take-over.'

'So the Japanese have become our Allies?' Lin Xiaobin's voice rose a pitch higher than usual.

'Avoiding loss of face is very important,' muttered Captain Fu. 'General He has said the Americans are insisting on this, not us. It seems the Japanese understand. They are now discussing where they will have dinner tonight.'

'Doesn't sound like General He needs protection.' Lin Xiaobin spat each word. 'I will confirm the time he needs us here tomorrow and we can return to our hotel.'

Later that evening Lin Xiaobin was sitting with the rest of the crews in the bar, mindful they would need to be on duty early next day.

'Hey there, Yellow Leader.'

Xiaobin turned to see Douglass's familiar face. His right

shoulder was neatly pinned beneath the epaulette with its eagle insignia.

'You made it to full Colonel as well?' Xiaobin gripped Douglass's left hand.

'Next step Brigadier General, eh?'

'Unlikely.' Xiaobin looked thoughtful. 'With the war over, there's going to be an over-supply of gold braid. Some of us will have to get used to life out of uniform. But what brings you here?'

'Chennault asked me to attend on his behalf, as he was called back to the States. I flew in yesterday and saw your name on the VIP list. Thought I'd do a stint at the control tower, surprise you.'

'You still in Zhijiang? Or back in Chongqing?'

'Chongqing. Part of Ambassador Hurley's liaison team. Did you know Mao arrived from Yan'an a couple of weeks ago for talks with the Generalissimo?'

'I heard he wanted to send Zhou Enlai in his place?'

'Yeah, he was worried about his own safety. They all remember the time Chiang Kai-shek was held by the People's Army in Xi'an. There's not a lot of trust between the Communists and Nationalists. But Hurley promised to guarantee Mao's safety. They're in talks about a coalition.'

'Thank God.' Xiaobin's response was heartfelt. 'Peace at last. A chance to build a united China.' He tugged at his queue, which was brushing the seat of the chair. 'Tomorrow I will be able to cut this off.'

'As long as Mao is happy. Remember I was heading to his place in Yan'an when we last split?'

'From Hengyang?'

The American nodded. 'Close shave, eh? I was on the last transport out, before you flew back to Zhijiang. I went to Yan'an as part of the Allied mission to case the joint.'

'What did you think?'

Dougie raised his eyebrows. 'Honest answer is very impressed. We were there a month. Mao met us at the airfield in person, made sure we saw what the People's Army had achieved. Some of the contrasts with Chongqing were pretty remarkable. No beggars anywhere and, although life was pretty basic, everyone was fed and clothed. There was huge support for Mao, wherever we went.'

Douglass recalled the heated discussions in the evenings among the members of the American and Soviet contingents, and the warning from Stalin's representative about not taking everything at face value. 'Vladimirov reminded us that, without the Kuomintang support in Burma, it's anyone's guess as to which flag would be flying in India right now. The Yanks recognise Chiang's military efforts, but hate the corruption. They want Mao involved in negotiations as an equal.'

It was after midnight before the two men climbed the wide staircase to their adjacent bedrooms. Xiaobin unlocked his door and turned to the American.

'Any news of Commander Winchester?'

Douglass shook his head. 'Not a peep. My cousin was shot down over Germany last year, not long after he'd met Harry, so no more news, I'm afraid. Now this show's finished, I'll try and make contact.'

'Give him my good wishes. He was a fine man.'

'He sure made a difference, wherever he went.' Douglass

hesitated outside his own room. 'I'll be leaving for Chongqing tomorrow evening, so may not get a chance to talk again. Once Mao and Chiang have agreed a deal, our job is done, so I'm likely to be posted back to the States pretty soon.'

Lin Xiaobin grasped Douglass's hand. 'Let's keep in touch.'

The American pressed his glasses against the bridge of his nose. He lowered his voice. 'Just watch your back, Xiaobin. There's already rumbling up north, where Mao has been moving troops into Manchuria. Although Chiang is seen as China's leader at the moment, I wouldn't bet my shirt on the outcome, if it comes to a punch up.' He looked directly at Lin Xiaobin for a few seconds and then closed his door.

Early the following morning, Colonel Lin was seated in the auditorium of the Military Academy. On the raised plinth between the columns that stretched to the glass dome, four flags were held upright by soldiers of the Chinese National Army. The Stars and Stripes and the White Sun were flanked by the Union Jack and the Hammer and Sickle of the Soviet Union. Either side were fourteen more flags. He recognised New Zealand, Canada, Australia, France, Korea and the Netherlands, but couldn't work out the rest, intrigued so many countries had claimed an alliance with China.

Five Chinese generals marched in and took their seats at the large table in the centre of the room. To the right, at a smaller table, seven Japanese generals were squeezed into line. Behind them stood a man with the rank of major. Xiaobin presumed he was there to translate.

At the stroke of nine, the soldiers were called to attention and the ceremony began. The Japanese came forward one at a time and signed the surrender. Finally, General Okamura handed the document to General He. The seven Japanese generals bowed from the waist. General He stared impassively back as the flashguns popped. There was no cheering or clapping, just a sombre silence as the Chinese generals studied the signatures.

General He spoke briefly, confirming that the War in China had finally ended, repeating the hope expressed by General MacArthur that a lasting peace would be sustained throughout the world.

Slowly the assembled audience filed into the adjacent hall, where tea was served. Lin Xiaobin observed the Japanese generals standing in a group with the Chinese top brass. He walked towards them, wondering what was in their minds behind the impassive masks. His fingers closed round the handle of the small pistol buried deep in his pocket. One bullet for each of the Japanese. Then it would be down to his bare hands. He looked up at the blue sky beyond the domed ceiling, allowing the image of Mei Li to fill his head. He stepped forward, loosening the gun from its padding.

'You find this difficult?' Xiaobin turned round to see the Major who had been standing behind the Japanese generals. 'Yet you are the victors.'

Lin Xiaobin studied the man's face. He recalled Harry's remark about not being able to tell the difference between Chinese and Japanese people. It was very obvious when you were close-up. The Major's eyes were large, with prominent lids, making it seem as if he was looking downwards. The face was heavier. He breathed in deeply, conscious of his finger round the trigger of the pistol.

'Where did you learn your English?'

'I went to school at Marlborough before the war. My parents were diplomats in London. I returned to Japan in 1940 to join the army.'

'I saw you in the hall.'

'I am one of the translators for the Japanese delegation. My colleague is doing it now, so I have a break. I arrived here last year from Manchuria, where I had been the liaison officer between the Japanese and Emperor Pu Yi. There we were able to maintain good relations between the local population and our troops.' His manicured fingers stroked his chin. 'Here was different though. I have heard awful stories about what happened after the Imperial Army entering Nanjing. I could only think they had been exaggerated.'

Lin Xiaobin recalled the train pulling away, pinioned to his seat by the strong arms of Herr Klein. How could he ever forget the look on Mei Li's face? His chest tightened. 'The Rape of Nanjing was a war crime, and the perpetrators should be brought to justice.'

'I agree with you in principle,' came the suave response, 'but two hundred thousand soldiers were involved. How can you ever identify them all?'

'Those in charge should be brought back to China. General He has already spoken with your General Okamura about Chen Gongbo, who took over as President after Wang Jinwei died. If the American occupation forces agree, he will be returned to China to face a firing squad.'

'It is understandable to seek revenge, but who does this satisfy?'

'I would find it very satisfying to line you all up against a wall.' Xiaobin's finger played with the trigger. He moved closer to the Japanese generals.

'It was war and it is finished. As victors you will write the history.'

'But war should be fought between men in uniform. Not innocent civilians.'

'I agree, Colonel. When I arrived in Nanjing, I ordered my men to respect the Bushido code for treatment of non-combatants.'

'There can't have been many Chinese left to respect.'

The translator's eyes narrowed. 'I think I know how you feel.'

'How can you possibly know?' Lin Xiaobin spat the words, as he edged backwards. If only he had more bullets. He clenched his left hand into a closed fist, remembering his training. When the ammunition ran out, one punch on the neck would be enough. Through the mist came the voice of the Japanese major.

'My family live in a town in the west of Honshu Island. We have a small house beside the old fishing harbour. I've not seen my wife and five children since I was posted to China three years ago. Because of the napalm raids on Tokyo, I heard that my mother and father had moved in with my family on Honshu. I prayed for their safety every night, and I received a message from my wife on the fifth of August saying they were all well. They were planning to visit my wife's parents in the mountains at the weekend.' He paused, and his eyes stared levelly at Colonel Lin. 'That was four weeks ago. I haven't heard from them since.'

Xiaobin had the seven generals in a line behind him. All he needed to do was swivel. But the major was still talking. It would be impolite to turn before he finished.

'I only want to know if they left Hiroshima in time.'

# Part Five

"Reality" is what we take to be true. What we take to be true is what we believe. What we believe is based upon our perceptions. What we perceive depends upon what we look for. What we look for depends upon what we think. What we think depends upon what we perceive. What we perceive determines what we believe. What we believe determines what we take to be true. What we take to be true is our reality.

Gary Zukav,
*Dancing Wu Li Masters: An Overview of the New Physics*

# Chapter Thirty-one

## London Airport:
## Thursday 23rd January 2020

The gate slid open and Sunny pulled her wheelie-suitcase to the line of people waiting to greet arrivals. Coffee from Starbucks wafted across in invisible threads. She searched faces. Late-afternoon sunlight refracted through high windows beyond the coffee-shop, sprinkling the floor with diamonds. She could feel her pulse race and took a deep breath, to more systematically scan the crowd.

Then she saw the banner held high above the crush of excited heads.

*Welcome Lu Chen Xi*

The Union Jack and Wǔxīng Hóngqí were emblazoned across opposite corners. In the centre was a photograph of a couple standing on a rope bridge. The roofline of the temple near Pingle was just visible in the background.

Sunny hurried forwards and Torin let the banner fall. She hesitated in front of him, registering the warmth in his eyes and familiar smile. She glanced down at the banner and then back to his face.

The voices in the arrival-hall faded, the clattering of cups and trays in Starbucks hushed, and the flight-announcements over the speaker-system quietened. The world was the space around them, with no space between.

'Can you roll that up?' A blue-uniformed security-guard, with a shaved head and G4S on his epaulettes, pointed at the photographs curling on the floor. 'Someone might trip over it.'

Torin knelt, fumbling for the corners of the banner to gather it into a scroll. He looked up at Sunny. There was an awkward silence.

'The indicator-board showed you'd landed at three, and then it was ages before the sign changed, saying baggage was being delivered.' He rose, holding the banner with both hands. 'Was there a problem?'

'Big queue for foreigners, and there was something not right with visa of woman in front. I think it finished.'

'You mean no longer valid?'

'Ran out mid-air. She was not allowed through. Must go back to Chengdu on the next plane. Husband very cross because he have to take the children on his own.'

'Not a great start to their visit.'

A smile creased Sunny's cheeks. 'I think she very happy to have a holiday back in China. Children supposed to be in first class with parents, but lots of running around near me.'

'You must be tired.'

'Stretched day. I hope sleep tonight.'

Torin glanced at his watch. 'We should be home around six o'clock, if we take the fast train to London, and then the tube.'

'Tube?'

'Underground… metro… don't know why we call it the tube. Maybe history?' He hesitated, floundering. 'Some of it was built more than a hundred and fifty years ago.'

'Chengdu metro ten years old. We underground baby of the world.'

It was nearly dark when the Heathrow Express pulled

into Paddington station. They walked along the concourse, so Sunny could be photographed beside Paddington Bear. Further up the platform Torin noticed a wreath on the memorial-plinth to the dead of two world-wars. Their shoes clattered on the steps and they crossed to the connecting slipway for the Metropolitan Line.

Minutes after the train slid into the tunnel, Sunny felt the carriage lurch and saw blue flashes light the snaking cables against grime-black walls. She wondered if something was wrong, but Torin was calmly studying the map above the seats. She closed her eyes, concentrating on her breathing. She felt Torin nudge her as the train slowed and realised she'd fallen asleep.

They came out of Mile End station to cross the main road. Sunny was floating. Everything felt surreal—traffic on the wrong side, street-lighting, design of houses, smells, trees, city noise, and a myriad of people from south Asia and Africa alongside women in niqabs, Europeans with large noses, and olive-skinned faces from the Mediterranean.

They walked along Eric street, past apartment blocks and the *Wentworth Arms*. On the corner Sunny noticed *Amin's Express* in green paint above the shutters of the convenience-store, and they crossed the road to a modern block of flats.

'Keats Court.' Torin tapped in the code and metal gates swung open to an entrance-lobby.

'We're on the fifth—right at the top.'

He pushed open the door of the flat and put Sunny's suitcase in the hallway. 'Just a small apartment.' His arm swung in an arc, indicating the four doors leading off the lobby. 'Sitting room and kitchen through there, bedroom, office, and bathroom in there.'

She took off her shoes, carefully placing them beside the front door. She looked at his pictures on the wall. A large map of the USA was dotted with blue pins, connected by a strand of wool from California up to Seattle, down the Appalachians to the Grand Canyon, and then across the southern states to New Orleans, before looping up to New York.

'Gap year.' He smiled. 'Drove across the States with a friend.'

'And this one?' She pointed at a map of the world, with coloured markers pressed into different countries. 'Places you've visited?' She noticed a yellow pin for Chengdu, and thought of her mother and father asleep in their apartment.

Torin switched on the light in the sitting-room, and she registered the kitchen area with a dining-table at one end, and French doors leading onto a balcony at the other. Sunny walked across the wooden floor and looked through the glass. In the building opposite many windows were lit. She saw a couple watching television in one flat, and next door a young girl on a rocking chair, stroking a cat curled on her lap. Below, she saw the tops of tree branches.

Sunny turned back to the sitting-room, where Torin was adjusting the flickering flames of the gas fire in the grate. Above the mantelpiece, framed photographs led in a sequence up to a mountain-peak. Sunlight glistened off the snow behind climbers, all wearing dark glasses. 'That's me.' He pointed at a grinning figure in a bright-blue bobble-hat. The mountaineering club at university had organised an expedition to Chile during his final year.

'Haven't climbed for years though. A bit out of shape, as you noticed at Dazhentou.'

'Need to keep fit.'

She felt Torin's arms around her and his lips nuzzled her neck. Tiredness rose like a wave. She knew she needed to lie down. She faced him, taking his hands. 'Sorry Torin. I'm floating, like balloon. Want to sleep. Nearly two o'clock in morning in Chengdu. Can I have water?'

'Of course.' He turned away to hide his disappointment, feeling churlish. He pulled her suitcase into the bedroom, then went back to the kitchen. By the time he returned, carrying a glass, Sunny was asleep on the bed, fully clothed. He watched the rise and fall of her breathing, thinking it had been several years since anyone had stayed in his flat.

It was still dark when Sunny awoke to strange sounds. She recognised the purr of an electric-motor outside the window, but could also hear jars rattling. There was silence for a few seconds, followed by a person whistling and bottles clinking. Silence again. Then more clinking and whistling. The motor whirred and the noises evaporated into the distance.

She turned to see Torin watching her. 'Milk gets delivered around six o'clock before people go to work. Then newspapers between seven and eight, letters at ten. Amazon deliveries during the day.' He glanced at the small clock beside the bed. The digital display showed 6.13. 'It's still early. Will you go back to sleep?'

Sunny lifted her head from the pillow. 'Feel awake now.' She was aware of Torin's feet across her stockinged toes. As she looked into his eyes, she was reminded of the tiny jade dragon beside her bed, its varying shades of blue and green, the polished whorls. She knew she had to ask. 'Tell me how you are.'

He hesitated. 'Not sure, Sunny. Less tired, maybe. Difficult to say. There's been a lot at work, clearing things to take three weeks' holiday.' He rubbed a hand across the purple scar. 'I've been taking Doctor Zhang's medicine and only had one episode since Chengdu.'

'And exercise? You said you would start running?'

'It's hard to be motivated when the mornings are dark.'

'Maybe I can come too.' She'd kept up her training after the Chengdu marathon.

'I've never enjoyed jogging. Might be different with you though.'

'I run not jog. But can go slow if helps. I very flexible.'

He chuckled, thinking about their last night in the St. Regis, when they'd fallen asleep as the sky lightened.

She squeezed his hand. The fog from the previous night had lifted. She was ready to talk, laugh, connect, discover. 'I must shower. Then I want to see all the sights in London. Whole *Monopoly* board. Need to be with you today.'

Torin thought he understood.

They emerged from the entrance of Green Park station, into the sunlight flickering through a line of plane trees that stretched down the slope towards Constitution Hill. Their feet brushed through fallen leaves, yet to be swept away with the first cut of grass. Towards the lower end of the park, they heard pipes and drums.

'Must be changing the guard at Buckingham Palace.' Torin hummed the tune.

'Just when we arrive?'

'I let the Queen know you were coming.' He smiled at her puzzled expression. 'Happens every day, same time.'

They watched the red-coated soldiers in their busbies march through the open gates, before joining the crush of bodies in front of the railings. Phones appeared above heads, between children on shoulders. Behind, people were standing on the Victoria Memorial.

Sunny was fascinated by the ritual of shouted orders, stamping feet, shouldering arms, and expressionless compliance, as the new guards replaced the old. Sunlight glinted on the polished rifle-barrels. A final command was given and the beating drums marked the end of the ceremony. Sunny filmed the men striding from the palace in perfect step, and texted a clip to her mum. 'Is Queen inside?'

Torin pointed to the Royal Standard fluttering above the roof. 'She must be here today, or the Union Jack would be flying instead. This is her office really. Lots happening about Brexit, so maybe she's with the Prime Minister.'

In the shop beside the Palace, they bought a book about the Kings and Queens of England. Sunny was delighted that it came in a bag emblazoned with the Palace logo. It was the start of a day that passed in a whirl of images, as if her English textbooks had come to life. The famous sights were no longer two-dimensional photographs, and she captured them all on her iPhone to send to her mother.

The pelicans in St. James's Park had beaks large enough to hide babies, like the story about Genghis Khan her mother had read to her as a child. The Mongol invaders swept through the Imperial Palace, determined to slay any young boys to prevent them growing into soldiers. While the Emperor's men ransacked the rooms, searching in vain for hidden princes, the pelicans watched impassively from the lake. After the murderous hordes galloped off, the magnificent, white birds opened their mouths to reveal small children curled up against their soft tongues, sound asleep.

They walked through the archway from Horse Guards Parade into Whitehall. The mounted guard in the box looked like the soldier in the poster on the wall of her office in Chengdu, with his red coat draped across the saddle. Now she could see his eyes staring impassively beyond the crowd. She smelt the manure scraped into a pile in the corner of the box, and heard the iron shoes scuffing cobbles, as the soldier steadied his horse against a barrage of photographers. She realised the face, framed by a strap holding the ceremonial helmet, was that of a teenager.

Beyond the policeman at the gates to Downing Street, the door to Number 10 was just visible behind a black limousine. There was an air of expectancy in faces pressing against the railings. Torin heard the man standing beside him tell his friend the Prime Minister was going to make an announcement about signing the Brexit withdrawal document, having been to see The Queen.

They eased away from the crush of bodies towards Parliament Square. Sunny stopped opposite Churchill's statue, to look up at Big Ben. Despite the scaffolding shroud, it was imposing. The sun behind the gold clockface, gave the tower a magical aura. She took a photo and sent the image to Huang Guo and Lin Ting.

Sunny turned to see Torin watching her. She held up her phone and touched the camera button. She was studying his face on the screen, when he took her hand and pressed her against the stone wall of the Treasury building, away from passers-by. As they kissed, the mix of relief and excitement was overwhelming. She struggled to stay upright. The sounds and smells of the city faded. She was aware of his lips, his taste, his scent, his nose brushing hers, the feel of his fingers wrapped between her own, coiling and uncoiling.

'I love you,' he whispered, after they broke apart, breathlessly standing close to the wall.

She thought her heart might burst. She wanted to hear him say it again, and again, and again. Wang Yi had used those words a lot, but she'd never believed it was about much more than physical desire, and she had been hesitant to echo the phrase.

Her fingers brushed his cheek. '*Wǒ yě ài nǐ*'

'Is that what I said?'

'Nearly, but different in Chinese. Not feel so real if I say in English.'

'*Wo ye ai ni*,' he repeated.

She smiled, nuzzling the blonde hairs on the nape of his neck. 'Stay with English. Sounds more true.'

He held her head gently between his two hands, looking into her brown eyes. 'I love you, Sunny.'

She could feel him against her and her breathing quickened. 'If continue, I not able to walk more.'

'We can go home any time.'

She hesitated. 'But if we feel same tomorrow, may never get to see London.'

'We have three weeks.'

'If you promise feelings stay till later, we continue.'

His smile broadened. 'The feeling will be there later.'

'One hundred percent?'

'Even more, if you want.'

'Not possible, but hundred will do.' She looked around the square. 'Can we find some food near here?'

They walked to Central Hall, across from Westminster Abbey, and descended stairs to the restaurant. It was nearly two o'clock, and the lunch-time queues had subsided. In a quiet corner, they shared a tapas platter and she showed him her photos.

'Have you sent some home?'

'Hundreds. My Mum excited at Queen's soldiers, and Huang Guo loving Paddington Bear. We saw film together last week.'

The sun was low behind the Houses of Parliament by the time they followed the crush of bodies through the pavement-bollards onto Westminster Bridge. To their right, they could see people on the Members' terrace, above the fast-flowing river.

London Eye loomed. Sunny looked up at the pods silhouetted against the clear, blue sky. It was hard to tell they were turning. The snake of people on the concourse reminded her of the crowds on the spiral staircase leading to the feet of the Giant Buddha at Leshan.

'We'll go there after the boat trip. I've bought tickets for both,' explained Torin.

The river-cruiser headed downstream under Hungerford Bridge. Sunny listened to the Mandarin commentary through headphones, as a guide regaled listeners in English with stories behind the buildings and skyline. Waterloo Bridge, Oxo Tower, Blackfriars Bridge,

Shakespeare's Globe, Southwark Bridge, London Bridge and HMS Belfast. Finally, the boat glided under Tower Bridge and they looked at the clear rectangle of walkway, to see pedestrians cross the river, hundreds of feet above. The boat circled St. Katharine's Dock, turning into the setting sun for the return trip along the north bank of the Thames, with more anecdotes between the Tower of London and Cleopatra's Needle.

Before they disembarked, Torin bought two ice-creams from the café below the promenade deck, and they strolled up the slipway towards the queue for the London Eye. Torin guessed it would be over an hour before they reached the ramp to the pods. He spotted an attendant holding open a barrier for a small group of Chinese families, squeezing in front of the main queue. Torin caught the young woman's eye, and pulled Sunny behind the people going through the barrier.

'You with this group in fast track, sir?'

Torin gestured at his girlfriend. 'Chen Xi is with China UK Ventures. Translation and interpreting.'

The attendant nodded, holding open the metal gate.

'What do you mean?' whispered Sunny. 'We not part of this group.'

'There's less than twenty,' he murmured in her ear. 'So, we help to make up their pod-numbers. We're shortening the queue for everyone.'

'Maybe.' Sunny looked unconvinced. 'You mistaken though. These from South Korea. I not understand what they say.'

The doors folded over the entrance of the pod and it started to lift from the crowds on the decking. They rose above the Golden Jubilee bridges and looked down the Thames, past the Shard towards the curve of the Isle of Dogs, to see the Millennium Dome rise through the gathering dusk beyond the skyscrapers on Canary Wharf.

As the wheel reached its zenith, they moved to the other side of the pod, to see Battersea Power station and Lambeth Palace. Finally, the Houses of Parliament came into view, as they approached the docking station.

They could hear Big Ben striking the hour, when they came out of the gift shop. Sunny clutched London buses for Lin Ting and Huang Guo, and Torin was holding the photo of pod 26, showing their faces pressed against the perspex.

'Six o'clock. Shall we go to Chinatown for food?'

'New Year in UK. So exciting.' Sunny held Torin's hand across Jubilee Bridge and down the steps onto Northumberland Avenue. They walked to the Pall Mall corner of Trafalgar Square, and zigzagged over Leicester Square into Wardour Street.

Passing the brightly-lit Qing Dynasty gates, they entered a world of red lanterns and haunting melodies of the bamboo *Dizi*. Chinese flags hung from every window, illuminating the Rats that graced the entrance door to each restaurant. In *Golden Dragon*, the waiter found a table for two in a corner. They ordered Beijing Duck and watched the opera.

Sunny took pictures of the changing face-masks and fire-eating till the food arrived, then wrapped pieces of duck in the wafer-thin pancakes, spreading them with hoisin sauce and slices of onion and cucumber.

They drank warm water and green tea.

On the tube to Mile End, Sunny opened the cardboard-packaging around one of the buses. It was a perfect replica. 'Good presents, but maybe scratch this out.' She held up the box.

Torin adjusted his spectacles to make out the wording, *Made in China*.

'Can't buy in Chengdu though. Factory in Shenzhen only sell to UK. Linda and Coco will know I bought them in London.'

This time Sunny enjoyed the walk along Eric Street from Mile End station. It felt familiar and she knew where she was going. She was curious about the random gaps in a line of terraced-houses, grassed over with shrubs and wooden seats. Torin explained about the wartime bombing that had hammered the East End. 'If no relatives came forward to claim ownership, the council had to do something with the space. I remember the landlord of the *Wentworth Arms* telling me Keats Court was built on an old bomb site. It was acquired by a property developer, who was able to prove his grandparents lived there during the War.'

Inside his flat, Torin lit the fire, while Sunny opened the wine and poured two glasses. They sat on the carpet, watching the flickering flames.

She turned to Torin. 'Still hundred per cent?'

# Chapter Thirty-two

## Rutland Mews, London: Sunday 26th January 2020

They turned into Rutland Mews North and stopped outside number twenty-eight. The front of the house was rendered in honeysuckle-yellow, with the curving arches above the windows picked out in white paint. A marble flagstone formed the step up to the black front-door, its polished-brass knocker in the shape of a lion's head. Wisteria climbed up the left of the porch, weaving its tendrils above the doorway and through the flaking branches of a grape vine, rooted in a matching tub on the opposite side of the step.

The adjoining houses were painted in pastels of greys and blues, and the cobbled street was empty of cars. It seemed to Sunny as if they had stepped onto a film-set. She glanced back at the entrance-arch, half expecting a horse-drawn carriage to clatter into the mews. 'Has your grandmother lived here long?'

'Fifty or sixty years, but the house is very old. You can tell from the style.' Torin pointed up at the line of sash windows. 'This was a magical place for a child, because it's close to Kensington Palace. Granny Mette talked about the princes and princesses who lived as neighbours, making up stories about the lives they led. I grew up believing Rapunzel was locked in the tower you can see from the attic.'

Torin looked at Sunny, standing on the marble step

above him. Her scarlet, woollen coat was unbuttoned to reveal a black jumper above a cream skirt. Below the hem, a pair of patterned tights ran down into the tops of brown, kitten-heel boots. A suede bag hung over her right shoulder, matching her footwear. 'I think you'll like Gran, but she sometimes has definite views about what's right and wrong.'

'Same with most old people. My grandparents always tell me skirt too short or hair too long. But I think if I grow skirt long and cut hair short. they still complain. I just smile and hug them. I know they love me really.'

Torin pressed the buzzer beside the brass strip engraved 'Rasmussen'.

There was a squawking the other side of the door. *'Just coming. Be there in a minute. Just coming. Be there in a minute.'* The voice had an odd register, barely human. Sunny moved back.

'Sorry, I should have warned you, Gran keeps a parrot as an answering machine, because it can take her a long time to reach the door.'

The latch slipped back and they looked up to see an old woman smiling down. She was wearing a beige knitted-cardigan over a grey blouse tucked into the top of a pair of tweed trousers. Her left hand grasped the carved head of a walking-stick. 'Come in, come in. Never mind Vestie. He won't bite.' She pushed the parrot back onto his stand with her stick, and the bird lifted his foot to scratch his ear, watching the newcomers as they stepped over the threshold. *'Wipe your feet, please. Wipe your feet, please.'*

'I'm Mette.' She extended her hand to Sunny. 'Very pleased to meet you. You look just like your name. So lovely. Thank you for sparing the time to visit an old lady.'

A smell of baking filled the hallway. 'I hope you like scones. I don't often get the chance these days, so thought I'd treat myself to the pleasure of using a rolling pin and cutting board, rather than rely on the delicatessen. It reminded me of making gingerbread-men with the children, when they visited from Scotland. Remember, Torin?'

He nodded, recalling the arguments with Emily about who would lick the remains of gooey batter in the empty bowl. They followed the old woman as she shuffled along the wide hallway in her flat-soled shoes, past a folded wheelchair and a gallery of black and white photographs, into an enormous kitchen. Mette hung her stick over the back of a chair.

Winter sunlight danced over the polished wooden-floor, cascading through the double French-doors that opened onto a small terrace. Sunny could see a pergola festooned with a dusty-leaved grapevine, trailing over a bench on which a cat basked in sunshine. Inside, a pine dining-table stood back from the patio doors, with a display of russet-coloured chrysanthemums in a vase in the centre. Three places were laid.

At the other end of the room, cupboards had been neatly fitted over granite worktops. Sunny thought of the new Ikea store in Chengdu. On top of the warm oven was a tray of scones. 'I love to live in a house like this. Everything perfect, and I like your paintings.' She pointed to the dining area, where framed pictures hung to one side of the table. Above the mantelpiece, a photograph of a thatched farmhouse reminded her of Du Fu's cottage. Tiny flames licked the glowing logs in the grate. 'Hen piaoliang. Very beautiful.'

Mette looked round curiously, as if seeing the room for the first time. 'I suppose I've had a few years to get it right.' Her fingers touched the silver brooch pinned at the top of the neckline of her blouse, matching a pair of earrings that flashed in the light from the ceiling pendant. She described the renovation work. It had been two separate rooms, each with a fireplace, but the dividing wall had been removed to make one room, creating a modern kitchen at one end. 'I'll show you the whole house later. First thing is coffee. I have not drunk any since breakfast and my body is suffering withdrawal symptoms.'

Torin could see Sunny was puzzled. 'Gran ingests coffee like it's going out of fashion. Very un-English in some of her habits.'

'That's because I'm a Viking at heart!' Mette thrust her chin forward. 'As well as sailing across wild seas in open boats, with upturned cow-horns on our heads to keep off the rain, we like our coffee strong and black. I may have been in London for seventy-five years, but I haven't lost my genetic coding. There are things you simply can't live without. Coffee is one. Rye bread is another.' She smiled at Sunny. 'Coming from China, you must find the same? What do you miss?'

'Spicy food. But my mum put chillies in suitcase, so all okay.'

'Sounds like a loving mother!'

Sunny nodded. 'She good.'

'I hope this is good too.' Mette pointed at the table. 'With cream and jam, because this is England. If you travel round the country, you will discover that different regions of the United Kingdom have their own specialities. I expect it is the same in China.' As she placed the food on the table and decanted the coffee, Mette took them through a culinary journey of the British Isles: Welsh cakes and larva bread; Cullen skink and haggis; Irish stew and colcannon; Cornish pasties and stargazy pie; Lancashire hot-pot and Yorkshire pudding.

Sunny studied Mette as she spoke. Although Torin had said she'd grown up in Scandinavia, there was no trace of an accent. She enunciated her vowels as clearly as The Queen, whose Tussauds' dummy she resembled. Despite a slight stoop, she was still taller than Sunny. Neatly-coiffured, white hair swept in gentle waves from a high forehead. Her blue-eyes sparkled. Sunny could feel the vitality emanating from the chiselled features. At the same time, she sensed a sadness behind the warmth.

Mette stood to refill the percolator. 'Tell me what you've been up to in London. Three days already? Has Torin shown you the sights?'

Sunny nodded, thinking about the whirlwind of images, captured in the hundreds of photographs on her iPhone. Mette was excited to see every picture and Sunny warmed to the older woman as they sat at the dining table. She was reminded of her great-grandfather on his farm, and the well of contentment that combined with an acceptance of the limitations imposed by age. *Zufu's* enthusiasm to hear about her activities was always affirming.

Sunny sensed a genuine interest, as Mette asked about her family, job and her thoughts. A smile creased the ageing face when she mentioned running and boxing. At the reference to *Weiqi*, Mette squeezed her hand. 'I used to play *Go* with a Japanese student who stayed here. I must dig it out and give you a game.'

The sun had long-gone from the terrace when Torin pointed to the clock above the fireplace. 'Sorry Gran, we've planned to go to the theatre tonight.'

'How exciting.' Mette's eyes flashed 'What are you seeing?'

'*The Lion King.*'

'You'll love it. Such energy. When does it start?'

'Seven thirty. We need to think about heading off, if we are going to walk there, and find somewhere to have food.'

Mette was still holding Sunny's hand. 'You haven't seen the house yet.'

'Maybe time now?' Sunny looked at Torin. 'Can we get Uber later?'

'Quicker by tube.' Mette stood and reached for her stick. 'Let's look round the house and have food here before you leave. It only takes a quarter of an hour on the District Line to the Embankment, which is ten minutes from the theatre.'

They walked through the connecting doorway into the sitting-room that ran the length of the house. Another pair of French windows led to the terrace at the back. The polished wooden-floor matched the dining-room. Sunny's eyes widened. She took in the carved, oak beam over the open hearth, with its basket of logs; a gilt-framed mirror above the mantelpiece that made the room seem even larger; upholstered sofas beckoning them to curl up; a glass-topped table with its bowl of half-open daffodils;

framed paintings on the walls; sash windows looking onto the terracotta mews-house opposite; discrete lighting from standard lamps; a crystal-glass chandelier hanging from the central rose; decorative plaster-moulding at the interface of ceiling and walls. In the corner beside the French windows, a bookcase stretched half the length of the room.

Sunny noticed many of the titles were not in English. 'Do you still read those books?'

'Not often, because my vocabulary is going. Sometimes I look at a word for ages, thinking I should know what it means.' Mette tapped the side of her head. 'It's the brain slowing up, although mine still seems connected, unlike many people my age.'

Another door led into the hallway; they followed Mette as she grasped the bannister-rail to climb the carpeted staircase to the first floor. Four white doors led off the landing.

'Here's the bathroom,' Mette pointed to the left of the stairwell. 'For years it had an original Victorian bath, complete with curved, brass feet. Do you remember Torin?'

He nodded, recalling the story about it being taken from a bombed building during the war. It had worked, although there was plenty of banging, clanging and wheezing in the plumbing system. His mother had insisted on paying for a revamp, as an eightieth birthday present for Gran. At the same time, builders put in a toilet off the entrance-hall, to save her having to climb the stairs.

'I never use it though when nature calls. Having to bend the knees for each step helps keep me fit, with my running days long past. At ninety-five there's not quite the same rush, but I arrive in the end. The only pity is my daughter never saw it finished.' She pushed open the door, so Sunny could see the whole room. On the left was a shower with Cotswold-stone panels and splash-tray. Beyond was a simple, white bath with curved handles along the rim. The wash-basin was large and square, supported by a unit that contained towels and an assortment of soaps and lotions.

Sunny was surprised at its size. 'Get baby in there.'

'I live in hope, Sunny.' Mette noticed the young woman blush, and moved onto the landing. 'Come and see my bedroom.' She stepped aside to let Sunny and Torin walk into the carpeted room. A king-size bed, draped with a white spread, looked directly onto the plane trees at the end of the terrace. On the side wall a built-in unit with mirror and drawers stood between two wardrobes. 'I lie here and watch the sun rise above rooftops in the spring and summer. So quiet.'

Sunny thought about her partitioned space in Chengdu. 'If I had such a room, difficult to leave bed. I always late for work.'

'One of the joys of being retired is I'm never in any hurry. When I finished my job fifteen years ago, I promised myself I would go with the flow.'

Sunny looked at the woman, resting her weight on her stick. 'You still working at eighty?'

'It was the year my daughter died. Has Torin told you about the Tsunami?'

Sunny nodded. 'A little.'

'He was fifteen and Emily seventeen. There were no other relatives, so I moved into their house in Scotland. But we realised it would work better if we came here. Torin went to the sixth-form college in Kensington to do A levels, and Emily attended Prior Park House, only a few-minutes' walk. It was like being a parent all over again, but with time to do it properly. I loved having them here.' Mette looked at the young man standing in the doorway. 'Understandably, once you started university, you wanted to live the life of a student, so you were here less often, and then you bought your flat in Mile End. By then Emily was making her home in New Zealand. Given what happened in Phuket, I was pleased that both of you had found your independence. But of course, the house felt empty.' Mette steadied herself against the bannister, to pull an embroidered handkerchief from the sleeve of her cardigan and dab her eyes.

Torin put his arms round his grandmother, feeling the frailty in the ageing body. He held her gently, pressing her head against his shoulder. Sunny moved closer and reached out her hands. The three of them shared the embrace in silence. Far off, a clock chimed the Westminster Quarters and then struck the hour six times.

'We'd better finish the tour, or there'll be no time for food. The room across the corridor was my daughter's bedroom when she lived here, and next door was for students on placement at the gallery. They became the children's bedrooms when we relocated from Forres. After they moved out, I turned Torin's into an art studio, and Emily's into an office. I call one the Matisse room and the other Picasso.' Mette led them up the final flight of stairs to the attic room. 'The Ancher room was my studio when Torin and Emily lived here, but now I just keep it ready for visitors—not that there are so many these days.'

Sunny looked through the velux window onto the roofscape. In the distance she saw the top of a tower, with a golden orb beneath a white cross. She squeezed Torin's hand. 'Is that Rapunzel?'

Mette smiled. 'You always loved that story, Torin. The truth is as powerful as the fairy tale. Queen Victoria had it built as a memorial for her husband Albert. She wanted to be able to see it from Buckingham Palace.

'She must miss him very much.' Sunny spun, arms outstretched, like a ballerina. 'So much space, Granny Mette.'

The old woman nodded. 'I keep thinking I should downsize, but this has been my home for seventy years. I'd rather leave in a box, than with the boxes. It needs to be more lived in though. My cleaner spends more time on this floor than I do.' She hesitated and her wrinkled fingers closed over Sunny's hand. 'I know what it's like not to see someone for a long time, so I understand why you both want to be alone. Next time you come though, it would be lovely to have you here, if you can put up with an old woman fussing round.'

Sunny pressed Mette's wrist with her free hand. She could feel the pulse beating strongly. 'I'd like that very much. It's such a beautiful house, I might never leave.' She paused, thinking about the names Mette had given each room. 'Why choose famous painters?'

Mette looked directly at Sunny. 'The simple answer is I didn't. Matisse and Picasso were both brilliant painters of course, but they owed their success to the women they were involved with—and that's the more complicated answer.' She sat on the edge of the large bed, holding

Sunny's hand, as she explained that Matisse had a daughter, Marguerite, who supported her father in his work, as well as being the model for his early paintings. During the War, when Matisse lived in Vichy France, Marguerite was a member of the Resistance and protected her father from interference by the Milice. Eventually she was captured and tortured by the Gestapo, then herded on a transport to Ravensbruck. Before it crossed into Germany, the engine was bombed by Allied planes, and she managed to escape and return to her father in Nice. Mette smiled. 'Incredible luck, eh? Matisse's reputation owes much to his daughter, so the room is named after her not Henri, and I've put her portrait at the centre of the collection.'

She paused, staring at the velux. Sunny sensed Mette was looking beyond Rapunzel's tower. 'Picasso's case is not the same because he had a rather different relationship with women.'

Sunny listened in silence to Mette's story of Francoise Gilot, the mother of two of Picasso's children and an artist in her own right. She met him at the time of the Allied liberation of Paris, when she was a twenty-one-year-old law student, and he forty years older. They lived together for ten years in a relationship that revolved around art, and included several meetings with Henri Matisse. When she left Picasso, taking Claude and Paloma, he did his best to ruin her career by instructing galleries not to exhibit her work. Eleven years later, Francoise published *Life with Picasso*, which included an account of her stormy relationship. In response, Picasso refused to recognise their two children as legitimate heirs to his estate, and Francoise used the royalties to pay for a successful legal challenge. 'So the room is dedicated to the Picasso children and their mother. It is Francoise's paintings hanging on the walls, above a copy of her book.'

Mette's blue eyes flickered from Sunny to Torin. 'I met Marguerite and Francoise in Paris in 1951. There was an exhibition of Matisse and Picasso at Galeries Nationales du Grand Palais. Both of them were present at the preview, and I was sent by my gallery to persuade them to exhibit in London. Matisse was very old by then and Marguerite wanted him to spend his final years without stress, but Picasso agreed.'

'Hadn't he gone to Paris to escape Franco's fascists?' Torin remembered doing the Spanish civil war at school. His history teacher had an uncle who'd fought with the International Brigades.

Mette nodded. 'Out of the frying pan into the fire. Paris was soon occupied by the Germans and he was subject to surveillance, as a communist sympathiser. Forbidden to exhibit, he was often harassed by the Gestapo. I was told by Francoise that during one search of his apartment, an officer saw a photograph of the *Guernica* painting that he'd sent to New York for safe keeping. "Did you do that?" "No," replied Picasso. "You did".'

There was a long silence. The sound of a distant car horn floated through the open velux. Torin thought about his grandfather, also killed in a bombing raid, leaving his grandmother as a widow for the rest of her life. How was it possible to spend seventy-five years on your own and not be bitter?

'What about this room?' Sunny was studying the

framed pictures. 'Also famous painter?'

'Anna Ancher was a Danish artist. She and her husband Michael belonged to a group called the Skagen painters, named after a town in the very north of Denmark. They lived at the end of the nineteenth century, famous enough to appear on a Danish bank note. I met their daughter Helga in nineteen sixty, on my first visit to Denmark since the war.' Mette described how Helga had helped arrange an exhibition of Skagen artists in London, despite being very old herself. 'We included some of her own paintings. These are Helga's.' Mette pointed to a row of four pictures under the eaves. 'They remind me of my homeland.'

'I thought that was Sweden?' Sunny frowned, trying to recall what Torin had told her.

Mette smiled. 'The only way to reach England during the war was via Sweden, but my family are actually Danish.' She pointed at a picture beside the wardrobe, of women on the beach in Skagen. 'That one is Anna's. Next to Michael's painting of Helga in their garden.'

'Are they originals?'

'All of them.'

'Downstairs too?'

'Oh, yes.' Mette laughed. 'Marguerite and Francoise wanted to make sure I had something to remember the London exhibition, so they each chose me a painting. The Matisse are all originals, as are the ones by Gilot I have collected over the years.'

'Have you always worked in the art world?' asked Sunny.

'After the war I managed a gallery in Fenchurch Street, in the old city of London. As well as organising exhibitions of well-known artists, my job was to introduce young painters to the public and give them a springboard for reaching a wider audience.'

'Sounds really interesting.' Sunny thought about her school friend, Zhao Chun Li, who'd moved to Beijing to study art. She'd stayed with her once and been taken to see the 798 Factory in Beijing's Chaoyang District. Till then she had no idea that such a place existed in China. She was amazed at the range of art, although disturbed by the grinning faces of Yue Minjun's characters.

'I met some famous artists, like Tracey Emin and other Turner prize winners.' Mette rattled off a list of names. 'I came to realise art can be a powerful mirror for wider society—both reflecting and initiating important changes.' She paused, thinking about the time she'd visited Guernica after Franco had died, and the shock of seeing the tiled replica of Picasso's painting at the entrance to the Basque town. She saw Torin glance at his watch. 'You must go, though. I talk too much, like all old people who live on their own.'

Downstairs, Mette quickly made sandwiches, while Torin went to the bathroom.

Sunny studied the framed pictures in the hallway. 'These look very old?'

Mette glanced up from the worktop. 'After my husband was killed in an air raid, I stayed on a farm near an RAF aerodrome. It was an exciting time, living so close to young men who were flying over Germany. I cut out those photographs from magazines, and framed them to remind me of that time.'

Mette came into the hallway, clutching a tupperware

box. Sunny was looking at a photo of a smiling woman holding a baby high above her head. 'That's me with Torin's mother on VE day.' As she stood beside the young woman, she thought about her thoughtless remark over the wash basin. She pressed the plastic container into Sunny's hand, hoping she could convey some reassurance through her fingers.

Torin appeared from the cloakroom, eyebrows raised, as he saw the box. 'Brie and cranberry,' explained Mette. 'Should keep the wolf from the door until you get home.' Vestie lifted its head from under its wing, as she slipped the catch on the door to the street. '*Safe journey. Thank you for coming. Safe journey. Thank you for coming.*'

Sunny hugged the old woman. 'I love your house, and your stories. I hope we come back soon?'

Mette smiled, eyes glistening in the yellow light from the street lamps. 'I will have the *Go* board ready.'

They turned at the corner of Rutland Mews to see her wave once more, before closing the door.

# Chapter Thirty-three:

## London:
## Wednesday January 29th 2020

'Doctor Smethwick will see you now.'

Torin stood, looking down at Sunny, who remained seated. 'What do you want to do?'

She shook her head. 'Not what I want. What you want.'

'I'd like you with me.'

'I with you then.' Sunny took his hand and they walked into the consulting room. She knew he'd had a restless night, tossing, rearranging his pillows, trying to find a comfortable position. At two in the morning he'd crept out of bed, whispering he was going for a glass of water. She slipped on a dressing gown and went into the kitchen to find him with his head buried in his hands.

'You worried about hospital visit?'

He nodded. 'Sorry about keeping you awake.'

'Not matter. I mind you troubling though.'

'I've pushed it to the back of my mind these last few days, but tomorrow I will know what's happening.'

'*We* will know,' she corrected.

He smiled weakly. 'You've been terrific, Sunny. I owe you so much.'

'Owe nothing, because we together. Maybe worrying is not necessary. How you *feel* is what matters.'

'I feel good, actually. The morning jogs make a difference.'

She had found a seven-kilometre route around Mile

End Park, which led up to Sutton Wharf and along the Regent's Canal to Limehouse, before following the Cut back to the maze of streets below Hamlet's Road. On the third day Torin appeared from the bedroom just as she was pulling her tracksuit-trousers over her knickers.

He noticed her tee-shirt printed with the words *'Take care of your body'*. In his hands he held a pair of dusty trainers. 'Can I come with you?'

Sunny nodded and they ran to the park and across the overpass, above the busy A11. She quickly registered how unfit he was and slowed the pace, shortening the route to three kilometres, by missing out the canal extension to Limehouse. Most of the way, Torin was looking at the back of her shirt, *'It's the only place you have to live.'*

'If you feel better, that best sign.' Sunny placed her hand over his. She talked about how feelings had always been an important thermometer of her health. She knew she was lucky, having a mother and father who practised *tai chi* every morning in the local park, silently moving through the sequences that harmonised mind and body. She had taken up running when she'd met Wang Yi, because he was a fitness fanatic. But he wasn't interested in learning how to connect his tremendous energy to his inner self.

'Listen to feelings. Share them and I can listen too.' She led Torin back to bed and took off her dressing gown, finally sinking together into a deep sleep, only interrupted by the radio alarm. Torin had set it for seven o'clock, to make sure they had time for a run, before catching the tube to Royal Marsden.

Doctor Smethwick stood as they came through the door, pushing his pebble-glasses back onto his head. He was tall, with a slight stoop, which gave him an angular appearance. His grey hair was swept back from his high forehead, gleaming in the light from the ceiling-bulb. He was wearing a pin-striped suit, with an open-necked, pink shirt. Sunny noticed the tiny buttonhole of flowers above the carefully-folded handkerchief in his breast-pocket, and the gold ring piercing his left ear.

He reached out his hand. 'Good to see you again Torin.' There was a hint of Lancashire in the vowels.

'And you. This is my girlfriend from Chengdu.'

The doctor pulled out a chair from the corner so Torin and Sunny could sit side by side. 'I did a placement in Chengdu Hospital of Traditional Chinese Medicine some years ago. I remember the hot pot! Aptly named. So spicy!'

'Can be okay for two tastes, as separate bowls are possible. Torin has not spicy half—me other.'

He smiled. 'I will remember for next time.' His eyes fixed on Torin. 'I've had the reports from your tests.'

Torin could feel Sunny's hand touching his thigh. He took a deep breath as the doctor continued.

'The problem is this is not an exact science. We tend to deal with percentages and probabilities in arriving at a prognosis, but each person is an individual.' His fingers played with his ear-ring. 'I know that's stating the obvious, but it's often the secret weapon. Last time we met, your condition seemed to be getting worse, with the blackouts increasing and the lymphoedema returning.'

Torin recalled the conversation in the spring, before he'd flown to China.

'I don't want to raise your hopes unnecessarily, but there

are positive indicators coming from the ECG tests and the MRI scan.'

Doctor Smethwick rested his glasses on the end of his nose to explain the diagrams. 'Nothing is conclusive, but I think something has happened to reinforce your immune system?'

Torin heard the inflexion in the sentence and felt warm fingers tighten around his hand. 'I met Sunny,' he said quietly. 'But we also consulted a Chinese medicine practitioner when I visited in September.'

The doctor's eyes flickered at Sunny and then back to Torin. 'Tell me more.'

He leant forward as Torin explained about the visit to Baisha village. When he started to describe the interview, Sunny took over. 'He sense Torin's level of energy.' She talked about how Doctor Zhang had felt the *qi* blockages, and meditated overnight about how to help it flow quicker. She guessed he had consulted his *luopan*. '*Qi* not easy. Mix of *tiān qi*, *dì qi* and *rén qi*. Heaven, earth and human. Two weeks ago, I visit Baisha again. Meet doctor for more medicine.' She lifted a glass jar from her small rucksack and placed it on the desk.

Doctor Smethwick studied the brown leaves visible through the thick oil. 'We had a whole module in Chengdu about geomancy and how blocked *qi* could stagnate and turn destructive. I was fascinated by the relationship with *feng shui*—negative *qi* travelling in straight lines and positive *qi* flowing in curves.' He looked directly at Sunny. 'We have much to learn from the Chinese approach to treatment.'

'Learning is both ways,' responded Sunny. 'West good

on evidence. You know rhinoceros horn not really help. But some Chinese men still believe.'

The consultant laughed. 'Viagra is cheaper, and better for the rhinoceros. Seriously though Torin, something has made a difference. The ECG is still registering unusual activity, but it is less dramatic than before. Clearly you need to keep taking the medicine.' He hesitated, glancing at Sunny. 'And, although I can't prescribe it on the NHS, it seems being together with your girlfriend is also making a difference.'

Outside the hospital, on the pavement, they stood a moment in the watery sunshine, sensing the promise of spring in the bracing air. Sunny put her arms around Torin and nuzzled her lips against his ear. 'Doctor say I good medicine.'

'I must keep taking you Sunny.' He wrapped his coat around her and they pressed close, oblivious of passers-by. Finally, they pulled apart and stood looking at each other.

Torin broke the silence. 'What do you think about the consultant?'

'He is good doctor.' Sunny was pleased Doctor Smethwick had acknowledged Chinese medicine. She knew Torin had been sceptical before going to Baisha, but thought he'd come away believing Doctor Zhang's approach might help. When they'd met at Heathrow, something was different about the smell of his skin. His spirit was brighter and his *qi* felt stronger. 'What do you think?'

Torin pressed his glasses against the bridge of his nose. 'It's hard to say, Sunny. When I first met Doctor Smethwick, he talked about some new treatment that may be possible in the States, but it is over a hundred thousand pounds, so out of the question unless I win the lottery. Which is why I wrote to you, thinking there was nothing that could stop things getting worse. But then you took me to Baisha's clinic. And now Doctor Smethwick says the ECG is more positive. Because I live with it every day, any improvement might be imperceptible to me. Have you noticed anything?'

Sunny described what she'd noticed at the airport.

Torin frowned. 'Smelling different sounds weird.'

Sunny chose her words carefully as she talked about the difference between eastern and western diets. 'Some girls not like smell of western men. Too strong. Chinese men drink no milk and eat less meat. So expect different smelling. If I eat garlic, you want to sleep in other room. But it's not just smell.' She described the aura of energy.

Torin rubbed his neck. 'Granny Mette always talked about the importance of diet. She has been vegetarian for as long as I can remember.'

'She smell good for old person. Like my great-grandfather. Now where can we go for lunch?' She looked along the street for a restaurant.

Torin suggested Covent Garden. They took the tube to Temple and walked up Arundel Street, past St. Clements' Danes into Aldwych and the maze of paths to Bow Street, so Sunny could tick off one more name on her *Monopoly* list. They rounded the Royal Opera House and stepped onto the cobbled surrounds of the old market.

In front of the entrance to the shopping-mall, two entertainers prepared their act. A woman in an embroidered cotton-blouse pirouetted in the sunlight to attract attention. Her blue plaited-skirt billowed to her waist as she spun, revealing bare thighs above purple woollen-stockings. The man wore a multi-coloured coat that flapped over a pair of red trousers and mustard-yellow shirt. To the edge of the space, a young girl in a peasant-smock pressed the knob of the sound system to start a drum-roll.

A plucked violin heightened the tension, as the woman elaborately blindfolded the man and helped him onto his unicycle. He rocked while she handed him a set of knives. She stepped away with a flourish of her arms and stood against a wooden board, pressing herself again the human outline painted behind her. Its hands were stretched above its head and its legs splayed like a starfish. By now a large crowd had gathered.

The drum-roll rose to a crescendo, and then there was silence. The man called out and the woman responded. He adjusted his cycle to line up with the board. He lifted his right hand with the knife held between forefinger and thumb, and swung it forward. It thudded into the board between her left arm and head, pinning the blouse to the wood.

He called again and the response rang out. A second knife thudded between her right arm and head. In quick succession the knives spun through the still air, marking out a starfish shape, as her blouse and skirt were pinned to the board. Another drum-roll echoed round the concourse as she drew her skirt up with her right hand, until the material was bunched beneath her crotch, showing the tops of her purple stockings. Silver flashed in the thin sunlight and the blade whacked beneath her clenched fist.

The girl in the smock quickly carried her upturned hat around the applauding crowd, catching people before they moved beyond the arc of entertainment.

They strolled the arcades, with Sunny tempted by lapis-lazuli earrings and a matching deep-blue stone in a silver necklace from a stall on the upper floor. She lifted her hair from the back of her neck so Torin could clip the catch of the pendant. He pressed his lips against the soft, fine down below her hairline and she turned to face him, laughing. 'You hungry?'

He bent his head close to her ear, so his voice was barely a whisper. 'I am feasting on the thought of you lying in bed, wearing this necklace.'

'More staring?' Her eyes softened. 'I like idea. Go home maybe?'

'Shall we get some food on the way?'

Sunny nodded. 'Hungry for that too. Maybe connected.'

Although it was one o'clock and restaurants were filled with people taking their lunch-break, they found a café in Neal Street with space in the basement. They sat in an alcove on some scatter-cushions, behind a small arch that hid them from other diners. The waitress set down two bowls of soup, a plate of tapas, and a basket of bread on the low, wooden table.

Sunny looked at Torin. 'I am so happy.'

'Me too.'

'Not want to end.' Even though she had arranged an additional week's holiday to add on the New Year, that still only gave her three weeks. She was due to fly back to Chengdu in a fortnight. 'Big problem in Wuhan though.

Government closed city.'

'What do you mean?' Torin spread smoked humous on the soda bread.

Sunny showed him the photos her mother had sent on WeChat. Wuhan was locked down, with residents not allowed to leave the city. All roads had been blocked and public transport mothballed. Planes were grounded at the international airport. 'Mother worried might spread. I explain Wuhan thousand kilometres from Chengdu, so should be okay.'

Torin recalled an email circulating at work about restrictions on travel to China. 'Is this something to do with contaminated food in a market?'

Sunny nodded. 'Maybe bats. They carry disease. It's like Sars again. I just nine then.'

'Let's hope they manage to sort it like Sars.' Torin remembered his father being invited to a conference in Singapore, and the whole family going for a holiday. As they approached passport control at Changi airport, they could see everyone's temperature being measured. Emily had been sick on the plane, so his mother was anxious she might trigger an alarm. She stepped out of the line and took his sister to the toilet, where she held her under the air-conditioning unit for ten minutes, before re-joining the immigration queue.

Torin looked at his watch. 'Shall we walk home past Granny Mette's old art gallery?'

'Is it on way?'

'Pretty much. I'd like to see the paintings she was telling us about.'

They walked up the marble steps to the Georgian

façade of the Fenchurch Gallery. The woman at the reception-desk smiled as they crossed the polished floor. Her brown hair was neatly cut so as to curve round the side of her cheeks, resting on the white collar of her blouse, open at the neck. Above her grey-flecked eyes, the lines on her forehead were just visible. Behind the desk, the walls were hung with a display of art work.

'Can I help you?'

'I hope so.' Torin explained the connection with his grandmother. 'She recommended we look at the Picasso and Ancher collections in the archive.'

'It's thanks to Mette we have those."

'Do you know her?'

'Know her?' The woman lifted her hands above her head. 'I owe my job to Mette. I'd been unemployed nearly a year after university when she took me on and gave me a chance. That was seventeen years ago. She taught me a lot about curating exhibitions.' The woman reached out her hand. 'I'm Leah. Mette rang this morning, so we were expecting you.'

'She rang?' Torin sounded puzzled.

'Yes, she thought you might be calling in.'

Sunny and Torin burst into laughter. He registered the bemused expression on Leah's face. 'Sorry. It's just we didn't know we were coming here till after lunch, and we haven't spoken with Mette for two days.'

Leah smiled. 'She always had an uncanny way of sensing the future. Anyway, it is very good to meet a friend of Mette's. We all owe her so much for establishing this gallery in the way she did.' Leah paused. 'I can show you round, if you like.'

'I'd appreciate that,' said Torin. 'I need someone to explain what I'm looking at. I think Sunny has more understanding.' He hesitated. 'But are you able, if you're on reception?'

Leah glanced at a wall clock. 'Maria takes over at three. Each of us four directors do a slot on reception. It's a legacy of when Mette was here. She wanted to make sure we remember that what matters most is the quality of the experience for visitors, not simply curating displays. Having expert knowledge at the desk makes a big difference to the start of the visit.'

Leah led them through a doorway. 'First the contemporary gallery, then we'll look at established painters. A lot of art appreciation is about knowing something of the context as well as content. Have you read any John Berger?'

Torin shook his head.

'Worth doing, if you're interested in the meaning of images. *Ways of Seeing* is a classic.' Leah was enthusiastic about Berger's writings. 'He is one reason I ended up here. Art can help us understand why we are who we are— something fundamental to being human.'

Finally, she took them into the archive section to upload Picasso paintings from 1953. 'This exhibition made the gallery's reputation.' She described how Mette had a knack for persuading risen talent to exhibit at Fenchurch, as well as spotting rising talent. 'Picasso was not the only top-flight name we've had, just the first. Since, there have been several Turner prize winners.' Torin had heard of one of the names Leah mentioned.

'Now I can show you Helga Ancher's collection.' Leah

projected pictures onto the display screen as she talked about the special light in Skagen, created by the confluence of the Skagerrak and the Kattegat around the Grenen sand bar. 'Extraordinarily atmospheric. You can feel something visceral in the landscapes. I think this touched Mette's own roots.'

It was dark when they left the gallery. A shower had dampened the tarmac, so lights from passing vehicles cascaded across the roads. They walked back to Torin's flat.

'Just like Gran to set that up. She was always a brilliant organiser. I can see why she made the gallery so successful.'

'She special woman.'

'I'd like to see her again this week, if that's okay, Sunny. I try and go over more often when I'm on holiday. Usually, I stay for supper, and we watch a film or play cribbage or backgammon. She enjoys the old games.'

'She must be lonely? Big house.'

'When I bought my own place and Emily confirmed she was staying in New Zealand after graduating from Otego, we thought Granny Mette could become quite isolated, because she'd already been retired eight years. But within weeks she let out our bedrooms.' Torin's surprise was clear in the pitch of his voice. 'The house was humming whenever I visited. Until I went to China in September, she was still taking students from the art college, but something must have happened, because she's stopped doing any of that.' Torin looked pensive. 'I wonder if there is some health issue, she's been keeping secret.'

'I happy to see her again. She lovely.'

Torin heard his phone beep, as they turned the corner from Eric Street to Keats Court. He glanced at the screen and smiled. 'Gran really does have second sight. She is asking if we'd like to go for supper on Friday. Says she hadn't realised last weekend was Chinese New Year. She wants to share in the celebrations, because it's her zodiac. Is that right?'

Sunny did a quick calculation. 'She correct. Nineteen twenty-four was also year of the Rat. It special on Friday, because Chinese people also celebrate end of New Year. Same as beginning. But I think Granny Mette wants to say something, not just rejoice. I felt her troubling.'

# Chapter Thirty-four:

## Rutland Mews, London:
## Friday 31st January 2020

They cleared plates from the dining-table and moved to the adjacent room, where a fire burned in the hearth. Sunny sat next to Torin on the sofa. On the low table in front, a cluster of small candles flickered beside a bottle of Gammel Dansk. Mette moved carefully with her stick across the room to select a disc from the rack in the corner. Incense hung in the air.

Torin looked at the framed photograph of his grandfather above the mantelpiece, hanging there for as long as he could remember. The ARP lettering was clearly visible on his warden's helmet above smiling eyes, as he faced the camera, the manicured moustache on his upper lip giving him the appearance of a film-star. He had studied the photograph often, willing some communication from the enigmatic ancestor. He wished he had more sense of who Stanley was, than just the few snippets his grandmother relayed. They'd only been together a short time, but it was surprising Mette had just kept one picture.

Dance music played from the speaker above their heads and he looked across to see Mette sway to the beat of the waltz. Her stockinged feet marked the timing, as she shuffled to her armchair. She smiled at the couple curled into the soft cushions. 'The nineteen forties big band is because I want to talk about the war.' Her eyes steadied on Torin. 'Meeting Sunny last Monday reminded me of a conversation with your grandfather seventy-five years ago.'

Torin blinked. 'You're amazing, Gran. I have problems remembering conversations I had yesterday.' He glanced at the face on the wall. 'I wish I'd known him though. He must have been a brave man to do that work.'

'You are correct. The man in the photo was very brave.' Mette's voice was matter of fact.

Torin registered the unusual choice of words, and looked closely at his grandmother. He could see a strange expression in her eyes. Sunny was right; something was troubling her. Instinctively, he reached forward and took her hand, noticing the mottling of age on the wrinkled skin.

'Stanley *was* courageous to go out during air-raids, especially as he was old enough to remember the Great War.' Mette paused, and Torin could feel the pressure increasing on his hand. He sensed something about to give way. 'But it's not him that I want to talk about.'

Torin looked at the photograph and back at Mette, waiting for the explanation.

'There are things I haven't ever mentioned within our family, and if I don't tell someone, they will go with me to my grave.' She took a deep breath. 'That may be quite soon of course and none of it is really that important now, but I think you have a right to know a little about the time I was living in Denmark during the war.' Mette's eyes flickered towards Sunny. 'Torin visited the farmhouse on Fyn as a small boy.' She glanced at her grandson, who nodded slowly.

'When Sunny showed me the thatched cottage of a Chinese poet, it reminded me of something I'd seen before.

Did my mother go as well?'

'We all went. Your father was invited to a conference at Odense University, and Johanne wanted to see the place where I grew up. The picture hanging in the kitchen was taken on that trip.' Mette's foot tapped the carpet, eyes focused on something far away.

'I was living there with my sister and our grandparents when the Germans occupied Denmark. I had started an art course at Ryslinge Folk High School, but as the Nazis imposed restrictions, I could see my grandparents finding it difficult to cope with the farm, so I took a job with a printing firm in Odense, allowing me to finish early. But it was still too much work for my grandparents; they moved to a cottage in the small town of Søndersø, and we sold the cows and sheep, concentrating on growing potatoes and vegetables, and keeping a few chickens. Lone and I managed the farm between us for several years. Then, one afternoon a British pilot appeared in the kitchen.' Mette sipped from her glass. 'He wasn't the first person the Resistance asked us to shelter. We'd already been involved in rescuing Jews.'

Torin and Sunny listened as she recounted what had happened in Denmark following Hitler's order to implement the final solution. Niels Bohr, the atomic scientist at Copenhagen University, had a Jewish mother, and received twenty-four hours' warning that his name was on a list to be rounded up. He fled to Sweden and persuaded King Gustav and the government to offer asylum to Danish Jews, like they had done for the Norwegians years before. Overnight, all the Jews went into hiding with local people.

Holger Danske organized a fleet of boats to take people from little fishing-harbours in Sjaelland across the Oresund to Sweden. Over seven thousand Jews made it to safety. Although there were informers, like a girl in love with a German soldier, who betrayed eighty Jews hiding in the attic of the church in Gilleleje village, the Gestapo only managed to round up five hundred in the end, and many survived the war because of interventions by the Danish government that ensured none ended in an extermination camp.

Mette reached forward to top up her glass. 'My boyfriend, Julius, was one of the first to leave, on an open boat that took four hours on rough seas to cross to Sweden. It cost him three thousand kroner, which was six months' wages, but at least he was safe.' Her lips tightened. 'I never heard from him again though. That was how it was for many people in the war and you just had to carry on somehow. I didn't even think about it at first, because Lone and I were concentrating on the family we sheltered in our farmhouse.'

The two girls had been careful to avoid arousing suspicion in the village, knowing not all farmers were sympathetic to the plight of Jews. The parents had two small babies, a five-year-old boy, and a grandmother in a wheelchair, so it was reckoned a rough sea-passage might not be safe. The Resistance decided to use the regular ferry between Copenhagen and Malmo. A truck took the family from Odense to the harbour in Copenhagen, where Holger Danske broke into a freight-van sealed by the Germans after they'd inspected it. They secured it with forged German seals to forestall further checks. 'Because I worked at a printer, I was asked to make sure the Nazi motifs on the seals would stand up to scrutiny.'

'*Det lykkedes*. It felt like a big victory.' Mette smiled. 'After this, Holger Danske often contacted me to produce travel documents for resistance fighters wanted by the Gestapo. And then, in the summer of 1944, just after D-day on the Normandy beaches, we were asked to help an Allied pilot. He was a breath of fresh air for us girls. We were only twenty and there was a shortage of young men on Fyn, especially ones that had led an exciting life.' Mette stared into the flickering flames, as she was carried back to the garden in Kirkenbjerg, listening to Harry talking about his exploits… teaming up with his navigator… patrolling the English channel… ferrying planes to Cairo… making a crazy bet in a poker game… flying over the Himalayas… fighting the Japanese in China… crashing after take-off… joining Special Operations.

The tempo of music changed and Mette returned to the present to see Torin and Sunny looking at her. 'Sorry, I was day-dreaming; I must finish the tale.' She took another mouthful from her glass. 'Every afternoon I hurried back from work to spend time with Harry before Lone returned. She was much more extrovert than me, and boys were always drawn to her if we were out together. I wanted him to myself without her around. As well as the usual things, we talked about our relationships, and discovered we'd both lost someone very precious. I guess we were like birds with broken wings, thrown together in the same nest.'

Mette described the afternoon she'd shown Harry her snakes and prepared *frikadeller*. 'After we'd eaten, we sat in the sunshine, listening to a gramophone record from the farmhouse. It was this music.' Mette gestured at the speaker in the corner of the room, remembering how they'd stood, swaying with the beat of the band. She could feel the sun on her neck and the scent of the lilac mixed with the fragrance of the orange blossom. His lips touched her cheek and she reached to lead him into the house.

'Then we heard a bicycle bell and Lone appeared round the side of the barn. It was our grandfather's birthday; she'd bought a present, intending for us both to pedal to Søndersø.'

Mette swirled the contents of her glass. 'But she'd hurt her leg at work and was obviously in no state to go anywhere, so I had no choice. I figured it would only take a couple of hours if I cycled quickly. I left them sitting in the garden. It was half an hour to Søndersø and I stayed a while to share the cake my grandmother made. It was still light when I set off back and I thought I'd be home before Harry went to bed. But I got a puncture a few kilometres from Søndersø, and had to push my bike the rest of the way. It was after midnight by the time I rounded the corner of the barn.'

Mette closed her eyes, recalling the silence as she crept through the kitchen. Lone's room was directly in front of the staircase and she could see a strip of light underneath her door. She knocked, but there was no answer, so she lifted the latch and pushed open the door. The candle in the lantern beside her bed flickered behind its glass shield, but the bed was empty. She wondered if Lone had gone outside to the closet, although that didn't make sense. Surely, she would have taken the lantern? She stepped back onto the landing and heard voices in the attic room.

'I was angry because I'd made it clear to Harry what I hoped would happen, when I returned from Søndersø. I felt embarrassed and foolish that I'd thought it meant anything for him. I stayed late at work the next day, and came back with Lone, so I wouldn't have to be alone with Harry. Lone had agreed to help a neighbour with his milking after supper, but I decided to visit a friend in another village. Harry came after me, and we had an awkward conversation at the start of the footpath, with Lone watching from the farmhouse. I was wary, but agreed I'd go to his room when I returned, so we could talk more. He promised he'd be waiting.

'On the way back from Tastrup, I met the neighbouring farmer, fishing in the small lake, fed by the tiny stream near our farm. Aage had separated from his wife the previous year, but I didn't know much else about him. He'd always seemed aloof, yet that evening, as I sat beside him, he spoke about his loneliness, running the pig units on his own, how he'd taken up angling as solace for insomnia. It took my mind off what had happened at the farmhouse.

'Eventually I said goodnight and walked home. It was quiet in the house. I was about to drop the catch and go up to Harry, when I realised someone was in the yard. Aage had followed me back. He came into the kitchen and tried to kiss me. I pushed him away, but he said I'd led him on, that I needed to be a good girl and finish what I'd started. I told him to leave or I would call Lone and we'd report him to the police. The hatred in his eyes frightened me, but he turned to go. Then he caught sight of Harry's boots, on the mat beside the door.' Mette closed her eyes, hearing the heavy breathing of the farmer as he stared at the large pair of muddy shoes.

'*Hvis er de støvler?*'

'*Roald is repairing the roof.*' She mentioned the village handyman. '*He leaves them here when he goes home.*'

Aage stroked his tiny moustache. '*Vil du ha' jeg skal tro på det'? I have been working on my pigsty beside the lane every day this week and have not seen Roald. Maybe he comes very early before you girls are out of bed? That would be interesting work.*'

She hoped her flushed cheeks weren't visible in the moonlight from the open door.

Aage's gaze was still fixed on the boots. '*I hear the Gestapo are looking for Jews again. Earlier this week I saw Lone with someone by the lake.*' His voice was low and menacing.

'*There are no Jews here, Aage. Most escaped to Sweden a year ago, as you know.*'

'*Thanks to you and your bitch sister.*' Flecks of spittle landed on the slate floor as Aage's eyes narrowed. '*We could have wiped out those vermin from the face of Denmark, but your socialist friends thought you could outwit the Germans. I would have reported you, but my stupid wife insisted I say nothing. Now she is gone, I can do what I want.*'

'*Skrid, din lort!*' Birgitte hissed through clenched teeth, but Aage stood beside the open door, stroking his tiny moustache. The silence was broken by murmuring from the top of the house. Was that what Harry meant by waiting for her?

Aage's lips curled. '*Perhaps we should call the police after all? I think they will be very interested in what is happening upstairs.*'

She laid her hand on the farmer's arm, forcing herself to

*stay calm. 'If you did that Aage, we girls would be arrested and unavailable. There is no need to tell anyone and I could come back to your house tonight.'*

*She saw Aage's wolfish eyes widen, as he grasped her meaning. Birgitte walked in silence beside him, along the winding lane, listening to the whispering poplars calling her name. Aage pushed open the hewn elm-door of his house and she followed him up the stairs.*

Mette reached for her glass. 'He wasn't the first man I'd been with, so, I thought I could just do what was necessary, go home and that would be it. But he insisted I return the following evening, holding out the threat of the police. I knew it would only be a few days before Harry was smuggled to Sweden, so I continued to go along the lane every night, even though what Aage wanted had nothing to do with making love. I could see why his wife had left him.

'Sankthansaften was different though.' Mette hesitated, struggling to remember the sequence of events. It was a bit of a blur. She had come back from the printers to discover the Resistance had arranged for Harry to board a ship leaving for Göteborg the following evening. Lone went upstairs to change, leaving her to sort Harry's hair.

She had massaged the peroxide into Harry's scalp. He'd knelt, resting his face in her lap as she rubbed the bleached locks with a towel. 'It looks pretty good. See here.' She reached for the mirror on the kitchen table.

Harry pressed his hands on her legs as he lifted his head to look. 'Needs the eyebrows as well.'

She nodded and carefully brushed loose strands from his forehead, applying the mixture. She could feel the warmth of Harry's head in her lap as she watched the peroxide take effect. She stroked the towel down the side of his face, mopping droplets from his cheek. He was still kneeling. She breathed in deeply as he moved his hands onto her waist. Her lips brushed across his forehead. He looked up at her and she understood his expression.

Behind her a stair board creaked and she spun round to see Lone framed in the doorway, saying something about Harry's looks. He responded by telling them it had been blonde once before, at his leaving party in China.

Mette looked at the logs crackling in the fire, recalling how her irritation had bubbled into anger, as Lone teased her for flirting to get hold of real coffee. She wanted to scream that stealing from Aage's larder had been some tiny recompense for what she'd had to go through to protect Harry. But she'd bitten her lip because he was standing a few feet away. It was only when Lone warned her not to get carried away, that her fury exploded.

'Should I take lessons from my big sister? You seem to have gone all the way!'

'So what? I wanted some fun and he was available.'

'You just can't resist any possibility. Even if it means pushing me aside.'

She remembered shouting at her sister for being a bitch on heat, unable to keep her hands off Harry. When Lone goaded her for being too slow with men, it was all she could do not to throw the hot coffee at her smirking face.

The argument continued on the bike ride with Lone dismissing what happened as harmless fun. She listened to Lone crowing about how she'd tricked Harry into bed, by telling him her kid sister was staying overnight at Søndersø. At her grandparents' house she laced Lone's currant juice with snaps, disguising the bitter taste with dollops of honey. She was determined to make sure Lone was in no state for a last fling, while she whimpered in Aage's farmhouse, to secure the final night's reprieve for Harry.

The music stopped and silence settled in the sittingroom. Mette looked at Sunny and Torin, gathering courage to finish the story. 'It worked. After cycling back, Lone was too exhausted to climb the stairs, and fell asleep on the downstairs sofa. In spite of my jealousy, I felt bad, because I knew Harry would be expecting her. I should have let Lone sleep it off, and woken her later. If I'd done that and walked to Aage's house as usual, everything would have been okay.'

She clasped her trembling hands. 'But I didn't go... I couldn't... not to Aage again.' She blotted her tears with a white lace handkerchief. Torin caught the scent of rose petals as she tucked the crumpled cotton inside the sleeve of her cardigan. 'Harry was my age you see, and I wanted him more than I'd wanted anyone.' Mette rested her hand on her grandson's knee, but her eyes were looking at Sunny. 'It was dark when I crept into his bedroom.'

Mette closed her eyes, recalling the quiet click of the latch on the door of the attic room, dropping her robe on the floor, sliding beneath the bedclothes, feeling Harry's arms wrap around her and his toes curl around her feet. She was breathing deeply, her chest rising and falling. Torin was struck by the beauty of her expression, a smile playing round the corner of her lips. In the hearth a log toppled softly on its side, sending a shower of sparks up the chimney.

When she next spoke, Mette's voice was resonant. 'It was absolutely *vidunderligt og uforglemmeligt*, as we say in Danish.' She looked up to see Torin and Sunny smiling. 'Hearing a ninety-five-year-old talking about great sex, might be a little shocking.' Mette shook her head slowly, chuckling. 'It took me by surprise as well. There was just one problem. Aage had made it clear what I was to do when we returned from the Sankt Hans party. Around midnight I heard footsteps on the gravel beneath the bedroom window. Harry had fallen asleep and I knew I ought to get up and walk along the lane, but can you imagine what it felt like? I was floating in a warm lagoon, safe and utterly content. I didn't want to leave Harry, so I just kept very still until the boots crunched away.'

Tears welled in Mette's eyes again and she tugged out her handkerchief. 'If only I hadn't been so selfish. It would have meant an hour of pain and humiliation to put things right. But I wanted the night with Harry to last forever. I didn't sleep; just lay there, savouring the warmth of his body till the dawn chorus. Then I crept from underneath the bedclothes before Harry woke. Lone was still out cold on the downstairs sofa, so I gathered my clothes and cycled to work. The morning sun was lifting the dew from the fields into a fine mist as I pedalled into Odense. It was such a beautiful morning and I was full of joy.

'Because I finished work early, it had been agreed I would be the one to go home and cycle with Harry to Odense harbour. I was carrying the forged documents. We had arranged to meet Lone in a small restaurant by the waterfront. The ship was due to sail at nine o'clock and we needed to smuggle Harry on board, before the German soldiers did their final checks.

'I came round the corner of the barn and saw Lone lying across the steps, with the kitchen door wide open behind her. I held her stiff body, howling, desperately wanting it all to be different, but the blood staining my clothes said it all. Her fingers were still touching the trigger of a gun.

'Then I heard a noise inside the house and looked to see Aage at the kitchen table, a Tuborg in his hand. In front was a line of empty bottles. He told me he'd contacted the police because I hadn't turned up at his house. Later, he'd seen a prison-van drive away and had come to discover Lone had been shot. He said it was my fault for breaking a promise.'

'*Naughty girls like you need to be punished.*' *Aage's voice rasped with menace.* '*You know I can do it in such a way that you will enjoy.*'

*Birgitte said nothing, wondering if she could run and grab her bicycle. As if he'd read her mind, Aage lifted the rifle in his right hand.* '*Wasn't it fun, playing undressing games? Putting you over my knee and making you plead for forgiveness. After you'd been a good girl, I always let you return home, didn't I? Don't disappoint me, like my stupid wife, or else I may have to teach you the same, ultimate lesson.*'

*Aage was smiling as he steadied the rifle.* '*Now you're alone, you are free to move in with me. We can play our little games whenever we want. No one else needs know about the other things you've been up to in your spare time. I am friends with the police commissioner. We are both members of the Waffen SS, so I can make sure the Gestapo won't trouble you.*'

*He rose and grasped her wrist.* '*Hvorfor ikke have det lidt sjovt. Nu er der jo kun os to.*' *Her body stiffened as he pressed* his lips against her cheeks. 'Playing hard to get, eh? My little girl needs encouragement.' Aage reached beneath his grimy vest to unbuckle his belt.

Birgitte spun to grab the gun beside Lone's body. Aage was still fumbling with his belt as she pulled the trigger. He fell, gasping, blood pouring from his chest. He crawled towards her, hands clutching her legs, saying he was sorry. She pointed the gun at his face, closed her eyes and pulled the trigger. She kept firing until the magazine emptied. When she looked and saw what was splattered across the kitchen floor, she was violently sick and passed out.

She came round to see the sun lower in the sky. Heat was draining from the day. The room smelt like a butcher's shop, with the remains of Aage's head congealing on the slates. Birgitte's mind raced. Lone dead, Harry arrested, and now a murdered man. The police could return any time. Where could she go? Søndersø? But they'd find her there, and it would just put her grandparents at risk. She wondered about Holger Danske, Lone would have known who to contact, but she'd never given Birgitte details. The less you knew the less you could be forced to tell. She thought about turning the revolver on herself, then realised she'd pumped all the bullets into Aage. Looking at the bloody pulp under the table, it was clearly not necessary.

Birgitte contemplated the line of kitchen knives on the shelf, wondering if she had the courage to stab herself. As she reached for one of the handles, she was aware of something rustling in her back-pocket. She pulled out Harry's forged documents.

Could she use them herself? Birgitte glanced at the clock. Nearly seven. Quickly she hacked at her hair with scissors and rummaged through the drawer of work-clothes they kept in *case her grandfather stayed overnight. She came back into the kitchen and stared at the carnage. She couldn't leave Lone lying on the steps. She lifted her body onto the downstairs sofa, and placed a blanket over her face.*

*Birgitte could hardly bear to touch Aage's remains, but knew she had to dispose of him. She managed to lift the corpse into the wheelbarrow for spreading compost. She covered it with a sheet, pushed the barrow along the lane to his farmyard, and kicked open the entrance to his new pig-sty. The animals came squealing over, greedily pushing their snouts against the legs of the barrow. She tipped Aage's body onto the concrete floor and shut the gate.*

Mette opened her eyes to see Sunny and Torin holding hands tightly.

'I pedalled to the harbour. The restaurant-owner accompanied me through the police control to board the ship, using the documents we'd prepared for Harry. He sealed me in the freight van. Next morning, I was in Göteborg, requesting asylum from Swedish authorities. From the safe house they found, I wrote to the family I had stayed with in 1938, and it was arranged for me to go there, once I had satisfied the refugee assessment-panel in London.

'I was in London for four months and arrived at the Cotswold farm in November. I changed my name to Mette Rasmussen to help shake off the past. The English family were kind and nurtured me through a really bleak period.

'The guilt was raw. I was responsible for Lone's death and for Harry being captured. My grandparents passed away before the end of the war, and I have always thought that was my fault as well—that they died broken-hearted for losing their granddaughters. Those have been my waking thoughts every morning, and still there in my head as I go to sleep.

'All my life I've felt I'd no right to happiness. Many times, I just wanted to end it. The only thing that gave me strength happened in March 1945. Johanne was utterly gorgeous. As she started to move and become her own person, I was fearful I'd see Aage, but her expressions and mannerisms reminded me of Harry. She inherited my hair and eyes, but the winning smile came from him. And you have it all, Torin.'

Mette reached into the pocket of her cardigan and pulled out a passport-size photo of a young man in RAF uniform. 'This was on the identity card I forged for Harry's journey to Sweden. After I'd bleached his hair, we took a picture and developed it in the dark room under the stairs. 'I have carried it with me since.' Tears pricked her eyes as she studied the image. She looked across at Torin. 'When I said meeting Sunny last Monday reminded me of a conversation with your grandfather seventy-five years ago, this is the man I was referring to.'

Mette placed the photograph on the low table in front of them. Torin was aware he was looking at a younger version of himself.

Sunny lifted the photo, staring at it in silence. Finally, she turned to Torin. 'Remember when we met my great-grandfather on the way to the restaurant? At air-raid memorial? *Zǔfù* was upset, and I was cross with him? He was pointing at you saying guǐ, guǐ, guǐ, which means ghost. He said he was convinced you were an English pilot he had met long, long ago at Fenghuangshan airfield; you came with him and other Chinese soldiers over mountains to join General Sun's army. He kept saying *tài xiàngle*, which means "so similar". I think maybe great-grandfather just believe all English people look the same. So, I told him he not right.'

Sunny paused, looking at Mette and then back at Torin. 'I was also confused because *Zǔfù* hadn't said anything about this when we stayed at Dazhentou. I think his brain going wrong, like happened with my great-grandmother. I tell him you exactly the same person he was so nice to at the farmhouse. You didn't change into different person after we come back to Chengdu on the bus. Then he remind me he broke glasses, feeding chickens before we arrived at Dazhentou.' She reached for Torin's hand. 'Do you remember he apologise when we meet him at front door? The whole time we there, you just big blur of man with nice voice. But at the air-raid notice, he was wearing his new glasses, and saw you properly for the first time.'

Torin frowned 'You never said any of this?'

'Because I didn't understand and I was frightened. *Zǔfù* tell me he never forget smile of man who sat beside him on plane to India' She turned to Torin. 'He kept saying *jīn tóufǎ* meaning "blonde hair".' Sunny described how she'd gone along the corridor to the restroom to look at the old photos her grandfather had talked about. They were mostly pictures of Chinese pilots, but there was one of a European, standing between a man with a traditional beard, and a young woman in a cheongsam. All three were laughing at the camera. The caption said Fu Zhe Ji and Li Ya Fei were the owners of the restaurant, and the Westerner was a pilot at Fenghuangshan.

'The pilot look like you, so I start thinking. Maybe the Englishman *Zǔfù* knew had come back to life? Last Monday, when we here first time, I was looking at the pictures in Mette's hallway. Something troubled me, but I not understand why. So, when we came this evening, I look again. I see your face in front of the airplane, except this time the pilot has dark hair.'

Mette put her arms around the young woman. 'I knew something had happened. I thought it was my careless remark about babies. I'm so sorry Sunny.' She stroked the young woman's arm. 'Most of the pictures are famous pilots I downloaded from Wikipedia, like Guy Gibson and Leonard Cheshire. But one *is* a picture of Torin's real grandfather, standing beneath the nose of his plane. We have a saying in English, that truth is stranger than fiction.'

'We learn same sentence in school, "*Xiǎo shuō yuan zi yú shēng huó*", responded Sunny.

'When we dyed Harry's hair for his escape to Sweden, he told us he'd done it once before, to surprise his men at his farewell party in China. He left the airbase several days later to return to England. That would be why your great-grandfather sat next to a man with blonde hair on the plane to India.'

Sunny breathed out slowly as the tension dissolved. '*Zǔfù* not crazy then. Everything connects. Story complete.'

'Not quite,' Mette pursed her lips. 'There is something else I have to tell you, but maybe you've heard enough for tonight? It is getting late. Shall we stop?'

Torin looked at Sunny, who shook her head. 'We not tired. This is important.' She put some more logs on the fire, while Mette refilled their glasses and sat back in her chair.

'Everything was fine for over fifty years, so more than half a lifetime, till the doorbell rang on a hot day in June 2000. It was the anniversary of that last night with Harry. I always placed lilac in a vase on my kitchen table, to remind me of Kirkenbjerg and sankthansaften.' Mette recounted what happened when she opened the door.

*On the step stood a man dressed in a finely-cut blue suit and open-necked shirt. He wore an elegant hat, with a wide brim that rested on large ears. He doffed it and inclined his head. 'Birgitte Vestager?'*

*Mette shook her head, trying to remain composed, holding down the turmoil welling inside her. 'You have the wrong house.' She made to close the door.*

*'I'm so sorry.' The man spoke softly. 'I know you are Mette Rasmussen now, but I have been searching for Birgitte for so long that the name slipped out without me thinking.'*

*Mette held her hand on the door, wondering what else he was going to say.*

*'I have come about Harry Winchester. I knew him during the war.' Mette could see the visitor looking into the hallway at the framed photographs of the second world-war pilots. 'Did you know them all?' His voice was tinged with surprise.*

*'None of your business!' Mette pushed the door, but his shoulder was already resting against the frame.*

*'It is definitely my business to see a photo of myself beside Harry Winchester.'*

*Mette thought she would faint, but the man reached out a hand to steady her. There was a gentleness that reminded her of Harry. She led him to the kitchen and made coffee.*

*Squadron Leader Standing talked about his life in Stalag*

*Luft Three after baling out from his Mosquito, his repatriation to England when the war ended in May 1945, and taking a job with Bristol Aerospace. He'd married, had children and retired to a village in the Cotswolds in 1990 at the age of sixty-five.*

*His wife and elderly mother had both died the year the Labour party won the election. With time on his hands, he decided to write a book about his wartime experiences, and wanted to include Harry's story.*

*Archibald had a friend, working at the Royal Air Force Museum in Hendon, who helped trawl archive material in their files. They had Harry's logbook, passed on by the station-adjutant at RAF Tempsford after the war. Reports had filtered to the SOE about Harry being captured and interrogated by the Gestapo, but there was very little detail. The documentation concluded: 'Harry was no longer in Dachau when it was liberated on 29th April 1945.'*

*Through the Prisoners of War Association, Archibald located a British survivor from Dachau. Brian had been incarcerated in the same barrack-block as Harry, and worked with him in the infirmary. He was involved in swapping prisoner-numbers to save those condemned to join the death-marches. Brian watched Harry amending the extermination list on that final morning and thought he was just faking another death. It was only when he saw Harry standing at the gate, he realised he'd substituted himself for another prisoner called Tomasz.*

*Archibald summarized what he had gleaned from the archives about the camp. 'There is no record of what happened to Harry after he'd marched out of Dachau. No one ever saw any of the men or the SS guards again. Distant gunfire could* have been approaching Allies. Three days later the Americans liberated the camp.'

Harry had told Brian about his escape from Belgium to Denmark, so Archibald travelled to Fyn to locate the farmhouse at Kirkenbjerg. He traced a woman who had grown up in the village during the war. She remembered Lone's murder and the disappearance of Aage. She also recalled a sister called Birgitte, but didn't know what had happened to her, although the rumour was that she'd fled with Aage.

Archibald thought it unlikely Birgitte would go off with her sister's killer, so he trawled the files about the Danish resistance in Odense's record office. He located a surviving member of Holger Danske, who confirmed that Birgitte Vestager had escaped to Sweden.

The Swedish embassy still had their wartime records, and gave him the address of the family in the Cotswolds. The parents had died, but one of the daughters lived in the family house. She told him where to look in London.

Mette stroked her white hair. 'Squadron Leader Standing really should have introduced himself as Sherlock Holmes; it had taken him eighteen months to reach the end of the trail. On the way he'd even tracked down Tomasz, because Brian was able to recall his home village had been near Treblinka.

'Tomasz was still married to his childhood sweetheart. They had five grown-up children and lots of grandchildren. Tomasz had downloaded the text of Harry's entry on Wikipedia and hung it in a frame in their sitting room, beside a large photograph of him in his RAF uniform. Their third child, who was born in 1946, was called Harry.' Mette paused and took a long mouthful from her glass.

'There wasn't much I could add that Archibald didn't already know, but I was able to tell him about Harry's time with Special Operations, and his escape from Belgium to Denmark. Most importantly perhaps, I relayed what Harry had said to me about the man he called Archie—that he was the closest friend he'd ever had. If Harry had dared to use the word love about another man, Archie would have been that person.

'We cried a lot, we held hands, we hugged, and there were many silences as we struggled with the memories. Finally, I told him about Johanne, and how she'd married late in life and had her own children. I showed him photos of you and Emily, and he remarked on the resemblance to your grandfather.

'It was then he produced an envelope from his jacket-pocket, with "*International Red Cross*" stamped at the top in faded letters. It was addressed in spidery, uneven writing to Mrs. Standing, Grange Farm, The Gib, Wiltshire. The postmark was September 12th 1944.

'Harry had written it on his last night in the Shell Hus. Archie found it when he went through his mother's things after she died. He couldn't understand how Harry had managed to get a letter out of that hell-hole. Archie researched the Copenhagen war archives. Although many records of the Shell Hus had been destroyed in the Mosquito raid of March 1945, there were transcripts of interviews with the guards tried for war crimes.

Mette related how Archie had paid a curator to go through them and see if he could find a reference to Harry. He turned up an interview with Knud Hansen, one of the warders at Shell Hus, a particularly sadistic interrogator.

Several survivors had testified about how he enjoyed inflicting pain, going back into prisoners' cells after bouts of interrogation to beat them with electric cables.

'Hansen had talked about a British agent, captured on Fyn, claiming he was an RAF pilot. The man had done a deal with the Gestapo to avoid execution. Hansen didn't know what was agreed, but the agent had been allowed to write a letter before being put on a train to Dachau. Hansen had been instructed by Oberführer Heydrich to deliver it to the Red Cross. Knud Hansen was shot by a firing squad in 1946, after the Danish government reintroduced capital punishment for war crimes. He was the first person executed in Denmark since 1892.

'Archie also discovered Heydrich had been caught by the Russians, trying to escape from Berlin in the last days of the war, having failed to buy a place on the last plane to Bavaria. He was shot by his Red Army captors.'

Mette patted her eyes. 'Reading that letter, fifty-five years after Harry sent it, was both awful and amazing. I could feel his pain in the spidery writing, but the words moved me to tears. He wrote about his last night at Kirkenbjerg and it was clear he knew who had come into his room, and what a powerful experience it had been.

'By the time Archie left. I felt I'd lived my whole life a second time that day. We became lovers.' Mette registered the expression on Torin's face. 'Yes, I was seventy-five at the turn of the century. When you are young, it is unthinkable that old people could be having sex. It happens though, and perhaps all you need to know is that it gets better in many ways.

'Archie wanted to marry me, but it felt too late for that,

and I didn't want the whole story about Harry to come out. Archie didn't see it the same way and helped me reframe my own thinking; but such a new perspective felt fragile, and I really didn't want to put it to the test in public. There was also the problem of telling Johanne I'd lied about her father—and by then you and Emily were growing up, believing your grandfather to be the man above the mantelpiece. Of course, Stanley *could* have been Johanne's father, because we did have a brief relationship, when I was at the refugee hostel for some months, while British Intelligence checked my status. He was attractive and funny and kind, so in naming Stanley on Joanne's birth certificate, I was at least able to bequeath her a father who'd died a heroic death.

'I lacked the courage to say "*yes*" to Archie, but we stayed friends, and he came to London a lot. The journeys became infrequent as we slowed up and joints wore out. After Archie had a stroke three years ago that left him in a wheelchair, we never met again, but we spoke on the phone and wrote occasional letters. I'm not sure his children ever knew about us. Then, last September he had another heart-attack, which paralysed him completely. That was the end of any communication.'

There was a long silence. Torin moved to sit on the arm of Mette's chair. He pressed his lips against the top of her head. 'Why are you telling us this now, Gran?'

Mette looked up. 'Meeting Sunny last week.' She smiled at the young woman. 'After I'd listened to you describing your great-grandfather's involvement in the War, I knew I had to say something about Harry. During our afternoons in Kirkenbjerg, he talked a lot about his time in China and his respect for the Chinese pilots he'd flown with. He also told me about meeting soldiers who'd fought alongside the British in Burma, and that very few people in Britain were even aware that China was an important ally. He wanted to make sure their contribution was not forgotten when victory came.

'In June 1944, after the D-Day landings, we all felt it was just a matter of time before Germany sued for peace. Harry was determined to go back to Chengdu and make contact with the men he'd met, particularly a Chinese pilot called Lin Xiaobin and an American air-traffic controller, Douglass Walters. Those names stuck in my mind, although I never did anything about it, until you came last Sunday.

'I Googled their names, but could find only a brief reference to Douglass Walters. There was a link to Alfred Douglass, from whom he'd got his name, and pages and pages about that man's struggle for the emancipation of slaves. For Douglass Walters himself there were ten lines and a photograph. He became a lawyer defending civil rights, as part of the non-violent protest movement in the United States, and was one of the marchers over the Pettus bridge in Selma in 1965. He was beaten by armed police, who wrapped barbed wire around the heads of their clubs. He died of a brain haemorrhage in 1967. The citation said he'd received serious head injuries during the war and these were exacerbated by the assault in Selma.

'There was a little more about Lin Xiaobin. He was a decorated fighter-pilot in the war of resistance, and became a senior general in the People's Liberation Army with a long list of battle honours. He retired from the military in the 1970s, and was invited by the local government in Nanjing to help create the Memorial Hall of the Victims of the Japanese Massacre, which opened in 1985. His daughter, Lin Ba, worked as one of the curators.'

Mette took a deep breath. 'And then there is this, which arrived three days ago.'

Torin registered the marbled parchment on the back of her hand as she passed him the brown envelope. He pulled out a thin booklet. 'Funeral of Squadron Leader Archibald Standing?'

'He died a week ago. It's in Archie's church at Castle Combe in Wiltshire. Even if we took my wheelchair, I couldn't manage the journey, but I would like you to go on my behalf.'

It was after midnight before Mette finished telling them everything she remembered from the conversations in the garden at Kirkenbjerg. When they finally stood up to leave, she looked lighter and taller.

As Torin tapped his phone to summon an Uber, Mette's hand closed over his. 'It probably seems a bit silly, but would you mind staying tonight?'

He hesitated, fingers pausing in their darting flurry across the screen.

'We will stay as long as you want, Mette.' Sunny was quietly assertive. She glanced at Torin, who pushed his phone into his pocket.

Mette blinked away the tears. 'It would be so wonderful to have people in the house again. I promise not to cramp your style. You can come and go as you want, and ignore me completely when you need to be alone. I may be ninety-five, but I haven't forgotten what it's like to be young and in love.

In the Ancher room you will be perfectly private.'

Sunny blushed and reached for Torin's hand. 'We can look for Rapunzel.' She was grateful Mette understood what she was feeling.

'There's just one other thing I want to give you.' Mette walked to the mantelpiece and picked up a package, which she handed to Torin.

He could see the Ace of Spades on top of a deck of cards, held together with a rubber band. 'Playing cards?'

'When he arrived at our farmhouse, your grandfather had his RAF identity, a photo of Amy, a poem, a commando knife, and this pack.'

'Was he a poker-player?'

Mette smiled. 'Maybe. I gather this secured him the flight over the Himalayas that began the whole Chinese adventure.' Mette relayed what Harry had told her about the origins of the cards and the events following the evening on the Nile houseboat.

Torin tipped the contents onto the glass-topped table. They were neatly sorted into four suits with the court cards uppermost. He laid them out in sets, glancing at Sunny as he came to the Hearts.

Mette rested her hand on his arm. 'Remember it was the 1940s, and everyone had a very different view of women. I think they all look beautifully coy, and I just love the hairstyles, especially this blonde one.' She pointed to the five of hearts, which showed a young woman on a motorbike, wearing a cap, with the peak pointing backwards. 'When Harry explained the provenance, it wasn't the Hearts that intrigued me, but the Diamonds. I recognised a few original Picassos but others looked more like Matisse. Neither name meant anything to Harry. He'd just inherited them from a fellow-pilot, who'd escaped Franco's Spain during the civil war.

'I used the equipment at the printers to produce an exact copy of the whole pack using high quality paper. I worked on it after lunch each day when most people had gone home. It suited me to stay later once Lone started with Harry. It was my own time, so there were no awkward questions. I had to photograph each card and design the pattern on the back to match. I was skilled at forgery by then, and used hot-foil stamping and embossing techniques to make a replica deck that looked exactly like the original. I even used a tiny filigree-pen to replicate the signatures of Matisse and Picasso.

'Harry had no idea how valuable they were. I was worried about the safety of something so precious, and thought I could return them to Harry once the war was over. It felt like a kind of talisman. I substituted my forged set for the originals in Harry's bedroom.'

# Chapter Thirty-five

## Castle Combe, Wiltshire:
## Tuesday, February 3rd 2020

On the train from Paddington to Chippenham, Sunny curled beside Torin, checking her WeChat messages, while he watched the changing scenery. The outskirts of Uxbridge gave way to the rolling landscape of the Thames Valley near Reading, past the rubble from Didcot's cooling towers, and then into the broad sweep of the downs around Swindon. The train gathered speed past the motorway, and Torin was thinking about his grandfather when Sunny interrupted his reverie.

'What does "autarkic" mean?'

'You mean Antarctic? Or Arctic? Both big oceans. One north, one south. Very cold.'

'That meaning not work. Your Prime Minister talking about Brexit. He speak about China, so it appears on my phone. Here, have a look.'

She passed the metallic-blue phone to Torin, to replay the YouTube clip. Boris Johnson appeared at a podium, emblazoned with the slogan '*Unleashing Britain's Potential*'. He was dressed in a dark suit, with a colour co-ordinated purple tie round the collar of a light-blue shirt. The knot was slightly askew, matching the carefully-disarrayed, blonde locks. He spoke about how tariffs in Brussels, China and Washington were suffocating trade.

*…we are starting to hear some bizarre autarkic rhetoric, when barriers are going up, and when there is a risk that new*

*diseases such as coronavirus will trigger a panic and a desire for market segregation that go beyond what is medically rational to the point of doing real and unnecessary economic damage, then at that moment humanity needs some country ready to take off its Clark Kent spectacles and leap into the phone booth and emerge with its cloak flowing as the supercharged champion, of the right of the populations of the earth to buy and sell freely among each other...*

Torin struggled with the image of the Prime Minister squeezing into a superman suit. He handed the phone back to Sunny. 'Funnily enough I do know what autarkic means. It came up in one of our economics lectures at Uni, and we all went around trying to slip the word into our conversation to impress friends. It describes an economic system that manages without outside assistance and doesn't rely on international trade. Small communities trying to be self-sufficient could be described as autarkic. I guess North Korea might be a good example of an actual country that practises autarky. To be honest, you'd only use the word if you wanted to show off.'

'I not want to be autarkic.'

'Same sort of isolation as Antarctic really.' Torin noticed the train slowing on the approach to Chippenham.

They took a taxi from the station, passing the terraces of Cotswold-stone houses in Yatton Keynell and The Gib, then down the valley into Castle Combe. Looking at the clock on the church tower, Torin could see they had time to wander the village before the service.

From the market-cross they followed the curving street of honey-coloured cottages, past the former post-office with its Victorian letter-box, to the bridge over the small river. They sat on the low parapet looking into the clear water. Trout darted between smooth, flat stones. Torin scrabbled in the bushes at the end of the bridge and lifted out two, small sticks. They held hands as they leant over the slow-moving stream and dropped the twigs. They hurried to the other side and peered down.

'It reminds me of the lanterns at Pingle, but I think maybe they drowned this time.' As Sunny finished the sentence, the sticks floated into view, locked together with a thread of weed, pirouetting slowly in the eddies of the current.

'Who win?'

'Both of us.' Torin smiled. 'You first and then they turn, so me first.' He glanced at his watch. 'Time for church.'

They walked on the other side of the street, pausing at the war memorial to the seven soldiers killed during the First World War, past the honesty-box of the cake-maker, to the church porch, where a couple in dark suits were giving out order of service booklets. The organ was softly playing as they took their seats halfway along the aisle of the vaulted nave, with its centuries of memories embedded in the carved walls.

Torin looked at the photograph on the front cover of the programme, and turned the page to see the service would begin with the *Dambusters March*, when the hearse arrived at the roadside. On cue, the organist changed pace and the first bars resonated through the church.

As the coffin, draped in a Union Jack, was placed in front of the altar, the congregation stood to sing *God is our strength and refuge*. The pall-bearers stepped back and saluted in unison as the final verse lifted to the rafters.

*Proudly, with high endeavour,*
*We, who are young forever,*
*Won the freedom of the skies.*
*We shall never die!'*

In his address, Archie's eldest son explained the choice of
Eric Coates's music, relating the time Harry and Archie
had flown with Guy Gibson when he commanded
Twenty-Nine squadron at RAF West Malling. 'On their
first sortie, they tested each other's knowledge of the secret
codes for the day, unaware their radio was switched from
receive to transmit, so that everything they said was
broadcast to the German listening posts across the
Channel. They were carpeted on landing. It wasn't their
finest hour, and certainly not mentioned in the citation for
the DFCs they were subsequently awarded.' The ripple of
laughter around the shaded church lightened the mood.
Celebration amidst sadness.

Torin studied Maurice as he clutched the sides of the
pulpit, noting similarities with the youthful face smiling
sardonically from the cover of the funeral programme—
forage hat at a jaunty angle, ears sticking out from the
unlined neck that sprouted from the collar of the military-
shirt, above a tie whose knot was slightly askew. *Swanton
Morley March 1944* was probably the last photograph
taken of Archie before he was shot down.

Maurice's mouth curved in perfect symmetry, as he
described his father's wartime antics in his battered Ford
Eight, including a group of inebriated friends lifting it onto
the roof of the entrance porch to the Officers Mess at
Swanton Morley, the day before Air Marshall Dowding

visited the station. At the end of his address, he encouraged the congregation to share memories before the final hymn, after which they followed the pallbearers outside into the churchyard. A neat mound of earth was banked up, several feet from the green baize covering the grave.

From where Torin stood, grey shingles of the church roof could be seen above the heads of the mourners at the graveside. The arms of the clock showed ten minutes past three. Wisps of smoke floated lazily up from a chimney-stack on a house burrowed into the hillside beyond the church. At the base of the tower, the first clumps of snowdrops enjoyed the final rays of early February sunshine, heads hanging gently in the still air. Wisteria branches twisted over the tiles on the porch, buds just visible at the tips of the grey-green fingers emerging from hibernation.

*'At the going down of the sun and in the morning, we will remember them.'*

Torin looked at the group beside the yawning grave, as the priest intoned the time-honoured phrases. Brown leather-straps, that had supported the coffin, lay scattered on the grass, threaded between the feet of the men who had lowered it through the mouth of the green material. The robed vicar and the six pallbearers stepped back, allowing family members to shuffle onto the sanitised covering.

Torin watched Maurice and another man link arms around an old woman in a wheelchair, who he guessed was the sister of the deceased airman. From the similarities of the arched eyebrows and jutting chins, Torin deduced they were brothers. Maurice's hand pressed down on the shoulders of his aunt, as if squeezing tears from her eyes. A droplet trickled down her cheeks and splashed the grass at her feet. She knelt unsteadily, supported by her nephews, to scoop a clod of cloying earth. The fingers in the gloved hand crumbled the red soil onto the coffin-lid.

Her nephews followed suit, and then led their aunt from the grave. Far off a pigeon called, and its mate responded across the churchyard, perched in the hidden depths of a yew tree. Torin watched the mourners leave the graveside and re-enter the church for refreshments in the vestry. He held back, thinking they should just slip away. They had done what Mette had asked.

Maurice broke from the group filing into the church and threaded through the cluster of lopsided tombstones. 'You must be Harry's grandson? I can see the resemblance with the man who has been in our house all my life.'

Torin struggled to make sense of what Maurice was saying, aware that the deep-brown eyes expected a response. 'Do you mean you *met* him?' How was that possible?

'My father hung a life-size photograph of your grandfather in our hallway, so we'd see it every time we went upstairs. He was as much a part of our life as Sandy, our Labrador dog.'

'They must have been very close.'

'I think they shared more nights together during the war than they did with girlfriends.' Maurice chuckled and rested his hand on Torin's arm. 'Are you joining us? We could talk later, if you stay a while.'

Torin sensed there might be other pieces of a larger jigsaw, but he knew the story was complete enough.

'Thanks Maurice, but we'll leave now. This event is for your father's friends and relatives. We just wanted to make sure there was someone from our family here. If it hadn't been for your father, Harry Winchester would never have survived the war long enough to meet my grandmother.' Torin smiled wryly. 'And I wouldn't be here...'

Maurice nodded slowly. 'That's true for me as well. Amazing luck, eh? I have something for you though. Can you walk to my car? It's just beside the church.'

Torin and Sunny followed Maurice along the path to where a black BMW was parked in the shade of a yew tree. Red berries were still visible through the leaves of the curving branches, a reminder of the Christmas not long gone. Maurice lifted a package from the boot of the car. 'My father wanted your family to have this.'

Torin unwrapped the hessian cloth to reveal a polished axe-head.

'The handle burned away. This is all that was left.'

# Epilogue

## RAF Museum, Hendon
## Thursday February 13th 2020

Torin pushed the wheelchair up the ramp and into the carpeted reception-area. The cushioned doors closed behind, shutting out the rawness of the February day, and allowing the warmth of the room to wrap around them.

They joined a queue for admission tickets, behind a man with three excited children jockeying for position to be first in the flight simulator. 'Me of course,' said the boy, whom Torin judged to be around ten. 'You girls'll crash for sure; then it'll be out of action.'

The frizzy-haired receptionist smiled as she handed the father their tickets. She adjusted her reading spectacles so she could look over the rim of the rectangular frame at the three children. 'Do you know which of the new intake at Cranwell was voted Top Gun last year?' She pointed to the life-size cut-out beside the desk, showing a pilot in a flying suit, helmet in hand, smiling at the camera, blonde hair cropped neatly above her collar. 'Flying Officer Jenny Wright is now with the Tornado squadron at RAF Lossiemouth.'

One of the girls poked her brother with her elbow. 'That'll be me.' The family walked through the sliding doors to the first exhibits and the room quietened.

Torin moved to the desk. He registered the Royal Air Force crest on the identity card hanging over her neat, black tie. Glancing sideways, he noticed Sunny had wheeled Mette away from the desk. 'I phoned yesterday, Dawn, and spoke with Mister Gwyn. We have an arrangement to meet.'

'And you are…?'

Torin gave his name. She checked her notepad. 'Yes, Mister Gwyn is in a meeting just now, but asked if you could text him when you are ready to go round Hangar Five.' She passed Torin a slip of paper. 'Here's his number. He'll join you with the photographer.'

Torin nodded. 'I expect we'll be a couple of hours looking round the other hangars.'

'Easily.' Dawn handed him a leaflet, explaining the museum layout. 'If you go this way, you'll see all the exhibits before Hangar Five.' She traced the route with a highlighter pen.

They walked round Hangar One, taking in displays and stories, and watching films about the people and partnerships significant to the Royal Air Force during the hundred years till its centenary in 2018. When they passed the flight-simulator, the young girl from reception was easing herself out of the cockpit. She was smiling as she stepped onto the floor, and gave her father a high five.

They followed the highlighted route through other hangars, captivated by the lives of the young men who had joined the Royal Flying Corps in the First World War, and their sons who had taken up arms twenty years later for the Battle of Britain. They walked in silence; for each of them the visit touched different chords.

At the entrance to Hangar Four, Torin texted the number he'd saved on his phone. The door behind opened and a silver-haired man in a dark suit appeared, accompanied by a young man carrying a camera. Melville Gwyn shook hands with Torin and Sunny and bent forward to greet Mette. 'You must be Mrs. Winchester. We are honoured to have you with us, madam.' The formality was from another era.

Mette glanced at Torin, then back to the man standing above her wheelchair. 'I'm Mette Rasmussen.'

Mr Gwyn frowned. 'I thought you and Wing Commander Winchester were—' he hesitated.

'I *am* Torin's grandmother, but I'm not Mrs. Winchester,' interjected Mette. 'I believe she died in 1944. I did know Harry Winchester though.'

The conservator recovered his poise. 'I do apologise Mrs. Rasmussen. We all have two grandmothers of course.' He took Mette's hand. 'The honour is undiminished. Thank you for sparing the time to visit our museum.'

Mette smiled. 'I have spent years curating exhibitions, so I understand the huge amount of work that goes into mounting displays. But nothing I did was on this scale. It is formidable.'

Melville Gwyn bowed in appreciation. 'That's very generous, Mrs. Rasmussen. I hope you will be pleased with the final part of your tour.' He led them into Hangar Five, past a Lancaster bomber and a montage of World War Two crews.

'We have had this display many years and there is still an airworthy Lancaster in the Battle of Britain flight. For years, we've been missing part of the story—the role played by RAF aircrew supporting the bomber streams over Nazi Germany. There were pathfinder squadrons, laying flares to guide bomber pilots, as well as those tasked with protecting the lumbering Lancasters from the Heinkels and Messerchmitts hunting them through the night skies.'

Mr Gwyn walked round the nose cone of the Lancaster and stopped in front of a twin-engine plane that towered above them. The three-pronged propellors were the size of a person. A purple cloth hung over a stand in front of the aircraft.

'Mosquitoes were made largely of wood, which explains why there are no original planes still in existence. We have had to reconstruct one from drawings in the archives of the de Haviland factory in Shenley. We completed this last week and would be grateful if you would do us the honour of formally admitting this addition to the museum.'

'Why me?'

'Your grandson said you knew Wing Commander Winchester and Squadron Leader Standing. This is the aeroplane they flew for twelve months, till that crash on New Year's Day. As far as we know, you are the only person alive who met them both. It seems fitting that you should inaugurate this exhibit.'

The belly of the aircraft curved to the cockpit above. She imagined Harry and Archie seated in the pilot and navigator positions.

Melville Gwyn stepped aside and passed Mette the cord to the purple cloth. 'James here will take some photographs.'

A small crowd had gathered, including the family they'd seen in reception. Mette pulled away the cloth to reveal a bronze plaque commemorating the aircrew. Beside the inscription, a tableau contained a series of photos. One showed Harry and Archie standing beneath the nose of their plane, a large 'B' painted on the underside.

'*Hold kaeft.*' The memory of that last night in Kirkenbjerg flooded back. Harry's arms wrapped around, as she sank down, feeling his energy and vitality rising into her. *Vidunderligt.*

'Gran, are you okay?'

Mette opened her eyes. Through the misty haze she could just make out Torin leaning over her. '*Vidunderligt og uforgllemmeligt,*' she whispered, wiping her eyes as Torin pushed the wheelchair behind Melville into a small meeting-room adjoining the exhibition-hall.

'I am sorry for my reaction. Mister Gwyn.'

'It must be a very moving experience, if you knew them both.'

'More moving than you can imagine,' breathed Mette, feeling the world closing in. She was conscious of an overwhelming weariness.

There was a long silence. Torin lifted a package from his pocket and passed it to Melville, who removed the brown paper and placed the polished axe-head on the table. 'This is all that was left after they crashed. You might want to include it in the display.'

'There seems to be another story here,' said Melville.

'Many stories,' Mette's voice was barely a whisper.

Sunny took Mette's hand and leant across to gently kiss the side of her face, catching a faint scent of rose-petals. She looked up at the display curator. 'My great-grandfather fought the same enemy as Harry. They met in China in 1942, when they were young men.'

Melville's eyes widened. He glanced at the clock above his head, showing nearly four o'clock. 'If you have time, I would like to hear more about that war. I can arrange for food while we are talking, and a car will take you home afterwards.' He gave instructions to James, and they were left alone in the cushioned quietness.

Melville listened intently as they shared their different stories. At six o'clock, an array of canapés was brought in on silver platters. 'We have our own chefs,' explained Melville, 'and they enjoy being creative for special guests.' He pointed at the mouth-watering snacks. 'Salmon and cream cheese, minced-beef pinwheels, parsnip blinis, brie and cranberry filos, prawn and pork lettuce cups, black figs and aubergines.' He hesitated. 'And some I don't recognise. But please enjoy.'

They continued to talk as they ate. At one point Melville produced Harry's logbook and they pored over the map stuck into the front, showing the south-eastern corner of the United Kingdom and the whole of Germany. 'I was going to have this as the centrepiece of the display beside the plane.' His finger brushed the hand-drawn swastikas with dates neatly inscribed beneath. 'But now I should like to extend the exhibition to celebrate these other connections you have talked about.' He looked at Sunny. 'I wonder if we could ask your great-grandfather to record his memories?'

'I am sure he would be pleased to do that,' she said quietly. 'I return to Chengdu on Sunday and can visit him at Dazhentou.' She took Torin's hand. 'I will also write down what he says.'

Through the window they could see lights being switched off in the hangars, and headlights sweeping across the glistening tarmac. 'Your car will be waiting at reception, but I look forward to continuing this discussion.' Melville accompanied them back to the museum entrance. He lifted his arm in salute, as the Audi drew out into the slow-moving traffic on the Hendon Road.

Mette reached into her bag and passed a slip of paper to Torin, who was sitting in the front seat. 'I have been meaning to give you this since Friday. And I'm worried I'll lose it.'

Torin studied the yellowing paper, embossed with faded crests of the SS Sudan and Thomas Cook.

'When Archibald asked me to marry him, he produced this instead of an engagement ring. It was the wedding present from General Chennault.' She explained how Archie had found it in Harry's logbook.

'Thinking we might use it fifty years on was a lovely idea, but even at that comparatively youthful stage in my life, I was not enthusiastic about an expedition up the Nile. You and Emily were barely teenagers, but I told him I would pass it on to one of you when the time was right. I phoned Thomas Cook last week to check they'd still honour it. See if you can use it while you're still young.'

Mette lay back against the headrest, content. The Audi crossed the North Circular and purred through Golders Green, where the street lamps along North End Road illuminated the inside of the car in waves, as if a dimmer switch was being turned on and off. Beyond the arc of yellow lights, darkness stretched across Hampstead Heath. The outline of naked branches was visible against the silvery sky. Sunny had covered her knees with a tartan rug, and silence thickened between them in the warmth from the heater. Mette was aware of feeling very tired. If she closed her eyes, she might sleep for ever.

Lying on the bed in their attic room, Sunny checked her phone. Through the velux window she could see Rapunzel's tower across the roof line, with its cross illuminated by a single floodlight. 'My flight to Chengdu has been cancelled.'

Torin looked up from the book he'd bought in the museum shop. 'Cancelled? You mean Sunday's flight isn't running? When is the next one?'

'There is not next one.'

'Not next one?'

'KLM saying no flights to China till end of March'

'End of March?'

'You are like echo with your questions.' She smiled, and showed him the text on her screen. 'See here. No plane before 28th March, because of virus.'

'But the government is saying it will all blow over very quickly. I listened to the Prime Minister yesterday.'

Sunny closed her fingers over his hands. 'This will not be over quickly. I read messages from friends in Chengdu. With us for a long time. Many deaths. Much unhappiness. World changing. But we have experience with Sars. We know we will come through.'

Torin put down *Pursuit through Darkened Skies* and turned towards Sunny. Her brown eyes looked steadily back. The connecting thread to China wound around them. For the first time in his life, he felt certain of something.

'I only have one other question.'

# Acknowledgements

This story has emerged from shared experiences and owes its appearance in print to many people, including:

Ejgil Aagaard from Odense, and Peter Kuenstler from UNESCO, whom I first met at a conference on Alternative Education in Copenhagen.

Dave Brockington, Brian Fletcher and Richard Pring, whose creative energies have been a source of inspiration.

Former ASDAN colleagues who encouraged me in wordsmithing, especially Mike Creary, Sue Downes, Sally Finn, Kath Grant, John Simpson, Maggie Walker and Bob Wolfson.

Arvon tutors over the years, particularly Anne Spillard, Clare Boylan, Penelope Fitzgerald, Hilary Mantel and Fay Weldon.

The students and tutors on Lancaster University's Creative Writing course (2006-2008).

Rana Mitter, from Oxford University for his book *Forgotten Ally: China's War with Japan, 1937-45* and his encouragement of this novel, and all of the authors whose books provided me with valuable background material, including John Berger for *Ways of Seeing*, Melvyn Bragg for *The Soldiers Return*, Vincent Brome for *The Way Back*, Pearl Buck for *The Good Earth*, Jonathan Fenby for *Generalissimo Chiang Kai-shek and the China he lost*, Richard Flanagan for *The Narrow Road to the Deep North*, Daniel Ford for *Flying*

*Tigers: Claire Chennault and his American Volunteers, 1941-1942*, Xiaolu Guo for *A concise Chinese-English dictionary for lovers*, Penelope Lively for *Moon Tiger*, Eric Lomax for *The Railway Man*, Franz Thaler for *Unforgotten: a memoir of Dachau*, and Geoffrey Wellum for *First Light*.

HarperOne publishers and Penguin for permission to quote from the *Dancing Wu Li Masters* by Gary Zukav.

Yang Ran, Vice Chairman of the Chengdu Writers Association, for *Pingle Ancient Town*.

Florence Ayscough for her translation of Du Fu's poem 'A Toast to Men' in *Fir-flower Tablets* (Houghton Mifflin 1921)

Project Gutenberg for the quotes of Kong Zi, translated by Leonard Lyall in 1909, and the quote of Lao Zi, translated by James Legge in 1897, used as epigraphs to Parts Two, Three and Four.

Harry White and Mike Allen, whose wartime experiences as one of the RAF's night-fighting crews, was often talked about around our dinner table, and which are described in Mike Allen's book *Pursuit through Darkened Skies*.

Diana White and my brothers, Mike, Andrew and Julian, for encouraging the telling of a story that draws inspiration from our father's escapades.

Caitlin White and Malin White for their enthusiasm for the whole project and their perceptive contributions at different stages of the writing.

Joe White and our daughter-in-law Xu Ting (Julina), for

introducing us to China, and Julina for advising on the Mandarin phrases used in conversations, and for her thoughtful observations about many aspects of Chinese life.

Our grand-daughter Xu Ru Xi (Ava) and all the Xu and Li family members for their welcome to Chengdu, and for opening the door to connections between us.

Liao Wang and Yichan Yuan from Seed International in Beijing, whose friendship and insights into Chinese history and culture influenced my thinking.

Gong Yaokun who arranged the visit to Sichuan Care Center for Veterans from the War of Resistance, and accompanied me as translator.

Mrs. Feng Xiao Yi, Chief Director, and Mrs. Wan Wu Yun, Associate Director of Chengdu Wanxia Social House, where the war veterans lived.

Zhang Li Yuan, Luo Jian Yuan and his wife Tang Guang Huan, and other veterans I met at the Center.

The Cultural Office at the Chinese Embassy in the UK, for advice about historical and contemporary references, and for encouraging the telling of a story that highlights the bonds of friendship between our two countries.

Zhao Laoshi (Sunny Hsu), my Mandarin teacher, for help with translation.

Daniela Gisella-Higgs and Johanne Sorensen, for enthusiastic engagement with the story, advising me on German and Danish phrases, and for thoughtfully correcting errors in respective histories

Kimberly Warner and Ginny Berg, for inducting me into Southern states diction and introducing me to phrases like "southside end of northbound donkey."

Ian Gregson, for his astute mentoring that helped shape the whole novel.

Jan Fortune, Rowan Fortune and Adam Craig at Cinnamon Press for supporting this whole project, and for the skillful editing, textual advice and creative design that has resulted in this finished product.

My wife, Chris, for sharing our many journeys to China and associated discussions, insightful editing and thoughts at various stages of the writing.

Despite all this support and input, there may still be errors— these are all mine!